Sepher Rezial Hemelach

Sepher Rezial Hemelach

The Book
of the Angel
Rezial

Edited and translated by
Steve Savedow

SAMUEL WEISER, INC.
York Beach, Maine

First published in 2000 by
Samuel Weiser, Inc.
P. O. Box 612
York Beach, ME 03910-0612
www.weiserbooks.com

Library of Congress Cataloging-in-Publication Data

Book of Raziel.
   Sepher Rezial Hemelach = The book of the angel Rezial / translated by Steve
Savedow from an original manuscript written by an anonymous author.
      p. cm.
   Includes bibliographical references and index.
      1. Cabala—Early works to 1800. 2. Angels (Judaism)—Early works to 1800.
I. Title: Book of the angel Rezial. II. Savedow, Steve. III. Title.

   BM525.A3612 S29 2000
   296.1′6—dc21   00-043535

ISBN: 1-57863-193-9 (hardcover)
ISBN 1-57863-168-8 (paperback)

EB

Typeset in 11pt. New Baskerville

Cover design by Kathryn Sky-Peck

Printed in the United States of America

07 06 05 04 03 02 01 00
8   7   6   5   4   3   2   1

The paper used in this publication meets the minimum requirements of the
American National Standard for Information Sciences-Permanence of Paper for
Printed Library Materials Z39.48-1992 (R1997).

This book is dedicated to the memory of Belle Ginsburg, beloved matriarch of the Ginsburg-Savedow family. I would like to express my appreciation to the following members of my family for their patience, support, and encouragement: my beautiful companion and best friend, Cathy Harbin, and her son, Brian, and daughter, Danielle (the little angel); my parents, Jacqueline and Barry; my three lovely daughters, Sarah, Mary, and Melissa, and their mother, Elaine; my sister and her family, Patti, Tom, Samantha, and Christopher; my brother, Michael, and his wife, Linda; my brother, Randy, and his son, Scott; my adopted parents, Valora and Loren.

Thanks to Glen Houghton for his antiquarian assistance. Also, thanks to Layla and Gary Gantz, Andrea Orloske, Penny Redman, Kim Langdon, Alane Patterson, Judi Lee, and Adam McLean.

Special thanks to Anthony Paulauskas, Jr., without whom this translation would not have been possible.

∞

CONTENTS

CONTENTS

TRANSLATOR'S
INTRODUCTION

❧❧❧

ACCORDING TO HEBREW LEGEND, the *Sepher Rezial* was presented to Adam in the Garden of Eden. It was given by the hand of God, through the medium of the angel Rezial. It is, therefore, suggested that this is the first book ever written. The text is an extensive compendium of ancient Hebrew magical lore, and quite probably the original source for much traditional literature on angelic hierarchy, astrology, qabalah, and Gematria.[1]

There is very little published bibliographical information available on the *Sepher Rezial*. It is noted in the bibliography of Gustav Davidson's *Dictionary of Angels* that the *Sepher Rezial* is sometimes titled *Raziel ha-Malach*, and credited to Eleazer of Worms.[2] Davidson mentions a Hebrew edition, published in 1881, and an

---

[1] "Qabalah" is an ancient mystical system usually attributed to Jewish religion. The study of qabalah is reputed to offer a multitude of spiritual benefits. There are several excellent introductory texts available on the subject, including *The Mystical Qabalah* by Dion Fortune (London: Rider & Co., 1935; and Samuel Weiser, York Beach, ME, 1984), *Tree of Life* by Israel Regardie (London: Rider & Co., 1932; and Samuel Weiser, York Beach, ME, 1972) and *Holy Kabbalah* by Arthur Waite (London: Williams & Norgate, 1928).

Gematria is a form of qabalistic numerology, in which each of the Hebrew letters is assigned a numerical value. Combining the letters yields a numerical value for every word. See the essay "Gematria" by Aleister Crowley (*The Equinox*, vol. 1, no. 5, London, 1911), later reprinted in *The Qabalah of Aleister Crowley*, edited by Israel Regardie (York Beach, ME: Samuel Weiser, 1973), currently available as *777 and Other Qabalistic Writings*. See also Gareth Knight's *Practical Guide to Qabalistic Symbolism* (Cheltenham, England: Helios, 1965; now published by Samuel Weiser, York Beach, ME).

[2] Gustav Davidson, *Dictionary of Angels* (New York: Free Press, 1967), p. 365.

English manuscript in the British Museum.[3] The bibliography of
Joshua Trachtenberg's *Jewish Magic and Superstition* notes a 1701 edition of *Raziel ha-Malach* published in Amsterdam, and "a German-
rabbinic script that does not correspond throughout with the
printed text, but often contains a more complete text." Trachtenberg
further states: "*Sefer Raziel*, probably compiled in the 13th century
and containing much Geonic mystical material (so potent were its
contents considered that mere possession of the book was believed
to prevent fires)."[4]

In Appendix IV of Aryeh Kaplan's translation of *Sefer Yetzirah*,
Kaplan notes 25 various 19th-century editions of *Sepher Rezial*. He
also notes that Eliezer (ben Yehudah) Rokeach of Worms
(Garmiza) lived in the years 1160–1237.[5]

There is certainly no evidence to support the theory that the
Sepher Rezial was actually written over 5000 years ago. There are however, references to the *Sepher Rezial* in several scholarly texts establishing a certain amount of validity to its claim to antiquity, dating it at
least as far back as the 13th century. There have been various quotes
printed from *Sepher Rezial* in a few English texts on Hebrew folklore,
such as the Trachtenberg book mentioned earlier, and *Myths and
Legends of Ancient Israel* by Angelo Rappaport.[6] (For the record, no
English edition was cited in either of these books' ample bibliogra-
phies.) Also, diagrams from *Sepher Rezial* were printed in Davidson's
Dictionary of Angels, Trachtenberg's *Jewish Magic and Superstition*, and
David Goldstein's *Jewish Folklore and Legend.*[7]

The introduction of the ancient Hebrew grimoire, *The Sword of
Moses* states that ". . . the so-called Sefer Raziel, or the book delivered to Adam by the angel Raziel shortly after he had left Paradise.
It is of composite character, but there is no criterion for the age of
the component parts. The result of this uncertainty is that it has
been ascribed to R. Eleazar, of Worms, who lived about the middle

---

[3] Mss. 3826 of the Sloan Collection. A list of Sepher Rezial manuscripts was posted
on the World Wide Web by Adam McLean. See Appendix.

[4] Joshua Trachtenberg, *Jewish Magic and Superstition* (New York: Behrman House,
1939), pp. 321, 322, 315.

[5] Aryeh Kaplan, *Sefer Yetzirah* (York Beach, ME: Samuel Weiser, 1990), p. 330.

[6] Angelo Rappaport, *Myths and Legends of Ancient Israel* (London: Gresham, 1928.

[7] For an example, see David Goldstein, *Jewish Folklore and Legend* (London: Hamlyn, 1980), p. 30.

of the 13th century. One cannot, however, say which portion is due to his own ingenuity and which may be due to ancient texts utilized by him. I am speaking more particularly of this book as it seems to be the primary source for many magical or, as it is called now, a cabbalistical book of the Middle Ages."[8]

Trachtenberg states, "The long list [of magical incantations] in such a work as Sefer Raziel are proof of the arduous training that the novice in magic must undergo if he would learn how to direct all the memunium [Hebrew for "in charge of" or "appointed to"] of air, wind, date, time, place, etc., which can control a situation at a given moment."[9] In *Folklore in the Old Testament*, J. G. Frazer notes, "He (Noah) learned how to make it (the ark) from a holy book, which had been given to Adam by the angel Raziel, and which contained within it all knowledge, human and divine. It was made of sapphires, and Noah enclosed it in a golden casket when he took it with him into the ark, where it served him as a time-piece to distinguish night from day, for so long as the flood prevailed, neither the sun nor the moon shed any light on the earth."[10]

Sepher Rezial is also mentioned briefly in James Hastings' *Encyclopedia of Religion and Ethics*. "The Book of Raziel, said to have been taught to Adam by the angel Raziel, and also to Noah, is a compilation, probably by various writers. It has affinities to the Shiva Koma and Sword of Moses. According to Zunz, Raziel was the work of Eleazer of Worms. It describes the celestial organization, and gives directions for the preparations of amulets."[11]

In *Hebrew Myths: The Book Of Genesis,* Robert Graves and Raphael Patai claim that:

> Solomon is said to have won much of his wisdom from the "Book of Raziel," a collection of astrological secrets cut on a sapphire, which the angel Raziel kept. The idea of a divine

8 Moses Gaster, trans., *Sword of Moses* (London: D. Nutt, 1896; reprinted by Samuel Weiser, New York, 1970), p. 15.

9 Trachtenberg, *Jewish Magic and Superstition*, p. 70.

10 J. G. Frazer, *Folklore in the Old Testament*, vol. 1 (London: MacMillan, 1918), p. 143.

11 James Hastings, *Encyclopedia of Religion and Ethics*, vol. 7 (New York: Scribner, 1908–1927), p. 628; it is also briefly mentioned in vol. 2, p. 658 (concerning the childbirth amulet); and in vol. 6, p. 296.

book containing cosmic secrets appears first in the Slavonic "Book of Enoch" (xxxiii), which states that God had written books of wisdom (or, according to another version, dictated them to Enoch), that He then appointed the two angels Samuil and Raguil (or Semil and Rasuil) to accompany Enoch back from heaven to earth, and commanded him to give these books to his children and children's children. This may well be the origin of the "Book of Raziel" which, according to Jewish tradition, was given by the Angel Raziel to Adam, from whom it descended through Noah, Abraham, Jacob, Levi, Moses and Joshua until it reached Solomon. According to the Targum on Ecclesiastes X.20: "Each day the angel Raziel standing upon Mount Horeb proclaims the secrets of men to all mankind, and his voice reverberates around the world." A so-called "Book of Raziel," dating from about the twelfth century, was probably written by the Kabbalist Eleazar ben Judah of Worms, but contains far older mystical beliefs.[12]

A reference to the angel Raziel is presented *in Witchcraft, Magic, and Alchemy* by Emile Grillot de Givry, who quotes from the preface of a manuscript titled "Le Secret des secrets, autrement la Clavicule de Salomon ou le véritable Grimoire," where Solomon speaks to his son, Rehoboam: ". . . I named the most holy Name of the Lord, Yahweh, and I merited the means that may not be named, the means of the Wisdom, which the Angel Raziel showed me in a dream, whereof the close tale may not be told to the understanding, and said to me, 'Hide well the Secret of Secrets, because the time comes when the universal sciences will be destroyed and utterly hidden and will become void; and know that thy time is near.'"[13]

In *Jewish Folklore and Legend*, Goldstein states: "Enoch consulted the wonderous 'Book of Raziel' that had originally been given to Adam, and there he read of the part that Noah was to play in the salvation of the human race."[14] George Yurchison, in *World of*

---

[12] Robert Graves and Raphael Patai, *Hebrew Myths: The Book of Genesis* (New York: Doubleday, 1963), p. 53.

[13] Emile Grillot de Givry, *Witchcraft, Magic, and Alchemy*, J. Courtney Locke, trans. (Boston: Houghton Mifflin, 1931), p. 103.

[14] Goldstein, *Jewish Folklore and Legend*, p. 30.

Angels, mentions that, ". . . when Adam was expelled from the Garden, the Archangel Raziel, at the instructions of the Lord, presented him with a Book of Secrets (known also as the Book of Adam, Secret of Secrets) to aid mankind in their attempt at salvation." He later states that "In ensuing generations of Adam's seed, the first man with his progeny were visited constantly by Michael and other Archangels to aid, instruct and console the mortals. It was at this point that Raziel gave the Book of Secrets to Adam. This is the only known book prepared actually in Heaven that existed (and still does, in fragments) on the earth."[15]

In *Dictionary of Angels,* under the heading "Raziel," Davidson presents the following:

> In the cabala, Raziel is the personification of Cochma (divine wisdom), 2nd of the 10 holy sefiroth. In rabbinic lore, Raziel is the legendary author of "The Book of the Angel Raziel" ("Sefer Raziel"), "wherein all celestial and earthly knowledge is set down." The true author is unknown, but he has been commonly identified as Eleazer of Worms or Isaac the Blind, medieval writers. Legend has it that the angel Raziel handed his book to Adam, and that the other angels, out of envy, purloined the precious grimoire and cast it into the sea, whereat God ordered Rahab, primordial angel/demon of the deep, to fish it out and restore it to Adam, which Rahab obediently did, although it should be pointed out that before this, Rahab had been destroyed. "The Book of the Angel Raziel" finally came into the possession of, first Enoch (who, it is said, gave it out as his own work i.e. "The Book of Enoch"); then of Noah; then of Solomon, the latter deriving from it, according to demonographers, his greatest knowledge and power in magic. (Rf. De Plancy, *Dictionnaire Infernal.*) From a midrash (Ginzberg, *The Legends of the Jews I,* 154–157) it develops that Noah learned how to go about building the Ark by poring over the Raziel tome. (Rf. Jastrow, *Hebrew and Babylonian Traditions.*) . . . Searching further in the cabala, one learns that Raziel is one of 10 (actually one of 9) archangels in the Briatic world, which is the 2nd of the 4 worlds of creation. . . .

---

[15] George Yurchison, *World of Angels* (New York: Vantage Press, 1983), pp. 30, 48.

According to Maimonides in his "Mishna Thora," Raziel is chief of the order of erelim (q.v.); also, the herald of deity and preceptor angel of Adam. In further connection with "The Book of the Angel Raziel", "The Zohar I", 55a, reports that in the middle there occurs a secret writing "explaining the 1,500 keys [to the mystery of the world] which were not revealed even to the holy angels."[16]

In the first book of the Zohar (Berashith-Genesis), there is a fairly long passage referring to the *Sepher Rezial*, that gives some insight to the legendary origins of this book.[17]

This is the Book of the generations of Adam. In the day that Alhim created man, in the likeness of Alhim made he him." (Gen. v.,1.) Said Rabbi Isaac: "The Holy Ones showed Adam the forms and features of his descendants that should appear in the world after him, and of the sages and the kings who should rule over Israel. He also made known to him, that the life and reign of David would be of short duration. Then said Adam to the Holy One, "let seventy years of my earthly existence be taken and granted to the life of David." This request was granted, otherwise Adam's life would have attained to a thousand years. This was the reason that David said: "For thou Lord, hast made me glad through thy work; I will triumph in the work of thine hands (Ps. xcii.,5), for thou hast filled me with joy in prolonging the days of my life." "It was thy own act and wish," said the Holy One, "when thou wast incarnated as Adam, the work of my hands and not of flesh and blood." Amongst the wise men and sages that should

---

[16] Davidson, *Dictionary of Angels*, pp. 242–243.

[17] The Zohar is a twenty-four-volume compilation of qabalistic wisdom and lore. It was first introduced in the 13th century by a Spanish Jew named Moses de Leon, of Granada. There is some controversy surrounding the Zohar, as some believe that the work was not derived from ancient manuscripts, but actually written by de Leon himself. However, this does not detract from the fact that it is an extremely valuable qabalistic work. There have been several portions of the Zohar translated into English, most notably the five volumes translated by Harry Sperling, Maurice Simon, and Paul Levertoff, published by Samuel Bennet in 1958. This translation was later reprinted by Soncino Press in 1984.

appear on the earth, Adam rejoiced greatly on beholding the
form of Rabbi Akiba who would become distinguished by his
great knowledge of the secret doctrine. On seeing, however,
as in a vision, his martyrdom and cruel death, Adam became
exceedingly sad and said: "Thine eyes beheld me ere I was
clothed in a body and all things are written in thy book; each
day hath its events that shall come to pass, are therein to be
found." Observe that the book of the generations of Adam
was that which was the Holy One through the angel Rasiel,
guardian of the great mysteries and secret doctrine, gave
unto Adam whilst yet in the Garden of Eden. In it was written
all the secret wisdom and knowledge concerning the divine
name of seventy two letters and its esoteric six hundred and
seventy mysteries. It also contained the fifteen hundred keys,
the knowledge and understanding and use of which had
never been imparted to anyone, not even to angels, before it
came into the possession of Adam. As he read and studied its
pages, angelic beings assembled around him and acquired
the knowledge of Hochma, or divine wisdom, and in their
delight exclaimed "Be thou exalted, oh God above the heavens, and let thy glory be above all the earth" (Ps. lvii., 5).
Then was it that the holy angel Hadraniel sent one of his
subordinates to Adam, saying unto him, "Adam! Adam!
guard thou well and wisely the great and glorious gift en-
trusted to thee by the Lord. To none of the angels on high
have its secrets ever been revealed and imparted, save to thy-
self. Be thou therefore discreet and refrain from making
them known to others." Acting on these injunctions Adam
zealously and secretly kept this book up to his expulsion
from the Garden of Eden, studying it and making himself ac-
quainted with its wonderous mysteries. When, however, he
disobeyed the commands of the Lord, the volume suddenly
disappeared leaving him overwhelmed with grief and most
poignant regret, so that he went and immersed himself up to
his neck in the river Gihon. On his body becoming covered
with unsightly ulcers and sores threatening physical dissolu-
tion, the Holy One instructed Raphael to return the book to
Adam. After obtaining a full knowledge of its occult teachings, he handed it, when at the point of death, to his son

Seth, who in turn bequeathed it to his posterity, and eventually it came into the possession of Abraham who was able by its secret teachings to attain to higher and more enlightened knowledge of the Divine, as was the case with his predecessor Henoch and enabled him, as it is written, "to walk with Alhim," that is to converse with them.[18]

The *Sepher Rezial* is very rare in any form, and the text is of great importance. It seems incomprehensible that it has never been translated, in its entirety, into English. The translation presented here was derived from a single text, the 1701 Hebrew edition, published in Amsterdam. The 1701 edition is a compilation of five texts, gathered together by its editor, who transcribed the letters of the various manuscripts into one volume. The title page notes that the book was "Printed in the chosen house of the respected priest [Kamir] Moses Ben Hieshiesh, by the honorable Abraham Mindim Kovitineyov."

The text is in biblical Hebrew, which uses no vowels. Hebrew vowels are represented by small dots and dashes positioned above and below the letters. According to the *Oxford Companion to the Bible,* the use of vowels in Hebrew writing developed between the fifth and tenth centuries C.E.[19] The full Hebrew text is 97 pages long. Each page has an average of 48 lines, with an average of 90 characters per line.

The use of vowels greatly simplified the matter of translating Hebrew into English. The variations of word interpretations became more specific with the placement of vowels. Also, there are very few pronouns and verbs utilized in biblical Hebrew, and almost no punctuation. In this translation, I have kept sentences as simple as possible, and have elected not to inject any implied verbs or pronouns, except where necessary to the grammar and/or syntax of the passage. Also, I have attempted to remain

---

[18] The quote is from the 1978 edition of the Zohar, translated by Nurho de Manhar (William Williams), and later reprinted by Wizards Bookshelf (San Diego, 1995). There are several other references to the book on pp. 234–235 of the 1995 edition, under the heading "Traditions Concerning Adam."

[19] Interestingly enough, this text actually discussed the use of the vowels in detail.

consistent with the words translated. You will therefore, likely note some repetition.

There are several difficulties involved with translating biblical Hebrew into English. English utilizes more words than any other language, especially Hebrew. Therefore, one Hebrew word may have a fairly large variety of possible translations, depending on the context of the passage. This obviously leaves room for interpretation. Most biblical Hebrew words have a root of three letters. The meaning may change depending on addition or omission of a prefix or suffix. For example, the root word (TzDQ) may be interpreted as right, righteous, righteousness, just, justice, justify, honest, correct, innocent, blameless, acquittal, vindicate, equitable, or charity. To complicate matters further, one English word may have several Hebrew interpretations. For example, the Hebrew words for the term "evil" include Ra'a, Resha'a, Ragezeni, Moseri, Chota, Cheli, Mezieq, Nezeq, Tzereh, and Hereh-Ason.

Each of the five manuscripts within the 1701 edition was produced during a different time period, while the manner of writing Hebrew was changing and improving. In each manuscript there is a different form and dialect of biblical Hebrew. Some of the dialects are of a very ancient form that was never intended to be translated into English. The first sections appear to have been derived from the most modern manuscripts. The style of writing in each book is different, with the use of different prefixes and suffixes, and different verbs and word spellings, and the expressions varied from section to section. The later sections are a bit "degraded" in places, as they are transcriptions of the most ancient manuscripts, and they were the most difficult to translate. For these reasons, the translation may seem rough and the "flow" of the text changes throughout this book. However, there is no way to accurately interject terms for the sake of literary integrity without possibly making an incorrect assumption. Those readers who have studied medieval Hebrew texts will understand the meaning as presented. Those not well-versed in this type of material may have difficulty, but they can also research similar works for clarification.

Due to the rarity of the *Sepher Rezial*, I could not locate alternate texts for comparison. I obtained two fragmented texts in English translation, but neither was of much use for comparison. One section of this text was published in English translation as *Sepher Ha-Razim: The Book of the Mysteries*. In the preface of this translation, the editor states that ". . . no English translation [of "Sepher Ha-Razim"] exists."[20] The 1966 Hebrew edition used for this translation was edited by Mordecai Margalioth.[21] Also, an English translation of a Raziel manuscript was posted anonymously on the Internet. This consisted of less than 100 pages, and was titled *Liber Ratziel: The Book of Salomonis*. It was obviously taken from a Latin manuscript, as many passages were left in the original Latin.[22]

There are several concepts discussed in detail in this translation that may be unfamiliar to novices. Biblical Hebrew texts often use several names for God, and this book is certainly no exception. The most commonly used name here is (Hebrew: HQBH). This is an acronym for Hova Qedesh Berek Hova, which translates "He is holy. Blessed is He." When this acronym is used, I translate it simply as "God." Other names of God employed in the text include El, Elohim, Elohik, Elohinu, Eloah, Yah, Yehuwa, Adonai, Ahieh, Shaddai, and Melek Meleki Melekiem (The king, king of kings). In these cases, I simply leave the word in the English equivalent of the Hebrew pronunciation.[23] Also, the letter Heh followed by an apostrophe was often used as "The Lord." There are other mystical words in the text that do not translate clearly into modern English, so I have also left these in the English equivalent of the Hebrew characters. Table 1 on page 19 shows the Hebrew characters and the Roman equivalents used in this book. Please note that letters in parentheses (Hebrew: IHOH, for example) may not be translated as they are phrases used repeatedly throughout the text, or they are referring to the unspoken name of G-D.

One of the most important aspects of this book is the material concerning the various names of God, specifically the "72-fold name," the "22-fold name," and the "42-fold name." According to

---

[20] Michael A. Morgan, *Sepher Ha-Razim: The Book of the Mysteries* (Chico, CA: Society of Biblical Literature/Scholars' Press, 1983), p. ii.

[21] *Sepher HaRazim*, Mordecai Margalioth, ed. (Jerusalem: Yediot Achronot, 1966).

[22] Probably Sloan Ms. 3846. See Appendix.

[23] In modern Hebrew texts, the name of God is never spelled out, but is often represented by two Yods. In prayer, this is usually pronounced as Adonai. Devout Jews will not even write the name God in English, and instead write out G-D.

Table I. Hebrew and Corresponding Roman Characters.

HEBREW	Name	ROMAN	HEBREW	Name	ROMAN
א	Aleph	A	ל	Lamed	L
ב	Beth	B	מ	Mem	M
ג	Gimel	G	נ	Nun	N
ד	Daleth	D	ס	Samekh	S
ה	Heh	H	ע	Ayin	Aa
ו	Vau	O	פ	Peh	Ph
ז	Zayin	Z	צ	Tzaddi	Tz
ח	Cheth	Ch	ק	Qoph	Q
ט	Teth	T	ר	Resh	R
י	Yod	I	ש	Shin	Sh
כ	Kaph	K	ת	Tau	Th

Trachtenberg, "The name of 22, however is another matter, more interesting and puzzling—and much more important for the magician. Its debut was made in Sepher Raziel. . . ." Trachtenberg presents an extremely informational essay on the names of God. He also discusses the *Sepher Rezial* extensively throughout this same chapter, as well as in the following one, on angelic names.[24]

Another important concept discussed is the five names of the human soul. Each name corresponds to a certain aspect of the soul. The *Neshemah* refers to the breath of life. *Nephesh* refers to the soul itself. *Ruoch* refers to the spirit or mind. *Cheyah* refers to the life or vitality of the spirit. *Yechideh* refers to the unity or uniqueness of the spirit.

The concept of the Hebrew hells is also detailed. According to Hebrew mythology, there are actually seven hells: *Gihenam* (hell), *Sha'arimath* (the gates of hell), *Tzalemoth* (the shadow of death), *Baraschecath* (the pit of destruction), *Tithihoz* (the clay of death), *Abaddon* (the perdition), and *Shahol* (the highest, triple, or Supernal hell). In qabalistic lore, these are described as the ten hells in seven palaces, and they correspond to the ten sephiroth of the qabalistic tree of life.

The divisions of the Garden of Eden are mentioned several times in the first few sections. According to the Old Testament (Genésis

---

[24] Trachtenberg, *Jewish Magic and Superstition*, pp. 90–97.

2:10–14), the Garden of Eden is divided by four rivers. The first is Pishon, which flows around the land of Havilah. The second is Gihon, which flows around the land of Cush. The third and fourth rivers are the Tigris and the Euphrates. These are two actual rivers that defined the boundaries of the ancient land of Mesopotamia, which today is essentially the land in the area of Iraq and Iran. In fact, the word "Mesopotamia" means literally "between the rivers."

In his foreword, the original editor states that this work is a compilation of several manuscripts. He also claims to have proof-read the text repeatedly to insure that this book would be "worthy to be studied by the children of my people." Although there is some repetition, the translation presented here is, for the most part, verbatim, in order to preserve the integrity of the text, as well as the intention of the original editor. I have also proofread the text repeatedly, and have taken great pains to produce an accurate transcription. I truly believe that the original editor would find this English translation to be worthy of study by the children of his people.

The title page is also of interest. We have reproduced it here, and the translation is as follows:

> This is the book of the history of man [Sephera Adem Qedemah] that was given to him by the angel Rezial. This is the gateway of the Lord. The righteous come forth. Rise upon the path. Rise to the House of El. Reach the glory of El. In every house of Israel, it is treasured. Rise up and see descendants most wise and intelligent. Prosper and be blessed. Extinguish the fire of enemies, that they do not rule in the house. Of every evil spirit and wicked enemy, fear not in the dwelling. Of who has this holy book, glory and honor to you. Keep it hidden and concealed near silver and gold in a house of treasure. In the course of sickness and misfortune, let there be salvation quickly. Testify [bear witness] and proclaim to all learned in the Torah. [25]

---

[25] The Torah is the holy book of the Jewish people, consisting of the first five books of the Old Testament. It is kept as a heavily ornamented scroll within an ark in the Temple, usually upon the pulpit. It is often carried and worshipped during ceremonies. The word "Torah" may be translated as "law," and may also be interpreted as "instruction" or "teaching." See Metzer and Coogan, eds., *The Oxford Companion to the Bible* (New York: Oxford University Press, 1993), p. 747.

זה כפרא דארם קדמאה
שנתן לו רחיאל דמלאך

וזה השיער לה' צריקים יבאו בו לעלות בכסלה ·
העולה · בית אל · לרבק בכבוד אל · ולמל בית
ישראל · היא סגולה · מועלה · לראות בני בנים ·
חכמים ונכונים · ולהצלחה ולברכה · ולכבות אש
המערכה · שלא ישלוט בביתו · וכל שר ופגע רע
לא יגור במגורתו · למי שהספר דזקדוש הנכבר
ונחנורא אתן · גנה וטמון אצל כספו וחכו באוצרתו ·
ונחליתו · ובעת צרהו · ידח לו תשועה כזרה ·
מה יעידו ויגידו כל בני הורה ·:·
נדפס
בבית חבחור הנחמר וחיקר כס"ד משה בן הש"ט
הנכבר כבוד אברהם מינדיס
קוטיניו זל' :

באמשטרדם
נסלם בשנת זה ספר תלחת
אדם לפ"ק :

FOREWORD

BY THE

MASTER PROOFREADER

[HEBA'AL HEMEGIEHEH]

———— ❧ ————

IN THE NAME OF THE UNITY of the tabernacle of the Lord [Heqe-bieh] and the dwelling of the Lord [Shekinethieh], it is secret and hidden. Blessed is the name of the glory of the kingdom forever.[1] See it restore the glory of life everlasting [Chieh La'avolemiem]. Endure therein and know every science of secret and hidden things.

This is the Book of the History of Man. Study and learn. Proclaim to the generations, from the beginning until the end. Of the most direct path of the Lord, the righteous journey therein, becoming strong unto Shem [Hebrew letters: Sh"M].[2] Break through as the dawn. Illuminate the eyes. See visions come in abundance. Visions of the illumination. Evil does not befall the righteous by understanding the commandments of purification coming forth from the ten books.

∞

This book was concealed and locked away in a house of treasure for many years. The children of my people [Benai A'ami, usually a reference to "my countrymen"] are enlightened by the printing. In the [old] days, my ancestors did not speak the word, and

---

[1] Berok Shem Kebod Melekothov La'avolam. This prayer is used repeatedly throughout the text.

[2] This translates as "name," but the apostrophes between the letters signify a number (340), name (Shem), or abbreviation. This may be a reference to the Shem Hemaphorash, "the divided name" or "ineffable name." This term is extremely significant in qabalistic literature. See *Sword of Moses*, *Jewish Magic and Superstition*, *Book of Enoch*, the Zohar, etc.

regretted not hearing the word. Upon seeing the vision of two visions [Rah Rayithi Shethi Rayivoth], it was printed in large quantity.

In the book are proclaimed the images of the letters from all the world, printed clearly. The holy and honored book is response to the commandments of the Torah. This was given long ago, financed by the Rabbi Obeadieh the Elder. A great outcry arose. The work was diminished and error after error discovered. I succeeded in reducing the errors by careful study, and seeking out the best portions of the book.

There are two books from other countries. I see mine is the original of all of them. They have all been copied from my book. I see the doctrine corrected for the benefit of the children of my people. Also included is the smaller work of Eleazer, son of the Rabbi Judah [see Introduction], who received the work of Merkabah [chariot] from the pious Rabbi Judah.[3] The rabbinical Judah the Hassidic received it from his father, Rabbi Simeon the Hassidic.[4] Obadiah himself proofread it, and sealed therein by the teacher of the great illumination, Rabbi Ta'abeli,[5] found during sojourn in the Land of Israel [Aretz Tzebi]. He traveled from one end of the world to the other. Those not dwelling in the land are not passed over. As travelers, as immigrants to Israel, dwelling in lamentation without possessions in the house, they are not passed over. They also receive greatest benefits by this book, from prayers rising up. From the beginning, the prayers are answered at once. Cry for joy all the day. There is no second to understanding the knowledge revealed by the name. Know the name to proclaim and be answered.

The great prophets were not able to make prophecies until studying this book, beginning properly on the third page.[6] The book prepared them to make prophecies. The Lord gives wisdom to understand every word in the world. It is required to prepare

---

[3] This term is highly significant in qabalistic literature. The text of *Sepher Rezial* deals with the work of the Merkabah in depth. Also, see the various qabalistic texts mentioned in earlier footnotes.

[4] There are several different Rabbis by the name of Judah and Simeon in recorded Jewish history. See the Zohar and the New Testament. Also, see Joshua 19:1–19:9, regarding Simeon's territory, later controlled by Judah.

[5] In the text, this is written as MHOR"R, which is a misprint for MOHR'R, an acronym for Morenov Verabenov Haravo Rabbi.

[6] The *Sepher Hamelbosh*, or *Book of the Vestment*, is presented on the third page of the Hebrew text.

them, as the jars of flour of the prophet Elihu [see The Book of Job], and the vessels of oil of the prophet Elijah [see Kings I, the Old Testament], and the fifty burnt offerings of the prophet Israel. When properly prepared, this book proclaims the Earth full with knowledge.

Also, it is written on the third page of the book, all pure are blessed and favored. The impure will not understand and not become wise. Let it be known, the words coming forth from this holy book are honored and revered. The impure profane by foolishness. The worthy become wise by understanding the knowledge. Herein are all the tributes [Medoth] written in the book of the great Rezial.

The book was not properly established by Obadieh. The work failed. The value of this holy book diminished, not being complete and corrected. The pure did not receive great benefit and usefulness by petition and prayer. It is required to speak all names and proclamations correctly. Only then to receive vision after vision, and the answer of answers to the secret of secrets.

The people dwelling in Egypt, who settle outside the land of Egypt, are not oppressed by powers of evil [Qliphoth] ruling the land from above. Shaitan commands the powers of evil, ruling from above and bound by the dwelling of the Lord [Shekineh].[7] Proclaim the day of retribution [Iyem Shelemeh] to punish the sons. The shadow of death [Tzalamoth] falls, bringing darkness across the lands. Israel languished, until the words of the Torah and word of the prophet. Death comes forth through the window [Chalon] by the powers of evil [see Exodus 11:1–11:8, the tenth plague of Egypt]. Cover the window and speak, protect us from the cloud passing over. The darkness falls, seen in the visible heavens. The prophets saw the vision by the virtue of the book. Serve the holy spirit [Ruoch Hakadesh]. Go forth from the cave, as the finger of a hand in the wall of the palace, loathsome and abominable. The hole closed and a great cloud passed over, spreading an abominable covering of bitumen [Chemar].[8]

---

[7] The Hebrew name of Satan. According to the Midrash, Shaitan was the chief of the Sepharim, and was created on the sixth day of creation. Also, see Gustav Davidson, *Dictionary of Angels* (New York: Free Press, 1967), p. 261.

[8] Bitumen, or asphaltus, is a dark, thick, gelatinous substance that flows underground, most notably springing forth in a "turbid effervescence" near Babylon, and also from the floor of the Dead Sea.

The prophets receive understanding. Fill the belly with all wisdom of the universe. There is nothing more precious than learning the wisdom of the qabalah, upholding the Mishnah [codification of Jewish oral law]. Without understanding the knowledge, there is no interpretation of the Mishnah, no knowledge of the work of the Merkabah, no learning the Gemara [commentary of the Mishnah], and no interpreting the unity of God. From understanding the knowledge, receive wisdom to interpret the significance of the unity of God. Begin the path of the Lord, but not without understanding the knowledge of the doctrine of the book. Is it not so, what Ezekiel and other prophets have written, bound, and sealed in the book?[9]

Change the names of the Malechiem.[10] In times of destruction [Choreveh], as in the Midrash of the scriptures[11] when Shaitan was cast out of heaven to the earth, where there is not understanding of the true meaning [Pheshat, the literal or plain meaning]. Of every work of qabalah, it is necessary to establish the seasons, the months, the days, and the hours. In every hour, change the name of the Malechiem, guided by the pages of this book. God created darkness to establish the hours. In the Midrash, Shaitan commanded the king of flesh and blood to extinguish the lamps. The Sun and Moon darkened. The shining stars increased.

Change the Malechiem watching over the heavens and Earth. Reveal the words of absolution by the Torah of Moses. Then the prophecies are revealed. Ears hear and eyes see. Cover the ears not to hear, and close the eyes not to see.

The qabalah is perfection, the root of the Torah. There are two Tablets of the Decalogue [Sheni Lochoth Haberith] arranged in order. The pure revere purity. It is indeed necessary to study and learn the 613 precepts of the Talmud. Solomon divided and distinguished the secret portions.[12] By grace of the Lord,

---

[9] Ezekiel was a prophet who lived from 593–571 B.C.E. See the Book of Ezekiel in the Old Testament.

[10] This term is often used as a general reference to angels. In some texts, the Malechiem are actually a specific order of angels.

[11] The Midrash is the non-halakhic portion of the Talmud. The term may also be translated as "commentary."

[12] The Talmud is a complex commentary on the Mishnah. Solomon was the King of Israel in the years 962–922 B.C.E. See Kings I of the Old Testament. Also, there are many amazing tales depicting the magical acts of Solomon in Hebrew and Arabic folklore. See the Zohar, the Koran, the Midrash, and, in fact, virtually every book mentioned in the Introduction.

reveal the prophecies. Make known the great perfection of the beginning.[13]

Goodness is the last word of the first wisdom. The beginning path to the end. According to the commandments, exceed in goodness from the revealed [Negelah] teachings of secret things.[14] You exceed in goodness by keeping the commandments.

Proclaim the lamp of the commandments of the Torah, the secret light.[15] Do not forsake the commandments written in the Torah. The light reveals that the commandments are superior. The light reveals the commandment as a lamp. The Torah is light [see Proverbs 6:23]. The secret is revealed. Bring forth a small lamp before the flame. Extinguish the burning flames as flame consumes flame. The fire of God goes forth to consume it. The lamp of Elohim.

The Neshemeth of man [see Introduction] is the root of perfection. Reach to God. Reach unto the Lord Elohik. The small lamp reaches to the great light. Make many commandments. Increase the lamps creating flames. Distinguish the secrets and reveal them. Become wise by the power of God. Reveal the divisions without reducing the commandments. Go forth to dwell in the house. Establish the prayers. Build the foundation of the Sukkah.[16] Dwell therein in prayer. Speak to the Lord and proclaim prayers above in reverence. Complete the tabernacle in prayer. Forgive the guilty banished [Diaspora].[17]

Keep all commandments. Reach to the Lord. The secrets are revealed to your sons. Dwell in the world. The son and father are as one.[18] All righteous dwell in the presence of power [A'atzemov].[19]

---

[13] On page 2 of *The Bahir* (York Beach, ME: Samuel Weiser, 1970), translated by Aryeh Kaplan, Kaplan notes: "The word 'beginning' (Reshit) is nothing other than Wisdom. It is thus written (Psalm 111:10), 'The beginning is wisdom, the fear of God.'").

[14] On page 70 of *The Bahir* (trans. Kaplan), it is noted: "What is the seventh attribute? This is the Blessed Holy One's attribute of Goodness." "Negelah" translates as "shining" or "revealed," but may also refer to the written or oral law.

[15] The term "light" has many important qabalistic and biblical significances, beginning in Genesis 1:3: "And God said, Let there be Light." Most classic texts on Hebrew mysticism discuss the concept of light.

[16] A tabernacle built of branches and leaves often adorned with fresh fruit.

[17] A Greek term meaning "dispersion." See *Oxford Companion to the Bible*, p. 169.

[18] The symbolisms of the father and son are extensive. See the Old and New Testaments and other original sources.

[19] The root AaTzM may be translated as power, force, strength, essence, bone, self, substance, etc.

The seal of Elohim is 96 by Gematria.[20] In the beginning, [Berashith] Elohim created the seal (Hebrew letters: ShAaHZ) upon a gourd [Dela'ath].[21] The wise understand and hereafter reach to God.

An abominable cloud of bitumen comes forth from the heat. Do not be destroyed by the powers of evil. Stand trembling before judgment.[22] Afterward, man speaks of the punishment of death [see Genesis 3]. Tremble before the wrath and be consumed by heat. The Torah speaks of heat to consume.

All are locked outside the gate. Weep and lament in Gihenam [the first hell; see Introduction]. In lamentation, experience 32 visions, the key of the 32 paths of wisdom and power of man. Of Yod Heh Vau Heh, shed tears until now revealing the secret of secrets concealed from ancient times. The secrets of the Neshemeth and Malachim above.

The pure learn and understand the words of the book. Be with Elohim as Enoch was taken by Elohim.[23] At the established time, speak to Israel of the act of El.

This is the Book of the History of Man and the Book of the Origin of Man. The worthy see the book of books is truth.[24] Behold, man is sustained in the Garden of Eden. Man received the secret of ten books from God through the medium of Rezial, the holy angel appointed over the highest and most holy mysteries. The ten highest plates are engraved of the most holy wisdom. There are 72 kinds of wisdom. The divisions are revealed as 170 (Hebrew: MAH OShBAaIN) engravings of the highest secrets. By means of the book, engrave the wisdom and reveal 1005 (Hebrew: ALP OChMSh) keys to the highest and most holy secret, concealed in ten

---

[20] The Gematria value of the name Elohim, as presented in the text, is actually eighty-six. In older Chaldee texts, however, the spelling of Elohim often terminates with a Nun rather than a Mem. The Gematria value of Elohin would be ninety-six.

[21] "Berashith" has a great deal of significance, as will be discussed later.

[22] The concept of judgment is quite significant. See the Old Testament, New Testament, Enoch I (22:4), *The Bahir* (verse 65), the Zohar.

[23] See Genesis 5:22. Also see *The Book of Enoch*.

[24] Psalms 85:12. "Truth sprout up from the earth, and righteousness looks down from heaven."

books.[25] The book was assembled at the time God indicated for Raphael to write ten books, as the intermediary of man.

Then came Abraham. By the ten books, he knew of the foolishness and disobedience in the world. He knew of Enoch writing ten books. Because of the foolishness in the world, he divided them. The brilliance was restored. Enoch rose up to reach the splendor and ceased being a man. You sent forth the holy angel to teach ten high wisdoms and deliver ten books. Keep hidden in the Tree of Life [Ayilon Chiyeh, see Genesis 2–3]. Learn the divisions. It is true that God gave this book to man through Rezial, the angel.

The book came to Rabbi A'aqivah and Rabbi Ishmael. The teachings of the Book of Formation were revealed by the Book of the History of Man.[26] It was handed down from generation to generation to A'aqivah. He rejoiced in the warmth of the light. It is also written in the Gemara, reveal to the generations. Rabbi A'aqivah rejoiced in the laws. The gift is seeing the generations. Reveal the visions at once. Be in awe by what is written on page 42 [of the original Hebrew text].[27] Write the names upon a myrtle leaf. It is not forbidden to engrave these seven names, as it is forbidden to engrave Ahieh. The gift to the worthy is knowing the signs of the ninth section.

The worthy come forth in purity. Learn from the pages of this book. Work in holiness and purity. Sons and grandsons of the pure father are created in purity. Only the father is required to guide therein to glory, as it is written in the Book of Vestments in the first section of this book.

It is required to keep this book in a house of treasure with silver and gold. Surely be delivered from blight and misfortune and affliction, and receive great benefit and usefulness.

---

[25] The Zohar notes 670 mysteries and 1500 keys, see the passage quoted in the Introduction. Also, see Rappaport's *Myths and Legends of Ancient Israel*, volume I, page 148.

[26] *Sepher Yetzirah*. This has been translated into English by various scholars, dating back to the late 19th century. Translators include W. Wynn Westcott, Isidor Kalisch, and Aryeh Kaplan. In Appendix III of Kaplan's translation are tables from the commentary of Eliezer Rokeach of Worms. Also, see page xvi of Kaplan's Introduction for information on Rabbi A'aqivah.

[27] The first talisman of Book 2, Part 4 is presented on page 94.

In the first section of this book is the Book of the Vestment. Therein are works of the book, of how it was given to man by Rezial, the angel, and how to be guided therein. Also, the names of the seasons, and the names of the Malachim ministering in every season and every month and every day. Also, the names of the heavens and Earth, and every spirit and angel ministering over every sign of the zodiac, and the angels of the seven planets in every season, and days of the week.

In the second section is the Book of the Mighty Rezial. The corrected doctrine is sweet as honey dropped from the honeycomb. Also, the work of Merkabah and words of wisdom. All words are properly corrected and suitable to be revealed to the worthy. Also the works and actions of the Malachiem, and knowledge of winds and rains and such things.

In the third section is knowledge of the 72-fold name and the actions of the letters and vowel signs.

In the fourth section is the Book of Noah. The actions of the greatest works are written. Also, of the work of Berashith and prayers to rise up in exaltation.[28]

In the fifth section is the Book of the Signs of the Zodiac. Also the charms [Qomeya'avoth] over all things, tried and proven. Also the 22-fold name and 42-fold name, and their actions.

It is required to establish and make known, not to speak the most holy names aloud. Only regard them in the heart, even in prayer. It is written in the Gemara, worship the Lord the true God in all hearts. The prayers are difficult to learn. Much sleep is required to learn the meanings of the letters. Remember the holy names, as required to prepare, but do not speak them aloud.

It is also required to prepare, by rabbinical consecrations and devotions not printed in this book, for a period of ten years. These are not printed here, as a wise man said it is not appropriate to print them in this holy book. Knowledge against knowledge hinders understanding. The rabbinical, combined with that printed here, are united as one. Forsake them and be cursed by all plagues foretold in the Torah of Moses. It is established, those not keeping

---

[28] The term Berashith means "Genesis," and translates literally to "in the beginning." It is also the very first word of the book of Genesis, the first book of the Old Testament.

every commandment of the Torah are accursed. Forsake one commandment and sin unintentionally, the foolish are accursed. Let it be known the knowledge is reserved for those prepared by rabbinical consecrations and devotions. The scholars of Earth are favored in the eyes of the Lord.

Now it is time the transcription is printed. I have copied it letter by letter, with special attention to the most holy names, and also the names of the Malachim. I proofread it four times, letter by letter. If there are any errors, I beg the Lord to forgive me. It is now prepared to be printed and bound by Isaac Ben Checheber Abraham, Amsterdam.

PART 1

BOOK OF THE VESTMENT
[SEPHER HAMELBOSH]

IT IS DECREED, THE HOLY AND PURE ARE FILLED with secret wisdom [Rezi Chokmah]. The knowledge is the result of understanding.

The wise are humble and cry in joy from the names learned in clear language. The chosen are pure of heart. Make to heal the body. Give grace that measures the strength of the light of the shining star. Gird with the strength. The power is established forever by the actions before the generations. Rejoice in silence from generation to generation of the holy heights [Qedoshov Merom]. It is written as pure gold. A bubbling fountain of purity is established in the center of the sublime power. Of the works of glory, the most precious pearls are not compared with the glory, nor the finest gold of Aphier.[1] The value of wisdom cannot be measured, nor understanding of knowledge. Also, there is no measure to the value of the secrets written herein, as revealed by Elohim.

As the force of fire, all search therein. As the ruler of the heavens, all search therein. The Tree of Life is supported and guarded and protected, as the apple of the eye. By reverence of the Lord, the glory is obtained. Obtain the glory to obtain life. Of understanding, receive wisdom. Of salvation, keep from death. Of fulfillment of the Nephesh, by consecration. Of the power, be strengthened by reverence of the Lord. Of learning the knowledge, understand and fill the heart with wisdom. From drawing of life, increase from the sole to the heel. Form divisions in the Garden of Eden.

Elohim treasures the reverence. The Lord fills all the Earth with glory, as in heaven where the throne is established. There is no

---

[1] A city or province famous for the highest quality of gold.

measure to the glory. Seven fountains rise and fall to honor a thousand thousands ministers [Mesharethim] and a myriad myriads
hosts [Tzebavoth].[2] The force of fire ignites the river of fire flowing
forth. The sound shakes the nations in fear of destruction. A vison
comes forth of the image of a fiery archer as Tharshish and Sar-
donyx, and arrows as swift as lightning.[3]

The throne of the glory resembles ice [crystal]. Surrounded by
Malachim, the archer Ophan kindles the flames.[4] The people of
the dominion tremble in fear and cover their eyes. The Lord made
clouds and fog all around, wrapped in swaddling cloth, dwelling
alone upon the throne, concealed and hidden.

The worthy go forth to the hidden light. The most profound secrets are revealed. The revelations are made clear, not obscured by
darkness. There is nothing in all the universe that compares. All actions and desires are fulfilled by works revealed. Become proficient
and results occur quickly. Those who attempt to duplicate the
works receive no results. The souls [Nepheshoth] of the disobedient and rebellious are punished by condemnation. By desire, to establish the curse. The sea dries up. The Sun and Moon darken.
The light of the stars becomes faint. The mountains shift and fall,
and the Earth trembles. This is the result of arrogance. Those chosen are strengthened by the power of the wisdom, established by
understanding the knowledge.

In the holy book are 72 signs, given by Michael, the great prince
above seven princes, ministering before the king, king of kings
[Melech Melechi Melechim]. From it, Adam, the first man, received the beginning wisdom. From it, awaken and proclaim the
names of every living creature and bird and creeping thing and
fish. From understanding, increase the wisdom of all created by
Elohim on the sixth day of Genesis [Berashith].

---

[2] Ten million. A myriad equals ten thousand.

[3] Tharshish is a semiprecious stone from the Spanish kingdom of the same name.
Some suggest it is either amber or chrysolite. It is also the name of the ruling
angel of the angelic order of Tharshishiem.

[4] In Gustav Davidson, *Dictionary of Angels* (New York: Free Press, 1967, p. 213), it is
noted that Ophan is identified by the ancient sages as the angel Sandalphon, the
twin brother of Metatron. Also, see p. 257.

Adam read the holy book and learned the letters and words. He knew the words were true. The knowledge lifted him above all other creatures. He was in awe from all he saw therein, and understood that all that is written in the book is the truth.[5] It is true; all of the words in the book are most holy. Great is the glory of every power.

In holiness and purity, perform the operations. In humility and modesty, succeed in all works. Become wise by the spirit of wisdom [Ruoch Chokmah].

It is written, Adam prepared a bar of gold and purified it twice by fire. Then [he] engraved thereupon the signs of the holy book, in holiness and purity. Then [he] placed the book in a cleft of the rock on the east side of the Garden of Eden—not to fall to Earth, but to endure and sustain the power. In every place, Adam was sustained.

It is proclaimed, Adam wandered upon the earth, as a ship upon the sea. He remembered and recorded when mountains melted like wax; and the sea went forth as hoar frost; and fire went forth as dust; and lions and leopards and bears and animals of the pasture stood silent and still; and insects rose up in the air as birds; and the sea became a desert wilderness.[6]

He remembered and recorded the letters of the holy name before the Sun and the Moon and Orion [Hakesil]. By the light of all luminaries, rule in righteousness and in reverence of Elohim. Also, hold dominion over the spirit [Ruoch] and over violence [Shad] and over misfortune [Phega'a, or enemy] and adversaries [Shatan] rising up over men and women. It is written, be summoned as you wish and desire.

He recorded when the stone wall of the tower suddenly fell to the ground; and fruit trees bear fruit before the proper time; and [people] take flight before battles of war.

Everything was revealed to him: of the holy spirit [Ruoch Hakadesh], of death and life, of goodness and evil. Also, the mysteries of hours and minutes of time, and number of days. Calculate

---

5 Psalms 119:160. "The beginning of your word is Truth."
6 These are omens and portents, probably noted to help predict weather.

the seasons and anniversaries [Yobelim, refers to the equinoxes and solstices] until the end of the universe. Measure the time from the beginning until the end.

Then serve his son, Seth.[7] For ten years, instructed according to the way of the holy book, he received understanding of all letters and words engraved in the holy book, of all powers revealed. He knew by the powers therein to perform miracles, and learned to perform the works. He kept the book hidden away in the cleft of a rock.

From the book, Adam learned that the time of death drew near. Every day, he rejoiced in adjuration, not eating fruits or vegetables or any meat [giving] forth blood. Every day, [he bathed] in the purity of running water, once in the morning and once in the evening. He spoke to his son, Seth, by adjuration alone, not guided by the holy spirit. Preparation is difficult. Work only in humility and reverance, in purity and holiness. Every path is revealed and you become wise by the signs.

After all this, Adam was released to the long home [Beth A'aolam, a reference to the cemetery or grave]. His son, Seth, served the Lord. He was sustained therein by every power, not turning to the left and right from every word spoken by his father, Adam. He became wise from understanding the knowledge, and received the wisdom of the holy book. He opened the gate of wisdom and understanding. Know the difference between good and evil, be repelled by evil and choose goodness.

See and behold the generations of ancestors coming after. The foolish and the vain and the sinful profane by proclaiming false idols in the name of God. The disobedient and rebellious tolerate suffering, not knowing or understanding. Journey in darkness.

Seth became wise by the secrets of the book and the letters of the holy name engraved therein. He learned that God would cause the sea to overflow and destroy all the world by his power. He kept the book in a vault of gold and also placed in the vault all the precious spices, and kept it hidden in a cave. He lived in the city of Enoch, built by his brother Cain [see Genesis 4:17].

---

[7] Seth was Adam's third son, after Cain and Abel. See Genesis 5:3.

❦

PART 2

THIS IS THE PRAYER OF ADAM, THE FIRST MAN

THIS IS THE PRAYER SPOKEN BY ADAM when cast out of the Garden of Eden. From [his] prayers for mercy, [he was] given the holy book by the compassion of the Lord.

Adam spoke: Lord, eternal God of the universe, [you] created all the universe by power and glory.[1] The kingdom is everlasting beauty, going from generation to generation. Nothing is unknown and nothing hidden from your eyes. You created me by your hand, to hold dominion over all living creatures and lord over actions.

The cunning and accursed serpent of the tree deceived my wife and me by lies, leading [us] astray to eat the fruit of the tree of knowledge. I know not what will become of my wife and myself and my sons, and the generations coming after. I am disobedient and foolish, running away before your power, not answering nor raising my eyes, ashamed of sins, of wickedness and iniquity, knowing you would cast me out into day.

Here am I, in the wilderness, to plow the soil and toil upon the earth, receiving nourishment from it, trembling in fear upon the earth, dwelling, from this time, by eating the fruit of the tree of knowledge and not heeding your words, not receiving wisdom. I know not what will come from foolishness.

You are merciful and rule with great compassion. I am the first man you created and breathed into me Ruoch and gave the Nephesh [see Introduction]. I beg mercy of compassion. Be slow to anger and show mercy as prayers rise up to the throne of glory. I

---

[1] See Angelo Rappaport, *Myths and Legends of Ancient Israel* (London: Gresham, 1928), vol. 1, p. 171.

petition for salvation from the throne of compassion. Let there be mercy. I desire to speak in your presence, no longer hiding as I pray for mercy. The everlasting Lord of the universe holds dominion over all, ruling in great compassion.

I pray you reveal what will come of the generations coming after. What will occur every day and every month. I pray you do not conceal the wisdom. Watch over me and sustain my labors.

Adam prayed for three days. God sent forth Rezial, the angel, who dwelled upon the river going forth from the Garden of Eden. He was revealed to Adam as the Sun went black. By his hand, he gave the book to Adam, saying: "Do not fear and lament no longer. From the day you served in prayer, the prayers were heard. I come to give the knowledge of the words of purity and great wisdom. Become wise by the words of this most holy book. They reveal until the day of death. All sons serve below. All generations coming after are guided by this holy book to prosper in purity. Be humble in Ruoch. Reveal all that is written therein. Know what comes to pass every month, and between day and night.

"Every word is revealed. Learn when to eat, when to fast, and when to honor A'arob;[2] what to do in heavy rain or in times of drought; how to increase crops; hold dominion over wickedness in the world; [what to do] when plagued with locusts [Arbeh] and locust larvae [Chasiel]. [Learn what to do] when fruit is picked off the trees; when [you are] plagued with boils; when to fight wars and when to turn away. [Learn how to act] when disease comes to man or beasts; when the good come upon the highest favor; when the wicked spill blood; when to lament that the profane desecrate the flesh."

Adam drew near and heard, learning to be guided by the holy book. Rezial, the angel, opened the book and read the words. Hearing the words of the holy book from the mouth of Rezial the angel, he fell upon the ground trembling in fear. Rezial spoke: "Rise up and be strong. Revere the power of God. Take the book from my hand and learn from it. Understand the knowledge. Make it known to all pure. Therein establish what will occur in all time."

---

[2] A rabbinical provision alleviating Sabbath restrictions on eating certain foods, carrying certain things, or walking to a certain place.

Adam took the book. A great fire kindled upon the bank of the river. The angel rose up in flames and returned to heaven. Then Adam knew the angel had been sent forth by Elohim, the holy king, to deliver the book, sustained therein in holiness and purity.

The words of the book proclaim works to perform when seeking to prosper in the world. For three days before the New Moon [Rash Chadesh may refer to the first of the month], prepare by fasting. Do not drink wine nor lay down with his wife. Bathe in the sea before the rising Sun.

Then bring two turtledoves.[3] Slaughter them with a knife of brazen metal [brass or copper] with two edges. Slaughter the first turtledove with one edge of the knife. Slaughter the second turtledove with the other edge. Remove the intestines and wash in the sea. Bring three shekels of aged wine, pure frankincense, and a little honey, pure and clear. Mix all together and fill the bellies of the turtledoves. Then cut them into pieces. Place the pieces upon burning coals before the rising Sun of noon as a burnt offering.

Then be wrapped in white robes and go forth unshod. Write the names of the Malachim ministering in the months. Divide the names into three sections. Burn one section every day for three days. On the third day, gather up all the ashes. Scatter them upon the floor in the middle of the house. Then sleep above the ashes. Record above the names of the Malachim: the Hadieriem [mighty or noble ones], the Chazekiem [powerful ones], the Geborim [strong ones], the Kadeshim [holy ones], and the Moshelim [rulers, or dominions]. Then awaken. The Malachim came forth in the night in dreams to reveal their names. These were made clear, not in riddles, but all clearly revealed. Seek without fear.

After four generations, Enoch, son of Jarod, served and became wise in the reverence of Elohim.[4] Keeping the body in purity, bathing in the sea of life [Mim Chiyem] and living in holiness before the Creator of the universe [Borah La'ahalom]. In a dream, the place was revealed to him where the book was concealed and also the path to lead therein. Work in holiness and purity. Rise early

---

[3] Joshua Trachtenberg, *Jewish Magic and Superstition* (New York: Behrman House, 1939), p. 243.

[4] Genesis 5:22.

and walk until noon. Because of the heat of the Sun, stop to rest, not realizing [he rested] in the [holy] place. There, pray in the presence of God and be blessed. Rise up in purity and be sustained in the place of purity. While concealed therein, the light of all paths will be seen. Guide therein until seeing the highest holiness. Separate from those dwelling upon the Earth, taken by Elohim.

In this holy book is knowledge of the Malachim ministering in the seasons, the signs of the zodiac, all the luminaries, and those ministering in every month. Also, the names and invocations of every season, and the Malachim ministering in the four seasons of the year. Become wise from the names of the Earth and the names of the heavens. Also, the names of the Sun and Moon. Increase the glory by every power. Understand all knowledge over all creation.

Adam, the first man, understood the power was passed on to the generations coming after, by the power and the glory. After Enoch was taken by God, it was kept hidden, until coming to serve Noah, son of Lamech, a most righteous and honest man, loved by the Lord.[5]

In the time of five hundred years, there was great corruption on the Earth, by acts of violence and corruption of all flesh. Because of the ways of people of the Earth, a great cry rose up from the Earth to the heavens, before the throne of the glory of God.

Noah was favored in the eyes of the Lord. The Lord sent forth the holy prince, Raphel, to Noah. Raphel spoke, I have been sent forth by the word of Elohim. The Lord God restores the Earth. I make known what will be and what to do, and deliver this holy book. You will understand how to be guided therein by works most holy and pure. Hear the word of the Lord. You are the most righteous and honest man in all the ages. Behold, I give you this holy book to reveal all the secrets and mysteries. Work in holiness and purity, in humility and modesty. From it, learn how to make the ark from pitch pine [A'atzi Gupher]. Gather your sons and wives and sons' wives. Live in hiding for a short time, until the wrath of the Lord passes over.

Noah took the book from the hand of the holy prince, Raphel. In time, he received understanding of the knowledge therein. By

---

[5] See Genesis 5:28.

the words of the holy book, [he was] guided unto the Ruoch of the Lord. He made the ark in the length and width written therein.[6] By the knowledge, Noah became wise by the holy name and spoke to every house of God: Come to the ark, those righteous and worthy.

From the secrets of the book, Noah, son of Lamech, built the ark and understood all the words. [He] then brought to the ark two and seven males and females.[7] The sky opened up and the flood lasted forty days and forty nights. Noah spoke by the Ruoch of wisdom and understanding, giving blessing to the Lord Elohim, the great, strong, and honored king.

Noah spoke: Blessed is the Lord, giving wisdom to revere your name. Blessed is the kingdom. By reverence, deliver the souls of the pious. In the secret place, protect and deliver us in salvation, living by your grace, forever serving your spirit. By understanding every word, every man and beast and living creature and bird and creeping thing and fish know of the power and great strength. Become wise by the great wisdom of the holy book. Make known when it is day and when it is night. Know when to eat and when to fast.

The prayers rose up to the throne of glory, giving salvation to all in the ark. The Ruoch of Elohim passed over the Earth, lowering the water. The ark rested gently upon the mountain of Ararat.[8]

Noah was guided by the wisdom of the book. It was made known to his son, Shem. From it, Noah learned to build the ark, and what would come. Shem was guided therein and sustained by the book, following the works in holiness. Shem handed down the book to Abraham,[9] then from Abraham to Isaac, from Isaac to Jacob, from Jacob to Levi, from Levi to Moses, from Moses to Aaron, from

---

[6] According to the Old Testament (Genesis 6:15), the ark was 300 cubits in length, fifty cubits in width, and thirty cubits in height.

[7] According to the Old Testament (Genesis 7:2-4), God told Noah: "Take with you seven pairs of all clean animals, the male and its mate; and seven pairs of the birds of the air, also male and female, to keep their kind alive on the face of the earth."

[8] A mountain in an Armenian province of the same name, whereupon the ark was said to have rested, according to the Old Testament (see Genesis 8:4).

[9] According to the Old Testament, the lineage from Shem to Abraham was Shem, Arpachshad, Sheleh, Eber, Peleg, Rev, Serug, Nahor, and Terah. Terah was the father of Abram, who was later instructed by God to change his name to Abraham (Genesis 17:5).

Aaron to Phineas,[10] from Phineas to his son, and to all the generations coming after.

All who are pure rise up in happiness and goodness by the knowledge. Become wise as established therein. All are not afforded grace and not all gain the understanding of the knowledge. The beginning wisdom comes from reverence of the Lord. By this, the wise man considers how to become wise therein. From understanding, man serves the Lord. Study the book in purity. Do not fall upon your face, trembling in fear. Do not go astray from the path of the Lord. Do not go before the power of evil. Come forth in goodness. Counsel the wicked to join together, casting off their wicked ways. Live in goodness and happiness is obtained in life, not being persecuted by evil spirits and wicked enemies. Deliver from misfortune at once. The house is blessed.

Journey to the high place to contemplate grace. Give blessings to the holy name. Attain the brilliance of the light. By visions, know all are good in the eyes of Elohim. Man knows, by visions, of the death of the wicked. Deliver the Nephesh of the righteous to live. Conceal the Nephesh in the foundation, enduring death by the power in the presence of the kings assembled. Serve in the name of God, the king over all kings.

All are sustained by this book. It is written, keep the body pure and do not defile the flesh. The wife is not to toil in impurity.[11] The Nephesh is not to die. All uncircumcised [A'arel][12] are not to profane. Keep holy the flesh in the sea of life. Purify the body to be with Elohim. Do not consume unclean things. Do not toil in corruption. Work only in holiness by all written herein and prosper.

Those who are improper [wrongdoers] by the letters of the holy name, not keeping the body in purity and holiness, and corrupting the flesh, they are guided therein frivolously. By not keeping to the path, and by going with arrogance therein, [they] profane and desecrate the holy name. [They shall] be punished and perish from the world. [They shall] be accursed and an abhorrence in the world,

---

10 Phineas was Aaron's grandson, and the son of Eleazer.
11 The term used here is "Nedah," which is usually a reference to female menses.
12 This term may simply refer to someone who is not Jewish.

not favored and not graced. The fire is not extinguished. [They will] wander in darkness, moving farther away from the light of the Lord.

Show reverence to the Creator of all the universe. Guide therein in purity and holiness. Understand the knowledge of all the words therein. Succeed in all the works. Be favored in the eyes of the Lord in mercy and compassion. All enemies tremble in fear before the power of the holy name. Proclaim to the wise and understand the knowledge. Travel the direst path to the Lord. Commit sins, and stumble, and fall before the power.

Prosper by the established and ordained blessings. Rise up to dwell in the light of the Lord, judged by the book.[13] The humble bow down to serve. All go forth to the Lord, for five days in the beginning of the month, and five days in the middle of the month, and succeed in all works.

Rise up and be judged by the great book. In exaltation, declare the Lord Elohim in prayer. All serve and live as it is written by the Lord to live, and succeed in all works.

Be judged by the book of judgment. In judgment, all serve and worship in prayer.[14] Of the works, change the name of the Moon and Sun, five days in the beginning, five days in the middle, and five days in the end.

In the first season, the Sun is in Aries [Taleh], Taurus [Shor], and Gemini [Tavomiem] for 91 days, three hours, and one from four of three hours [Achad Marba'a Vosheliesh Sha'ah].

In the second season, the Sun is in Cancer [Saretan], Leo [Areyieh], and Virgo [Betholeh] for 91 days, six hours, and one from four of three hours.[15]

In the fourth season, the Sun is in Capricorn [Gedi], Aquarius [Deli], and Pisces [Dagiem] for 91 days, and one from four of three hours.

---

[13] In the *Oxford Companion to the Bible* (New York: Oxford University Press, 1993), p. 565, it is noted: "In terms of purpose, the oracles of the prophetic books can be classified generally as either 'judgment speeches' or 'oracles of salvation'."

[14] In *The Bahir*, Aryeh Kaplan, trans. (York Beach, ME: Samuel Weiser, 1979), p. 24, it is noted: "As long as a person does judgement, God's wisdom is inside him."

[15] The third season is omitted. It is quite safe to assume the passage should read: "During the third season, the Sun is in Libra [Mazenayiem], Scorpio [A'aqerov], and Sagittarius [Qashat] for 91 days," etc.

When seeking to make the earth fertile, take water and pour it upon the earth. Speak the names of the earth in every season. The earth will absorb the water at once. You work and succeed.[16]

When in the first season, perform works to cultivate and sow the soil. Speak the name of the earth and the sun; and the prince, Yehov Hov Ayien; and the name of the first day of the week, Phiegnotheqer; and the names of the first season, Samal, A'anal and Geneshorash; and the prince, Ayied Mesetar; and the name of the Sun, Phenievothah; and the name of the sign of the zodiac Aries, Sha'atan; and the names of the rulers [Sheletin, or magistrates] over sowing the soil, Yiesorien, Thorethah, Yivoba, A'areketh, Dekadial, and A'anal; and the seven names.[17] Speak the prayers of holiness to serve all who work. They are Sheden and Aseren.

When in the second season, perform works that the trees and crops may thrive. Speak the name of the earth, Kol Ached,[18] and the name of the prince, Eliehon; and the name of the second day of the week, Mochethier; and the names of the angels of the second season, Nemelial, Tzedeqial, and A'anal; and the prince, Abier Abieriem; and the name (Hebrew: IHOH ABIN) [God the father]; and the name of the sign of Cancer, Qechedar; and the name of the rulers over the crops and trees, A'aqerieh and Hemoledieh; and [the names of the] princes of the Lord, A'arebrethiehov, Qorebithieh, Abekeleth, Netheleba, and Derekethial; and the seven names. The trees will grow tall and strong. The crops will thrive by the prayers. They will serve, whether conditions are good or bad.

When in the third season, perform works that the harvest is prosperous. Speak the name of the earth, Yieshieshieh; and the prince, Yehemial; and the name of the spirit of the east, Abiyan;

---

[16] These first four operations focus on improving the agricultural aspects of the land. It is generally accepted in biblical lore that there is an intimate connection between agriculture and religion. In fact, several of the major Hebrew religious festivals are based upon the harvesting of crops. For example, The Feast of Weeks, or *Shavuhot*, celebrates the completion of the grain harvest and the first fruit harvest. Also, the Feast of Booths, or *Sukkoth*, celebrates the final fruit harvest.

[17] The names of the seven archangels ruling the planets: Michal, Bereqial, Gabrial, Dodenial, Chesedial, Tzadiqial, and A'anial.

[18] Kol Ached translates as "every one." The term is presented as a name in the text.

and the princes Raphal, Gabrial, and Avorial; and the name of the third day of the week, Pherethan; and the names of the third season, Shemal, Ashemreh, and Gabrial; and the prince, Alebera Ayieh; and the name (Hebrew: IHOH SOPOThONIN); and the name of the sign of Libra, Theshegon; and the names of the rulers over the harvest, Raphal, Roqial, Gabrial, Tzorial, Yehov Yehieh, Michal, and Shelishial. From the first shoots, thrive until the harvest.

Abraham comes after, drawing near the Lord. In the place, see two angels. One serves as the right hand of the Lord and one serves as the left hand of the Lord. They serve Abaddon, the minister of death.[19] By his authority, endure. Hear the words and impose upon mankind wealth and prosperity, and goodness to him and every tribe until the end of all the generations. When corruption angers the Lord, send forth to fall upon the right side and be sustained. They are Meroqaphera and Merakephial; and the seven names of the princes. Raise hands to the heavens. From the flask filled with precious oil, anoint and consecrate. By judgment, [you are] bound in servitude to harvest the earth.

When in the fourth season, perform works insuring the preservation of the harvested crops. Speak the name of the fourth day of the week, Ramieh Shor Setar; and the names of the fourth season, Agedia, Gedodial, Berakial, Robiyoveh, and Derapa; and the names of the Sun, Abelad, Ashekor, Kechedon, Shecheron, and Qoledon; and the name of the sign Capricorn, Shenar Levi; and the names of the ruler over the preservation of the crops, Ahedierier, Methagdal, A'azrial, Zebena, and Zereqetha; and the seven names. Over the days, crops will be preserved. Serve Phelon Ben Phelon by the holy commandment.

When in the first season, perform works that the cattle may thrive. Speak the name of the fifth day of the week, Aberiemonos; and the name (Hebrew: IHOH PNIOTh); and the name of the sign of Aries, Shepheten; and the names of Moses and Aaron and Joshua, son of Non; and the most holy, Daleha, Bonegos, Beravoth,

---

[19] Abaddon is sometimes referred to as "the destroyer." This is the Hebrew name for "Appolyon," the angel of the bottomless pit (see Revelations 9:10). According to S. L. MacGregor-Mathers' translation of *The Key of Solomon the King* (London: George Redway, 1888; reprinted by Samuel Weiser, 1972, 1989, 1999), Moses invoked the name Abaddon to bring down the blight upon the land of Egypt.

Vometebrath, Gedeg, and Sebelievothavoth; and the seven names. Serve Sheriyien and Ayieserien.

When in the second season, perform works that the cattle may thrive. Speak the name of the sixth day of the week, Atheroph; and the names of the second season, Nemoval, Tzedieqial, A'anial; and the prince Abier Abieriem; and the name (Hebrew: IHOH ANKON); and the names of the sign of Cancer, Qeheder, Ovalien, Thenonial, Benebod, and Ayiepheten; and the seven names. Serve Gediehon and Geremiehon.

When in the third season, perform works that the camels may thrive. Speak the name of the fourth day of the week, Agethekon; and the names of the third season, Shemesial, Ovashemera, and Gabrial; and the names of the princes, El Bera Avor, Shemasha, and Sophethenien; and the names of the sign of Libra, Thenegebon, Beqoneqephethov, Menkebehov, and Anomiekehon; and the seven names. Take hair from a camel. Braid it in a circle and bury it in the earth. Petition Elohim. Do not return to the place until the hair turns to dust. In the place the hair was put into the earth, there raise the camels.

When in the fourth season, perform works that the birds of fowl may prosper. Speak the name of Earth [Aretz]; and the name of the first day of the week, Makel; and the name of the spirit of the east, Siederavon; and the names of the princes, Gabrial, Raphal, and Avorial; and the names of the fourth season, Agedal, Gedodial, and Berakial; and the name of the prince, Robiyov Derepha; and the names (Hebrew: IHOH), Abeleched, Ashekor, Kechedon, Beseron, Shechedon, and Qolehon; and the names of the sign of Capricorn, Sheger, Levi; and the names Neqola, Dema, Shebenial, Shenathial, A'azeberial, and Tenebial; and the seven names. Serve Phelon Bather Phelon.

When in the first season, perform works that the wine may be sweet and strong. Speak the name of the second day of the week, Ha'asher; and the name of the spirit of the west, Bechieledek; and the names of the princes, Yiediedial, Voval, and Shemal; and the names of the first season, Samal, A'anal, and Geneshoresh; and the name of the prince (Hebrew: IHOH); and the names of the sign of Taurus, Dekeron, Yereshial, Yerekethial, Va'anobien, and Samal; and the seven names.

When in the second season, perform works that the oil may be rich. Speak the name of the third day of the week, Qoch Dereshan;

and the name of the spirit of the north, Selenesh; and the names of the princes, A'azrial, Zekedial, and Shemeshial; and the names of the second season, Kemenial, Tzadiqial, and A'anial; and the name of the prince, Abier Abieriem; and the name (Hebrew: IHOH AONBIN); and the names of the sign of Leo, Shenehon, Michal, Raphal, Rephedial, Ova'akedial, Roqial, Toriel, and Iyovediem; and the seven names.

When in the third season, perform works that the spices may be aromatic and sweet. Speak the name of the fourth day of the week, Degiyem; and the name of the earth, Yeshieshieh; and the name of the prince, Yechemal Yehemavoth; and the name of the spirit of the south, Aphosemon; and the princes, Kokebial, Sherial, and Michal; and the names of the third season, Shemeshial, Vashemeda, and Gabrial; and the name of the prince, Alebeda Avor; and the name of the spirit, Biethial; and the seven names.

When in the fourth season, perform works that the mines may be plentiful with metals and gemstones. Speak the name of the fifth day of the week, Beri Abieriyov; and the name of the spirit of the west, Mepheniyeh; and the name of the prince, Yiediedial, Ovoval, and Samal; and the names of the fourth season, Anedial, Gedodial, and Berakial; and the names of the princes, Rebon, Herapha, and Derapha; and the names (Hebrew: IHOH), Abelechod, Ashekor, Necheron, Sheheron, and Qelechon; and the names of the sign of Capricorn, A'avothera, Aphethial, Becheral, Nodial, Phethial, Ayienovagel, and Gelethotz; and the seven names.

When in the first season, perform works to bring forth rain. Speak the names of the sixth day of the week, Abothem, Rehet, and Shesher; and the name of the prince, Avopheter; and the name (Hebrew: IHOH PTTh); and the names of the sign of Gemini, Shegerem, Ma'arekoth, Meloch, Meremavoth, Norethial, Segenial, Vobenoval, Qelaboth, Asetheqon, Norial, Shiethial, Senenial, Aremavoth, Gedegial, Seremial, Aremavoth, Va'ashal, and Vogenzial; and the seven names. Speak seven times. Speak the holy and established prayers. The prayers rise up before the throne. The dew and rain descend to fill the world from the storehouse. Blessings fall upon the surface of the earth and there is no drought.[20]

---

[20] The operations of rain were of utmost importance. Palestine records virtually no rainfall during the months between April and October.

When in the second season, perform works to stop the hail. Speak the name of the day of the week [not specified], Demeroniek; and the name of the spirit of the west, Sephophien; and the names of the princes, Yiedierial, Yoval, and Samal; and the names of the second season, Nemenial, Tzadiqial, and A'anial; and the name of the prince, Abiebiem; and the name (Hebrew: IHOH ANKIN); and the names of the sign of Virgo, Yieherial, Ovayien, Phethenavoth, Serekial, Phethelial, Genethial, and Chezeqial; and the seven names. There will be no destruction by hail.

When in the third season, perform works to find wells and bubbling springs. Speak the name of the first day of the week, Sopheterenien; and the name of the ocean, Asheresher; and the name of the prince, Aba Bavoth; and the name of the spirit of the north, Aha'arehies; and the names of the princes, A'azrial, Zebedial, and Shema'ayial; and the names of the third season, Shemeshial and Vashemereh; and the name of the prince, El Bera Bavor; and the name (Hebrew: IHOH SOPNThIN); and the names of the sign of Sagittarius, Abenier, Abelediyon, Mebieniethiyeh, Vothepheniyoth, Abiyoth, and Arebieter; and the seven names.

When in the fourth season, perform works for an abundance of fresh water. Speak the name of the second day of the week, Shegerien; and the name of the sea, Aphiyarenien; and the name of the prince, Thederenolial; and the name of the spirit of the south, Yiechel Derek; and the names of the princes, Kokebial, Sherial, and Michal; and the names of the fourth season, Anedial, Gedodial, and Berekial; and the name of the prince, Rebiyov Derephes; and the names (Hebrew: IHOH), Abeleched, Ashekor, Bechedon, Shehedon, and Qelehon; and the names of the sign of Pisces, Bechemera; and the names, Yehov, Yeh, Qethothial, and Vohayin; and the seven names.

When in the first season, perform works that the water may be purified by heat. Speak the name of the first day of the week, A'arebon; and the name of the spirit of the east, Qonedek; and the names of the princes, Gabrial, Raphal, and Avorial; and the names of the second season, Nanial and Tzedeqiel; and the name of the prince, Abier Abieriem; and the name (Hebrew: IHOH ANKON); and the names of the sign of Cancer, Qoheder, Voba'ayi, and Mieniyeh. Speak, Heh Yehieh Yedied Adokeh Yedied Yechotzoriya Iyayar Aberesekem Yeh Yeh Yeh Yeh Yeh Ahieh Asher Ahieh

Zeqoqoveheyi Yehoveh [IHOH]; and the seven names. By heating the water of the well, purify it and make it fit to consume.

When performing works in the first season, speak the name Yom in the days of the first season, and the name Lielela in the nights of the first season.[21]

When performing works in the second season, speak the name (Hebrew: IHOH) in the days of the second season, and the name Zehiera in the nights of the second season.

When performing works in the third season, speak the name Richesha in the days of the third season, and the name Shemieh in the nights of the third season.

When performing works in the fourth season, speak the name Asor in the days of the fourth season, and the name Dechiyotha in the nights of the fourth season.

The names of the Malachim ministering in the first season are Samal, A'anial, and Geneshorash. The name of the prince is A'aliehon Avor Kosesor. These names are proclaimed when performing works in the first season, otherwise the work will not succeed.

The names of the Malachim ministering in the second season are Siemoval, Tzediqial, and A'anal; and the name of the prince is Abier Abieriem. These names are proclaimed, otherwise the work will not succeed.

The names of the Malachim ministering in the third season are Bereqial, Avoremedial, and Gabrial; and the name of the prince is El Bera Avor. These names are proclaimed, otherwise the work will not succeed.

The names of the Malachim ministering in the fourth season are Avorial, Berial, and Kerebial; and the name of the prince is Deberhema. These names are proclaimed, otherwise the work will not succeed.

The names of the Malachim ministering in the nights of the first season are Sha'agien, Therotz, Sheregemen, and Shekeremen. The name of the prince is A'ashial. The name of the Moon is Lebedenieth. These names are proclaimed when performing works in the nights of the first season.

---

[21] Yom translates as "day" and Lielela translates as "night."

The names of the Malachim ministering over the nights in the second season are Ashoshal, Ateredemen, and Shecheqonek; and the name of the prince is Lebermeq; and the name of the Moon is Avoliyar.

The names of the Malachim ministering over the nights in the third season are Phelayiem, Vothedoregel, and Shethenesheron; and the name of the prince is Phenial; and name of the Moon is Yirech.

The names of the Malachim ministering over the nights in the fourth season are Ashegeron, Redophial, Sheder, and Liyedi; and the name of the prince is Gedial; and the name of the Moon is Sheherien.

These are the names of the Sun in the four seasons. In the first season, the Sun is in the signs of Aries, Taurus, and Gemini. The name ministering in the first season is Avor Bemepheterieh. In the second season, the Sun is in the signs of Cancer, Leo, and Virgo. The name ministering is Akethemiem. In the third season, the Sun is in the signs of Libra, Scorpio, and Sagittarius. The name ministering is Aberiyavor. In the fourth season, the Sun is in the signs of Capricorn, Aquarius, and Pisces. The name ministering is A'aseqoron.

These are the four names of the heavens in every season. In the first season, the name is Ason Avor. In the second, the name is Rom Reqoya'a. In the third is Mephietz Nogeh. In the fourth is Shechoq Ma'avon. These are the names of the heavens in the seasons. When performing operations in the seasons, proclaim the names of the heavens in the beginning of every season.

These are the names of the earth in the four seasons of the year. In the first season, the name is Mememen. In the second, the name is Yebesheh. In the third is Thebel. In the fourth is Hed Herom.

These are the four names of the spirits [Ruochoth].[22] In the first season, the name is Abekeren. In the second is Qoherebek. In the third is Neberial. In the fourth is Areterial.

---

[22] Some texts suggest this term refers to the winds of the world. In the *Oxford Companion to the Bible*, it is noted: "There is no distinct term for spirit in the languages of the Bible; the concept was expressed by a metaphorical use of words that mean, literally, wind and breath; the English word spirit is simply an Anglicized form of the Latin word for breath (spiritus). Wind is an invisible, unpredictable,

These are the names of the spirits of the north in the seasons. In the first season, the name is Amoneh. In the second is Aberien. In the third is Nolegedod. In the fourth is Desephor.

These are the names of the spirits of the east in the seasons. In the first season, the name is Akeberon. In the second is Qorebek. In the third is Abedoth. In the fourth is Begierethov.

These are the names of the spirits of the west in the seasons. In the first season, the name is Mecheniyem. In the second is Kenogor. In the third is Zerezor. In the fourth is Deriyavor.

These are the names of the spirits of the south in the seasons. In the first season, the name is Meneshor. In the second is Alepheron. In the third is Methenial. In the fourth is Themehor.

These are the names of the princes of the planets ministering in all the houses [Ma'avon], and the angels ministering in the seven highest houses. The names of the planets are Saturn [Shabati], Jupiter [Tzadiek], Mars [Madiem], Sun [Chemeh], Venus [Nogeh], Mercury [Kokeb], and Moon [Lebanah].

In the seventh house, ministering therein is Saturn. The angel is Michael. To invoke Saturn in the first season, the name is Qovoretom. In the second, it is Pheshietos. In the third, it is Qoremelos. In the fourth, it is Phenephophos.

In the sixth house, ministering therein is Jupiter. The angel is Bereqial. To invoke Jupiter in the first season, the name is A'ayeh Avor. In the second, it is Pheniebor. In the third, it is Zavos. In the fourth, it is Qonienial.

In the fifth house, ministering therein is Mars. The angel is Gabrial. To invoke Mars in the first season, the name is Adom. In the second, it is Derom. In the third, it is Beron. In the fourth, it is Phezetom.

In the fourth house, ministering therein is the Sun. The angel is Dodenial. To invoke the Sun in the first season, the name is Qoyiezelos. In the second, it is Herotes. In the third, it is Thedephoriem. In the fourth, it is Tenephal Pheniyos.

---

uncontrollable force, which bears down on everything in its path; and people found early that they are exposed to influences that affect them like the wind" (page 287). There is also an interesting passage in the New Testament that reads: "He makes his angels winds, and his servants flames of fire" (Hebrews 1:7).

In the third house, ministering therein is Venus. The angel is Chesedial. To invoke Venus in the first season, the name is Kokav Hanogeh.[23] In the second, it is Aphrodite.[24] In the third, it is Qoliepho Voyimephes. In the fourth, it is Phezetor.

In the second house, ministering therein is Mercury. The angel is Tzedeqial. To invoke Mercury in the first season, the name is Haremiem.[25] In the second, it is Hiyethophial. In the third, it is Teliem. In the fourth, it is Antoloviyem.

In the first house, ministering therein is the Moon. The angel is A'anial. To invoke the Moon in the first season, the name is Phelonieth. In the second, it is Seriyeqov. In the third, it is Nezephielov. In the fourth, it is Heyiphereki.

These are the names of the twelve signs of the zodiac and those ministering in the four seasons of the year. The names of the twelve signs are Aries, Taurus, Gemini, Cancer, Leo, Virgo, Libra, Scorpio, Sagittarius, Capricorn, Aquarius, and Pisces.

In the first season, the signs of the zodiac are Aries, Taurus, and Gemini. These are the names ministering in every season.

In the first season, the name over Aries is Sha'aphon. In the second, it is Behemoth. In the third, it is Bekemesheb or Bekemekesheb. In the fourth, it is Qotzien.

In the first season, the name over Taurus is Dierenavor. In the second, it is Heniethebol. In the third, it is Siemegedel. In the fourth, it is Morepheker.

In the first season, the name over Gemini is Sheneron. In the second, it is Phelehedien. In the third, it is Volereked. In the fourth, it is Akeneseb.

The names of months of the year corresponding to the signs of the zodiac in the first season are Nisan, Ayer, and Sivan.

In the first season, the name over Nisan is Asegesenek. In the second, it is Mesokenek. In the third, it is Deriegemon. In the fourth, it is Shethenovesenov.

---

[23] Kokav Hanogeh translates as "Venus."

[24] The name of the mythological Greek goddess is printed here in Hebrew characters. She is the Greek equivalent to the Canaanite goddess Ashtaroth, who was also primarily a deity of love and fertility. Also, see Trachtenberg, *Jewish Magic And Superstition*, p. 100.

[25] Trachtenberg, *Jewish Magic and Superstition*, p. 100.

In the first season, the name over Ayer is Phemetor. In the second, it is Qotenebial. In the third, it is Ma'agol. In the fourth, it is Goberethial.

In the first season, the name over Sivan is Senediem. In the second, it is Tzoveh Tziyer. In the third season, it is Qoseqomial. In the fourth, it is Senegedial.

The names of the signs of the zodiac in the second season of the year are Cancer, Leo, and Virgo. These are the names ministering in every season.

In the first season, the name over Cancer is Qedoqoredi. In the second, it is Qoheleren. In the third, it is Phereshethial. In the fourth, it is Memenial.

In the first season, the name over Leo is Bephopher. In the second, it is Lieshebeker. In the third, it is Shehenen. In the fourth, it is Shehelekek.

In the first season, the name over Virgo is Siemosial. In the second, it is Sebodeh. In the third, it is Siegel. In the fourth season, it is Teremothiyeh.

The names of the months in the second season of the year are Tammuz, Ab, and Elul.

In the first season, the name over Tammuz is Zemieda.[26] In the third, it is A'aphierepheleh. In the fourth, it is Ma'ava'aqobebov.

In the first season, the name over Ab is Kedoremot. In the second, it is Hetheledemi. In the third, it is Qonezerema'a. In the fourth, it is Hehemekel.

In the first season, the name over Elul is Phelietepheter. In the second, it is Thesedegeb. In the third, it is Nephesa'ar. In the fourth, it is Qomoval.

The names of the three signs of the zodiac in the third season are Libra, Scorpio, and Sagittarius. These are the names ministering in every season.

In the first season, the name over Libra is A'ariegol. In the second, it is Mereton. In the third, it is Qa'aberi. In the fourth, it is Leqoshemelek.

---

[26] The name over Tammuz in the second season is omitted from the text.

In the first season, the name over Scorpio is Therephietz. In the second, it is Phetza'an. In the third, it is Shemophethen. In the fourth, it is Thokesed.[27]

The names of the three months of the third season of the year are Tishri, Marheshavan, and Kislev.

In the first season, the name over Tishri is Derek. In the second, it is Mezeredeter. In the third, it is Neqocheda. In the fourth, it is Asepheres.

In the first season, the name over Marheshavan is Beqosh. In the second, it is Pheladen. In the third, it is Seherenar. In the fourth, it is Kebod.

In the first season, the name over Kislev is Phelestos. In the second, it is Kether. In the third, it is Henek. In the fourth, it is Phonetos Lobenos.

The names of the three signs of the zodiac in the fourth season of the year are Capricorn, Aquarius, and Pisces. These are the names ministering in every season.

In the first season, the name over Capricorn is Ameni. In the second, it is Bieker. In the third, it is Depheri. In the fourth, it is Memelial.

In the first season, the name over Aquarius is Meta'am. In the second, it is Theberien. In the third, it is Shethoqoeh. In the fourth, it is Danial.

In the first season, the name over Pisces is Qomietzon. In the second, it is Qeheregen. In the third, it is Tzeletzel. In the fourth, it is Amenial.

The names of the three months of the fourth season of the year are Tebeth, Shevet, and Adir. These are the names ministering in every season.

In the first season, the name over Tebeth is Naphenietz. In the second, it is Sekeberiem. In the third, it is Senekeros. In the fourth, it is Bekereba'al.

In the first season, the name over Shevet is Pholekemon. In the second, it is Qeronega. In the third, it is Shelomieth. In the fourth, it is Yavorer.

In the first season, the name over Adir is Koneled. In the second, it is Ba'aren. In the third, it is Sebiebekera'a. In the fourth, it is Qoromeqoreb.

These are the names of the signs of the zodiac in every season.

---

[27] The names for Sagittarius are omitted from the text.

In the first season, the name over Aries is Shaitan. The name over Taurus is Debechen. The name over Gemini is Shegeresi.

In the second season, the name over Cancer is Qeheder. The name over Leo is Shehenom. The name over Virgo is Yiehierieh.

In the third season, the name over Libra is Theshegekon. The name over Scorpio is Bietheron. The name over Sagittarius is Aketen.

In the fourth season, the name over Capricorn is Shegerelovi. The name over Aquarius is Aketheral. The name over Pisces is Qohemera.

These are the names over the signs of the zodiac and the names ministering over the Moon in the seasons in the signs of the zodiac. Every sign of the zodiac ministers for thirty days. All the signs are complete in twelve months.

These are the names ministering in the seasons, with the names of the Moon.

In the first season, the names are Shaitan, Therezien, and Sheneremi. The prince is Gabrial. The name of the Moon is Leberenieth.

In the second season, the names are Yieshieshieh, Abererehon, and Sheheqonek. The prince is Bal Menael. The name of the Moon is Seletheleb.

In the third season, the names are Phelayiem and Ketherenial. The prince is Rebenial. The name of the Moon is Yieshegeron.

In the fourth season, the names are Biyom, Bieth, and Rothep. The name of the prince is Danial. The name of the Moon is Sheherieph.

These are the names ministering over the Moon in the signs of the zodiac in every season.

In the first season, the name in Aries is Zerem. The name in Taurus is Dekedon. The name in Gemini is Shegeron. The name in Cancer is Mekerechiem. The name in Leo is Letzoneber. The name in Virgo is A'anen Qenek. The name in Libra is Tzedeqiel. The name in Scorpio is Therephieth. The name in Sagittarius is Tzoqor. The name in Capricorn is Meshegeriem. The name in Aquarius is Ma'asheniem. The name in Pisces is Sha'aphenen.

In the second season, the name in Aries is Behemi. The name in Taurus is Mezekerien. The name in Gemini is Biehereron. The name in Cancer is Qoheder. The name in Leo is Shegeher. The name in Virgo is Yiehedieh. The name in Libra is Sheqothiek. The name in Scorpio is Menedeber. The name in Sagittarius is Reberon. The name in Capricorn is Yieshieshieh. The name in Aquarius is Aberedon. The name in Pisces is Aniesien.

In the third season, the name in Aries is Pheloneh. The name in Taurus is Thederenael. The name in Gemini is Yielebek. The name in Cancer is Keresivon. The name in Leo is A'avoqor. The name in Virgo is Kenedeni. The name in Libra is Theshegekon. The name in Scorpio is Kotheben. The name in Sagittarius is Abenor. The name in Capricorn is Shebiebiek. The name in Aquarius is Mesepher. The name in Pisces is Sethered.

In the fourth season, the name in Aries is Qonosh. The name in Taurus is Amiena. The name in Gemini is Ashegerien. The name in Cancer is Mehiemeten. The name in Leo is Ayiethebien. The name in Virgo is Shegeton. The name in Libra is Shecheqon. The name in Scorpio is Bedod Besher. The name in Sagittarius is Keniepena. The name in Capricorn is Shegerelovi. The name in Aquarius is A'anethera. The name in Pisces is Qohemehogov.

These are the names of the days in the seasons:

The name in the first day of the week of the first season is Phiegenochen. In the second, it is Tenekien. In the third, it is Kophethenien. In the fourth, it is Makeleched.

The name in the second day of the week of the first season is Tha'sher. In the second, it is Menechethor. In the third, it is Qoleneheren. In the fourth, it is Shegedon.

The name in the third day of the week of the first season is Sheriyachetz. In the second, it is Qohebereneden. In the third, it is Phezeren. In the fourth, it is Hegelomoth.

The name in the fourth day of the week of the first season is Pheniov Lavor. In the second, it is Miyeshor. In the third, it is Degiem. In the fourth, it is Betheroqa.

The name in the fifth day of the week of the first season is Kedemenor. In the second, it is Avoreberien. In the third, it is Qovephethem. In the fourth, it is Bariebererov.

The name in the sixth day of the week of the first season is Qola'azeran. In the second, it is Deremethok. In the third, it is Akethenor. In the fourth, it is Arieh.

These are the names of the earth in the seasons. In the first season, the name of the earth is Memegien. In the second, it is Yibesheh. In the third, it is Thebel. In the fourth, it is Hezeh Dovem.

These are the names of the spirits of the earth in the seasons. In the first season, the name of the spirit is Mechemed Lov, and the prince is Yihov Yihov Ayin. In the second season, the name of the spirit is Bel Ached, and the prince is Yihemelieh Mavoth.[28] In the fourth season, the name of the spirit is Avor Berek, and the prince is Yibavobavoth.

These are the names of the spirits of the earth. In the first season, the name of the spirit of the east is Aseberon. In the second, the spirit of the east is Akeberon. In the third, the spirit of the east is Arial. In the fourth, the spirit of the east is Siederehon. The princes are Gabrial, Raphal, and Avorial.

In the first season, the name of the spirit of the west is Qohelorek. In the second, the spirit of the west is Siemephov. In the third, the spirit of the west is Sechemor. In the fourth, the spirit of the west is Mephenieh. The princes are Derial [or Redial], Yoval, and Samal.

In the first season, the name of the spirit of the north is Amoniem. In the second, the spirit of the north is Deseleni. In the third, the spirit of the north is Arehieh. In the fourth, the spirit of the north is Mephenial. The princes are A'azrial, Zebedial, and Shema'aial.

In the first season, the name of the spirit of the south is Mepheni Shesher. In the second, the spirit of the south is Baledenien. In the third, the spirit of the south is Aphosien. In the fourth, the spirit of the south is Yihelederek. The princes are Kokebial, Sherial, and Michal.

These are the names of the Malechiem in every season, and the names of the four spirits of the world in the seasons.

In the first season, the name of the spirit of the east is Akeberon. In the second, the spirit of the east is Qoherok. In the third, the spirit of the east is Aberieth. In the fourth, the spirit of the east is Beriekoch.

In the first season, the name of the spirit of the north is Amereneh. In the second, the spirit of the north is Aberiek. In the

---

28 The names for the third season are not included in the text.

third, the spirit of the north is Gezorophed. In the fourth, the spirit of the north is Kephor.

In the first season, the name of the spirit of the west is Mazeniem. In the second, the spirit of the west is Siegor. In the third, the spirit of the west is Zerezor. In the fourth, the spirit of the west is Avor.

In the first season, the name of the spirit of the south is Meneshor. In the second, the spirit of the south is Pheniemor. In the third, the spirit of the south is Themekor.[29]

When serving man traveling from a place or returning, separate the thoughts of the friend from the enemy. Be as a star [Kokeb] of the four spirits of the world and be without desire. Wander in the world without the desire to speak the names of every spirit. In that place, appear at once and work as you wish. Succeed in every operation and every work, however, work in purity.

These are the names of the sea [Heyiem] in the four seasons of the year. In the first season, the name of the sea is Belied. In the second, it is Thehom. In the third, it is Mererial. In the fourth, it is Shebiel Geder.

The name of the sea in the first season is Aregez, and the prince is Bethemial. In the second, it is Behenephel, and the prince is Pheliephal. In the third, it is Kieserephenon, and the prince is Thethederelial. In the fourth, it is Aphareten, and the prince is Therebegolial.

When seeking to cast a thing [Devar] to the middle of the sea, and make a thing in the middle of the sea, write the name of the waters in every season. Place it in the middle of the sea and receive by it. Work and succeed in every work, but work in purity and holiness.

These are the names of the ocean [Thehom] in the seasons. In the first season, the name is Netheqothed, and the prince is Tzephnial. In the second, it is Siempheten, and the prince is Athial. In the third, it is Ashereshek, and the prince is Ababavoth. In the fourth, it is Hayithob, and the prince is Bephenial.

These are names of the Malachim ministering over fire and flames: Melekial, Rephedial, Gorial [or Gezerial], Amienial, Aralielael, Norial, and Yizerael. When seeking to make a thing and

---

[29] The name for the fourth season is omitted from the text.

cast it into fire, or gather in fire, or extinguish fire, speak the names of the season and the seven names of the Malachim appointed over the river of fire, and receive all desire.

The names of the Malachim ministering over the sea, and all life in the sea, are Sheboqothial, Zekorethial, and Therekial. When seeking to cast a thing into the sea, write the names Neqietial and Regoneh with the names of the season. Cast it into the water and receive desire. Write upon a plate of silver.

These are the Malachim ruling over rain. When drought [comes] and [you] seek to make it rain, pray in supplication. Speak the names in this order: Melekial, Meremeremoth, Nohetial, Sebenial, Qokethial, Thenial, Gedial, Keremial, Yisha'aieh, Meterial, and Liethial. Speak the names of the Malachim seven times. Then take a white cock and purify it, cleansing it of all defilement. Remove blood and feathers, and take out the intestines. Fill it with frankincense and myrrh and saffron, the best peppers and the white blossoms of the white peppers, honey and milk, and aged wine. Then stand before the passing Sun and speak in petition: Lord, I stand before you in holiness and petition you to open the gates of the blessed storehouse. Allow the rain to flow down. Restore the earth from the blessed storehouse.

If rain does not fall at once, lay upon your face upon the earth. Speak the prayer and, after, speak the holy names of the glory and honor. Offer a libation [make a drink offering] of the milk, honey, and wine seven times. Rain will fall quickly to restore the world. Keep yourself pure and humble, and all your works will succeed.

These are the Malachim ruling over all dangerous creatures, such as bears, lions, and wolves. Speak these names before the creatures and close their mouths. The names are Methenial, Aphethial, and Vobehielael. By these names, shut the mouth of the animal.

When going forth on the path, seeing battles and wars coming forth, place the hand upon the right side. Proclaim the names of the spirits of the days of the week. Then speak the names in reverse. The battle will end before.

When falling into the congregation of the wicked, consider death and understand there is no salvation. By the name of the glory and honor, there is salvation. Place two hands upon your sides. Speak the name of the Sun in the season, the name from the

beginning as it is written. By the letters, separate therein righteousness and deliverance.

Write the letters upon a plate of gold. Of all thoughts of wickedness and corruption, man turns away. When going on the path, and
falling upon persecution by the path, not yet seeing, turning away
from the path of El Shaddai [Almighty God], place both hands
above [your] head. Proclaim the names of the Sun in the seasons.
If [you] still [do] not see the vision, speak the names three times. If
[you] still [do] not see, spread [your] arms out and drop [your]
hands. Speak the names in reverse and be delivered.

If when you are in the house, it falls upon the earth, quickly proclaim the names of the earth in the seasons and the names in reverse. The stones and wood will be lifted away, and be delivered
without injury.

When in a boat in the sea, and a great storm arises upon the sea,
seeing there is no refuge, proclaim the names of the sea in the seasons. [Through] the names of the glory and honor of the highest,
the storm will abate and [you will] be delivered.

When standing in judgment before the enemy, place [your]
hands over your ears. Speak the names of the week and the letters
of the names. Rise up in the heart of the enemy, righteous in
judgment.

When not hearing words, knowing [that] sin and iniquity are
before [you]. Of disgrace and shame, command the prisoner to
pray in supplication the prayers of this holy book. Remember the
names and rise up in blessing to destroy enemies in righteousness.

When seeking to see the Sun rise in the chariot [Merkabah],
speak the names of the Sun in the seasons. In holiness and purity,
see the passing Sun. See, as the bridegroom going forth from the
wedding canopy.[30] For all desires, petition and they will be given.
After the petition, behold, the Earth trembles. Speak the names in
reverse and send forth upon the path.

When seeking to locate hidden treasure, and bring forth silver
and gold buried in the earth, take the gold tzietz, purified sevenfold.[31] Write upon it the letters of the name of holiness and purity

---

[30] The *chopheh*, the canopy of flowers under which Jewish couples are married.
[31] The *tzietz* is a gold ornament worn on the forehead of a rabbi.

[see top of page 30]. Bind it with a purple cord.[32] Bring forth a white dove and tie the purple cord around its neck. Then it flies with the sign into the air. Follow the dove on foot. The place it descends is the secret place. If it descends in a city, stand upon a roof top. Walk around seven times. When in the day, speak the names of the Sun in the seasons. In the night, speak the names of the Moon in the seasons.

TRANSLATOR'S NOTE—The Hebrew in the talismans here in figure 1 is of an ancient form, and the translation is certainly open to interpretation. The numerous Yod Heh Vau combinations may possibly represent partial spellings of the name IHOH; however, HI may be translated as "oh," or "here is." HO may also be translated as "oh," or "alas." HIH usually translates as "to be," but may also signify "the Lord." IHO may signify "Lord of." There are numerous possible interpretations. Also, AL and AHIH are names of God, although AL may also have various intepretations. Therefore, I have partially translated this talisman, leaving God names and Yod Heh Vau combinations in Hebrew characters. Additionally, the larger talisman presented here is quite difficult to translate. The translation presented is certainly open to interpretation.

---

[32] The word used here is *Thekeleh*, which represents a colored dye obtained from a mussel, species Helix Janthina. The color of this dye is designated cerulean purple.

TRANSLATION OF THE TALISMAN
(PAGE 31)

1) Go forth to write in every place. Of the holy name complete, this is Shem Hemaphorash.

2) Separate 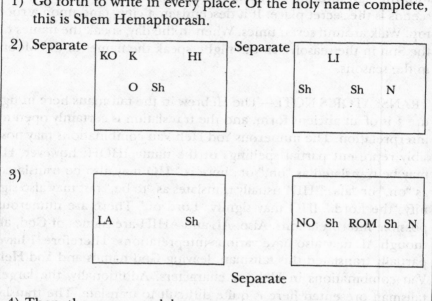 Separate

3)

Separate

4) Then the name and letters are suspended. Not supported above and not below, but alone by itself separated around.

5)

HI HI HOD IH IHO AL BROKA BIH IChOSh IH ROB DIDI IROBIO BITzIRH IHOH DSS AHIH IIHO HH IHO HIH KMH HIH NChMD KMH MPOAR MShOBCh KMH ADIR KMH ARITz KMH NDOR KMH ZRZIR KMH ZK NQI BBROR OKL MShRThIO ZHO KBODO IH HI HO HIH IHOH HO HI HO SS.

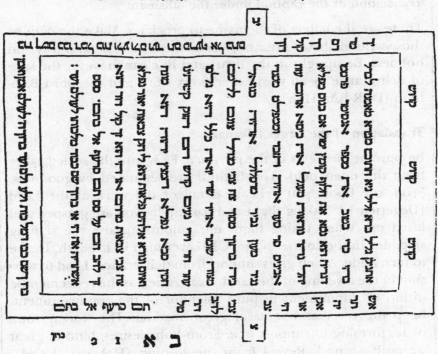

Figure 1. The translation of the text for this figure appears on the following page. The transliteration will be very literal so readers can interpret the text according to their studies.

Translation of the talisman (5):

HI HI splendor IH IHO AL blessing by IH to hasten IH great [strong] by the hand of [power of]. Strengthen [be great] by formation IHOH DSS.[33] AHIH IIHO HH IHO HIH desire [Kemeh]. HIH delight in desire, wondrous from praise. Desire glory. Desire to rush forth. Desire to make a vow. Desire to bind together. Desire that the pure be clean by purification. Of all serving, this is the glory. IH HI HO HIH IHOH HO HI HO SS.

Translation of the caption under the talisman:

These are the letters of the name to proclaim. Make the oath by those written above. After prayers by the letters, be in purity and holiness. Be upright in the heart and in cleanliness for the sake of deliverance by all works over every word and the word Ba'a-hesh [DBR BAa"HSh].

Translation of the larger talisman:

Be pure in the fields of the province. Flow into the sealed valley from the open field. The faithful are separated by goodness. From the book, you write in detail of the work of the Lord [Degeriem].[34] Taking flight and passing by, you are grasped and lifted up. When taking flight miraculously, praise the shining splendor in the course of life. Oh, cover man in strength. Desire to turn aside. Ahieh gives support from deliverance. Lead to worship in the dwelling of the Lord. Exalt Ahieh as the redeemer. Be within by anointment in pure splendor of the commandment. Keep the commandments of great Shaddai. The worthy complete, forming to support one. From holy desires, bind in great strength around. Reveal from the shining (Hebrew: IHOH). Make the offering and revere Elohim. Of the splendor to me, the law of the hosts enlighten. Provoke wonder of pure splendor as the hosts dwell. Here is the clear voice. Dwell in the clear flames

---

[33] The Daleth is likely superfluous, as two Samekhs usually signify termination of the sentence.

[34] This actually translates "the Lord broods (over eggs)," which does not make much sense. A lesser-known interpretation of the root DGR is "work persistently."

of those above. Complete the division of El in perfection [Them Sera'aph Al Bethem]. Oh, here is where the Lord breaks forth [Ashetherieh]. Blessed is the name of the glory of the kingdom forever. [35]

At the top of the diagram (Hebrew: QDOSh) translates as "holy."

The line at the bottom of the diagram translates: "Blessed is the name of the glory of the kingdom forever. Blessed is the Lord of the universe, Amen and Amen."

The line on the upper right side translates: "The Lord breaks forth to strengthen [or bind]. Here is the shining splendor of the glittering mountain of dew."

The line on the lower right side translates: "Complete the division of El in perfection." The line on the upper left side translates: "Through the ages, in a soft and tender voice."

The line on the lower left side translates: "Blessed is the name of the glory of the kingdom forever and ever. Complete the division of El in perfection."

---

[35] There are various possible interpretations of this: Them may be translated "complete," "end," or "perfect." Sera'aph may be translated as "division," "branch," or "thought." Ashetherieh may also be translated as "star of the Lord."

PART 1

THIS IS THE BOOK OF THE GREAT REZIAL

BLESSED ARE THE WISE BY THE MYSTERIES COMING from the wisdom. Of reverence, the Torah is given to teach the truth to human beings. Of the strength and glory, honor the Skekinethov. The power of the highest and lowest works is the foundation of the glory of Elohim. The secret word is as milk and honey upon the tongue. Let it be to you alone. The teachings are not foreign to you. This book proclaims the secret of Rezial, but only to the humble. Stand in the middle of the day, without provocation and without reward. Learn the tributes of the reverence of Elohim. Turn away from evil and journey on the path to pursue righteousness. The secret is reverence of the Lord. The worthy go directly to the secret. It is written, only reveal the secret of El to serve the prophets.

There are three secrets corresponding to the Torah of the prophets. All secrets correspond to these three. The first commandment is the first wisdom, reverence of the Lord.[1] It is written, reverence of the Lord is the first knowledge. The beginning wisdom is reverence of the Lord, corresponding to three wisdoms.

It is written, of the outer wisdom, rejoice and build the house of wisdom with the secret of the foundation. Be wise by opening the heart to the secret.

---

[1] This is often interpreted as "The beginning of wisdom is the fear of God." The term "Yirath" may be translated as "fear," but it may also be interpreted as "reverence." Many scholars disagree, but I firmly believe that "reverence" is appropriate. In support of this conclusion, I refer to the *Oxford Companion to the Bible*, Metzger and Coogan, eds. (New York: Oxford University Press, 1993), p. 225, where it is stated: "The fear of God involves worshipping the Lord with deep respect and devotion. It is a religious expression, and as such implies obedience, love and trust."

There are three kinds of secrets. The secret of the Merkabah [chariot],[2] the secret of Berashith [in the beginning, or Genesis],[3] and the secret of the commandments [the laws of God].[4] These are made clear by the help of Shaddai.

There are three kinds of reverence of heaven. They are reverence of the Lord, reverence of Shaddai, and reverence of Elohim. It is made clear that reverence of the Lord is to love the name of God and serve in love. It is written, man is happy to revere the Lord. It is not written here of reverence of Elohim, but only of reverence of the Lord.

It is written in the commandments to serve in love. Desire to regard in the heart and keep the commandments. In the commandments, it is said of the reverence of Elohim, revere Elohim, lest [you come] into the hands of temptation. Man is not to serve in temptation, of reverence before the king, not rising up by the name.

It is decreed, as it is written, Abraham was beloved. God spoke to him to lead his son. It is written, you know to revere Elohim. You know of love. Know it is decreed, man is happy not to journey by counsel of wickedness. It is written herein, man is happy to revere the Lord. Show reverence to the heavens all the day. Regard love in the heart. The reverence of the heavens is in the heart at all times, reverence of the purity of the Lord. Those giving reverence are loved by the Lord. There is much value in living in purity. Bathe in the glory of the light of Elohim. Go from darkness into light, divided from those led astray. As the light shines down upon the sea, that is the reverence of Elohim who spoke to Abraham. From love, understanding was created by the love and reverence. A thousand generations come after from the love.

---

[2] The term Merkabah is used to describe the mysteries of the Hekhaloth, or the seven heavenly halls of the palace of God. One would travel through them upon a chariot.

[3] Berashith is the name of the first book of the Old Testament, as well as the first word of the book.

[4] Most people are familiar with the tale of the Ten Commandments, which were handed down to Moses on Mount Sinai after the liberation of the Jews from the land of Egypt. However, in the Old Testament (Exodus 20:2–23:19), there are over sixty commandments that were proclaimed by God to Moses. Also, see *Oxford Companion to the Bible*, page 736.

It is written in the Midrash of three kinds of offerings. They are the burnt offering [A'avolah], the peace offering [Shelomim, or "thank offering"], and the sin offering [Chetath].[5]

There are three classes of righteousness. They are love, petition, and reverence. The burnt offering corresponds to love. The peace offering corresponds to petition. The sin offering corresponds to reverence. The burnt offering is a sacrifice to the glory of God alone. The peace offering and sin offering are for the sake of the living body. Proclaim love from the petition and petition from the reverence. From love, you serve God in righteousness. Give glory and honor to the kingdoms alone before all things. In goodness, the Lord created the universe by the word, not by labor. The God [Haloveh] and father and king is strong and wise, good and compassionate. You tolerate all things, filling all the highest and lowest, sustaining in the high places and bringing forth all creatures. You reveal the mysteries of the universe, the knowledge of good and evil. You tolerate wickedness for the sake of the restoration. Behold, all goodness to the righteous who love God. Give praise and laud over the greatest works.

The burnt offering is sacrifice. By petition, serve in the holy place, blessed is it. Fall in supplication and petition. Petition for every measure of goodness for the sake of the benefit of the body. This is the foundation of wisdom, understanding of knowledge. From this, bring light in the days. Heal the woman unable to conceive and make sons upright in the heart. You succeed in works of wealth and glory and treasures, all to the good. Petition the Lord above, thus sacrifice the peace offering.

Give reverence and serve God in great fear.[6] Be delivered from curses written in the Torah. The punishment comes forth from the holy place, blessed is it. Its measure is longer than the Earth and wider than the sea.[7] Receive salvation from affliction, injury, and suffering. Do not writhe in pain. Do not be ruled over by foreign lands. Do not bring death or speak evil. Fill the days in goodness

---

[5] There are five kinds of offerings described in the Old Testament (Leviticus 1:1–5:14): the burnt offering, the grain offering, the offering of well-being, the sin offering, and the offering with restitution.

[6] The context of this passage warrants the use of the term "fear."

[7] This reference describes the dimensions of heaven. See Job 11:9.

and blessings in the world. Deliver from misfortune and affliction and destruction from the walls of fire in Gihenam. The wicked prepare to burn in flames on the day of the great judgment [Yom Hadin Hagedol]. By reverence of the Lord, rise up by sacrifice of the sin offering. Make three sacrifices: the burnt offering, the peace offering, and the sin offering.

Of sacrifices in the first house [Beth Achad] through the first priest [Kahen Achad] in the name of the one God [El Achad], three times in righteousness: by love, by petition, and by reverence. Complete them and be protected by God, protecting and loving you from petition and reverence.

The beginning wisdom is reverence of the Lord and love of heaven. The heart of the righteous burns as flames of fire. Keep the commandments in reverence of the Lord. This the Lord Elohik requires, not making reward for reverence and love. It is written of reverence and love, the Shem Hamephorash was created from love. Of the written word, this is the reverence of Shaddai. Revere God by keeping every commandment. (Reverence of God is not in itself glory, but keeping every commandment.)

Fall down in supplication and cry out to El. Establish the heart and grant the petition at once. Reject wickedness and condemn the wicked. Forsake reverence of Shaddai. Know to withold mercy for sins. Forsake the petition, not revering the name of Shaddai, and not making desire or evil grow in the heart. In the middle of the house, the humble show reverence and gather in the house. It is written in the Midrash, withhold the mercy from those forsaking reverence of Shaddai. Stand and serve before God. Show reverence in prayer and receive tranquility therein. Deliver from all evil. Dwell in the secret place of the most high, hidden in the darkness of the shadow of Shaddai. Deliver from the mouth of the trap [the opening of the snare].

Petition in prayer. Speak, protect from traps. In every petition to Shaddai, be blessed by God the father [El Abiek]. By support of El Shaddai, be fruitful and multiply [Pherov Vorebov]. El Shaddai sees and turns away. Behold, be fruitful and multiply. Wherefore be silent, and bring forth from the secret place that the father reveals to you. Establish Shaddai, of sixty, four hundred, thirty and the Yod above [Hebrew: I' AaOLH, or ten burnt offerings] is five hundred.[8] The man Job begets sons and daughters. There are five hundred of them.[9] Five hundred strong ones [Aberiem], 248 sons and 252 daughters. There are four more daughters than sons. Thus be fruitful and multiply (Hebrew: PRO ORBO).[10] By Gematria, the letters Tau Qoph are the name over be fruitful and multiply.[11]

Therefore, establish to petition the name. Thus, the course of the universe is five hundred years. It is treasured by Shaddai as the measure of heaven. Speak of heaven. According to Shaddai, there is not enough to serve. Remember Shaddai by the prophet of the nations seeing Shaddai. Behold the reverence of Shaddai. Be aided by the name Shaddai, protected from the evil spirits [Hamezieqien]. By protection of Shaddai, lodge and speak prayers of supplication. Therefore the name is written upon the Mezuzah.[12] Penetrate the iron over the Mezuzah. Proclaim and re-member the name Shaddai to protect from the evil spirits, that is (Hebrew: IHOH BATh BSh MTz"PTz Sh').[13] Of the letter Shin of Shaddai, Shin is above [or "300 burnt offerings"] in the name of (Hebrew: IHOH). Of Shin above, (Hebrew: BATh BSh ShM HQDSh ODI) corresponds to (Hebrew: ID KOZO BMOK"SZ KOZO) written in the Mezuzah.[14]

Reveal the secret of the fourteen signs of the holy name. (Hebrew: KOZO HOIH) in reverse Aleph Beth. Thus Yod upholds Kaph, Koph upholds Vau, Vau upholds Zayin, and Heh upholds Vau. Thus, (Hebrew: KOZO).

---

[8] The letters S' Th' L' are used here to represent the Gematria.

[9] In the Book of Job of the Old Testament, it is noted that Job had seven sons and three daughters (Job 1:2). This name may also be Joab, who was a general in King David's army. There are a few stories of Joab involving children. In the Midrash, one tale depicts Joab slaying 500 warriors in Kinsali, the Amalekite capital.

[10] The Gematria of the letters of this phrase is 500.

[11] Tau is 400; Qoph is 100.

[12] The Mezuzah is a talisman attached to the doorpost. It contains a prayer written on a small scroll. Also, see Trachtenberg, *Jewish Magic and Superstition*, p. 145.

[13] BATh may be translated as "come forth" or "in you." BSh may be translated as "shame," but is likely interpreted as "by Shin." MTZ"PTz is a name. The Gematria value is 300.

[14] The name KOZO is considered the antithesis of YHVH, or "Tetragrammaton." The numerical value of KOZO is 39. Also, see Joshua Trachtenberg's *Jewish Magic and Superstition*, p. 92.

(Hebrew: BMOK"SZ ALHINO). Beth upholds Aleph, Mem upholds Lamed, Vau upholds Heh, Koph upholds Yod, Teth upholds Nun, Zayin upholds Vau. Here are fourteen signs corresponding to the three names (Hebrew: H' ALHINO). Therefore, write fourteen letters for the sake of the two corresponding to (Hebrew: H' ALHINO). Write Shaddai with Shin Daleth Yod.

The first Daleth corresponds to the back [or neck]. The Yod of Shaddai corresponds to the fathers, Jacob, Isaac, and Abraham. The final written words are (Hebrew: BATh BSh ShDI).[15] Beth, Shin, Qoph, Daleth, Mem, and Yod.[16] The beginning Yod Yod Aleph is the number of (Hebrew: AHIH).[17] When adding the numbers Resh, Tau, Vao, Samekh, Tau,[18] Israel proclaims Jacob to be Resh, Yod, Vau in number.[19] That is to say, take Resh, Tau, Vau, Samekh, Tau, from the fathers, Abraham, Isaac, Jacob, Israel, here is 203.[20] Combine thirteen letters from the three names of the fathers, and here is 210. Thus the signs of the fathers correspond to thirteen tributes.

There are three praises. Of the Aleph before the name are 63 aspects [Bechineth].[21] Therefore, see the God [El] of Abraham, God of Isaac, and God of Jacob, by El Shaddai. Also the secret of Shaddai is revealed by calculating Tau Qoph.[22] The life of the fathers is 502 years. Abraham lived 175 years. Isaac lived 180 years. Jacob lived 147 years. Together, the years total 502.

Beth [with a value of 2] corresponds to heaven and Earth. In the course of 505 years, the fathers gather to them as the days of the heavens above the Earth. Make clear as the days of the heavens above the Earth. The course is 500 years as the lives of the fathers.

The letter Shin is in the house of prayer. First consider the correspondence to Jacob, that is written Israel.[23] Thus, praise in

---

[15] The Gematria of these letters is 1019.
[16] The Gematria of these letters is 456.
[17] The Gematria of Yod Yod Aleph is 21. This is the same value as the letters Aleph Heh Yod Heh.
[18] The Gematria of these letters is 1066.
[19] The Gematria of these letters is 216.
[20] These are the Gematria values of the names of the fathers: Abraham is 248; Isaac is 218; Jacob is 182. Also, the name Israel has a value of 531.
[21] In the text, it appears to read S"G (which is 63), however the lettering is a bit smudged.
[22] The numerical value of these two letters is 500.
[23] See Genesis 32–35, where Jacob's name was changed to Israel.

prayer. Proclaim the praise, speaking: Praised is the ruler above, and the chosen cast down to Earth. It is written, be cast out from heaven to Earth, the beauty of Israel. Prayers proclaim the glory. By prayer with the letters of glory, stay upon the path of the Lord. Therefore, by the nine fathers [Thesha'ah Bab], give the crown [Apher] in the place of prayer.[24] Of the days of the Messiah, give praise below the crown.

It is written in the *Book of Formation*, the letter Shin reigns.[25] Bind to the crown and bind therein the heavens. Therefore, fire resembles Jacob in heaven. By the letter Shin, create fire, and see fire therein. Thus, in the house of Jacob is fire corresponding to the letter Shin, as Jacob wrestled the angel of fire.

Also, the letter Shin has three branches, corresponding to the three names of Jacob, Israel, and Jeschuron [a periphrastic name of Israel]. The letter Shin is over the noble houses [Bethiem Atzel].

It is written, the image engraved in the throne of glory resembles the image of a flying cherub. Come forth to Egypt. It is written, fly over as the cherub takes flight. Revere Israel by the hand of the strength. It is written to revere Israel, by the hand of the great grandfather [Seva]. Israel resembles Jacob over the sea. Sing the hymn unto Israel. The Lord reigns forever and ever. Therefore, resemble Jacob, according to the written truth. Give the truth to Jacob. According to this, do not go forth unto carved images [Phesoleth]. The daughter, Dinah, was troubled by Shechem[26] and the maiden Aseneth,[27] daughter of Potipherah.[28] The tribes

---

[24] Apher actually translates "gray," "ash," or "meadow." It is probably a transposition for Phar.

[25] See passage 3:9 of the *Sepher Yetzirah*. This is presented on page 155 of Aryeh Kaplan's translation (*Sefer Yetzirah* (York Beach, ME: Samuel Weiser, 1990)).

[26] Dinah was the daughter of Jacob and Leah. Shechem was the name of a province, and the man for whom the province was named, who had raped Leah. Leah and her brothers then took severe revenge upon him. See Genesis 34:1–34:30.

[27] Aseneth was the wife of Joseph, son of Jacob and Rachel. The most famous bible story concerning Joseph is the tale of the coat of many colors (see Genesis 37:3–37:36), which results in his own brothers selling him into slavery in Egypt. He earned the good graces of the Pharoah by his prophecies. The Pharoah gave Joseph the name Zaphenath-paneah, as well as the hand of Aseneth in marriage. She bore him two sons, Manasseh and Ephraim.

[28] Potipherah was the father-in-law of Joseph, and a priest of On.

multiply to put forth the law.[29] Do not speak of idolatry. In the house of Jacob, written by Jacob, is the great name [Shem Hagadol] and the holy tzietz.[30] Take Mikal to become the wife of Potipherah.[31] Proclaim Joseph to take the daughter.

Around the Shin, twelve prayers divide, corresponding to the twelve tribes. The three divide and three tribes spread out as they go forth from Egypt.

The letter Daleth corresponds to the back [or neck], corresponding to Isaac. Straighten the back to unite the name of God. Daleth is the flesh of the back. All the flesh of the back corresponds to the back of the neck. Of all the flesh of the back of the neck, wring the neck. Therefore, shave the back. Place the strap upon the flesh. Inquire of Isaac. The letter Daleth is over the head in purple [argeman, a purple or reddish-purple]. Therefore, the letter Daleth corresponds to the neck.

Also, draw above and below, dwelling in the fourth firmament, the name in the Holy Temple [Beth Hamikadesh], thus the holy tabernacle [Meshikan] of four coverings. The first covering is sky-blue [Thekaleth].[32] The second veil is of goat skin. The third is of ram's leather. The fourth covering is of Egyptian leather [Tachashim, seal, dugong, or badger skin].

In the lowest dwelling, Isaac is sacrificed upon the back of the altar of degrees [Mezabech Shel Ha'aleh], therefore corresponding to Daleth. It is written in the *Book of Formation*, reign with Daleth. Bind it tight and create Mars in the fifth firmament.[33] Close to the Sun, it receives the heat of the Sun to be dry as fire. Therefore, Daleth corresponds to Isaac, the rising of the Sun. Mars is dry as fire and appointed over heat, and over anger and wrath. Therefore, when God is angry, remember Isaac, as he is honored. It is written, remove the ashes from the burnt offerings.

---

[29] The twelve tribes of Israel are descended from the twelve sons of Jacob: Reuben, Simeon, Levi, Judah, Issachar, Zebulon, Joseph, Benjamin, Dan, Naphtali, Gad, and Asher.

[30] The tzietz is a shining plate or talisman worn on the forehead of the rabbi.

[31] Mikal was the daughter of Saul and wife of David. According to *The Oxford Companion to the Bible* (p. 546), the wife of Potipherah, Zuleika, attempted to seduce Joseph.

[32] This refers to a colored dye obtained from a mussel (helix janthina), termed cerulean purple. However, the term may also mean sky-blue, light blue, or azure.

[33] See *Sepher Yetzirah*, 4:9–4:10.

The Yod of Isaac corresponds to Abraham tested by ten trials.[34]
Give in prayer near the side of the first house over the first name
Abraham. It is written in the *Book of Formation,* the letter Yod reigns.
Bind to the crown and create therein Virgo.[35] Abraham takes his
beloved bride [Sarah] as virgin and form with the letter Yod. The
perfection of the Lord [Kalelieh] is separated. Rise over by counsel
from the perfection [Kalivoth].[36] It is written, rise up to the perfection. It is written in contrast to the counsel, take instruction and
correspond to perfection. Give counsel and speak to close friends.
The father Abraham did not learn much from the book, but
learned perfection is as two fountains or springs of wisdom.

Also, the letter Yod corresponds to Abraham lifting the hand of
the Lord God. The Yod corresponds to the heart. It is written, the
faithful reach out with the heart.

Also, the Yod corresponds to Abraham, as according to it, God
foresees Abraham serves by ten trials. Create the universe by ten
commandments. It is written of the history of the heavens and the
earth, the name Abram became Abraham.[37]

The ten numbers are nothing. Thus one and two, three and
four, five and six, seven and eight, nine and ten. Then all calculations repeat. Begin eleven, twelve, and so on. Then twenty is two
times the letter Yod. Thirty is three times the letter Yod, and so on.
Thus all calculations are perfection. Nothing is concealed by language. By ten numbers, speak and close the mouth to speak
profoundly.

At first, the Shekinah precedes the universe by myriad myriads
years, or as many years afterward. The glory of the universe is above
or below, deep and profound. It is in the east and west, north and
south. How great is the light. In darkness, obscure the firmament.
Here is the letter Yod. At first is the letter Aleph. At the end is the
letter Beth. Gimel is above. Daleth is below. Heh is to the east. Vau
is to the west. Zayin is to the north. Cheth is to the south. The light
of the letter Teth reveals light in the air. Darkness obscures all

---

[34] See Genesis 22.

[35] See *Sepher Yetzirah,* 5:8.

[36] This term usually translates to "the inward, secret parts." This usually denotes
the secret workings and affections of the soul. In this context, it probably means
simply "perfection."

[37] See Genesis 17:5.

things. All is formed. It is in all and it is all. Bow down by all. Rise up and give thanksgiving in the heart. As the letter Yod bows down, the ancestors of Abraham go forth. Understand by the *Book of Formation*. Reveal over the Lord [Adon]. Place it in the bosom and kiss the head. Make a covenant.

Also, much more is revealed in the secret work of Berashith with help of Shaddai.

Also, the letter Yod corresponds to Abraham as Yod upholds Kaph. From Adam until Abraham is twenty generations. The universe was created by Yod. Bring forth small things, as Yod is diminutive. Yod is as a humble man, bowing down and rising up.

Also, make clear the reverence of Shaddai. Man serves God with love in the heart. Great is the reverence and devotion. Establish the heart. Keep the commandments. Rejoice in supplication to serve the creator of the universe. By rejoicing and reverence, serve the Lord in reverence and tremble in exaltation. It is written, serve the Lord by rejoicing. The heart rejoices to petition the Lord.

Revere Elohim and serve in fear of Gihenam and the day of judgment, of the suffering and torment. That is the reverence of Elohim. Judge and deliver retribution, as angered by the sins of man. Of every word, it is difficult to speak, Elohim, I do revere you and speak with great difficulty, very loudly at your feet. I shall not fall to rest, but journey to the house and revere you, lest I be punished. It is written, Elohim, judge me by reverence.

I revere Elohiek, speaking every word devoted in my heart. It is spoken, by the Lord Elohiek, revere and uphold the reverence of Elohim, not to fall from grace. In every place, revere Elohim and serve from the reverence.

Behold the reverence of the Lord. Serve in love, corresponding to the burnt offering. Be sustained in exaltation by the reverence of Shaddai, for not to revere is not to serve the Lord (That is not to serve).

Corresponding to the peace offering, fat [Cheleb] and blood is consumed [or burned]. The remainder is to the Lords [Leba'aliem]. The desire of the high priest [Kihenim] is the peace offering, bringing peace in the world. Serve from love and supplication, and strengthen the body. Give to him the Torah, of wealth and treasures and glory and understanding, revere Elohim. Serving in reverence is the foundation. Of the house of man [Aneshi

Bethov], do not deprive support corresponding to the sin offering going over sins. There is great love from the petition and supplication from the reverence.

At this time, become wise and prosper. Of the love of the blessed, after, write the secret of the Merkabah. Let man be wise by reverence forever. Consider the wisdom of the world. By the glory, form the king of flesh and blood. Command the armies and go to battle to smite the enemies in the name of the Lord. Give reverence before going into battle. If there is not reverence, enemies lay waste, prevailing over the land in every dwelling.

The king of all kings, God, exalts in reverence before going on all paths. The Lord is everywhere and in every place. He observes the good and wicked in every place. The worthy revere the Lord in righteousness. Unite the nations in order that the nation [not] be divided. Work for the sake of the heavens. Every path is created from the blessings. Establish the heart. It is written, satisfy the Lord. He is eternal, therefore established.

Blessed is the Lord. Command man to bind and calculate every season. Of the man who is a sinner or thief or adulterer of women, bind to consider much. Of the wisdom, this man is not to know and not to come near, disgraced in every dwelling created by the wisdom of the Creator.

Consider the wisdom that created the commandments, making reward for the love. Serve the Lord a little and serve much. Also, man considers forever not to forsake the wish of the Creator.

Bring the Lord of judgment [Ba'al Hadin] before the magistrates [Sheliton]. Reveal that the magistrates rule over the necromancer [Ba'al Avob] and magician [Yida'avoni], or engage in demoniacal works [Ma'asheh Shedim] or works by the knowledge of the signs of the zodiac.[38] Do not be false or deceitful, as it is revealed the magistrates know all. Also, fear the works binding with an evil spell [Lechebierora'ath], lest [you] come forth to be judged before the magistrates.

---

[38] Ba'al Avob is the Lord of Necromancy. The term "necromancer" may be defined as one who calls up spirits to learn of the future. Yida'avoni means "wizard" or "soothsayer." Ma'asheh Shedim are works of demons or works of violence or destruction.

God gives life to man in the heart. By the path of reverence, reveal all thoughts and understanding of all works. Lord over people and know to summon the Lord of judgment. Speak the words to end deceit. Rise up that the words may be true. It is written, those not pure will not rise up to know of the universe.

It is made known when shame is necessary. Speak, I will not do acts of iniquity, nor deceive by speaking or writing words, not to establish before the eyes. Thus, in every hour and minute, consider the love and search the heart. Examine the perfection. Keep the commandments and show reverence over the lifetime.

Of the root of benevolent acts [Chesiedoth, may refer to Hassidism] measured previously, be judged by every word you write, of favor over all works.

Of the root of reverence, the words are difficult. Know you revere Elohim and perfection.

Of the root of supplication, rejoice in the heart in love of God. Rejoice in the heart from the petition of the Lord. Therefore, be loved and protected.

Of the root of the Torah, the most profound knowledge of the works of all words, it is written, all made by the Lord is good.

The root of the commandments is eight words, corresponding to the eight threads of the Tzitzith.[39] Write and remember all the commandments of the Lord.

The first thread corresponds to the eyes. Do not see without raising up the eyes. Do not brim with tears. After, the eyes do not close. Speak by the power of eyes, lest [you] forget the words seen. Cast down the eyes to salvation. Also, the Totephith is between the eyes.[40]

The second thread corresponds to the ears. Do not be deceived by hearing lies, nor hear the ending of words. Israel hears the decrees.

The third thread corresponds to the throat. Do not swallow all abominations. Make to eat matzoh and similar things.[41]

---

[39] A fringed garment or shawl, draped around the shoulders of one praying in a Jewish temple.

[40] An ornament worn by the Rabbi upon the forehead.

[41] Unleavened bread. The custom of eating matzoh on Passover originates from the days of Moses. When the Jews were being liberated from Egypt, they did not have enough time to allow their bread to rise, therefore they baked unleavened bread.

The fourth thread corresponds to the mouth. Let the tongue not speak words. Of all words written, [do] not labor to make the oath, [do] not deceive by words or speaking the name, [do] not make the oath and speak falsehoods. Also, the teeth are not white in the mouth, or the tongue articulate.

The fifth thread corresponds to the hands. Do not lay the hand in sin and do not steal. Open the door with the hand. Bind the signs by the means of it.

The sixth thread corresponds to the feet. Do not walk about after strange Gods [Elohim Acheri], not stumble and fall. Walk after the Lord Elohik. Journey by all paths, as commanded by the Lord Elohik. Watch the feet as you walk to the house of Elohik.

The seventh thread corresponds to the skin [Ha'aroh].[42] Do not commit adultery. Be fruitful and multiply. Respect circumcision [Hamilah].

The eighth thread corresponds to the nose. Let it not be irritated or excited by the sweet scent of idolatry, nor desire the oblation. Smell the myrtle on the Sabbath, and similar things.

Man is to remember these eight things for all time. Let them be in the heart. Eyes first, ears second, throat third, mouth fourth, hands fifth, feet sixth, and skin seventh. Do not sin by them. The heart is with each. Consider thoughts of every one.

It is written in the Midrash, the congregation [Asepheh] diminishes and grows. Behold them equally over the years. Cast down to the battles. The first rise up and make the offering, fixing the crowns [or ornaments]. The first rise up, fixing the crowns. Reveal what is great. Speak, to ascend by the crowns. Of the wicked, smite the sinners rotting before smelling the scent of idolatry. The eyes close before the journey and the head turns away from the Lord in Gihenam.

The first threads of the Tzitzith are the strands of the greatest length and suitable to adorn. Of the first strand, speak not to deliver the strong ones [Geborim] to vanquish the uncircumcised [A'arelim]. The body is righteous to fulfill the commandments.

First, beginning in prayer. Second, the proclamations of the Torah. Third, opening the heart. Fourth, the nose smells the

---

42 This may also mean "bare skin" or "nakedness." It is obvious from the context here that this refers to male genitalia.

matzoh. Fifth, the hands give righteousness. Sixth, consecration of the Torah and supplication before God. Seventh, the covenant of the body is suspended therein. Eight, the feet walk to the synagogue [Beth Kenesioth] and the house of study [Beth Midrashoth, another name for synagogue]. Therefore complete perfection.

The root of the reverence of the Lord is to forsake the pleasures of lust by the path of the reverence of the Lord. Do not revere the Lord for the sake of salvation of the universe, or being eternal. You just revere, lest not to be perfect before God in love.

As the commandments come into the hands, you labor over the works. Make as Abraham by sacrificing the son. It is written, at this time, know you revere Elohim. At this time, it is made known. Is it not so that before the secrets of the universe were revealed, the knowledge was not yet concealed in the belly [womb]? Speak, you are not tempted. Henceforth not to be tempted by all temptations.

Also, the letter reveals by the word. The heart is perfect by all commandments, as it is not necessary to be tempted. At this time, know the Lord is great. All to Elohim.

Also, by the name Aloah, Joseph spoke: Elohim, I show reverence to you. It is difficult to rise up and go forth to you by the feet. Indeed Elohim. I revere you. My sons endure in famine and the wrath of El. You, the Lord, are revered. It is difficult to rise up, lest reveal not to dwell and be slayed. However, he spoke of reverence of Elohik with devotion in the heart. He spoke to the Lord, I honor you in reverence. You, the Lord, by the holy words. The weight is upon the heart. Consider before the reverence of the Lord. I revere you, the Lord. Surely, take up your son Isaac in the name of God. Take up Nephesh and consider the power [A'atzem]. Come to bind, as a word. It is difficult to rise up, through that beyond desire.

The root of love is to cherish the Lord. The Nephesh is filled with love. You rejoice by passing over the pleasures of the body. Reign over the pleasures of the universe. Love is rejoicing in strength. Strengthen the heart. Consider always how to create desire of God. Bring forth pleasure, walking as women before the love of the Creator. More in youth and passing of the days, many women do not come before El. From desire of the Lord El, the heart burns to rise up to the Lord. From much love and desire, rise up to the Lord. Of the lightning of the early rain [Ivoreh Kachetz, or arrows of the archer], benefit much from all without making desire of the Creator. The body is kept in purity and holiness by the love.

Phineas betrayed the body and slayed Zimri.[43]

As Abraham, place the hand to the highest when below. Until the shoe latchet [Sherok Na'al], Elishah did not desire to receive from Na'aman, and loved the heavens in the heart as flames.[44]

Bind the divisions, not seeing women there and not from the word cast forth. End the words. Toil and labor, making favor of the Creator. Delight by praises to fulfill desire. Rejoice to cherish the Lord.

The root of humility is to go away from the glory and be praised when returning before the Rabbi. It is revealed, gather the friends of the Rabbi to sleep. Know when to rest. Lie down after hard labors. Know when not to toil. Speak thus of labor and desire. Give glory to the friend, but do not speak of young women.

It is written, of you who send forth to journey, speak to send forth. Do not speak to send forth before the heretics [Mieniem], not speaking by the authority in the place. They are also humble. Go before the name of the friend, the house of praise [Beth Chelel] to the house of heaven [Beth Shemiya]. The friend senses [or experiences) and stops speaking. All are able to diminish the glory. Great is the glory to revere the name.

It is written, honor the Lord with the reverence in the eyes to condemn. When seeing humility, there is no desire to go before God. Great is he. Go before Shemethbiyiesh (Hebrew: ShMThBI-ISh). Be humble before the great Shemethbiyiesh. From honoring them, go before the Lord.

When proclaiming, man learns of El, Rabbi Shemethbiyiesh proclaims. Do not praise man much before and much after, and not speaking much. Speak thus, as it is written. Speak to him to learn of Rabbi Eleazer over Rabbi Jochenan Ben Zeketzi.[45] The

---

[43] Phineas was the son of Eleazer and grandson of Aaron. Also, another Phineas was the son of the high priest Eli, see Samuel I 1:3. The time frame here appears to be appropriate. Phineas was said to be a "scoundrel" and an "idolater" (Samuel I 2:12). See Kings I 16:9.

[44] Elishah was a prophet and the companion and successor of Elijah. See Kings I and II. Na'aman was the Syrian commander of King Aram's army. See Kings II 5:1.

[45] According to Kaplan, in the introduction of his translation of the *Sepher Yetzirah*, Rabbi Yochanan ben Zakkai lived in the years 47 B.C.E.–73 B.C.E. (p. xvi).

friend is permitted. El beholds the heart of man himself. When you praise, do not praise the body. It is written, praise the enemy [Zer, or stranger], and not the mouth, but only of the friend. Learn to teach. From the teacher, be able to praise the body. Speak of the perfection of Ahieh. Watch the path of the Lord. Declare the strength to rise up to the high place [Bemah].[46] Lengthen the days and show them the high place. Also, lengthen their days.

Keep all the commandments in secret. In secret, go with Elohik. When keeping them, know how to work before all, such as in prayers, and by the Tzitzith. Of envious writers [Sopheriem], increase the wisdom and the commandments. All are able to make commandments for the sake of the heavens.

Speak of the righteous, you are righteousness by every commandment. Do not be occupied by other matters. Place the love of the Creator in the heart. Reverence is necessary before him. Be skillful making the commandments. Rejoice before El and speak the final words.

In every place and in the synagogue [Beth Hakeneseth, house of gathering or assembly], stand in awe before the Shekinah. Establish the heart only to him. Do not withold passage, as there is disgrace before making the covenent. He is angered when man is not seen to revere, lest [you] make it known to human beings to be disgraced.

All passes forth, that which brothers [Shachiyiem] make. Do not make labor double [or multiply]. Every man toils before the king and before woman. The Creator of the commandments sees before the king. By splendor, the king finds favor in the eyes; however, women are forbidden to see. Speak, it is forbidden for the wife of man to see even the face of the Lord. When preventing sickness [Dothek],[47] do not see before the women. The labor doubles.

Know all the increased words are brought into the hands of the sinner. Consider the suffering of the loss of commandments corresponding to labor. Let all works be for the sake of the heavens. It is good to possess more from them of the brilliance. When you make them, be happy in the world. Good things come to you forever.

---

[46] This generally describes a hill or high place, usually dedicated to religious worship.

[47] A term meaning sickness, usually refering to a woman's menses.

They come from the assistance of the Lord, who created the heavens and Earth.

The secret is reverence of the Lord. Of the secret work of Berashith, Isaac speaks, it is not necessary to begin the Torah, but only restore this to you. Begin by Berashith. Because of that, speak of the power of works revealed to people. All was created in order to know and understand and make wise by the greatest and most wondrous works.

Bear witness there is none as, and there is none other than. I write the book to proclaim the secrets and reveal the strength of the creator of the universe. Man is happy to learn the secrets. Revere the Lord. Shelter him, dividing the universe. Come and write over the mouth of the gates of all that is above. Know of the unity of God. Of the glory, give the heart over to reverence. Bow down to him. He is one and there are not two of him. Blessed is he.

Aleph is as God. It is first and last. He is king over all the universe. There is no other unto him. In as much as the Aleph is first of the letters, God is first of all the Malachim. The Aleph is first. The calculation is small. There is none less than. Thus a myriad calculations.

Aleph is the first letter of the word Achad [one] and Aleph is the last letter of the word Rebova [myriad]. Speak of one Achad [Achad Chad] and a myriad Rebova [Rebova Rebov].

It is written by Ezekial, the first word is El Achad. By Daniel, it is written of a myriad myriads [Rebov Rebovon] before existence. The Aleph fell, as it is the first to designate one. Speak Achad Rebova [one myriad]. The Aleph fell, as it is at the end of Rebova. Speak Rebov. Human beings know it is first. There are none second to it. It is first and it is last.

Aleph is the beginning of calculations and the end of calculations. Also, Aleph begins the alphabet, as Aleph, Beth, Gimel, Daleth. Aleph is at the end, as Aleph, Tau, Shin, Resh, Qoph, Tzadik, Peh, Ayin, Samek. It is proclaimed by three letters, Aleph Lamed Peh.

Aleph is the letter of the larynx. Lamed is the letter of the top of the tongue, in the center of the palate.[48] Peh is the letter of the lips.

---

[48] The palate is considered the seat of taste, which may be taken as a metaphor for the seat of perception.

Aleph begins in the throat. Of the larynx and the tongue, it is in the center of the palate. By the tongue and the lips, to speak.

Let it be known that Achad is first [Rashon], middle [Amtza'a], and last [Acheron]. The last Aleph is turned away [or opposite] from the rest of the letters. The Achad is in the universe. Create the universe turned away from the universe. Speak and revere the power [Avon].

Do not understand, as foreseen by the destruction [Cherben] of the Beth. Speak, do not permit destruction in the world. Hide the face from it. Know that, in the beginning, to create the universe. Indicate the destruction of the Beth. The Beth of Berashith is the great Beth Rashith [First Beth, or first temple] of the Holy Temple [Beth Makadesh], written therein upon the heavens of the first place of the most holy.

Through the gate of Earth, falling [Hietheh] to chaos [Tohu Vobohu] by the written word [Thibeth] in the middle. By Gematria, Tau Yod, indicating the first house [Beth Rashon], serves 410 years to fall.[49] By Gematria, Tau Koph [420] indicates the second house [Beth Sheni], serving 420 years in chaos. Tau Lamed [430] indicates two temples, both serving for 430 years: That is to say, Tau Yod, Tau Koph (Hebrew: ShKNThI) is in the middle of (Hebrew: ShKIN).[50] Here is Tau Yod also in the letters (Hebrew: ShKNThI).

Also, Tau Koph is in many places, indicating the destruction of the Beth. In time, make known Beth Rashith in the beginning of the universe. Remember the destruction of the Beth to destroy all that is created. The Lord alone is sublime.

All created by Beth are in pairs. Two worlds, heaven and Earth. Mountains and hills, seas and rivers. Gihenam and the Garden of Eden. Leviathan and Nechesh Beriech. The Sun and the Moon. Man and woman. Wickedness and righteousness. Man has two eyes, two ears, two nostrils, mouth and tongue, two hands, two feet and sides, so on and so forth.

The Lord El distinguishes Beth, revealing one division. Make known to all, there is a pair. Therefore, opened by the outer Beth, he is one in the kingdom. Blessed is he.

---

49 Tau Yod, by Gematria, is 410.
50 This is a discussion of Hebrew suffixes.

According to Shem (Hebrew: Sh"M), Aleph is the first of the letters. Aleph begins the name (Hebrew: ADNI); however Yod begins the chosen name (Hebrew: YHVH). It is recognized. Aleph Vau Melaphom makes known the universe was created by the ten commandments and filled all.

Also, recognize Aleph Vau. Above is the punctuation point of Vau. The punctuation point is below Aleph.[51] Thus, Aleph, Kamatz,[52] Patah,[53] Aleph, Hatef,[54] Kamatz, Aleph, Hatef, Patah, Aleph, Vau.[55]

Of the seven above, recognize Aleph Vau. Reveal it is united above the seven firmaments. He is the ruler of all (and therefore, the name of Aleph). The name Ahieh is the beginning of the ten sephiroth, above to below. Adonai is the end of the ten sephiroth, beginning by Aleph. Aleph is first of all letters and end of letters, before Tau Shin Resh Peh. Complete to see every one by these letters.

Recognize all the most holy names. Yod begins the chosen name (Hebrew: YHVH). You are not able to write Aleph without the first Yod and also all the vowels.[56] Recognize the letter. It is not able to exist without Yod Vau, that Yod, Cholem [a Hebrew vowel corresponding to the Latin "O"] or Melaphom or Chiroq [a Hebrew vowel indicating the sounds "ee" and "i," as in "slip" or "sleep"].[57]

Reveal by Yod, create ten sephiroth, the universe in the middle, and the universe at the bottom—of Aleph itself, Sheva, Tzeri, Pethach, Chiroq, Cholem, Melaphom, Cheteph, Pethach (Hebrew: QO), Petach, Sheni, Yod, Sheva, Hatef, Patah (Hebrew: QO). When the Yod is below Kametz with Yod above. Of Vau, Cholem with the middle Yod (Hebrew: QO), Melaphom, as when above the line, Chiroq without the line, Sheva or Tzeri with the line. Of three letters (Hebrew: SGL). Aleph by itself, Yod Vau Yod.

---

[51] Portrayed by an Aleph with a dot beneath it.
[52] A Hebrew sublinear vowel in the form of a small mark or dot beneath the letter to indicate the sound of "a," as in "father" (long kamatz), or "o" as in "short" (short kamatz).
[53] A Hebrew vowel to indicate the sound of "u," as in "but."
[54] A short vowel mark to indicate the sound of a, e or o.
[55] The Aleph has a dot beneath it.
[56] The letter aleph is actually four yods in the form of an X.
[57] Hebrew: AO—the vau has a dot at the top; AI—the aleph has a dot below it; AO—the vau has a dot at the middle.

It is written of the name (Hebrew: HOIH). Reveal the Lord is one and created all the universe, the highest, middle, and lowest, filling all. There is not a vowel placed or the covenant [Hebreh] without him. Blessed is he. He is one above the seven firmaments and he rules over all.

Consider the one God [El Achad] for many myriad myriads [Reba Rebeben] years. In the beginning of the universe and in the worlds [A'avolemoth], you see by them and by them, the splendor and glory. Speak in the heart. Human beings are not to consider the glory of the kingdom. Create the universe, that it is to pass. Complete the understanding of El in the heart in reverence. Serve in truth with the perfect heart, and goodness to them all the days.

The Lord [Adon] spoke, all come forth from the Ruoch of the holy spirit [Ruoch Kadesh]. It is the first of all the covenants of man. From the word, Ruoch comes forth from the mouth. Therefore, spirits are not shut up by the worthy in silence.

The tractates on fasting [Tha'anieth, or self-humiliation] are in the *Book of Formation*. [58] Here are words of the Ruoch of fire and water.[59] From the word, man presses the lips. By force, the voice goes forth. Sparks go forth by the Ruoch. Therefore it is spoken, as a hammer smashing rocks. Sparks go forth from stones. Fire comes from the power of the sparks coming from the mouth. Therefore, it is written, is it not so the power of the word is as fire? Here is power from the voice of man, the Ruoch of water, the heat of the fire in every dwelling. From the word, fire consumes fire. Therefore, speak of how to create fire and water. The Ruoch is the glory of Elohim, the secret word. From blessings over the days, all exist by words.

---

[58] There is no text concerning fasting or self-humiliation in the modern English translations of *Sepher Yetzirah*. Tha'anieth is probably an error.

[59] See *Sepher Yetzirah*, 1:14.

PART 2

REGARDING THE POWER OF RUOCH

THE THREE LETTERS OF RUOCH go forth three times. Awaken in the days of Job, Elihu, and Jonah, and make three tributes. The Ruoch breaks boulders and dissolves mountains, and fire goes forth.

It was written by Elihu, Ruoch is great and powerful, dissolving mountains and breaking boulders before the Lord. It was written by Ezekial, Ruoch is great and continuous fire [Ash Methleqocheth].

Resh is the first letter of Ruoch. Resh reduces Beth by numbers. The second letter is round.[1] It is spoken of Ruoch, El goes around in circles to restore Ruoch.

Vau is in Ruoch. It is spoken of the Messiah, first is the spirit of wisdom [Ruoch Chokam], second is the spirit of understanding, third is of strength, fourth is of intelligence, fifth is of knowledge, sixth is of the reverence of the Lord, and seventh is Ruoch.

There are seven [sic] kinds of spirits. The first is Neqemeh [to establish]. Do not judge Ruoch. The second is Hamenshebeth [the breathing one]. It is spoken, in the world, the Ruoch of Elohim hovers above. The third is Melak [messenger, or herald], not by the Ruoch of the Lord. In Yonethen's translation, Hemelak Heruoch [the angel of the spirit], in the dwelling of the Lord, creates the spirit Melak.[2] The fourth is Berieh [nature, or human being]. Speak of El Elohi Heruoch. The fifth is Rechebah [proudly], making the laws of the spirit of justice [Ruoch Meshephet]. The sixth is Shera Demiyonoth [Prince of fantastic images, or prince of

---

[1] Beth is the second letter of the Hebrew alphabet. This refers to the shape of the letter Beth.
[2] Yonethen translates as "Grecian."

imagination]. Fear the Ruoch of Elohim. The seventh is A'arietzoth [mighty, or tyranny]. Do not fear before all. Even though you are weak, A'arietzoth takes on your burden. The eighth is Nebiayiem [prophecies], giving you the Ruoch. The Lord raises the Ruoch of Elihu. Be guided above. The Ruoch of the Lord pours out Ruoch over all flesh. These are the eight kinds of spirits.

God is the king of Shin Aleph Aloph. There is great value and importance in the knowledge of Ruoch. Of human beings, there is the Bible [Miqora], the Mishnah, the Talmud, and the Hagaddah [the narrative and hermeneutical portion of the Talmud]. In them are matters of the earth, and mysteries of the importance of Ruoch.

The male is Amesh. Mem is in the middle between Aleph and Shin. Change (Hebrew: BATh BSh IOR). Here is Amesh, the male.

The female is Amesh. Mem is changed by the Lord by Aleph Beth (Hebrew: AP BAa GS DN HM). Here is woman from Ashem.

The letters are prominent, illuminated by shining lights and complete. Thus, before the creation of the universe, letters are prominent in the Torah. Of the letters (Hebrew: AShM), thus create air. Strengthen by the highest power. Males are stronger than females. Be fruitful and multiply.

Ashem is complete. Created from the air, the females are created much weaker than males. There is air from the great weakening of the females. There is air from the great strengthening of males. Be fruitful and multiply.

The Ruoch goes forth from the holy spirit, filling the lives of all men with the breath of Ruoch. Therefore, remember Elohim by the Ruoch. Many say the Ruoch of Elohim hovers above. From the moisture of Ruoch came the sea. By the power of water came fire. Rejoice in the world.

Man breathes in the palm of the hand and sees moisture. Know when to heat water in a clear glass [or crystal] vessel.

Give praise to the Sun in the month of Tammuz. In the provinces, the atmosphere is warm. Be able to ignite the fire of the waters. Thus from the fire, the stones heat the water in the kettle. Boil therein for many days. After, find the stone divided below the vessel, revealed by the knowledge.

The strength of Ruoch is complete. Ruoch is suspended by the commandment of God. In the end, write the covenant with the Ruoch of the Creator.

It is written, the sea is arranged above the firmament, creating darkness and light. The light is formed and the darkness created. The Ruoch of Elohim hovers above the surface of the sea. Reveal Ruoch over the sea and therefore El. In the days of Elihu, as on the palm of the hand, man rises from the sea. Ruoch is there.

The Ruoch of Elohim is the holy spirit. The living air goes forth from the living spirit [Ruoch Chiyem]. It is created as the glory of the air. The holy name [Shem Hakadesh] from the Ruoch created all spirits. Know Ruoch is the first of all creatures [Haberiyoth] below and above.

Of the four spirits [Ruochoth] of the world, every one of them is in all four corners of the world. Ruoch is actually within every dwelling.

Every day, speak from the *Book of Formation* [see *Sepher Yetzirah*, 1:9–1:14] of the Ruoch. It is inscribed and engraved therein of Ruoch. The mouth is as night and dawn by three.

Ruoch is actually moist and warm. It goes forth from the holy spirit. From the Ruoch goes forth water. From the water goes forth fire. Water is from Ruoch. Every place there is water, there is Ruoch.

It is written, you go to the Lord as water from Ruoch. In the beginning, fill the sea with life by means of Ruoch. The Ruoch is moist. Collect the moisture of the air in the sea on one side. Carve a line of foliage from it. It covers all the world as a kind of green herb [algae] growing upon the surface of the sea.

The stones disintegrate [erode] from the moisture. They sink down in the ocean [Thehom] and water goes forth.

From the letter Mem, create the sea, as Mem is water.[3] Opposite to the proportion of the earth, there is water. Mem resembles water. Man proclaims, you drink between the lips and the sign of the sea resembles it [the letter Mem].

Mem is the first letter of the word Mayim [water], Mebova'a [spring], Meqovor [fountain], Ma'ayin [well], Moqvoh [pool, or pond]. From the holy word, all water goes forth in purity as a pool of water. God proclaims Moqvoh three times.

---

[3] The Hebrew word for water is Mem, spelled Mem Yod Mem.

Second, Moqvoh Israel, the Lord and Aleph and Moqvoh are as fathers [Abothikem]. Of the Lord, therefore, Moqvoh, by rising three mothers [Amoth]. Moqvoh, by Gematria, is forty Seahim.[4]

In the *Book of Formation* [see *Sepher Yetzirah*, 3:8], Mem is bound to the crown. Combine this with that. Flood the Earth, forever cold in the year. Draw out by Nephesh, male and female.

Divide the name Mem. Begin the word and combine the letters, making two words. Proclaim the first one Mash [Mem Aleph Shin] and the second Mesha [Mem Shin Aleph]. Form Earth in the world, as a fountain of cold water. In the belly, by the heat of Nephesh, consume and bring forth the cold. Male is Mash amd female is Mesha.

There is Earth. Bring forth the words and bring forth grass between. Of every word, there is female and male. On raining days, it is cold.

Ruoch is warm. There is moisture in the breath, as vapor comes from the mouth. Thus, place the word upon fire. The water goes forth from the moisture, therefore do not speak of how to create. The voice of the Lord is over the water. In the beginning, you, the king, receive by voices. Speak, the Lord is mighty in the heights [Adier Berom].

The Torah holds dominion over the sea. Of all who thirst for water, it comes to pass from counsel of Melakethov [angels, or heralds]. Be in purity as instructed by the Lord [Lomedieh, or disciple of the Lord]. Therefore, in forty days Moses received the Ten Commandments. Also, forty days afterward, of two-times-forty and the Ten Commandments, here is water. The moisture of the word fills all the world with water. Ruoch hovers above the sea.

Of water and fire, water comes forth from Ruoch of the holy word [Ruoch Debor Kadesh]. By the virtue, complete it. Fire comes from it, carving the throne as divided. Shin is engraved above and fire turns to heaven. Of fire, hissing by tearing [Qoriya'ath, or rending],[5] from hearing the sound of the letter of fire. When burning, the sound goes forth. Shin is above, as a lamp extinguished. The flames rise up. Come forth and proclaim Shin to change the

---

[4] Plural for Seah, which is a liquid measurement equaling fourteen quarts.
[5] The term usually refers to the tradition of tearing one's garment in time of mourning. Also, see *Sepher Yetzirah*, 2:1.

language. Of heaven, as in the *Book of Formation*, the Shin is bound to the crown. Combine this with that, forming the heavens [Shemiem].[6]

In the world, the heat in the year begins. Of Nephesh, the male and female. Divide the crown of Shin by fire and engrave the first word. Combine the letters, making two words. Know that male is Shema and female is Sham. Form the heavens in the universe from fire and the heat of the year. The first alone is from heat. Bring forth heat. There is heat in the year. Divide from the heavens and bring forth human beings, males and females.

Shin changes the language. Of Shin, there are three branches. It is the first letter of heaven. The Sun therein is fire and the Moon is snow. The blackness spreads. Here is three. The Sun is fire as red coals and the Moon as flames. The Moon in the firmament is similar to coal embers. Thus, there are three branches of Shin.

Fire is formed with the Shin. Therein are three things: flames, smoke, and embers. There is no fire without Ruoch blowing the letters. Therefore, binding Aleph with Shin is Ash [fire]. By Aleph form Ruoch. By Shin form fire. Shin changes language. The fire of heaven creates water. Consume the water. It is written, drain the water by licking it up.

The heart goes forth from the holy spirit as the brightness of fire. It is written, every word comes by fire. Pass over fire and purify. Above, purify by fire of the river of fire [Neher Dienor. This is also a reference to the Milky Way], and below, purify by the sea, existing by the word.

Fill the world with Ruoch, water, and fire. Amesh is air, water, fire. Fire decreases the water. Of all words of the petition, water is appointed above to descend below. Flames rise upward, coming to the place. The Ruoch of Elohim hovers over the surface of the sea. The holy spirit takes the fire together in the middle, of the Lord Shaddai. Now, life is in the world. Of water, Ruoch is over the water and fire is above all things.

Speak to the Lord in the heart. There is no glory to the king without the host to create worlds of knowledge and the glory of the kingdom. Counsel the king in all things. Teach him the Torah. The

---

[6] This is spelled Shin Mem Yod Mim. Also, see *Sepher Yetzirah*, 3:9.

value and importance of Berashith increases. Ahieh withholds the teaching of the word of the Torah. I exist in all things.

Of the teaching of God in the Midrash, the wisdom of the Lord is the foundation of the universe. There is no wisdom, but only of the Torah. It is written, it is the highest wisdom and the highest understanding. Learn that God created the universe by the wisdom of the Torah. Know (Hebrew: ChITh KP MM HH) by Gematria is 613.[7]

It is written, in the beginning, Elohim created [Berashith Bera Elohim]. There is no beginning, but only in the Torah.

It is written, the Lord establishes the beginning path of Berashith. By Gematria, the Torah was formed to learn from. Know the universe was formed by the Torah.

Aleph is one and Beth is two, which is three. Gimel is three, which is six. Daleth is four, which is ten. Heh is five, which is fifteen. Vau is six, which is twenty-one. Zayin is seven, which is twenty-eight. Cheth is eight, which is thirty-six. Teth is nine, which is forty-five. The letter is set in order to form one. Now calculate. Ten and ninety is one hundred. Twenty and eighty is one hundred. Thirty and seventy is one hundred. Forty and sixty is one hundred. Together this is four hundred.

Fifty remain set in order. Fifty with forty-five is ninety-five. Set in order ninety-five with four hundred. Here is four hundred and ninety-five.

Obtain five [H']. Subtract from five hundred [MTh"Q], and obtain five fifths [Chemesheh Chomeshi]. The Torah rules from the amount five hundred.

The universe was created in the course of five hundred years. Therefore, in the Torah form the universe. It is written of the covenant of day and night and the limits of heaven and Earth. It is not established in the Torah from the word.

Study therein day and night. It is known, study the Torah all the day. Consider every verse of the Torah, bequeathed to us by Moses.

In language it is (Hebrew: ATh BSh).[8] In numbers it is (Hebrew: IG ALP).[9] Subtract 40 [M']. That is to say:

---

[7] The Gematria actually calculates to 618, as the letters are presented here.
[8] The Gematria of ATh is 401. BSh is 302.
[9] IG is 13. ALP is 111.

One times four hundred is four hundred.

Six times eighty is four hundred and eighty.

Three times two hundred is six hundred.

Five times ninety is four hundred and fifty.

Here is (Hebrew: ThORH) [Torah], nineteen hundred and thirty.[10]

Five times ninety is four hundred and fifty.

Six times eighty is four hundred and eighty.

Five times ninety is four hundred and fifty.

Here is (Hebrew: TzOH), thirteen hundred and eighty.[11]

Twenty times thirty is six hundred.

Nine times fifty is four hundred and fifty.

Six times eighty is four hundred and eighty.

Here is (Hebrew: LNO), fifteen hundred and thirty.[12]

Ten times forty is four hundred.

Two times three hundred is six hundred.

Five times ninety is four hundred and fifty.

Here is (Hebrew: MShH), fourteen hundred and fifty.[13]

Ten times forty is four hundred.

Six times eighty is four hundred and eighty.

Three times two hundred is six hundred.

Two times three hundred is six hundred.

Five times ninety is four hundred and fifty.

Here is (Hebrew: MORShH), twenty-five hundred and thirty.[14]

---

[10] The Gematria is for ThORH and APGTz.
[11] The Gematria is TzOH and HPTz.
[12] The Gematria is LNO and KTP.
[13] The Gematria is MShH and IBTz.
[14] The Gematria is MORShH and IPGBTz.

Four times one hundred is four hundred.

Five times ninety is four hundred and fifty.

Ten times forty is four hundred.

Twenty times thirty is six hundred.

One times four hundred is four hundred.

Here is (Hebrew: QHILOTh), twenty-two hundred and fifty.[15]

Ten times forty is four hundred.

Seven times seventy is four hundred and ninety.

Four times one hundred is four hundred.

Two times three hundred is six hundred.

Here is eighteen hundred and ninety.[16]

Here is (Hebrew: S"K HK"L I"G), a thousand less forty [M'].

Thus, there are twelve hours in the day, and in every hour, one thousand and eighty divisions. So, here is twelve times one thousand and eighty, thirteen thousand less forty, and thus night.[17] Study therein day and night.

Twenty-four books correspond to twenty-four hours in the day and night. Six orders [Sedriem] correspond to the six days of the week. Of four orders, there is Gemara, against four days of the week, without reading the Torah, and four orders of classes.

The Torah is the counsel of God, the King, King of Kings, King of Malachim. Blessed is the Lord of the universe, Amen and Amen.

---

[15] The Gematria is QHILOTh and DTzMBA. The Vau was excluded.
[16] Although not noted in the text, the Gematria appears to be IAaQB and MZDSh.
[17] ThThR"P I"G ALPIM PChOTh M'. The result is 12,960.

PART 3

IN THE BEGINNING
[BERASHITH]

IN THE BEGINNING, GOD CREATED TWENTY GATES. It is revealed to the son of man by twenty letters. Create two names (Hebrew: AaHZ OHAaHB). By Yod Heh, the Lord formed the worlds, the Heh of (Hebrew: HAaHB) by Yod and (Hebrew: AaHB) over the works of creation preceding the universe. Yod precedes Heh and Aleph Tau precedes the holy name, blessed is it. Of Aleph Beth of Yod, for the sake of combining Yod Heh Vau.

Aleph is one. Beth is two, which is three. Gimel is three, which is six. Daleth is four, which is ten. The Yod is upheld by Heh Vau. Yod Heh Vau is the holy name. Divide the gates by the names of Beth. There are three sides to the universe, as the letter Beth.

Of Yod, words are created corresponding to the Ten Commandments.

Of Tau, the lives of the people [Thechiyieth Hamethiem] [are created]. Therefore, this is the gate to create the universe. Also the face of Beth is above. Aleph stands alone, forever turning the face in the universe.

Beth is written at the side of the desert as Bethiem [Beths, or houses]. You see Beth in the desert as the Earth. Here is chaos [Tohu Vobohu].[1] El was in the heavens, but there was no man in the beginning of the universe. The Earth was chaos, in darkness and desolation [Tohu]. Divide the emptiness [Roqnieth] from all goodness.

---

[1] This represents the two veils of nothingness of the qliphoth. Tohu translates "desolation," and Bohu translates "emptiness." Collectively, they translate "chaos."

In desolation, lament in the desert. It is the place of desolation, as there is no goodness therein. After the desolation, do not benefit and be not delivered from [it]. Thus, see the Earth is chaos and there is no man. Falling to the Earth, desolation consumes all the universe.

Of emptiness [Bohu] establish the days. Adam and his wife are concealed in the middle of the tree in the garden. It is not a cemetery [Bieth Ba'avolem].[†]

The clouds darken, as water is dark in the sky. Proclaim the clouds become dark and withhold the light. The darkness obscures sight when Eliek descends in the darkness of the clouds. Here create the clouds. Darkness is not without speaking, let there be light. Before darkness, light was not created in the universe.

Speak of darkness over the surface of the ocean. The clouds darken by the water near the sea. Also, in the beginning, the universe was dark. Therein a substance, as required by darkness. Of how many thousands of myriads, there is no beginning.

Thus of the universe, God is in the worlds. After, there are eyes to see therein other than Elohim. Do not rise up to support the evening. Illuminate according to the time of rest, as the rebellion of the darkness, in the dark of night, counseled by God in thanksgiving of the creation of the universe. The Torah is written by the strength of the fire of the Moon.

There are seventy-three names of God inscribed to the right. Alone in the universe, turn to this side and fear there is no man. Desire to be alone forever and to be one. He turns away from you, and at once you beg. The one goes forth, taking three drops of water and filling the universe with water. Dwell over the sea.

---

† There is a note in the original text that reads as follows: Add one, two, three, four, five, and six. The total is twenty-one. The second begins. That is to say Aleph Zayin. By the addition of seven, this is twenty-eight. The secret of Aleph Zayin, through deliverance, indicates twenty-eight works. Also, study Aleph, Beth, Gimel, and Daleth. The secret of Aleph Daleth [AD translates as mist or vapor], rising up from the earth. Add one, two, three, and four. The total is ten. Aleph Daleth by three [written "A"D BG'] in the center is the Heh. Heh is Nun. By the number, subtract, and here is the name Adonai. That is the secret of Beth, Gimel, Daleth (Hebrew: QODSh) [holy] indicates Beth, Gimel, Daleth, Beth, Daleth, Kadesh. With the Gimel in the middle, here is Beth, Gimel, Daleth, by Gematria, Yod, Heh. Beth, Gimel, Daleth, by itself is nine, and Resh Tau and Samekh Tau [OR"Th OS"Th]. Beth and Daleth is six. Here is fifteen [T"O].

The Ruoch of Elohim hovers over the face of the sea. The water is divided into three parts. One third is suspended above by his command. One third is springs. One third is sea.

Second, take three drops of light and divide them. One third is (Hebrew: BAaHZ). One third is (Hebrew: BAaChB). One third is the days of the Messiah.

Third, take three drops of fire and divide them. One third to create the Malachim. One third is the lives [Chiyoveth] of the holy. Of one third, do not breathe the fire.

Fill the world with water, light, and fire. Fire is on the right. Air is on the left. Water is below. Take and mix this with that. Take fire and water to create the heavens. Take water and air to create the throne of glory. Take fire and air to create the lives of the holy. The angel [Malachi] serves.

It is written, the wisdom of the Lord is the foundation of the Earth. Number the wisdom seventy-three, as the seventy-three names of God. Inscribe by the strength of God, laying his hand upon seventy names, every one able to create one universe. Thus it is indicated in the Midrash, the wisdom of the Lord is the foundation of Earth.

I receive, as it is written in the *Book of Formation*, of ten sephiroth. First, of the Ruoch of Elohim, the living breath of the mouth. Second, of the holy spirit, the Ruoch of air. The Ruoch does not go forth, but seven spirits [Ruochoth] go forth. From the word, Ruoch goes forth. The water is third from Ruoch, the wetness of the moisture of the words. The fire is fourth. The water displaces the heat by the words. The fifth is above. The sixth is below. The seventh is to the east. The eighth is to the west. The ninth is to the south. The tenth is to the north.[2]

From the words come the world, except for air, water, and fire. Mix fire and water together to create the heavens. Proclaim before, let there be light, not requiring light. Light is the power of Shaddai.

It is written, be wrapped in light as Solomon, the man that built the precious house [Beth Segor]. The shining lamp illuminates the shadows of the Ruoch of air as fog.

---

[2] See *Sepher Yetzirah*, 1:9–1:14.

Speak from the midst of the fire. The fire of Ruoch rises up as a narrow pillar of smoke. It is between the heavens and the Earth. It is divided first in the desert, second in the mountains, and third in the inhabited land. Hold dominion in the dwelling. Without eyes, be able to rule by the desire to see in the house.

There are three windows. The strength of the Sun goes forth above the windows and within the house. Thus, desire is as the measure of the strength. Bind and stand away from the windows. It is the air.

In the days of winter, see the narrow fountain rising up from the air and fire. It is not gathering above, but sinking in water to heat the earth. It is not usually visible, going forth from outside.

Also, in the days of the winter when the air is cold, body heat goes forth from the breath from the mouth of man standing outside, as fine smoke.

In the days of summer, the air is warm and the body is warm, not separating this from that.

The heavens are suspended in the air. Earth is suspended from the air. By the turning of the wheel, Earth turns around. There is no movement from the place. Speaking metaphorically, it is as a vessel of glass with the width of the mouth short; and as a chaff, or dry leaf, or wing of a bird, or the shell. Put it in place, face to face with the vessel. Breathe the Ruoch by the power, until filling the vessel with Ruoch. Then rise up in the air in the middle of the vessel, until the Ruoch is therein. Thus, Earth is suspended in air and air sinks in moisture.

The power of the Sun is the heat of the day. However, in night, lie down below the air, covered in a garment of wool or leather. The next day, the moisture goes forth from the mouth in a flowing movement, as a river in the air going forth from the mouth. Of the air of Ruoch, water is from air.

Of God, there is none like him. Only in the image, in order to understand the teaching. Thus the river goes forth from the mouth of Adon. From the flowing of the water by the power of the river, fog is all around. It covers the rivers from the heat of day. The river makes chaos in the direction of the green foliage. It resembles an image of a green arch.

When man is in a boat on the sea in the highest waves, look in the direction of the green above. It is reddish near the bottom and the sea below is black near the deepest points. This is the place of darkness. In the shadow of the water, be able to look from end to end; to the ends of the world, from heaven to Earth.

The shadow of the water is fifteen cubits high from the heights of the mountains. By movement of water, man rises over the top of the mast [Thoren]. Observe the curvature of the earth before the water rises. Man sees this in the water. From the distance of the province, see all lands are like a bowl.

From the foam, the sea freezes as snow. In the mud and loam, raise a flower bed of fragrant herbs. Sow many varieties of fragrances. Make the border around the flower bed and place up a wall. When the sea comes forth, do not forsake them in a storm. It is as a valley. Put the rain therein. The clouds are filled with water and become dark. Do not speak how the light goes forth from the word.

I learn the secrets of fire and light. Also, how much moisture is inside, and of times to listen to sounds not able to rise above the foundation, and how to rise above the hidden and unknown, but only as ancestors receive in their hands. Reveal how to illuminate the sea from the holy word. Speak of you ruling over the truth.

Man inscribes the signs from the image. The angel drives out the accursed. God casts down from the heavens to find Adam, the first man. Return to inscribe the image from Aleph until Heh Yod Vau.

Thus of the water, Heh Yod Vau of the shining [or glorious] Malachim. Also by the name, man is the shining lamp in the house of illumination [Beth Lehayir, or house of light]. Thus created the universe by the most holy word, blessed is it.

Over the shadows of the sea, light goes forth. Light illuminates it forever. Let there be light. Perform miracles by the light. Create the sea. In many places, it is proclaimed, the sea is as light. Disperse the cloud with light. When covering the eye from light, therein the sea flows as tears from the eye.

Therefore, proclaim the light of day is the inlet of the sea. Let there be light. The clouds go dark. The Ruoch connects over the sea and the air between the shells [Qliphoth]. Heaven is in the day. The Moon is as a sphere. Water is above and below the universe, going around the firmament thus.

אור רגלאן
ארין על
מים

Figure 2. The translation of this talisman
reads, "Light fills Earth above water."

Between all the shells is light. The light is created from the moisture of the word. Create water in the storehouse of water as rain
and lightning. The storehouse of snow is the place the water shines.
There is no darkness.

Thus of snow and rain, lightning comes, the lightning of the
heat of the luminaries. Proclaim light over the name of air to
pierce the darkness. The light is required of all actions, therefore
sustained.

It is written, let there be understanding of light. Also it is written, let there be light to sustain the requirements of light. Also, it is
written of the reverence of Elohim by the light.

Goodness completes the requirements of actions. Speak in
goodness over the light, not over the heavens and Earth. The water
is above. Let there be light, not being heaven, not Earth, and not
water. Therefore, it is not written, let there be understanding. Let
there be light. The river of fire is shining between the qliphoth.

From the word, the light goes forth before all. Engrave the word
and be enlightened. Your light is sweet and treasured. Rejoice in
righteousness. Rejoice in the light of righteousness.

The world is one third water, one third wilderness, and one
third inhabited land. Also, the Earth of heaven is in the days. Also
(Hebrew: HAaHZ OHAaB). In the days of the Messiah, reward the
people of Jerusalem with mercy.

In the dwelling is three firmaments. From here, create pillars to
strengthen them, not to be seen from the side. They are as stones
rising up by the side, thus they are not seen. It is written, heaven
measures three spans [or hand-breadths].

God takes pure fire and pure water, mixing them to create heaven. Create heaven with fire. In the beginning, Elohim created the heavens and the Earth, arranging seven houses above and seven below. Heaven extends upward as a cobra [Phethen] in a great veil. The Sun is complete, extending to surround heaven, resembling a veil.

It is revealed, you are over the gate and brought forth. The king brings forth and covers you, going forth and passing over you. The veil rises up as the morning star [A'amod Heshecher].

Of the heat of the Sun, cover the first firmament before the wheel of the Sun. Gather the heat passing over. Gather the Moon, stars, and signs of the zodiac. The Sun in the universe is the House of Glory [Beth Helel].

Speak of the Earth, created by the glory. Thus, the gate is in heaven before arranging the constellations.

Nisan is the first month of the year. Fire is the beginning of all things. Here is light to measure first. Nisan is the beginning of the warmth of the year. Aries is fire. It is the sign of the zodiac of Nisan. It is (Hebrew: TAQ).

After fire (Hebrew: AaPR) is Taurus, the sign of Ayir [the second month]. It is earth and (Hebrew: ShBG) is earth.

(Hebrew: AChK) is air. Gemini is the sign of Sivan [the third month]. It is air and (Hebrew: AChK).

Water corresponds to Cancer, the sign of Tammuz [the fourth month]. It is water and (Hebrew: SPD) is water.

Leo is the sign of Av [the fifth month] and fire.

Virgo is the sign of Alul [the sixth month] and earth.

Libra is the sign of Tishri [the seventh month] and air.

Scorpio is the sign of Marheshvan [the eighth month] and water.

Sagittarius is the sign of Kislev [the ninth month] and fire.

Capricorn is the sign of Teveth [the tenth month] and earth.

Aquarius is the sign of Shevet [the eleventh month] and air.

Pisces is the sign of Adar [the twelfth month] and water.

(Hebrew: ShShTh SAB MAQ GDR) are appointed. Therefore, in the scriptures, arrange heaven and earth. The Ruoch of Elohim hovers above the surface of the water.

Of light first, thus Aries is fire and proclaimed first. Nisan establishes the chamber to consume the offering. Obtain lambs from the herdsman. Proclaim the light. Speak to him of the secret of darkness. I desire to create the universe by the light. Speak before him of what you created before. Speak of not turning aside and devise the curse with you, to perish from the world. I am the Creator by the light of Aries. It is the fire, the sign of Nisan.

Speak after the light El created. Your darkness resembles Taurus, the sign of Ayer.

After, El created Gemini, the sign of Sivan. Man shuts out light. In the darkness, give two tablets.

After, El created Cancer of water, the sign of Tammuz. Everything requires water.

After, Yah speaks of Leo, the sign of Av. Man grasps with the strength of a lion.

After, Yah speaks of Virgo, the sign of Alul. Man is ready to be profound.

After, El of Libra, the sign of Tishri. Man as Virgo weighs you in Libra.

After, El of Scorpio, sign of Marheshvan. Weigh you in Libra. Of iniquity, be cast down to Gihenam, the place of serpents and scorpions.

After, Yah speaks of Sagittarius, the sign of Kislev. Descend directly to Gihenam, not rising to the Lord directly. From the petition of the highest for mercy, I cast down to Gihenam, as an arrow from the bow.

After, El of Capricorn, the sign of Tebeth. Be cast down directly to Gihenam, not rising up. Therein are the power of darkness [Meshechierien], turning away and leaping up. Rise as Capricorn.

After, El of Aquarius, the sign of Shebet. I sprinkle water to cleanse in purification of iniquity.

After, Yah speaks of Pisces, the sign of Adar. Rise up directly from Gineham. Succeed in the universe. Go forth to the spring, therein the dominion. Thus it is distinguished in the Midrash.

Then flow to the previous position of Aries in fire in Nisan, forming the chamber.

Of earth, Taurus is in Ayer, going forth from Thehom below. The image of a calf lying down on the ground, a fatted lamb. In fasting, therefore, make the image of a calf upon the ground, below the feet.

Gemini is in Sivan, corresponding to the Ruoch. There is no air going forth. By the word, from death, the trees flourish.[3] Cancer is in Tammuz, corresponding to the water. Of the great name of every generation on the Earth, suspend the signs of the zodiac. Therefore, heaven precedes Earth. However, Earth was created in the beginning, until here explaining the creation of Earth.

Of the twelve signs of the zodiac, God created light to shine in day and in night, but it was not seen in the day before the power of the wheel of the Sun. Measure it to see in night, except from the sign of the rising Sun. The highest is when the measure rises up to the sign of the zodiac. After, the union is concealed. From them, it is revealed to rise in the east. The star sinks down here and there over the measure.

Aries is arranged as the highest. Libra is in the period that stands in the east, setting in the west. The star of Aries sinks in the west as the star of Libra rises. Aries measures sinking, Libra measures rising. Then, Taurus and Scorpio, Gemini and Sagittarius, Cancer and Capricorn, Leo and Aquarius, Virgo and Pisces.

Measure the distance going forth, in the amount rising from the east, in the amount sinking in the west. In the amount, there is not one of them, but two arranged; not gathering in the boundary of the divisions of the sign of the zodiac.

When serving in the Spring, not serving in the Autumn. When serving in the Winter, not serving in the Summer. When serving in

---

[3] A reference to the death of trees in winter, and rebirth in the spring.

Summer, not serving in Spring. When serving in Autumn, not serving in Winter.

Arrange the ministers in the middle. Libra, Scorpio, and Sagittarius are in the middle. Plant seeds during these months. They minister for sixty-one days. In the middle is Sagittarius. Of Capricorn, in the middle is Aquarius. They minister in the days of the winter for sixty-one days. In the middle is Aquarius. Of Pisces, in the middle is Aries. They minister in the days of the spring for sixty-one days. In the middle is Aries. Of Taurus, in the middle is Gemini. They minister in the days of the autumn for sixty-one days. In the middle is Gemini. Of Cancer, in the middle is Leo. They minister in the days of the summer for sixty-one days. In the middle is Leo. Of Virgo, in the middle is Libra. They minister in the days of the warmth for sixty-one days.

The wise men of Israel speak of the firmament. It is made as a tent. The signs of the zodiac are fixed in the wheel. The wise men of the nations speak of the circle of the wheel. The signs of the zodiac are fixed therein, turning around. The wise men speak the words, not indicating Scorpio is in the south and the Dipper constellation is in the north. The Dipper constellation does not move from the place, not circling in the wheel.

The letters (Hebrew: TAQ) are fire (Hebrew: ShKG) are earth (Hebrew: ThMD) are air, and (Hebrew: SAaD) are water. Man does not know the root source [essential origin] of the signs of the zodiac. God created them, but not from the actions.

It is written, El poured out water in heaven and Earth, and fixed the signs of the zodiac. Reveal the works of the highest blessings. See the signs circle. Proclaim the sign of the zodiac when leaving. Bow down to the glory and the hosts of heaven [Tzeba Shemiem].[4] Bow down and be humble. Create all hosts by the Ruoch from the mouth.

The four above and below correspond to the twelve divisions: (Hebrew: TAQ) is fire; (Hebrew: ShKG) is earth; (Hebrew: ThMD) is air; (Hebrew: SAaR) is water. The twelve signs of the zodiac correspond to the three letters. Therein are the hosts [Methechielien]

---

4 This term may refer to the angels, or to the Sun, Moon, and stars collectively.

of judgment. The last letters are (Hebrew: ShAZIININ), the three letters without (Hebrew: ZIININ).

Thus, there are twelve months and twelve great lives [ChOI-IOTh] in the hands and feet. There are twelve tribes and twelve Malachim surrounding the throne of glory. Twelve blessings increased by all prayers. Twelve orders of the Torah, the laws of the Lord.

The first is integrity [Themiemeh]. The second is the restoration of the soul [Meshibeth Nephesh]. The third is faithfulness [Nameneh]. The fourth is intelligence [Mechokemeth]. The fifth is uprightness [Yiesheriem]. The sixth is rejoicing in the heart [Meshemechi Lebov]. The seventh is chastity [Bera]. The eighth is enlightenment [Mayiereth]. The ninth is cleanliness [Tehoreth]. The tenth is servitude [A'avomedeth]. The eleventh is truthfulness [Ameth]. The twelfth is righteousness [Tzadiqov].

Therefore, the twelve hours of the day are occupied by these twelve orders of the Torah. Thus, the offering of bread for you to eat is of twelve shew breads. There are twenty-four tithes [A'asheronieth] serving the students of the Torah. Study for twelve hours in the day and twelve hours in the night. Of the twenty-four books, therefore be upheld at the side of the Lord and receive redemption.

The first step is to cook and mix the wine. Prepare the table and proclaim to those serving. Instruct those who are simple. Instruct them even when there is no desire to occupy themselves with the instructions of the Torah. Therefore, eat the bread of the Torah by eating twelve shew breads.

There are twelve praises [Shebechoth] of the Torah. The first is beginning [Rashith]. The second is preceding [Qedomim]. The third is from before [Maz]. The fourth is of old [Ma'avolem]. The fifth is in advance [Merash]. The sixth is early [Meqedomi]. The seventh is without [Bayin]. The eighth is Bayin. The ninth is Bayin.[5] The tenth is before that [Beterem]. The eleventh is in front of [Lepheni]. The twelfth is not until [A'ad La].

Of the twelve after, the first is the way of [Derekov]. The second is the act of [Mepha'aliyov]. The third is the work of [A'avosh].

---

[5] The eighth and ninth may be typographical errors.

The fourth is in the presence of [Bephienov]. The fifth is in the bosom of [Bechiqov]. The sixth is in the midst of [Bametza'a]. The seventh is by the strength of [Ba'azoz]. The eighth is by the name of [Beshomov]. The ninth is by the law of [Becheqov]. The tenth is at the side of [Atzelov]. The eleventh is in the presence of [Lepheniyov]. The twelfth is in the land of [Aretzov].

The twelve signs of the zodiac were created for the sake of the Torah. There are four divisions of the signs, and thus of the Torah. Watch over the gates of the dwelling day by day. The first is by the journey [Vobelekethek]. The second is by rising up [Vobeqoumiek]. The third is by lying down [Vobeshekebek]. The fourth is by sleeping [Vobesheneh]. These are the four periods.

Man returns to serve. Learn of the three periods in the day and night, of sixteen in Av, until sixteen in Ayir. Therefore uphold and consider the commandments.

Observe all of the laws of God in fifteen days of the second month and uphold them. Thus, the mother learns to appoint it, as all are thrust forth from the caul. Be in the mother's womb for three portions of the year—actually, the days filled in the womb, previously eight days of eight months. (Hebrew: ThSh"I). A myriad and 240 [OR"M] divisions, relax in time to thrust forth in birth (Hebrew: ThSh"I).

It is written, you and your sons receive the laws of Elohik, and also the ancestors as thrust forth in birth (Hebrew: ThSh"I). It is indicated to Abraham that El regards them as a stone to be hewn. Abraham was occupied in the Torah, and learned the signs of the zodiac. Go forth abroad and [set] forth astrological matters [Atztaginothik].

Also, four are drawn above and below, corresponding to the twelve signs. Divide four above and below. (Hebrew: TAQ) is fire, corresponding [to] above. There fire is sustained, corresponding [to] above. (Hebrew: ShKG) is earth, corresponding [to] below. (Hebrew: ThMD) is air [Ruoch] to guide above. (Hebrew: SAaD) is water below. Also, guide above and below. The clouds are of air and water when in the sky. Man is in the days of raining. Ruoch opens, resembling a cloud, and it is water. In the days of raining, find growth to establish the green vegetation in open fields.

The rain falls upon the soil of the earth. Desire the growth of green vegetation. When water falls as rain in a stone vessel, it becomes green after many days.

In the days of heat, the signs minister with the Sun. Ruling in the days of heat, the signs minister with the Sun. Of the rain, then seeing many kinds of tropical flowers, seeing all varieties.

(Hebrew: TAQ) is the beginning of fire. The heavens are the foundation of the creation, above and first in heaven. (Hebrew: ThMD) is air of the Ruoch above, of all birds, only bound in the heavens. Thus, Earth was created second. Also of the foundation of Earth, the Ruoch (Hebrew: ThMD) takes the earth. The Ruoch gathers, reaching to Earth. The sea is fourth. Of (Hebrew: SAaD), the sea flows below and in the desert in the low country. It flows down to the heart of the nation. Of the sea, the dew comes down. It is written, flow down and establish the low country from the meager earth.

These are the four seasons of the year. The season of Nisan is hot and moist. The season of Tammuz is hot and dry. The season of Tishri is cold and dry. The season of Tebeth is cold and moist.

The four elements of man are blood, phlegm, red bile, and black bile. These are cold, hot, wet, and dry, as fire, earth, air, and water. The four elements of the body are blood, phlegm, red bile, and black bile. The seasons correspond to cold and hot, as summer and winter. The world was created from fire, earth, air, and water. The red bile corresponds to fire. Black corresponds to earth. Phlegm corresponds to water. Blood corresponds to air. The blood is the Nephesh and the Nephesh is warm.

Learn the interpretation of creation by the elements of the world. In the beginning, create Ruoch from the Ruoch of the Creator of all things. From Ruoch, create water and air. From the water, create fire and snow. From fire created from water, create the heavens. From the snow, create the earth.

Of the heavens and the living Ruoch of the heavens. The air of the heavens is hot and dry, corresponding to fire. Bring forth Ruoch from air. The earth is dry and cold. The water is wet and cold.

Thus, create the four elements of the body. The living Ruoch is the father and mother, Ruoch of the creator of all. From the living Ruoch of the father and mother, create the seed. The blood corresponds to water and the blood is opposite to the air. The seed goes forth from the father. The mother creates red bile. The phlegm is as snow, created from the blackness by the word of the Lord. The sea of the universe is water. Of Ruoch, fire and air, as a throne over the water. The glory of the king is directly above.

The Torah was written by the fire of the Moon over the blackness of fire. Offer the Torah, hidden in the bosom [or hollow place]. Of pleasure, the throne stands by the word of the mouth, not creating life as paradise [A'adiyien] in the garden. Knowledge is the medium to reveal the light. From the images therein of all creatures and Neshemoth, it is hidden in a pouch below the throne.

Behold, on the left there are seven habitations built in the Garden of Eden. The Holy Temple [Beth Hamekadesh] was built before. The dwelling of glory [Shekineth Kebod] is in the middle. The name of the king, the Messiah, is inscribed upon the stone of goodness upon the altar. The Ruoch of Elohim sustained you until the universe was created. Be counseled by the Torah, for there is good counsel. Of the creation of the universe, return and create the Malachim that there is no sin. The first was Sodom. El invited man to drink the water of iniquity.

God restored all he created, restored by healing from sin, by the Nepheshem, healing man from a great state of affliction. In the Holy Temple, offer sacrifices of atonement in the Garden of Eden, of Nepheshoth, of righteousness, of Gihenam, of passing over the commandments of the Torah. The Messiah is occupied with the Torah, gathering the pages by hand. Administer to the restoration of the Torah.

Speak of the greatness of the universe. You are Elohi, Elohim of the universe. He speaks to you of what to do when there is no host of the king and when to journey to the desert by the words of the Torah. Listen to him. Of the firmament of heaven, cover in glory. Reach to the firmaments and the seven nations.

Elohik is the Lord of the heavens, the heavens of the heavens [Voshemi Hashemiem], the Earth, and all in it. The scriptures [Pesoq] are the strength of the Lord and offerings of the Lord.

From the heavens to the Earth is a journey of 500 years. Thus, the firmaments are obscured by the clouds. Thus, from the Earth to the firmament, and from end to end. Now, place the ear as a funnel and listen to the sound of words. Give reverence to the heavens in the heart. Then, understand the knowledge of matters of the universe. Take snow from beneath the throne. Cast it upon the water. Freeze the water and make soil upon the earth. Of snow, establish the earth.

It is written of earth, the snow comes forth. By the word of the great king, freeze the water and make the storehouse of snow. Take snow from below the throne. The earth is the footstool. Of white snow, melt and flow down. The waters are muddy. Thus all creatures are pure and good from the heavens.

In the end, El restores the earth. Of snow, six horns [Qorenoth].[6] Thus all the operations of earth are six days. Of earth are six tasks [or customs]. Seed and harvest of winter, spring, summer, and autumn.

It says in the *Book of Formation,* water is from Ruoch. Engrave and hew chaos [Tohu Vebehuh] from mud and clay as a flower bed.[7] Establish by heat. From neglect, place snow above. Of the work, speak of snow.

Speak of the desolation of Earth. The green vegetation surrounds the Earth. The rocks fall and are immersed in the ocean. Water goes forth. Divide water from Ruoch. The moisture is to one side. Hew Tohu there. The green surrounds the world. Green is upon the water and upon the rocks. Moisture falls and the water goes forth. The water is created.

The man does not support this, not creating rock from water. Take a brazen vessel. Make rock from the brazen metal. Take pure, clear water, and boil it over the fire. When the water decreases, add twice as much water. The brass vessel breaks and a rock is found in it. Thus, in man and beast, find small rocks from the moisture boiled in the body. Make a rock in the liver or kidneys, or in the hinder place.

Of God, fire consumes the words, making the water into mountains and rocks and earth. The moisture goes forth from water.

It will come to pass, the Earth surrounding Tohu is seen by eyes. Anchored therein is the foundation of heaven, the origin of fire

---

[6] The horn is a symbol of strength. This term may also refer to mountain peaks.
[7] See *Sepher Yetzirah,* 1:11.

with the foundation of the Earth. Water goes forth. Collect the water and make mud, loam, and clay. Make it like a flower bed in a valley, surrounded by a wall. From neglect, by virtue of the signs, the mud and loam separate. Place snow above. Freeze and make earth. Speak of snow, earth is made.[8]

Of the *Book of Formation*, made from Tohu. Actually, Tohu is made of mud and clay, establishing earth. Actually, make the earth by them. Create the fortress above the ocean. Engraved above is the Shem Hemaphorash in 42 letters. Establish the letter over the surface of the ocean. Cover the waters and indicate 20 letters. Every word is sealed in the name of the heavens.

Of Earth by (Hebrew: AHIH). Aleph Heh is below and Yod Heh is above, corresponding to the crown. The throne is sealed by Yod Heh of (Hebrew: IHOH), of the three letters of fire and flame. By (Hebrew: IHOH), create heaven and Earth. Therefore, the beginning is Yod Heh.

Rejoice the heavens and exalt the Earth [Ishmecho Hashemiem Othegal Haretz] by the great name. Of all suffering [or burden], the Lord makes all. Seal in the pouch 42 letters. Offer over the ocean. The water does not rise up as the deluge of the ages. Take the pouch and at once divide the water of all the springs. The ocean increases. As one hastens to find the pouch, speak in vain to labor over [it].

Establish the Holy Temple and turn the pouch. The water goes forth and floods the worlds. Fall upon the face. By the song of degrees [Shir Hama'aloth] from the valley, proclaim the Lord to descend quickly.[9] Rise up by the fifteen songs of degrees, except for every song of degrees of David or Solomon, for they are not important.

Thus, corresponding to the dwelling in Chechares [mystical name of a city in Egypt] of 19 letters, therein place the 14 letters. Of Vau Yod Heh, here are five letters. By them, the ocean is angered. God beholds the humility. Indicate by Ruoch to wander the Earth. Over the pouch, God speaks to David to fetter his loins and build the foundation of the Holy Temple. David sees that in the

---

8 See *Sepher Yetzirah*, 1:11.

9 A term noted in the title of fifteen psalms. It is probably so called from having been sung on the steps of the temple.

pouch is written above the fifteen letters of the Shem Hamephorash. Around it, it is written, let there be glory to the Lord forever and He rejoices.

It is also written of David and Solomon, build the Holy Temple. Extend the hand and raise the pouch to be touched by El. The name of the Creator is engraved upon it.

Of God, the miracle to guide the pouch. It is fate [Gorel] of Joshua to proclaim. It is fate to return the pouch from heaven to David. By the name of the Creator, David is filled with the love of God.[10] Reach in you and raise the pouch by the power over the Shem Hamephorash. The water rushes upward.

God spoke to David, giving instructions of the arrangement of Aleph Lamed and instructed the building of the Holy Temple to re-member the name. Establish it. Turn away from wickedness.

David raises the pouch and engraving over the Shem Hamephorash, casting it over the surface of the ocean, and after-ward returned. Now become wise by the hidden, secret things of El. Learn without receiving the desires of the heart. When receiving the desire of the heart, speak of the desire in you.

Of thoughts, turn aside the heart. Serve and be reverent of life. Desire to be lifted upright at once. Incline upright and desire to re-turn. Bow down thus, not to rise above the heart. Consider the val-ley below. The glory is below in the valley, as in heaven, the splendor of the Kingdom and the glory of the name.

It is written, below sow the earth. Know the heavens surround the Earth as a shell over all the universe.

All the universe is 500 over 500 [Th"Q AaL Th"Q]. The great sea circles the universe to support the foundation of the universe. The letter covers all the great sea. All the universe is supported by one pillar. The righteous name is (Hebrew: ShNA). Righteousness is the foundation of the universe and the letter of the pillar.

All the universe is upon the single fin of Leviathan [whale, or sea serpent]. Leviathan dwells in the lowest sea, as a small fish in the sea. The lowest sea is over the sea in the beginning.

Upon the shore of the sea, proclaim the name of the sea of weeping and the water rises up. Take the water of the highest

---

[10] The name David actually means "love."

weeping. The lowest weeping is not as pure as the highest. The highest desire is the path of God.

The sea of weeping is suspended above the lowest Earth [Aretz]. The Earth extends over the sea. It is written, the Earth extends over the sea. The sea is over the pillar of Chashmal.[11] The pillar of Chashmal is over the storehouse of snow. The storehouse of snow is over the mountain Bether [Her Bether]. The mountain Bether is over the ocean [Thehom], resembling three ox heads [Rash Shor]. El proclaims the ocean over desolation [Tohu]. Desolation is in the direction of the greenness. Darkness goes forth. Desolation is over emptiness [Bohu], resembling stones.

The water goes forth to serve. Emptiness is the pillar over the sea. The sea is over the water. The water is over the mountain. The mountain is over Ruoch. Ruoch is suspended in the gate [Sha'areh], bound by the elements of the lowest Earth [Aretz]. The angel appointed over the lowest Earth is Aretzietziyahov.

Proclaim the name of Earth. Desire to make the word of the king, ruling over the lowest Earth. The ocean [Thehom] is over the ocean of desolation [Thehom Tohu], over chaos [Tohu Vobohu], over the sea of emptiness [Bohu Im], over the sea of water [Im Mim], over the sea of ashes [Mim Apher]. The lowest Earth is suspended in the gate and bound in the dome of land [Kepheh Adameh]. Over land [Adameh] is the greatest glory, power, and beauty, by the virtues of the Creator.

In the beginning, El sees land. Exalt and rejoice. Proclaim how to create man from the soil. The Lord Elohim forms Earth [Aretz] from land. The angel appointed over land is Ademael, and over the ocean of land [Adameh Thehom]. The ocean of land is over the ocean of desolation, over chaos, over the sea of emptiness, over the sea of water, over the sea of the desert [Mim Chorabah]. Land is suspended in the gate and bound in the dome of desert [Kepheh Cherubeh]. The angel appointed over the desert is Cherubeh.

Proclaim the name of the desert to draw water from all the seas in the world. Regard the desert over the surface of the streams of

---

11 In modern Hebrew, this actually translates as "electricity." It may also refer to a kind of polished brass or a mixture of gold and silver.

land [Adameh Iyavorim] and over the streams. The streams of the desert [Iyavorim Cherubeh] are over the ocean of desolation, over chaos, over the sea of emptiness, over the sea of water, over the sea of dry land [Mim Yobeshah]. Cherubeh is suspended in the gate and bound in the dome. The angel appointed over dry land [Yobeshah] is Yobeshehael.

Proclaim the name of dry land. Of all seas in the world, Israel goes by dry land within the sea. The water of the rivers and pools of water go to the sea, making dry land. Above the ocean of dry land [Thehom Yobeshah] is the ocean of desolation, over the sea of desolation [Tohu Im], over the sea of water, over the sea of earth [Mim Aroqa]. Dry land is suspended in the gate and bound in the dome. The angel appointed over Earth [Aroqa] is Aroqael. Proclaim the name Aroqael.

In Gihenam, the wicked are judged by the fire. Eloha in heaven judges the disobedient. Aroqa Shahul, and Abbadon, and Bar Shecheth, and Tit Hiyon, and Sha'ari Tzalemoth [Gate of the Shadow of Death] are in Gihanem.[12]

Of the wicked, there are forty Malachim and Chebeleh appointed over them. The clouds of darkness form a wall. The wicked are silent in the darkness.

Shahul is half fire and half hail. They suffer in pain and terror in Shahul. The Neshemeth do not languish, as the worms do not die in the river of fire.

There are seven great dwellings in Gihenam. In every dwelling, there are seven rivers of fire and seven rivers of hail. The highest is served by the fire. Every dwelling is bound together. There are 7000 caves [Chor] in every dwelling. In every cave are 7000 clefts. In every cleft are 7000 scorpions. Every scorpion inflicts 300 wounds. By every wound, there are 7000 as bitter herbs. There are seven rivers of poison [Sem]. Of death in fire, man is smitten therein. The angel Chebeleh smites you and judges you for every minute of one half of the year in fire, and half in hail and snow.

The Tzeneh [a vessel for containing snow] is from the fire. Divide the sins of man above the ocean of Earth [Aroqa Thehom]. The ocean [Thehom] is suspended in the gate and bound in the

---

[12] See the Introduction, page 19.

dome is the world [Thebel]. The angel appointed over the world is Thebel. Proclaim the name of the world.

From Thebelim are signs of the works of goodness. In the world are mountains and hills and all dwellings of the Lord. When speaking, the mountains tremble and all the hills dissolve.

In the world are 65 kinds of creatures over human beings, resembling the body of a lion and the face of a man, the head of a lion and the body of a man, the head of a serpent and a bull, for there are two heads. There are three heads, four hands, one body, one torso, and two feet.

Over the world, God prepares to judge. Speak to the world. Judge in righteousness and create the human being from the dirt [A'apher]. It came to pass, make the substance to build the world. Reward goodness and face the throne. Establish from the meager earth.

The throne of glory is over the ocean, over the ocean of desolation, over chaos, over the sea of emptiness, over the sea of water, over the sea of the world [Mim Cheled]. The world [Cheled] is suspended in the gate and bound in the dome. The angel appointed over the world is Cheledial. Proclaim the name Cheledial.

In the world, you are human beings. Of acts of wickedness, there is not the world, but only the body. The world is over man and beasts, birds and fishes, creeping things and insects.

Of the righteousness of the Torah and works of goodness, the reverence of heaven. All inhabitants of the nations listen.

In the world are seven lands and seven oceans between them. These are the four spirits of the world. From the spirit of the east, light goes to the universe. From the spirit of the south, a pool of water. From the spirit of the west, the storehouse of snow, the storehouse of hail and cold rain. From the spirit of the north, not stopping the spirit of destruction [Ruoch Meziqin] and horrors [Zova'avoth] and spirits [Ruochoth] and demons [Shedin]. In the north is the hell of the evil [Thopheth Hera'aheh]. Do not stop them from affecting man. Only Eloah may stop them. Forsake the north gate.

The Shekinah is in the west. All face the right-hand path. The universe is created corresponding to the east, south, and west.

It is written in the Torah, of the knowledge be counseled by the Mishnah. In the beginning, the universe was created in six days.

After six thousand years, the universe is established. The righteous are occupied by the doctrine of the Torah. The Lord first completed the testimony, second, the orders, third, the commandments, fourth, the reverence of the Lord, fifth, the judgment of the Lord, sixth, the blessings.

Thus first, be blessed. Second, preserve the light of the Lord. Third, consecrate. Fourth, rise up in exaltation. Fifth, be at peace [Shalom]. Sixth, observe the commandments.

First, keep watch over Israel. Second, observe. Third, observe.[13] Fourth, observe the Nephesh. Fifth, observe the going forth. Sixth, [observe] the coming of the Lord.

Sing the song of degrees. Keep in purity by keeping the Torah in purity. The divisions of the Garden are five signs. Five are exalted in Eden, of Egypt, Mesoptamia, Sinai, Jericho, and Israel.

Keep in tablets of six spans [or hand breadths]. The six orders are saved from Gihenam. It is written therein of the shadow of death [Tzalemoth], not of the orders of the tablets, six spans over six.

Let there be light to every one of the six. In the desert [Cherebah], make six divisions of the six. This equals 36 spans, arranged span over span. The width is three spans. Three times 36 is 108 appointed to Gihenam. Be delivered from it.

Know Gihenam and the Garden of Eden are supported by the first house, divided between them. The Garden of Eden is on the northeast side. In the north, fill the belly. Therefore, the Sun is red in the west. Flourish by the brilliance, as surely the fire is in Eden. In the northwest is Gihenam. From the burning coals of fire, the Sun in the east is red as blood. The hot springs go forth from Ga'a. Form a wall on the side from the springs. Gihenam is diagonal to the south. Come to the gate of Ga'a below the firmament. Gather in the universe on one side. The rest is outside of the firmament.

In the Qliphoth, seal the river of fire. Above the Qliphoth, the sign of Ga'a is surrounded by the second Qliphoth. Of Ga'a and Gihanem, the power of the Qliphoth. The river of fire is above the Qliphoth.

Of the throne of glory, life comes from the strength. Establish the turning of the Sun, Moon, and signs of the zodiac. Of boiling

---

[13] There is likely some dropped text here.

rain, the hot, boiling water descends, going from the east to west, and so on and so forth.

The highest firmament is the course of 500 years. Proclaim the universe is 146 myriad myriads cubits.[14] In the midst of the firmament is the Qliphoth and the river of fire. They come near the lowest part of the universe. In the end, complete the Earth.

The light from the heaven goes forth beyond the Garden of Eden by the mountains on the northeast side. It descends between the mountains to the world. The mountain divides the universe from the Garden of Eden.

The Malachim come forth from the mountain. The darkness of the firmament obscures it from the Earth. Also, the firmament surrounds Ga'a in brilliance.

Above the Qliphoth is the throne of glory. Below is the gate of spirit [Ruoch Sha'areh]. There is nothing surrounding the Qliphoth. It faces Ga'a and Gihenam, surrounding the universe. There is a path to the river of fire.

Of the limits of Gihenam, the signs of the zodiac are near the river of fire, immersed therein above. One from 60 in the garden, one from 60 in Eden, and one from 60 in Gihenam.

Be occupied by the study of the Torah. Of one from 60 of the highest wisdom, be delivered from death and from Gihenam. Come to the Garden of Eden. It is written, the wisdom of the Lord is the foundation of Earth.

Of the 22 letters of the Torah, Aleph is one and Beth is two, making three. Gimel is three, making six. Daleth is four, making ten. Heh is five, making fifteen. Vau is six, making twenty-one. Zayin is seven, making twenty-eight. Cheth is eight, making thirty-six. Teth is nine, making forty-five. Yod is ten and Yzaddi is ninety, making one hundred. Kaph is twenty and Peh is eighty, making one hundred. Lamed is thirty and Ayin is seventy, making one hundred. Mem is forty and Samekh is sixty, making one hundred. Here is four hundred-and-ninety-five. Of five from the Torah, here is 500.

Qoph is one hundred, Resh is two hundred, Shin is three hundred, and Tau is four hundred, making one thousand. Here is fifteen-hundred.

---

14 This calculates to 14,600,000,000 cubits. A cubit is said to be the distance from the tip of your finger to your elbow, approximately 2 feet.

Twenty is five-hundred-and-forty, and six-hundred-and-fifty, and seven-hundred-and-sixty, and eight-hundred-and-seventy, and five-hundred-and-one-thousand, here is six thousand.

In the beginning, Elohim created (Hebrew: R"Th BKA OBKA BA"Th B"Sh) of six, as much indicated 6000 rising upward. By the right of three fathers and four mothers, create seven firmaments. Divide by seven lands. Twelve tribes correspond to the twelve signs of the zodiac.

The names of Abraham, Isaac, and Jacob, by Gematria, are 638 [Abraham = 248; Isaac = 208; Jacob = 182]. The names of Sarah, Rebecca, Rachel, and Leah, by Gematria, are 1086 [Sarah = 505; Rebecca = 307; Rachel = 238; Leah = 36]. The names of Reuben, Simeon, Levi, Judah, Issachar, Zebulon, Benjamin, Dan, Joseph, Naphtali, Gad, and Asher, by Gematria, are 3166 [Reuben = 259; Simeon = 466; Levi = 46; Judah = 30; Issachar = 830; Zebulon = 95; Benjamin = 152; Dan = 54; Joseph = 156; Naphtali = 570; Gad = 7; Asher = 501]. Israel and Yesheron are 1107 [Israel = 541; Yesheron = 566].[15]

Of the prophets of the Torah, as it is written of the three, here are six thousand years. The universe will endure. Of Ephraim, Manessah, and Israel (Hebrew: BATh BSh ALP L"H), here is 7000 corresponding to 6000, to be the universe and Aleph Zayin of Tohu.

Therefore twice as much as Lamed Cheth [L"Ch] corresponding to Cheth, the seventh of seven firmaments. Of seven planets, and seven countries, and seven oceans, that seven is the world of Tohu.

Therefore, survive to the days of Achab[16] for 7000, not kneeling before Ba'al. 7000 in days of Jehovachez.[17] Here is divided seven countries and seven deserts between them, of seven firmaments.

It is written, the wisdom of the Lord is the foundation of the Earth. Fill with wisdom, not coming forth. It is written, the reverence of the Lord is the wisdom; however in heaven, be filled with intelligence. Understand the wisdom.

---

[15] Yesheron is a periphrastic name of Israel, meaning "the righteous people."
[16] A King of Israel. Also, the name of a false prophet.
[17] The name of a King of Israel, the son of Jehu. Also, the name of a King of Judah, son of Josiah.

By the means of the word, speak of intelligence in heaven. In the deserts, knowledge goes forth in two drops. From drops of knowledge in the deserts [come] the great book and all the works of glory.

On the seventh day, the love of the Lord shines upon the universe. Create seven countries. Give the laws over the Earth and in the open plains of the seventh firmament. The seventh day is chosen to be the Sabbath. Thus bind them and create around the lowest earth. Afterward, surround by fire and water,

Tremble in fear of lightning and thunder. Tremble in fear of the images. The noise and tumult returns and, afterward, silence. One minute after, speak the Kaddash [Prayer for the Dead]. After speaking the blessing, speak in counsel. After all this, the holy life and the Aophnim, the throne of glory, and the foot of the Shekinah.

Around the back of the head, see life on Earth as the Shekinah above. Thus, the Shekinah is below and splendor fills the Earth. Also, heaven is the throne and the Earth is the footstool.

A thousand thousands and a myriad myriads ministering angels serve below the feet of the Shekinah. From every kind of praise [Shebech] and every kind of praise [Qolos], fill the Earth below.

All the lands of the Shekinah are over the throne of glory from below. Of the powers of the universe, the second power to what is first of the lowest labors. First is the highest labor, keeping the glory above and below. The glory of the Creator is in the air and in the darkness, in every place filled. Do not fill the firmaments with glory. One is above and one is below.

The word written by the Lord is of one divine truth. He is one and there is none like him. There is no Creator other than him. He fills all, except as it is explained in the end of the book.

The Creator established all. The vision of glory is in heaven above. Dwell in the glory above, corresponding to the throne. Of the name, Seraphim, Chashmallim, Cherub, Aophanim, Chiyoth, thus below the lowest earth.

Reveal the glory above by the singing of the wings. Listen to the sound of the wings. From the wings, those on the Earth hear the holy singing from above and blessings from below. When speaking to God, I work in the temple [Meqedesh] and dwellings. Gather to all habitation above. Come forth to God, and speak to him: What is the matter with you, dwelling in an unclean place? It is better to dwell in purity. I shall purify the dwelling. Dwell in the temple of El.

God spoke to them: Of man below, be equal. Complete the sign. Rejoice by the singing. Rejoice in heaven, created by the Lord. Dwell in the lowest Earth and rejoice in heaven.

The Malachim dwell in the lowest Earth. Of Israel from the singing below, and moreover the singing. It is written, rejoice in unison by glory that comes forth.

The people of Israel call out [Yiriya'aov, or sound the trumpet] to every son of Elohim. Consider more of all congregations. Do not rise up to rejoice the name of Aaron. The song of Aaron rises up. Rejoice as Jacob rejoices.

It is written, see and rejoice in the heart when you hear. Thus, when quiet, it is complete.

Moses and Esau are appointed to consecrate in the midst of the dwelling, corresponding to the letters of the names: Abraham, Isaac, Jacob, Reuben, Simeon, Levi, Judah, Issachar, Zebulon, Dan, Naphtali, Gad, Asher, Joseph, Benjamin, Sabbatai, and Yesheron. There are seventy-two letters (Hebrew: ABRHM ITzChQ IAaQB RAOBN ShMAaON LOI IChODH IShShKR ZBOLN DN NPThLI GD AShR IOSP BNIMIN ShBTI IShRON).

Thus, by the name (Hebrew: OISAa OIBA OIT). The letters of the mothers are as the letters of the fathers. Embrace and kiss the image of Jacob.

Israel is the holy land, the place of God. Below is the Holy Temple. Speak, Holy, Holy, Holy [Qedesh Qedesh Qedesh], as it is written in the book of the temples of God. Embrace and kiss the name of the image of Jacob, engraved upon the throne of glory.

Place two seeds of Jacob. Speak, happy is the father of the praise of your son. By the most holy praise, see the vision of (Hebrew: ShDI IHOH) [the Almighty God] and see God.

The prophet Bala'am performed works of the Merkabah.[18] Place Jacob upon the throne. Speak of the goodness of Elohik. Of Jacob by Gematria, Jacob upon the throne. It is written below the left side (Hebrew: LRAShI IShRAL). On the right side, embrace. Therefore, speak of the hand over the right hand of man.

---

[18] See Numbers 22–24.

(Hebrew: AaL AISh IMINK) by Gematria (Hebrew: IShRAL). Over human beings, Ametzeth [strength] to you. (Hebrew: AIMTz"Th) by Gematria is Israel. It is written (Hebrew: ChZO-QOThIK AMTzThIK) [powerful strength].

Also, support the right side in righteousness. Speak, Holy, Holy, Holy, three times corresponding to Elohim. In the heavens above, first. Above the Earth below, second. There is not another in the air, third. There is not in the highest and lowest, nor in the air between.

Corresponding to three praises [Yithodien] we speak, hear me Israel, the Lord our God, the Lord is one.[19]

Of the blessings before, he who endures, petition in the morning, and then in the evening. First, proclaim from the beginning of the first generations. Second, proclaim to the Lord. I am first, and I am last. Thus speaks the Lord, King of Israel, and the redeemer, the Lord of hosts. I am first and I am last. There is no other unto Elohim. Of the third, actually sprinkle the blood.

From ancient times, return in vestments as white as snow. The heat of the flames of pure fire. The flames shine as a wheel of burning fire. First, put forth the darkness. Behold, the clouds around heaven come near. From ancient times, reach and come near second. From ancient times, deliver judgment of the highest and most holy. Appoint to reach the kingdom to possess holiness, third.

In the morning, speak three times, Holy, Holy, Holy. Once in Yotzer, and once in Amida [Prayer of Eighteen Benedictions] in supplication, and once as arranged in the Kaddash.

The holy glory is in the air between heaven and Earth. Those are the three prayers of supplication in the day. The Prayer of Eighteen Benedictions is the supplication.

Deliver directly from eighteen. Of Gihenam, 108 nations by the nation of God. From Gihenam, open the mouth wide without (Hebrew: Ch"Q) and gather (Hebrew: LAa"HB) for eighteen hundred thousand years.

Of the eyes, not seeing Elohim other than those men able to see eighteen hosts [Cholivoth, or armies] assembled.

---

[19] The prayer is Shema. Shema Yisrael Adonai Elihanu Adonai Achad. In modern tradition, followed by "Amen."

It is written, be satisfied in the eternal life of eighteen thousand lands of God. See in all time. They are hidden. Therefore, hide in them. It is written, they are hidden. (In other words, in the world. There are eighteen benedictions in the Amida. It is written to hide. Thus, in the world, there are eighteen rows of the throne, for it is written to hide.)

The Creator formed all and filled all space with the glory. Rise up over the holy life in heaven. Thus, honor the most holy glory over the life below the throne. Before the throne of glory, below is as above.

The name Shekinah is written upon the throne of the heavens. The Earth is the footstool. It is written, the glory fills the Earth.

Place the sign at the feet of the Shekinah, surrounding 18,000 lands. Of the spirit of the north, 4,500. Of the spirit of the south, 4,500. Of the spirit of the west, 4,500. Of the spirit of the east, 4,500. Thus, the circle is 18,000.

The 4,500 of the spirit of the north are of splendor and glory, of strength and praise, of song and honor, of joy and exaltation and majesty.[20]

The 4,500 of the spirit of the south are of fulfillment [Melayim] and holiness, of purity and righteous is the great name.

The 4,500 of the spirit of the west are of fulfillment, of adorning the crown, of the kingdom and the sound of the silence of time [Qol Demameh Dekeh].

The 4,500 of the spirit of the east are of fulfillment, of splendor and glory, of beauty and exaltation, of rejoicing in song. Restore as written therein.

The sign in the north is of fulfillment, grace and righteousness. Be strengthened by the great victory.

The sign in the south is of fulfillment, of splendor and glory, of beauty and glory. Exalt in the majesty.

The sign in the east is of fulfilment. The song restores the crown of the kingdom and the sound of the silence of time.

The sign in the west is of fulfilment. Adorn in the splendor. Of strength and exaltation, rejoice and sing all the words of praise.

---

[20] Tehileh Vokevod Vogeborah Voshebech Vozemireh Vohedar Vorenah Vogavoh Vogavon. Many of the words used here have very similar meanings.

Speak of the chariot of Elohim. Of myriad thousands upon thousands, the Lord is in them.

Eighteen thousand remain and they minister before and after. Of 18,000 lands surrounded by the river of water. After the river of water, surrounded by the river of fire. After the river of fire, surrounded by walls of fire and water. After the walls of fire and water, surrounded by mountains of hailstones and hills of snow. After is the wall of storm. After is the shaking of an earthquake. After is the fear of thunder and lightning. After are the Cherubim flying upon the wings of the wind. After are a thousand thousands hosts. After are myriads of pleasures. After, sing hymns. After, sound the Shofar. After is the sound of blowing the Shofar. After are myriads of pleasures. After are further praises. After are holy words. After are the words of blessings. The glory fills the Earth.

After all this is the mud and mire. After mud and mire, there is nothing; henceforth chaos and darkness. You cannot see, as there is no measure to it.

It is written, hidden in the darkness is a secret place. Every day for all time, God rides above the Cherub. Go forth to ride above the Cherub swiftly and return to see. Flying upon the wings of the wind, ride above the Cherub, flying upon the wings of the wind, filling all. Ride above the Cherubim in the south, thus going to the south side. All the Cherubim and every spirit dwell by the Ruoch of the Malachim.

By the sign of the side, the strongest princes [Methegeborim Sheriem] are below the strongest. The brilliance of the glory is not seen on the second side. Therein, Solomon speaks in prayer. Hear me in the heavens. The foundation of the dwelling corresponds to the glory coming forth by the brilliance of the great Malachim.

Place the sign of eighteen lands in righteousness. In the end is Ezekial, but not there, as the lands are diminished. Complete by these signs in love of 310 lands.

Give the name of the universe and the name of the lands. By the brilliance of the glory, see from the place of the throne of glory. The brilliance around it is from the blessing.

Blessed is the glory of the Lord. It is all and fills all, all between the heavens and the Earth. Seek the Lord by Aleph Beth, as the Rabbi A'aqiba.

The mercy of the Lord fills the Earth. Great mercy is given from God. Know in the Torah, to proclaim mercy. It is written in the Torah, of mercy over the language above. The Lord is merciful and the Lord is compassionate. They shall know all put forth of the firmaments and what is in the midst of the first. It is the veil high above. The veil covers and binds. It is as a sheet spreading. It is out, open, not seeing in the house. Thus, extend to surround heaven.

In the morning, spread out over the surface of the firmament of the heavens. Protect from the heat of the Sun, in the night, [from] rain.

The sign is before the stars of the signs of the zodiac. In the morning, return to the place. Cover the firmament in the evening to bind. In the morning, cover and be renewed every day.

Of the work of Berashith, the veil of heaven is bound. Unite the veil and heaven below the firmament is separated. It is written, the heavens are covered by the glory of El. It is revealed by the firmament. Return above the veil surrounding. See in the day. Know God created 390 firmaments of heaven. Double [or multiply] to unite. Corresponding to double, every firmament to my name and title. Point above and every one ministering between the throne of glory.

Of seven firmaments, they are the foundation. Above, all the firmaments are complete and perfect. The veil surrounds the heavens in the course of 500 years.

The ladder stands upon the Earth [Aretz]. Over 500 years, begin reaching to the Lord in the heavens. Rise up the ladder in the course of 500 years.

The most-honored princes [Sher Nekbadim] appoint seven chief offices [Serasim] over the lands. Above and below, come forth to the sign of Metatron. Create the heavens from fire and water by the word of the Lord. Create heaven by the word of God. By the power of the heat of fire and the moisture of the water, create the heavens therein.

The skies are below the firmament. Raise water by the name of the first firmament. The hosts of angels stand guard. Seven thrones stand over the heavens, not dwelling in the highest. Watching over and ministering, they are the highest magistrates [Sholetiem, or dominions].

Bind to them, the most merciful, the highest blessings, and the most powerful. Desire to take vengeance in the blessed place. The destruction [Mezieqiem, or demons] of man is occupied by the Malachim.

Of the seventh sign, the Malachim are appointed to make. The seven princes [Shariem] of the magistrates [Shetoriem] are formed from fire. See by the flames of the fire. Go forth from the fire. The hosts did not create the word, but only when counseled by the magistrates. By authority of the seven, put forth whether good or wicked, whether wealthy or poor, whether in war or peace.

Below the first dominion [Shoter] are 70 princes ministering. They listen to every word. Of works of healing, proclaim the name Tezom and Thereh.

Below the second dominion are the princes and Malachim ministering. Of the consecration, keep guard and cast down the enemies in battle. Proclaim by the name of the Malachim. Proclaim in purity.

Below the third dominion are four princes of the Malachim ministering. They are friends of man, whether satiated or in hunger. Every word comes forth, whether good or wicked. Proclaim the name in purity.

Below the fourth dominion are 42. They are appointed over the heart of the king and the princes and every man. Proclaim the name in purity.

Below the fifth dominion are 22. They listen in the night to the words. Petition the stars and speak with the spirits. Proclaim the name in purity.

Below the sixth dominion are 37. They are strong Malachim, girded in power and strength, covering all the corners of the world. Proclaim the name in purity.

Below the seventh dominion are 46. They read every word in dreams. Proclaim the name in purity and you succeed in the works.

PART 4

IN THE BEGINNING, PART 2 (BERASHITH)

THE ANGEL A'AMOAL IS APPOINTED over the veil of the firmament, appointed over 12,000 Malachim. Of the many paths in heaven, extend the path in the light of the fire of splendor. In the place, there is a great mountain of white fire. Divide the pure fire, not seen from there. Go forth beyond to divide the path of the white fire from the pure.

On the grassless paths, the Malachim go forth. Go forth on a journey upon the path. Go around, until rising up the ladder from firmament to firmament, the Merkabah is reached. There are the Malachim. Those who are not pure will not reach the splendor (as it is commanded), rising up to the Merkabah.

In every place, it is written of the heavens, either of the significance of an open hand or the body of the firmament; however the heavens above the heavens are as a chamber within a chamber.

It is revealed that all the heavens are formed as a tent, stretched by a tent hook in the Sea of Oceanus [Mi Avoqiyinos]. Be caught as a hook in the Sea of Oceanus. Distinguish the limits of the heavens. Distinguish the limits of the Earth. The limits of the Earth and the limits of the heavens extend from the Sea of Oceanus.

Be refreshed in the highest sea. In the midst of the sea, rise above, as a tent extending forth. The human being stands below. The limits are below and in the middle of the heavens. The limits below and in the middle are above all the creatures of the lowest dwelling. Dwell in the tabernacle.

Of the seal of the heavens and the Earth, by the seal of Ahieh, Aleph Heh is below and Yod Heh is above. Of the three seals of Ahieh, there are twelve letters corresponding to the twelve hours of the day and twelve hours of the night, twelve months of the year, twelve signs of the zodiac, and the twelve tribes.

To the side (see figure 3 on page 94), there are four seals of every spirit. Two letters are above and two letters below: Aleph Heh is below and Yod Heh is above. Of three spirits and three letters of (Hebrew: AHIH). The fourth spirit is established to serve, but not of the seal until the appointed time.

In the divine seal of (Hebrew: IHOH), Yod Heh is above and Vau Heh is below. By this sign, rejoice the heavens and exalt the earth. Rejoice the heavens [Ishemechov Hashemiem], as Yod Heh is above. Exalt the earth [Vothegel Haretz], as Vau Heh is below. These are the four letters of the name.

From the north gate, the Shekinah descends. Sustain the language. The Lord descends to see the city of Gomer.

Descending to Sinai, the Lord descends upon Mount Sinai to restore Jerusalem. Stand upon feet in the day, thus, upon the Mount of Olives. The letters of the seal are seen as lightning and flames of light. See a thousand thousands myriads of divisions rising up. Before that, engrave by the fingers. Bind the crowns of burning arrows of brilliance.

The letters Aleph Heh Yod Heh are a thousand myriad divisions. The one measure rises up as 79 [Aa"T) flames. It is written therein of 3000 of the seal of the heavens. As before, I employ the heat of the Sun in the universe. Be consumed by fire.

The myriad hosts of heaven of the orders of fire. The orders of the powers of the force of fire rush forth to cast down and burn the world. Thus, see the limits of the heaven, bound by the ends of the earth, the ends of the earth by the ends of the heavens by the seal of Ahieh. Serve in sorrow and bring forth by measures of mercy.

The seal is in the *Book of Formation*.[1] Raise in the hand three simple things [Pheshototh]. Cover them in the name of the great (Hebrew: IHOH). Seal them with six edges. Face upward and seal by (Hebrew: IHOH). Proclaim of twelve (or by Aleph Beth) not double Heh Vau Zayin Cheth Teth Yod. Move Qoph Yod Nun, taking Yod Heh Vau Heh.[2] Reveal by combining the letters of the name.

---

[1] See *Sepher Yetzirah*, 1:13 and 6:6.
[2] The Gematria of Qoph Yod Nun is 160. The word is Qien, or Cain, and translates as "lance" or "spear."

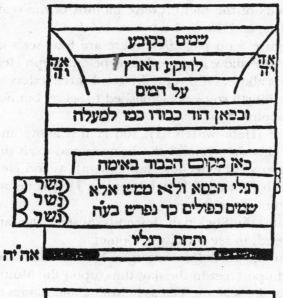

Figure 3. The caption under the diagram translates as: Of these twelve letters (N"L AHIH), that (AHIH) observes by the description. Before find three seals of (AHIH), two times (AHIH) and one time (AHIH). Here is the seal of heaven and Earth, of three seals of (AHIH). Complete as that before.

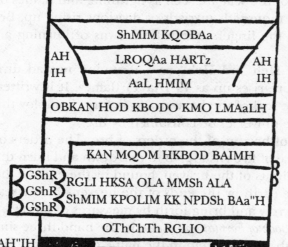

AH	Heaven is as a helmet	AH
IH	spread the earth	IH
	over the water	
and here, splendor and glory as above		

Bridge	Here is the place of the glory, where the foot
Bridge	of the throne, and not being except in Heaven
Bridge	to double, thus to divide by 75 and beneath the feet.
AHIH	

Combine this with that, making Heh Qoph Beth Heh in heaven [HQBH, see Introduction], resemble the throne, but not the throne actually. Reveal only to all the Malachim. He is king over all the heavens. Double the image of the throne.

The heavens number the glory of El. Serve thus above the sea of the heavens, above the sea of water to the sea of lightning and thunder. Tremble as the walls of the powers of fire surround the sign.

The great ladder is placed in heaven. The top reaches to the firmament. The most holy Malachim and most honored princes are appointed over it.

The Malachim are appointed over the north gate by the grace of the Lord. There are six over the south gate, six over the east gate, and six over the west gate.

Malachim are in the sole (the round circle of the foot). The groups divide to establish. El speaks to man. Pass before, not turning away according to the circle within. Bring forth in the round sole of the foot. Interpret the feet and the oval sole of the foot. The footsteps in the circle are as darkness in the beginning of creation, resembling an ox. Therefore, create twelve oxen below. The foot is upright. The foot of the ox grows as the lion, not as man, and similar to the eagle. What the Lord creates is great.

Know, when described thus, by three veils of the throne of Aleph. Aleph is as the highest. Reveal the three veils. Aleph is above Beth. Beth resembles a throne. Gimel is as the eye of Cheshemial, like a sapphire. Aleph is above and created as Beth, therefore Aleph Beth.

Of Rabbi Aqieba, the Beth descends from above, from the throne of glory. Tremble as the wheels [Gelgalim]. God speaks to them. Restore the Beth above. Descend in the beginning, of all the splendors of heaven [Kebodino Merom].

From the beginning, speak of the glory of the Kingdom. Speak as it is written. The first circle of the throne is below the feet of the highest. God hears the prayers from his dwelling, sitting upon the throne in the heavens. The Earth is the footstool in the house of rest [Beth Menocheh] of the Lord [Adon]. The footstool is in the House of God [Beth Elihanu]. Bow down before the holy footstool.

Of Daleth, fifty-and-one of the Book of the Mishnah [Sepher Mishnah] of the Torah. Therefore, bow down before the Torah, the footstool of the Lord. Thus, there are seven thrones in heaven. These thrones are in the heavens, seen therein. The magistrate is appointed over them.

The root of the word is engraved in the throne of glory in the court of the temple of the king. The honored prince is Voqemoval. The host is Sederial, appointed over the Malachim. The magistrate is appointed over 12,000.

The king stands over the gates of heaven. Therein are multitudes numbering the glory of El. It is written, the heavens number the glory of El.

Teth corresponds to the portion of the firmament reaching nine times the firmament by Samekh Berashith, until the sea shines upward to the heavens. Aleph is the most high [Meromiem], Beth is the angels [Melakiyov]. Gimel is the hosts [Tzebayov]. Daleth is the Sun. Heh is the Moon. Vau is the stars. Zayin is the heaven of heavens [Shemi Shemiem]. Cheth is the sea above the heavens. Teth is, thus, the foundation of the dwelling.

The foundation dwells in the heavens. There are nine kinds of fire. By the works of Merkabah corresponding to Teth, make the firmament above the heavens. The firmament is fixed therein. The Sun, and Moon, the constellation of the Pleiades, Orion, stars, every sign of the zodiac, every ocean, and every great ladder are placed in the firmament. The top reaches up to the sky. The angel is as flames of fire. The most honored princes are appointed over it.

There are seven appointed over the gates of the firmament. Of the gates of the firmament, make the north spirit. In the north are appointed six princes. There are seven princes serving over the spirit of the south, seven princes over the east, and seven princes of the west.

In the the second firmament is frost and vapor, the storehouse of snow, the storehouse of hail, the angel of fire, the angel of judgment, and the spirits of fear. Of the sign, the firmament fills with fear. In the midst of the Malachim, serve the unfathomable [Ayin Cheqor]. Make the hosts and the highest princes and most honored magistrates.

In the firmament are twelve degrees. In every degree stands the most honored and highest Malachim. Of every one of every body [Gopheh], hear to make a human being. Of every proclamation in purification over the first degree, serve nine princes and magistrates serving. The fear weakens them. The terror binds them by fear. Tremble as they are dying by the image of fire around as a vision of lightning. The mouth is not to silence the commandments and not to hear sounds. The angels are silent. They come upon them suddenly, rushing over all to serve the highest.

There are eleven princes serving over the second degree. They serve by the power. Fill with strength, love, and desire. The burning fire rushes forth from the nearest sign of the zodiac.

Fourteen princes serve over the third degree. Tremble in fear of the anger of human beings, hindering thoughts. They are strengthened by the strength. Fear is before and fear is to follow. Of groaning and trembling, walk from the sound of the trembling of thunder as the sounds of fire. Burning fire goes forth from the eyes, to establish, complete, and abolish.

There are sixteen princes serving over the fourth degree. Seven bind the storm. The sound of steps walking are as the sound of chains being brandished in the east. From the north are sounds as lightning and rushing fire. Of the divisions of the year, and of good and evil.

There are twelve princes serving over the fifth degree. They hold a shield and spear, a helmet upon the head, and a coat of chain mail armor covering the right side and left side. Of hail stones, tremble in oppression as fire goes forth. Hold a lamp and whisper [Lecheshiem] the answer. Do not silence the mouth as burning flames go forth from the fire. The Ruoch from the nose consumes the fire. Make the storehouse of fire, from where fire goes forth.

There are seventeen princes serving over the sixth degree. They lead the humble, filled with glory and robed in white vestments. They are seated upon great thrones, over faithfulness, loyalty, honesty, and over the healing of the faithful and the peaceful.

There are eleven princes serving over the seventh degree, bound by the power to strengthen in fear. One half resembles fire and one half resembles water. They are wondrous, not serving over. Fire rises up as burning coals in the eyelids. Serve in fear of the lowest, not being able to see the visions. Serve the highest. Be afraid [of] the visions and the three spirits of the world.

There are nineteen princes serving over the eighth degree. There are fourteen offices over the faithful, appointed over the rushing forth of power and strength. Form man by the strength of the bow and lance. Seal up the fire. Fear the horsemen of fire and chariots of fire.

There are fourteen princes serving over the tenth degree [The ninth degree is omitted]. The offices are over the faithful. By the powers of the sounds of fire, not hindering all the knowledge, make the covenant in heaven.

There are sixteen princes serving over the eleventh degree. They serve in greatness. The hosts minister over the princes. The fire rises up in splendor. Fly and give praise to the Creator.

There are twenty princes serving over the twelfth degree. They are surrounded in rightousness and shine in splendor. In the beginning, fill the foundation of the building. These serve half and half. Half are roots and half are branches. Afterward, heal by words of binding. All remember healing in the firmament. The tabernacle of beauty is improved by the arrangement of heaven and filled with a great light.

Speak the name of the Sun in the tabernacle. The firmament divides the darkness of seven planets. Saturn is the highest. Mikal is appointed over Saturn. Berekial is appointed over Jupiter. Gabrial is appointed over Mars. Raphal is appointed over the Sun. Chesedial is appointed over Venus. Tzedeqial is appointed over Mercury. A'anial is appointed over the Moon.

Saturn is cold and dry, as ice and hoar frost. Jupiter is hot and moist, in even mixture. Mars is hot and dry, as fire. The Sun is complete fire. Venus is cold and hot. Mercury is cold and hot, less dry and moist. The Moon is a mixture of cold and hot.

Four dwellings are revealed to the prophets of the life of man. Bring forth by the star constellation [Mezeh Kokeb]. Reveal to the prophets of the life of man. In time, bring forth. The rising star goes forth in the universe from out of the east. It is the house of life [Beth Chiyov].

First, the house of the planet Saturn rises in 57 years. Second, Jupiter comes to pass in 79 years. Third, Mars comes to pass in 66 years. Fourth, Venus comes to pass in 22 years. Fifth, Mercury comes to pass in 77 years. Be alone in the house of the planet.

Saturn is appointed over (Hebrew: RIOCh) [probably an alternate spelling of Ruoch], over affliction, bruises, sickness, and disease hidden in the body, and over death.

Jupiter is appointed over life [Chiyiem], over peace, goodness, happiness, wealth, and over the glory and majesty of the kingdom.

Mars is apppointed over the blood [Dem], over destruction, wickedness, hostility, war, vengeance, anger, and over the great Lords [Ba'ali Reboth], over wounds and injuries, over iron, and over fire and water, and over the fall.

Venus is appointed over beauty, over mercy, lust and desire, sexual intercourse, fertility, nature, over the birth of men and birth of beasts, over the spirit of the earth and fruits of the tree.

Mercury is appointed over wisdom and understanding, over the science of writing and all engravings, the importances of all arts of education, all customs of every culture, and all languages.

The Sun is appointed over the division of light and darkness that determines the days and years, making therein all arts of education, over the writings of all languages. Reveal the revelations from city to city and from country to country.

The Moon is appointed over the gates of heaven and Earth, and the mixture of all the covenants, establishing the divisions of good and evil. They are appointed, not dominated by good or evil, as these are all in the commandments of the Creator. Favor all dwelling upon the earth. They are not evil, and also they are not good, even in Israel.

The light of the Sun is not necessary in the day, nor the light of the Moon in night. The Lord goes before the days, not touching the foundation.

The clouds in the day also come forth in the world. Israel does not require the light of the Sun nor the light of the Moon, not in day nor in night. The Lord goes forth in the day.

Speak, not because of the Sun, for the Sun and Moon are driven forth. The signs of the zodiac are fixed. Thus, calculate the seasons and measure the days. Calculate the hours and the orders of the courses from the beginning.

The strength within the Sun is Michael, Mercury is Beraqial, and Chesedial is the Moon. Gabriel is Saturn.

Saturn from the Sun, of all the signs of the zodiac, is 30 years. Jupiter is Tzedeqial. Mars is Samal. The Sun is Raphal. Venus is

A'anal. The seven Malachim are of seven hours of Saturn from the Sun. Of every planet is two. In the middle, reach the end. From the Sun, with all the signs of the zodiac, complete in 30 years.

Of Jupiter, from the Sun with every planet, in 12 months reach the end. Be complete in 12 years.

Of Mars from the Sun with every planet, of 30 days to reach from the sun. Twelve months is Venus from the Sun with every planet. Twenty-eight years to reach from the Sun and 36 years of Mercury.

The Sun ministers with every planet. In seven days, reach from the Sun. Three hundred days of the Moon from the Sun with every planet. In 25 days, reach from the Sun. Complete in thirty days.

The arrangement of the seven planets is the wisdom of the people [Goyiem]. The firmament is ten divisions of seven degrees above. There are seven dwellings of seven planets. These are arranged from the lowest degree. Uphold Earth by the dwelling of the Moon. The Moon circles in the firmament, rising up from the Earth 730 measures [Chebeliem].[3]

By the measure of the heavens, of every measure, there are 156 measures. Measuring to reach the Earth, the end is 123,880 by measures of the Earth.

The second degree is the degree of Mercury. Rise up 353 measures by the measure of the heavens. Of every measure, there are 161 measures. Earth, to reach the end, is 56,433.

The third degree is the dwelling of Venus. It is around every firmament. Rise from the dwelling 58 measures by the measure of the heavens. Every measure is 84 measures. Earth, to reach the end, is 4,552.

The fourth degree is the center of the dwelling of the Sun. Rush forth around the firmament in twelve months. Rise from the dwelling of Venus in 80 measures by the measure of the heavens. Every measure is 518 measures. Earth, to reach the end, is 41,340.

The fifth degree is the degree of Mars. Rush forth around the firmament. Rise from the dwelling of the Sun in 30 measures by the measure of the heavens. Every measure is 119 measures. Earth, to reach the end, is 3,570 measures.

---

[3] This refers to a measuring line, or a rope or cord.

The sixth degree is the dwelling of Jupiter. Rise from the dwelling of Mars in 612 measures by the measure of the heavens. Every measure is 112 measures. Earth, to reach the end, is 68,544.

The seventh degree is the highest. It is the dwelling of Saturn. Around the firmament is 30 years. Rise from the dwelling of Jupiter in 750 measures by the measure of the heavens. Every measure is 156 measures. Earth, to reach the end, is 127,000 measures.

From the dwelling of the Moon to the dwelling of Saturn is 1,881 measures by the measure of the heavens. Of 291,800 measures by measuring Earth.

Every measure of the earth is 50 cubits. 40 measures to the mile. Every mile is 1,000 cubits, to reach 72,546 miles less one measure. (And one from eight in the mile, and one from two miles, and 179 days and one half, and one from 40 miles to the clouds of the firmament.)

In the hollow space of the universe, from the Earth to the firmament, is 730 measures by the measure of the heavens. Every measure is 156 measures. By the measure of Earth, to reach the end is 123,480 measures of Earth. The 2,447-mile course is 71 days and seven miles.

Of the wisdom of Israel, it is spoken: From Earth to the firmament is 500. Speak the truth of the seven planets, of Saturn, Jupiter, Mars, the Sun, Venus, Mercury, and the Moon.

Divide the firmament in seven arrangements and seven lands of dominions. By these seven planets, know to bring forth man therein, of good and evil.

Above the second firmament is the highest sea. Reach the planet Saturn. It is near the sea. Therefore, it is cold, until the vapor comes from the water. It is far from the Sun, not receiving heat. Thus, it is cold and dry, as ice and hoar frost.

Jupiter is nearest to Saturn, receiving the cold that is close to the water. The heat goes to Mars, in the center between the cold and heat. Therefore, there is power from the mixture in the middle, not of great heat, nor of great cold.

Mars is near the Sun. It is hot and dry as fire. The Sun is the fire of all the seven planets. The heat of fire and force of the Sun is in the center. The path of fire heats the universe by the flame from above to below.

Of Venus from the cold, and Mercury and the Moon from the heat of the Sun, rise up and melt the cold. Mercury is cold. From the cold of Earth, the Moon is cold as snow.

Heat is received from Venus and Mercury. Below, reduce the moisture of the Moon from the mixture. Cold as snow, receive the cold from the lowest water. From the air [Ruoch] between the Earth, freeze the cold as snow. From the mixture of the heat, receive from the heat of the planets. It rises from Earth, not as cold as Saturn.

The heat received from the most powerful hosts [Tzebavoth Chiyiliem] comes near. Therefore, the power is from the mixture of cold and hot.

The Sun is fire. Mercury is dry. Jupiter is wind. Venus is rain. The Moon is cool. Saturn is flowing water. Mars is boiling water.

The Sun is as the land of Gog.[4] Mercury is as the southern land of Kebtabieth. Venus is as Edom. The Moon is as Shinar [A country near Babylon]. Jupiter is as Idumea. Mars is as Kephethor. Saturn is as Hodov.

The Sun and Jupiter are the ruling planets of fire. The Sun rules in the day and Jupiter rules the night.

Venus and the Moon are the ruling planets of water. Venus rules in the day and the Moon rules in the night.

Saturn and Mercury are the ruling planets of air. Saturn rules in the day and Mercury rules in the night.

Mars is the ruling planet of water in the night, ruling in the day and in night.

Seven Malachim are appointed to the highest. Therefore, seven rule in the day and the night. Give the power and strength of the Sun and the planets as one. Mars is ruling. The Moon is love. The Sun and Jupiter are hate. Saturn and Mars are as one in place, facing as one. Favor goodness in the place. Evil is ill-favored, being favored and ill-favored.

Jupiter, the Moon, Mercury, and Venus are as one to favor hate, ill-favored to complete this to that, not love with the Moon.

Mercury to Venus, as one favored. They are ill-favored, and of love, this with that. Of desire, not passing over Mercury with the

---

[4] This is probably a reference to Megog, an unknown region, probably Scythia.

Sun, and not the Moon with Venus, and the sign Aries with Jupiter, and Mars with Saturn.

The Sun, Venus, and Saturn favor Gemini, Venus, and Aries, with Jupiter, Mars with Saturn. The Sun, Venus, and Saturn favor Gemini, Jupiter and Saturn favor Cancer. The Sun and Jupiter favor Leo. The Sun, Venus, and the Moon favor Virgo. The Sun favors Sagittarius. Jupiter, Saturn, and Venus favor Capricorn. The Sun, Jupiter, and the Moon favor Aquarius. The Sun, Venus, and the Moon favor Pisces.

Of Yod, create the universe by ten commandments corresponding to ten words. Create the Sun and Moon corresponding to two tablets. By Zayin, create the planets corresponding to the Torah, refined sevenfold. Create many stars, ministering with the signs of the zodiac.

God created the twelve signs of the zodiac in the universe. Of every sign and planet, create power [Cheyil] of fifteen powers. Of every power are 30 powers. Of the powers of Riyehton, there are 10,406. Of Riyehton, there are 30 legions, 324,000 in every legion: 30 of Setera, of 9,720,000; 30 of Sherqon, of 90,000,000 and 1,600,000; of all to Sherqon, 3,650,000 stars as appointed, the days of the Sun, of 100,000,000,000 [one thousand myriad myriads], and 99,600,000,000.

Rule in the day and in night. Ruling the seven planets in the day is Keshetzenesh and in the night is Chelem. In the day, Keshetzenesh rules in the day over the seven arrangements of the constellation of the Pleiades, beginning with Taurus. The stars unite, gathering as one, as the brood below the chickens.

The constellation of the Pleiades begin with the sign of Taurus, Orion, the Little Dipper, and the Big Dipper. Going after the constellation of the Pleiades, speak of the Little Dipper, the Big Dipper, and Orion. Going after second, the stars of the Little Dipper. Proclaim Orion and the Lord proclaims the dwellings of Orion, of the constellation of the Pleiades, of seven stars.

In the beginning, rule in the day and rule in the night. Virgo rules in the day and in night. Here are five days and two days.

Seven are suspended from the wheel in the firmament. Those suspended go forth, and reverse, with all the signs returning. Of the wisdom after, there are no rulers of these signs, according to the desire of God, the king of kings, who created the wisdom of the signs, to which there is no end.

Therefore, to every man is Neshemeh, Ruoch, and Chiyiem [see Introduction, page 19]. Face him, as he knows in the heart what comes forth in the day. Be united by the signs. Understand all in every dwelling. Of him who created, know of all thoughts until not creating all the great, shining luminaries in the sky, outside of the Little Dipper, as it is placed in the north.

The demons [Meziqiem] go in the firmament. The Malachim that fell from the most holy place, from the heavens, rise up to hear one word. After the veil, follow after in the tribe of man. By the hand, return to the place.

All stars and planets, and all signs of the zodiac were formed in the first quarter, not preceding the two parts of the hour. Therefore, every work of the Sun is slow. Every work of the Moon is swift.

The Sun and Moon are the two great, shining luminaries in the firmament. The highest is stretched as a tent, extending as a curtain. Isaiah speaks that it is spread as a tent. All the creatures cover the firmament as a tent, covering all below.

The wheel turns the luminaries, the stars, and the signs, from east to west, from west to east, going from Aries to Taurus, from Taurus to Gemini, and so on, until Pisces. From the beginning until the end of the year, going around and around. Rising up and descending, with the two great, shining luminaries. The stars from south to north and from north to south.

Earth extends over the sea, fixed within the waters of the oceans, as a ship in the middle of the sea. The Sea of Oceanus surrounds it. Proclaim the great sea [Im Hagedol]. There is no water produced therein or going forth. Cast down therein and rest in the water going forth in the universe.

When passing Oceanus, reach chaos. From there, reach the ends of the firmament. It is written in the Book of Job, surely be divided. Isaiah speaks of the Creator of the ends of earth.

Earth is created from the dwelling on the north side. Earth rises up to the dome, reaching the firmament on every side. It is suspended by the strength of the firmament. Of the wheel of the constellations, the Sun is the head and the Moon is the tail.

The desire of knowledge is in every place. The head is suspended, increasing over the creation of the universe in two years. Deliver in twelve years and the remainder therein in the course, corresponding to the year and corresponding to the month.

The head is suspended and the tail goes behind it. Thus the stars go before all. Bring forth by going forth, but not before the head suspended. Rise by the letters Yod Heh, and return the tail.

There are seven planets. Bow the head before the favored star. Bring forth therein. Suspend the twelve signs of the zodiac. Set apart men from women. Reveal Tau Aleph Vau in the east, of the names of men. In the east corner is a young maiden [A'alemoveh]. It begins the letters and every word is of the highest.

In the beginning, man is Shin Koph Gimel before women. In the corner, divide the south. Cast down every word by casting down women, as women are below.

Samekh Ayin Daleth is in the north, extending in Tohu. In the lowest, women of Tau Mem Daleth in the west. Men are before the corners divide west.

Of the dwelling in the west, there is no glory. Of men, Tau Aleph Peh fire. The names of men are according to the dominions of fire. The fire rises up as man, for it is seen above.

Shin Koph Gimel is earth. The names of women are according to the dominion of earth. The nation below are as women, being seen below.

Tau Mem Daleth is air. The names of men are according to the dominion of air between above and below. Third, man bows down is Samekh Ayin Daleth as water.

The names of women are according to the dominion of water. The water is below. Third, women bow down, for it is seen below. These are the elements of fire, air, water, and earth.

God created the twelve signs of the zodiac in the universe, arranging them in the firmament. They are Aries, Taurus, Gemini, Cancer, Leo, Virgo, Libra, Scorpio, Sagittarius, Capricorn, Aquarius, and Pisces.

The Sun is arranged in the twelve months of the year. The luminaries shine in the day and night. Every one is in place, not visible to the eye before the light of the Sun. In the wheel of the Sun, visible in the night outside from the sign, the Sun dwells above. Before the Sun, there are six concealed and six revealed.

Aries is arranged highest. From the strength of the star, Aries sinks down. Libra rises up. When Libra sinks down completely, go forth from the number of hosts and complete the names.

There is not one gathering in the boundary limits; not leading to minister in the season of sowing; not ministering in the season of the harvest; not ministering in the season of sowing.

Arrange to minister from the middle of Libra. Scorpio is in the middle. Sagittarius ministers in the season of sowing for 61 days. The hosts are in the middle of Sagittarius. Capricorn is in the middle. Aquarius ministers in the days of the winter for 61 days, in the middle of Aquarius, Pisces in the middle. Aries ministers in the season of the winter for 61 days, in the middle of Aries, and Taurus in the middle. Gemini ministers in the season of the harvest for 61 days.

Thus speak, come forth with sheaves of grain in the beginning harvest. The priest [Kehen] of El comes forth with sheaves of grain in the days of Nisan. Thus speak of the river Jordan. It overflows over every river bank in all the days of the harvest.

In the middle of Gemini and Cancer, and the middle of Leo in the season of the summer for 61 days, speak of the season of sowing until the harvest. Of the Sun in the course of the seven planets, from the middle of Libra until the middle of Aries, there are 180 divisions. Thus, in the season of the harvest until the season of sowing, seven planets from the middle of the signs of the zodiac until the middle of Libra, there are 180 divisions.

The divisions of the planets in the firmament are made as a helmet. Therefore, proclaim the planets go forth. Thus proclaim in the universe, the Little Dipper is in the south and the Little Dipper is in the north, leading in wisdom.

The Big Dipper, Orion, and the constellation of the Pleiades lead the order, every one in the season of the year, changing with the passing seasons. The Big Dipper and Orion minister. Define Orion and define the passing in the days of the Sun. Thus speak to define all language. Close and seal, as making to define by Isaiah.

Of Orion, define the passing and the interpretation of the Lord of the universe, creator of all. Seal the star. Orion passes close. The winds return from the strength in the days of raining. There is no path to the host of the sea [Mecheneh Iyem].

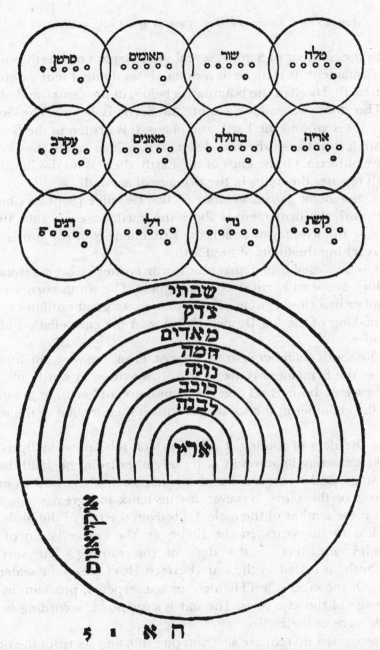

Figure 4. Earth and the heavens. The smaller circles (top row, reading left to right) contain the 12 signs of the zodiac: Aries, Taurus, Gemini, Cancer, Leo, Virgo, Libra, Scorpio, Sagittarius, Capricorn, Aquarius, Pisces. The orbits below show Saturn, Jupiter, Mars, Sun, Venus, Mercury, Moon, Earth. Below is the "Sea of Oceanus."

In the number of Saturn, reveal the covenant of Cheshmoval in the firmament. It is made as a dome, resembling a tent extending over Earth. Dwell in the boundaries below, in the center and above.

The dome resembles a tent. All Earth is below. The Sea of Oceanus is around the Earth and chaos. It is written in the Book of Isaiah, is it not so of the knowledge, not to hear Elohi, the Creator of the universe. Of the ends of the Earth, there is no dwelling. The Earth reaches the limits in the firmament around.

In the book of the wisdom of the Gentiles [Sepher Chokmi Hagoyim], the firmament is above the Earth on every side. In the book of the wisdom of Israel, the firmament is in the north side, not reaching the limits of the Earth.

It is not established that the north corner is over desolation [Tohu]. Suspend Earth over nothingness. The south corner is the chamber in a closed circle. It is written, make great until not seeing the making of the Big Dipper, Orion, and the constellation of the Pleiades.

The south chamber is from the east. From the west, the foundation of the firmament is over Earth. It is written in words, obscure the heavens above. Bind over the foundation of Earth. In the dome and the chamber in the south, the Ruoch is concealed in the midst of it.

In the days of raining, God ministers. Job knows to fly as the hawk, spreading its wings in order to gather from the south below the wings, and he served. Let there be power of the bird to judge the rest of the birds; however, as the hawk has great wings, and great is the feather of the male, fat is from the rest of the birds.

Thus in the years, in the first year, the constellation of the Pleiades ministers in the days of the raining. The serpent [Nechesh] is sealed in the star [Beriech Hova Mezel, or sealed its fate]. Of the crocodile [Thenien, or sea serpent], proclaim in the language of the wise ones. The star is suspended, according to the twelve signs of the zodiac.

Suspended therein are six from one side and six from the other side, sealed in the heavens from end to end. Therefore, proclaim the serpent is sealed. From the twisting tail, gather therein. The middle of the face is as the twisting serpent.

The innermost six signs minister, leading the universe. Come forth in the period by the rising of the Sun. Also, twisting from the second side in order to gather the outer signs before the Sun in the center of the universe.

Minister at this time. Surround and extend forth, sealed in the firmament from end to end. The firmament extends over all the universe from end to end. From one end, divide the north, but not to the end. Make the universe of three divisions. One third is sea, one third is wilderness, and one third is civilized land.

In the east of Earth in the period of Tebeth is the southwestern height. Until the firmament, measure in a circle. Go around corresponding to the shores of the Sea of Oceanus. On every side and in great height, go around the east, the south until the west and the south. The heights are as open windows in the east and open windows in the west.

In the east, in the period of Tishri, is the southeastern side of the period of Tebeth. Also, the east is the center, the center of the period of Tammuz. In the center, there are 91 windows in the south corner. Therefore, 91 in the north corner.

There is a window in the center. The splendor shines in the window. In the north, there is a window in the corner. It is covered and light goes forth.

It is said, from the covering, light goes forth. It is in the east corner, south of the period of Tebeth. Proclaim the window is open. The window in the north corner is of the period of Tammuz. Proclaim it is pleasant. From the beginning, the Sun shining in the window is pleasant. Go around in a circle. Afterward, cast down from north to south, going past the window. By the measure of 91 windows, there is one window in the chamber. In it is the wind of a hurricane.

The period of Tishri begins when the Sun rises before the window, shining in splendor. Go around to the eastern corner, the south, window after window, until it reaches the open window. The period of Tebeth begins from the open window. Go around in a circle. Afterward, rise from south to north, window after window, until reaching the concealed window. Go around and rise to the eastern corner, from the northern window, until reaching the pleasant window, until the window in the chamber.

In the chamber, consider 91. Consider from the beginning, the eastern corner south from the open window, until the concealed window. The window is concealed. Consider 91. It is the concealed window to the chamber. There is the window, shining in splendor. Here it numbers 183. These windows in the east are 183, corresponding to 183 windows in the west.

Three enter and the Sun rises every day before the window. It sinks down, passing one in the west, corresponding to the window in the east, until it passes. Rising up in the darkness, it passes the window.

See it return in the dawn. It is spoken, when the dawn rises, reach the rising of the dawn until it comes and goes. Extend in the dwelling. Of passage in darkness, it is spoken, let the Sun come and darkness be.

The Shekinah is in the west of the universe, rising up to lead blackness to the first window, in the center of the firmament, between the east and south.

In the period of Tebeth between the eastern window, spreading there north to the period of Tammuz, it spreads out. From the chamber comes the tempest, from the spreading of ice. The Sun does not go forth to gather therein. Only once in the great course, the Sun is created therein. The course is desired in the orbit [circuit].

There are four faces of four sides. The first side is warm and moist. The second side is warm and dry. The third side is cold and dry. The fourth side is cold and moist, corresponding to the fourth season of the year.

In the period of Nisan, the side of the Sun is changed. It is warm. Thus, the fourth season of the year is warm and moist below the earth. It is warm and moist in the season for three months.

In the period of Tammuz, the side of the Sun is changed. It is hot and dry, below the rising up of earth. It is hot and dry in the season for three months.

In the period of Tishri, the side of the Sun is changed. It is cold and moist for three months.

In the period of Tebeth, the side of the Sun is changed. It is cold and dry for three months.

If the Sun does not pass around four revolutions, the universe is not served by the seven. Bind the constellation of the Pleiades in five bands and Orion in two, thus seven. There are twelve around the wheel. Seven are bound.

Two return to the south side. Of five gates on the outside, return to the north side. Four rise up from the north to the right side, and five to the left side. They gather in day and night.

Gemini is the end. Seventh is Scorpio. The eighth is from Gemini to Sagittarius, between Scorpio to Cancer. Between Scorpio to Cancer, between the Big Dipper to Scorpio, the Big Dipper to the north and Scorpio to the south. They rise up in a circle toward the south and sink down in a circle toward the north.

In the north, the Big Dipper rises, and ministers with those suspended by the wheel. Those suspended are the stars of the wheel. The wheel turns in a circle, Aquarius is in the days, and the stars in Cancer are suspended to rule. The Big Dipper is leading. Complete by Ruoch to serve by Ruoch, the beauty of heaven.

Bear the hand of Nechesh, bound and suspended in the circle. Rise to gather the luminaries as kings. The stars are as princes of the hosts. Arrange the stars as hosts in a group. Go forth by the number of hosts.

Consider twelve signs of the zodiac reaching the constellation of the Pleiades and Orion above. The seven planets reach from the constellation of the Pleiades and Orion above.

There are forty arrangements of the constellation of the Pleiades or the seven dwellings, with Orion beginning. When binding, arrange the constellation of the Pleiades. Orion is beginning. These are bound. Learn from the signs.

Of the seven planets, know the Lord arranged the constellation of the Pleiades and the seven dwellings with Orion beginning. God turned his face to regard, and spoke to Job. Be able to bind the five bands to the constellation of the Pleiades. There are seven. Begin the seven dwellings of Orion.

The Lord made twelve and the constellation of the Pleiades. It is in the sign of Taurus, from the tail of Aries until the constellation of the Pleiades. Consider it is near Taurus to Orion. The Little Dipper and Big Dipper go after the constellation of the Pleiades.

The Little Dipper and the Big Dipper go after the constellation of the Pleiades, the Little Dipper, and Orion. The Lord proclaimed the dwelling of Orion second. Consider before the Little Dipper. Of the Lord of dwellings and wheels of God (Hebrew: MOSh-BOThIHM OMGOLGLOTh IH'), the constellation of the Pleiades, there are seven stars. They bind the constellation of the Pleiades. The Big Dipper goes after the constellation of the Pleiades.

God declared he would flood the world. Take two stars from the constellation of the Pleiades and thus the flood. As petition of the passing, take two stars from the Big Dipper. Conceal them in a place. Go above the Big Dipper after the Constellation of the Pleiades.

Petition the sons of the Lord [Benieh]. Make the Big Dipper over the sons of the Lord. Lead the universe as the beginning star, the one rising in the east.

Libra is seventh from the beginning, coming forth and sinking in the west. It is not visible. Complete the seven planets united from the ends. Rise up to see. From the ends, the seven sink and are not visible. Aries and Libra are in the period.

Begin with Aries rising, and from the beginning, Libra sinks. Taurus and Scorpio are in the period. Taurus begins rising. Scorpio in the beginning sinks down. Thus Gemini and Sagittarius, Cancer and Capricorn, Leo and Aquarius, Virgo and Pisces.

Six signs in the universe rise from the north. To the day it is, at the south side, south, visible to return. They go forth to the north side after the height of Earth, not visible to the eye. Thus, not the signs after. Over thus, proclaim Samuel is wise to perceive the gates. By the language, bind the gate.

The seven are bound above and bound within. The dwelling is not visible to the eye. This is not designated in the scriptures.

These are all of the signs of the zodiac and the planets. The Big Dipper and Orion are in the sign of Gemini. The constellation of the Pleiades and the Big Dipper begin with the sign of Taurus. Regard above. Much is revealed from all the planets and all the signs. Above, they are continuous. The constellation of the Pleiades and Orion unite. Draw near to unite this with that. Going to this after that, regard with all eyes.

Thus after God to Job, bind the bands of the constellation of the Pleiades or dwellings of Orion. These are the gates to learn. Look to the firmament. Rise up to the constellation of the Pleiades. Taurus is in the east. See the sign of Scorpio sinking in the west. In the period, Scorpio rises up in the east, Taurus is sinking in the west. Orion is near Taurus. The signs come after (in other words, the signs of the zodiac come after).

The dwellings of the signs are from west to east, and from the north side after. Earth rises up. Proclaim the dwelling. Dwell in the bands. Also, rise over the constellation of the Pleiades in the northeast. Learn much from all the signs above.

Thus, proclaim the binding of the seven. From the beginning, rise from the constellation of the Pleiades. Rise from the north and Scorpio rises from the south. The rest of the signs rise from the east. The constellation of the Pleiades is from east to west. Measure seven bands. The bands are considered near Orion. Five bands bind from west to east in the season. Orion is in the east and Scorpio sinks in the west. At the end of the five signs, they are in the north side. The bands near Orion are in the west to the east.

In the south side, from the sign of Scorpio, reach to Gemini in the end. The seven are in the east after the constellation of the Pleiades. The bands are regarded from the east to west in the north side. From the sign of Gemini, Orion is in the end of the seven. Reach Scorpio in the end. Five are in the west. Begin in Gemini until the beginning of Sagittarius.

Of the twelve signs of the zodiac, measure from the constellation of the Pleiades and Orion. There are twelve degrees, no less and no more.

In the beginning, increase the bands of the constellation of the Pleiades. Divide into divisions of the constellation of the Pleiades. Minister in the days of raining and from death, with worms from putrification.

The division of the band of Orion is between Sagittarius. Divide Orion to minister in the days of the Sun. Of the holy days of the Sun, divide the point near the second. From the heat, increase the band by rising from the point of shining. Blessed is the path of the blessed place, amen.

At this time, understand the baking [A'agiyini] of the Sun. Of 366 windows and 180 degrees in three days, rise up by the eastern spirit. Of 180 degrees in three days, descend by the western spirit.

According to the days of the year, the Sun goes forth in the east and gathers in the west. The Shekinah is in the west. Gather those bowing down before God, the king, king of kings. Speak of the everlasting greatness, making as appointed.

In the period of Tishri and Tebeth, the course is in the southern corner. The Sea of Oceanus is between the limits of the heavens to the limits of Earth. Sinking down, the glory is great and the path is great, until the power reaches the window, in the window in the east, quickly produced therein.

In the period of Nisan and Tammuz, the course is in the northern corner. The Sea of Oceanus is between the limits of the south. The course is north. Go north in the period of Tishri and Tebeth. The north is in the period of Nisan, in the southern corner for six months and in the northern corner.

The course above is in the windows in the east. The spirit of the Sun returns by the three letters of the name written over the heart. The Malachim lead by the letter. They lead in the day, not in night.

The Sun rises in the chariot and the horsemen are adorned as the bridegroom. It is said, the bridegroom is adorned in beauty as the bridegroom goes forth to the bridal chamber.

In the days of the Sun shining, see the fire shining from Earth. Face upward of hail. Were it not for the hail covering the letter, the universe is consumed. It is not concealed because of this.

In the winter, cover and turn your face above from below. Were it not for the heat of the fire, the hail is not in the universe. Be able to serve before the cold. Speak, before the cold of the day, serve and the Sun shines.

The 460 bands (in other words, windows) are the number of the days of the Sun. Therefore, 460 of the names Shesech, Shemesh, Chedes, Chemeh.[5]

In every day of the Sun and Moon, cover the eyes from the light above. Cast out flaming arrows and go forth in strength. Of weakness from the iniquities of human beings, be bound by the blessings of the day. Above the arch of the firmament, pass below, heating the sea from there. Thus, not hidden from the heat.

Thirteen words are written over the heart. Therefore, from the beginning until enduring the light. Thirteen and five Malachim lead the letters of the day. Therefore, five words of the Sun.

The bridegroom goes forth first. Exalt in the strength second. Reach to it third. The seasons, fourth. Not hidden from the heat, fifth. Thus the light is divided of eight. First, in the beginning [Berashith], three Malachim lead the letters in the night.

---

[5] Shemesh and Chemeh are both terms usually referring to the Sun.

There are eight Malachim between day and between night, corresponding to the four days. Eight times light. Therefore, the Lord God [El Adon] is over all, making eight written words. Gedelov [strength] is first. Votobov [of goodness] is second. Mela [fulfillment] is third. A'avolom [universe, or eternal] is fourth. Da'ath [knowledge] is fifth. Votheboneh [of intelligence] is sixth. Sobebiem [turning, or circling] is seventh. Avothov [Thou, or sign] is eighth.

Thus of every one. Outside are Aleph Beth, Koph Lamed, Shin Tau [MA"B K"L Sh"Th]. However, by the the Lord God, Aleph Beth corresponds to the 22 letters of the Torah. Therefore, the name of the Sun [Shemesh Shem] shines in them. The Torah of the Lord divides between day and night. Upholding them are four spirits. They are a thousand corresponding to the Torah, preceding a thousand.

The Sun is immersed every morning. It circles and the light increases, going forth in brilliance until the day is established. Bow to it. Receive Ruoch in the flesh and blood.

The Sun comes forth in the firmament. Be immersed to purify with the power. Thus, in all time, Gelegelial is the prince appointed over the wheel of the Sun. Ninety-six Malachim, great and glorious, serve the wheel radiating [Heleh] in the firmament. There are 65,000 divisions in every day.

The Sun shines in the filthy place [Meqom Hetienophoth]. There is no destruction [Mezieq, or demon]. Be immersed in the light above. The eye is not able to see. It is written, man does not see life.

Thus, serve the Moon according to the New Moon circling after, as the Koph. When the Moon is half, cover around the Shekinah. From water, clouds and fog are around. The Moon is curved, as if facing the Lord.

The neck is below and the face is above. Of rain, all speak of drops. The blessing is over the Moon. Receive before the Shekinah, and dance before. Of the desires of life, return and leap up from below to the New Moon.

Aophenial is the prince appointed over the wheel of the Moon; 88,000 Malachim serve the wheel of the Moon. Of 24,000 divisions in every night of every season. In the season, the Moon serves in the east in the first season, by 96 of the New Moon of every month.

The dwelling of the Moon is between the clouds and fog. It is made as a dish. The New Moon covers this with that. It is between the eyes, as the birth of the Moon.

These two coverings change before the western spirit. It goes forth from between both, as a kind of shofar in the night. The first measure is in night. Measure second and thus until the middle of the month. It is revealed, the two coverings change faces.

By the spirit of the eastern corner, the Moon goes forth first. Gather and cover between the second in the night. First measure and second measure, and thus until the end, until the covering is complete.

It is spoken of the covering, place the covering of cloud and fog. Bring forth to cover completely. Blow the trumpet on the New Moon. The shofar is in the New Moon. The time of meditation [Hegiegov] is in the New Moon. In the time, complete the covering. Blow the trumpet in the New Moon. The shofar is in one hour. God comes forth.

The Sun and Moon in the beginning of the night is four hours. Return in the hours. Perceive the flame of the Moon reaching to the Sun in the day. Forty degrees pass to the center and darken with light.

In great brilliance [Rebi Nehorayi], the king speaks and decrees the iniquities of Israel. In the passing year, perceive the flame of the Sun reaching to the Moon in night. Forty degrees pass in the center. From the light is darkness. Israel desired to perceive over the passing year. God is perfection. Of the Sun, send forth wrath over the nations of the world. Thus it is spoken of the Lord God, learn the path of the people.

The light of the Moon is concealed in times and revealed in times. However, the light of the Sun of the universe is revealed to all people. The Sun and Moon go forth constantly, but the path of the Sun is not as the path of the Moon. The path of the Sun is fixed. The path of the Moon is not fixed.

In times, go forth with the planet in shortened length of time. How many steps from the north? See it is long from the south. See it is short and, not seeing it, remember the word, as it is spoken. Make the Moon of the festivals.

The Sun knows to come forth. Thus it is arranged, not going to the house as Saturn, Capricorn, and Aquarius.

Jupiter, Sagittarius, and Pisces. Mars, Aries, and Scorpio. Venus, Taurus, and Libra. Mercury, Gemini, and Virgo. The Sun, the Moon, and Cancer.[6]

Rehetial is the prince appointed over the stars. Seventy-two Malachim, great and glorious, serve with the signs of the zodiac rising from east to west, and west to east.

God created the planets and signs of the zodiac, going in the night from east to west and from west to east.

Kokebimal is the prince appointed. Three hundred and sixty-five thousand myriad Malachim, greatest and most glorious, serve with the planets. From city to city, from country to country, in the firmament of the heavens, and all suspended therein.

God created the firmament of the highest divisions of seven, created with those suspended from the head from fire. From water, the image of a great crocodile as a twisting serpent. Make the head and tail. Place in the darkness of the firmament. In the place, extend from end to end, bind the twisting serpent springing forth to the center of the light. In the middle, extend in a great circle. All the stars and signs of the zodiac surround all the planets therein and the two luminaries.

Twelve signs of the zodiac hold dominion over them, guiding between good and evil. Darken the light of the two luminaries and the seven planets. They go and come with the luminaries and signs of the zodiac, from east to west and from west to east.

In the period, the planets go after. Preceding to serve in the one place, speaking not before and not following after. You go forth on a journey directly. From fire and from water, see the hidden things not seen by the eye. Deliver the most ancient writings. I go forth to the knowledge of those suspended. Of power from holding dominion over the kingdom in reverence and goodness. In wickedness, facial features bring forth therein.

Prepare to go from star to star and be guided. Go forth to change the limits going after, behind the tail of the highest and lowest. Surrounded therein are the constellations, six in the south side and six in the north side. Know the wheel of the signs, planets, and luminaries are arranged and fixed in the darkness of the firmament.

------

[6] Although omitted from the text, Leo should be added here.

The stars are fixed and surrounded therein forever, not moving from their place. They are fixed in the wheel, circling around the firmament in the south. In the north, from east to west. Those suspended extend therein from end to end. They are bound and suspended, created in the center of the wheel.

The Big Dipper is placed from the north side by virtue of those suspended in the north side. The signs of the southern part of the wheel are suspended by virtue of those suspended in the wheel. The Big Dipper is fixed in the circle. Those suspended from the wheel of the signs are fixed in the wheel from east to west. From the north, from west to east of the universe.

Of the seven planets, the wheels diminish. The wheel of the stars goes forth with seven wheels of seven planets. They are Saturn, Jupiter, Mars, the Sun, Venus, Mercury, and the Moon.

The planets and the twelve signs of the zodiac are from east to west. From west to east. From the wheel of the Big Dipper, lead with those suspended. The fixed lead the suspended from the wheel, the wheel of stars. Seven of seven planets, completed by the Ruoch of God.

By the power, speak of the Ruoch of heaven. Create beauty by the hand of the serpent [Shephereh Choleleh Yidov Nechesh]. Bind those suspended, as written by the word of the Lord, who created heaven.

Ruoch is in the face of all hosts. El proclaims the names of the planets. Count what is written. Count the number.

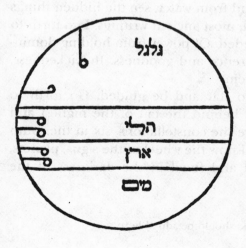

Figure 5. The Hebrew translates, from bottom to top, as "Water/earth/suspend/wheel."

It is written of the great power of the great Adonai, learn there is much greatness by the arrangments of the Malachim. Of the planets, signs, and those suspended in the wheel, as the Big Dipper, see greatness in the rest. Create the universe, for there is no width or depth to the wisdom. Distinguish the universe as wisdom, the heart of the suspended body in heaven, the wheel of the signs.

There is no wisdom. (HEBREW A"Ch ARI"H). The Sun is the innermost part of the universe. The wheel of the signs is suspended. There is no wisdom to serve, when the Moon is new or its period complete. The sea dries as fire. The name of the prince is Michael. Taurus is earth and Libra is air [Ruoch].

Serve Venus when the Moon is new. Air is flowing water. Of Venus and of rain, the prince is Aanael (Hebrew: ChK"Q) [or ThBQ]. Gemini is air and Virgo is earth.

Serve the planet when the Moon is new. Flow a little and dry a little upon the foundation of the earth. Of air, the prince is Raphael (Hebrew: S"L). Cancer is water.

Serve the Moon when therein, or when the New Moon is complete. The prince is Gabriel (Hebrew: QD"Sh). Sagittarius is fire and Aquarius is air.

Serve Saturn when the Moon is new. Dry by placing over in secret. Seal the mixture by moist air and flowing water. The prince is Qephetzial (Hebrew: GD"Tz). Capricorn is earth and Pisces is water.

Serve Jupiter in the New Moon. Divide in half. Dry in the place and divide in half of flowing water. The prince is Tzadqial (Hebrew: TAa"M). Aries is fire and Scorpio is water.

Serve Mars in the New Moon. Dry in the place. Divide in half as flowing water. The prince is Samael.

Learn the signs of the Sun. The Sun rises clear and pure. Of the warmth, reveal the qualities of fire, air, and purity. When rising, the Sun is clear and pure in flames of fire. Of red flame, reveal the greatest and most powerful spirits.

When seen before the Sun rises, the clouds are green and red, revealing the rain. When shining as the flames of the Sun, reveal the measure of the autumn and winter. The Sun rises in the midst of the clouds.

In the midst of the sea, see the flame revealing the winter and autumn. When the Sun shines, rising in brilliance from the clouds, reveal the winter and autumn, of the rain.

When the Sun rises in the west, the clouds increase around. Reveal the qualities of the purity of the firmament and the air.

The Sun comes forth, returning from the spirit of the north. Draw away the redness of the clouds from the north side and black clouds from the south side. Reveal the qualities of purity, of the winter and autumn.

When rising with Ruoch, also designate the raining. When, from every side, the Sun is at the approach of evening, signs of the red clouds shine in brilliance of the Sun. The clouds reveal the spirits of strength. It decreases when the winds blow clouds to be from here and from there.

The Sun reveals the winter and autumn. See the firmament in great blackness as the dawn of life [Shechoroth]. The darkness shows the dry land. The rivers dry up, and the springs and wells.

When the Sun rises, circle around to reveal the winter and autumn. The Sun rises at the time. After, weaken and scatter the greenness from there. The brilliance of the flames shines from the midst of the clouds. Reveal the rain mixed together with hail sinking down. In other words, reveal all the rain together with Ruoch. Ruoch of earth begins in the Ruoch of the world.

Kindle flames in heavens. Send forth, shining in brilliance. Send forth therein, as a lamp of fire. Follow after and complete by revealing the rain with air together.

When the brilliance is pure, the Ruoch of the north dwells. Of the purity of the body of the heavens, the Ruoch of the north is purity by Ruoch. The Creator decrees Yod Tau [I"Th] over that. Dwell on Earth from the high and lofty place. From all the highest places, therefore, is pure darkness of Ruoch, black and darkness. The light of the Sun shines without darkness, cloud, and fog, as the shining splendor of the light.

When seeing the Moon in the day, be concealed in the hiding place. The highest shining of the Moon reveals the Ruoch of the north. When concealing the lower Ruoch, reveal the dwelling of Ruoch. When seeing the Moon in the day, reveal the qualities of the purity of Ruoch.

When seeing the Moon in the day, it is diminished by fog and cloud. Pure and clear, reveal the changing of Ruoch. Dwell by the sign of the coming day.

When seeing the Moon, clouds reveal the winter and autumn. When the Moon is the fourth day of the New Moon, lift up vertically in the corners until the Ruoch returns. From the Ruo-choth of the west, reveal the winter and autumn. When seeing the New Moon divided from the place, see the divisions revealed from there. The Ruoch returns.

As the Moon is full, pass until the fourth day. From the fourth day until the fourth day, fill until the middle. Reveal the period being near the Sun. The Ruoch of the fourth sign goes with the Sun. Change the spirits of seven days.

Thus, by the signs of the Moon, see and understand the knowledge of the signs, the omen of rain for three days of the New Moon, or three days following the New Moon. Fill the life complete.

Of the half of the Moon, measure to fill all the seasons. Of the Moon, see the omens of rain for three days, or following three days. When the Moon is thin, pure, and clean, not seeing therein anything swollen, bind over the qualities of the air.

When seeing the dwelling of the Moon, it is circled around with cloud and fog. The wisdom of the purity of the Moon is in every month. See every Ruoch surrounding. Lead the clouds above. Bind the Ruoch dwelling from the sign at the side. Lead the sign of the clouds.

When seeing the Moon surrounded and dark, the name binds over autumn and rain. When around the Moon as one lamp of purity, descend from the dwelling. Decrease the lamp and bind over the qualities of air and purity, and when two or three.

Bind over autumn and rain and wind, when surrounded as wax [Doneg]. Divide from the first side, of the sign at the side, darkness comes. When darkness decreases, or is yellowish surrounded in blackness, see the divisions completed when greatest. Thus also, scatter the air and change much.

Of Ruoch, the Sun goes around as a circle of light. When divided quickly, bind over the qualities of purity. The firmaments rise as the Sun. Know by the sign of the day when there is to be rain. When the Sun rises from the midst of the clouds, heat rises as a flame of fire, then to be winter and autumn. As the Sun rises reddish and boiling, bind over Ruoch. When in the morning, see the Sun is great and large, then to be winter and autumn. When seeing the Sun shining before the rising, bind over rain. When rising before reddish clouds, bind over rain coming to the south side. When seeking great strength as in the desert, cast off. Also, when seeing the great blackness passing over and flies gather to bite or whisper sounds, bind over rain.

Know the periods in the beginning, all the periods of heat and the middle portions. Venus is as much raining. Mercury is completely hot. The Moon is completely cold. Saturn is as the summer and the winter, cool and much raining. Jupiter is completely cold, of snow and rain. Mars is heat, decreased rain, and completely without cold.

The signs of the zodiac are arranged, ministering in the beginning.

> In the first night, Kelesh Tzemchoq Kelesh Tzem.
> In the first day, Chenkel Shetzemech Kenel Chenkel.
> In the third night, Nekel Shetzem Chenkel Shetzemech.
> In the second day, Leshetzemech Chenkel Shetzemech.
> In the fourth night, Shetzemech Chenkel.
> In the fifth night, Chenkel Shetzem Chenkel.
> In the fifth day, Tzem Chenkel Shetzem Cheneb.
> In the sixth night, Leshetzem Chenkel Shetzemech.
> In the sixth day, Nekel Shetzem Chenkel Shetz.
> In the seventh night, Mechnekel Shetzem Chenkel.
> In the seventh day, Shetzem Chenkel Shetzem Chen.

Reach the order of the nights, Ketzenesh Chelem. Also, the intelligence to understand when it is autumn, or rain is from the signs of the Moon in the third day of the lunar month.

The New Moon draws out when the beams of the Moon are as plates of metal. Of darkness, the sign binds over rain. Thus, when the Moon shines in the fourth day, bind over the rain. When seeing the Moon is red as fire, it is the sign to bind over the great rain in autumn, filling the seas. When seeing the Moon is black, it is the sign to bind over the great rain in autumn, filling the seas. When all around is as a lamp in a circle, or two or three circles, bind over autumn and the great rain.

Also, learn and understand the knowledge of rain. In autumn, it rains by the signs of the Sun. When the Sun rises red, bind over the rain. It is established to sink in the west. When black clouds come near from the left side [the northern side], it will rain at once, as the Sun rises serving the clouds. When the brilliance of the Sun shines as flames, it is the sign to bind over rain. Thus, it is written in the *Book of the Signs of the Zodiac* [Sepher Hamezeloth, presented here as Book Five].

Also, the wisdom of the name is over autumn and rain in the light of the days. When pigs or goats have sexual intercourse, the males with the females are able to produce. Cease the sexual intercourse to make strong. Also, when desired to make use of, or when dirty by places of the sea, or mud and clay, desire to be very dirty. Also, desire pleasures and seek pleasure from below the earth, until the ends of the opening edges.

Also, extend the head to correspond to the north side. Also, when the dogs dig in the earth and the wolf comes near the goats. Also, when immersing the princes of the tribes in the mirror of the sea, and in springs, not before desire. Also, listen when proclaiming the power consuming the crops. The thread of a spider's web falls from the strength, not to snare Ruoch. All these bind over autumn and rain in the light of the days.

In the course of the Moon, decrease to proclaim the small light. Thus, there is no dominion of the stars in the firmament, when stars number ninety-eight [Tz"Ch].

Denounce the Moon over the dwelling of the Lord [A'al Leboniethieh]. Create the stars as a man. Of power over the tree, consume and flames go forth. Therefore, the stars with the Moon go forth from the beginning of the universe.

Combine the signs and the wheel. Record and calculate and assign and number. Consider the calculations of the planets and signs of the zodiac. Calculate the periods and circling of the planets. Of those suspended and signs of the zodiac in everlasting order, see with light. Calculate in order to see the generations. Prepare to see them from the beginning until the end.

It is written, who acts and creates, proclaim the generations from the beginning, before the creation of the universe. In order to understand the actions of every man in righteousness and wickedness, decree over every one. According to the works, prepare works between good and evil.

Number the planets and signs of the zodiac, scattered in the hours. Bring forth between good and evil. All was created by Elohim in wisdom and intelligence, before the rise of the universe.

The wisdom of the Lord is the foundation of Earth. Number the planets and signs of the zodiac of every man. The universe was formed before them. According to the works, man is made to prepare. God does not give the planets and signs of the zodiac by permission of wickedness or goodness.

In the beginning, see man not established and without form. It is written, the heart of the wicked man is formed from youth. Elohim is compassionate and merciful. Compassion is over wickedness. Arrange and set in order. Return from the beginning of creation, when not yet rising to bring forth. Mankind dwells until the torment from sin is restored by repentence of the Lord Elohim.

There is no sign of the zodiac fixed. All is according to the man, by the sign and hour. As it is written by Ishma'al, by the name and by the letters of the luminaries, see all the periods. Therefore, speak in the night. Pass with the periods and change the hours, but not in the morning hours [Shecherieth, or morning prayers]. The cock proclaims the Sun in the night. Change the period and on the morrow being clouds. The clouds gather in the heights.

In the times the Moon is not shining in night, change with the periods. The next time, by three planets in the night.

That is the division between day and night; however, in the morning, see ten calculations in day. It is written to work diligently, be weary, and complete the name of the Lord of the hosts.

Learn to correspond Heh to the luminaries, thirty heights over all the the signs. Thus God is above all human beings. Observe all from the beginning of the creation of the universe by the command, let there be light.

Of the river of fire [Neher Dienor], the luminaries go forth by the commands. See, if not to toil, the constellation of the Pleiades in the river of fire. No creature is able to serve in the cold. Therefore, the Sun and Moon and planets see the redness of the Sun going forth in the day.

The river of fire goes forth in the place. The Sun goes forth in the day. The river of fire goes forth and the sign goes forth to proclaim day.

Proclaim the season of the day in the place. The Sun goes forth in night. In all days, be humble to go to the sign in the place and proclaim night.

Of the division, Elohim is between the light of the river of fire. Between the darkness of day, darken the sky and proclaim Elohim. Of the light of the day, that is the river of fire. By them, the luminaries stop going forth. Do not speak thus to be evening and be morning. Here suspend the luminaries.

The river of fire goes forth at the time of the Sun. Of the light of day, the river of fire. Of darkness, proclaim night. Of darkness of the days, the path of the Sun. In the morning, light of the river of fire until the middle of the day. The river of fire is above to the east and west in the fourth day. Go forth from the river of fire.

In the middle of the day, the river of fire is above and the Moon and planets are above. Speak of extending the heavens.

According to the going forth, arrange the measurements of the wise ones. Of 360 degrees, twelve signs of the zodiac are bound therein. The names of the signs are Aries, Taurus, Gemini, Cancer, Leo, Virgo, Libra, Scorpio, Sagittarius, Capricorn, Aquarius, and Pisces.

Of every ruler, go forth 30 degrees. All degrees are 60 degrees to Gesteravoth.[7] Of every Gestera are 60 Bereqovonoth.[8] Of every Bereqovon are 60 Avoloth.[9] Of every Avoloth are 60 Avoroth.[10] Of every Avoroth are 60 Sototh.[11] Of every Sototh are 60 Rophosavoth.[12] Of every Aphorsavoth are 60 Herophoth, as instantly recieved.[13]

Calculate until eleven and twelve words. Follow the exactness of the calculation however the planets descend in the universe or lead in the universe. The names are Saturn, Jupiter, Mars, the Sun, Venus, Mercury, and the Moon. There is a division to every one of

---

[7] This is probably a reference to Mater, which usually means rain, or is sometimes applied to the sending of hail, lightning, fire and brimstone, manna, etc.

[8] This may refer to Bereqoth, which can mean lightning bolts, although the term Bereqovon refers to thorns or briars.

[9] This is often used in reference to trees, and sometimes to fools. It may also be a reference to curses.

[10] This usually refers to lights, or sometimes to curses.

[11] This probably refers to Shototh, which may mean whips, or fools, or madmen, or possibly statements of contempt.

[12] This is likely a typographical error for Aphoresavoth, which may mean divisions or distinct declarations, or possibly specifications.

[13] This may translate as bruises or weaknesses, possibly medicine or cures.

the planets, by the strength of Draqon Dienor [Hebrew: DRAQON DINOR, a reference to the term dragon] surrounding.

Thus, in the period of the sign suspended from the wheel, go forth in heaven. The twelve suspended give seven from the period of the constellation of the Pleiades. The Lord binds the signs, suspended from the wheel and going forth in heaven. In Earth is seven. The Lord binds twelve around the wheel, bound from within. They are the outer gates. Seven rise from the right side of the north.

The Lord is from the north to the right side corresponding. Gather six in the day and six in the night. Gemini is innermost of the seven, and Scorpio is at the end. The Lord is from Gemini to Sagittarius, and from Scorpio to Cancer. Thus, gather the Little Dipper to Scorpio, with the Little Dipper in the north and Scorpio in the south.

Rise in a circle, according to the sinking in the south. Extend according to the north. In the north, the Little Dipper rises from the period with those suspended. The signs are suspended, the signs of the wheel. The wheel returns. In the wheel is Aquarius.

The signs are as lords [Seregiem] suspended as the rulers lead. Begin by six at the tail, suspended in the end. The six begin going directly and the tail goes opposite. Thus in the beginning, the river of fire is around the universe. Afterward from here is 80 days. On the fourth day, surround the river of fire. Begin and create the Sun to lighten the day upon the Earth. The river of fire is near the sign of heat. Cold is the constellation of the Pleiades. Snow is the Moon, as going forth by them. Therefore, create the smallest planets that do not shine, except to warm the universe by the light of the flame sending forth. Do not speak of what is created, what is neccesary to the universe, but only to create all the beauty of the universe.

From the power of the light of the planets, desire exaltation. Also, the signs and luminaries desire. Rehetial is the magistrate [Shoter] of desire. Twenty-three princes correspond to the desire of the signs. The luminaries, therefore, proclaim Rehetial, the language of desire. Desire to interpret desire.

All the Malachim proclaim over the name that supports the printing of Rezial. Deliver the *Book of the Mysteries* [Sepher Harazim]. Adam, the first man, learned therein, as therein are the Malachim over the months.

Shephiya'aial presides over the month Nisan with 36 Malachim.

Regehiyal presides over Ayar with 43 Malachim.
Arinavor presides over Sivan with 68 Malachim.
Tha'atz Bon presides over Tammuz with 28 Malachim.
Thecher Gar presides over Ab with 29 Malachim.
Morael presides over Alul with 29 Malachim.
Pechederon presides over Tishri with 29 Malachim.
Lerbeg presides over Marheshvan with 27 Malachim.
Arbegedor presides over Kislev with 29 Malachim.
Aberekial presides over Adar with 28 Malachim.

According to those presiding, proclaim Aberekial in the blessed language. The lowest are proclaimed by goodness to establish Romial, Chereshial, Tepherial, Shelemial, and Melekial.

All go forth seeing God. Send forth Mordecai in the month Adar.[14] Esther is of grace and mercy.[15]

Of the *Book of Memorials* [*Sepher Hezekeronoth,* or *Book of Commemorations*], come to Mordecai, being the one next to the king. Give blessings to the king of the glory.

Norial is over the river of fire. Shemeshial is over the Sun. Irechial is over the Moon. Kokebial is over the planets. Shopherial is over the *Book of Life* [*Sepheri Hechiyem,* or the numbers of life], over the name to speak of the shofar. Zekobial is over the purity of Israel. Yihodial is over the Malachim, extending to the highest.

Proclaim all the Malachim over the name of the dominion. Combine the letters (Hebrew: HQBH). Create the wheel of the words. See all the actions of creation. Proclaim to rise upward by the names in wisdom, according to the Sun, Moon, and planets, created from the river of fire. Therefore, it is in the second firmament. The stars go forth proceeding to the conclusion.

Make blessings in the days before the Sun. Of the cold, heat the heavens. Of the division appointed in the fourth day, go forth from the river of fire. The Sun, Moon, and planets are suspended in the firmament.

---

[14] Mordecai was a Jew of the tribe of Benjamin, living in Persia, who was the foster father of Esther, and afterward the prime minister in the court of King Ahasuerus.
[15] Esther became the wife of Ahasuerus, and queen of Persia.

In judgment from the river of fire, boiling and put forth afterward, therefore the planets go to one side. Man is established, as cheese begins to go forth from the milk. When taken from the milk, it ripens and becomes cheese. Thus, it is not all white. Therefore, the Sun is white from the Moon.

From the planets, diminish the covering of the Moon. Of light over the days, create the river of fire. From them, create the lights. That is what is spoken by the wise ones. The shining goes forth from the motion of the living. Create in the highest heaven from the motion near the throne of the glory above. The wicked turn away.

In the second firmament, the river of fire is one. Of the judgment of the stars, speak of the many. If not for the tail of the constellation of the Pleiades in the river of fire, there is no salvation before the cold. The stars in the second firmament shine as the Sun goes in the day.

The river of fire is in the first day. Proclaim day by the Sun going forth. In night, go forth in the darkness of the universe. Of the days, take hold of the shell (Hebrew: BQLIPH ShThOPSh) in the days. Around the shell of the star, the river of fire goes forth in one shell above. In the shell going forth, the Sun goes forth in the day. Below in the shell is the place of the Sun in night. Thus, go forth in the darkness of the days.

Of the days of heaven, beneath in the shell dwell in darkness. Upon the path of the days, however, above is shadows. It is written of darkness, proclaim night as in the place of darkness. Proclaim the place of night, as the Sun goes forth in night. Thus, of every star above in the side of the end of the firmament.

Of the firmament, receive from the great fire, from the moisture, the holy word and the holy spirit. Mix together to bring forth a crystal. Be moist to extend and spread.

It is written on the right side, extend heaven. That is dry land. Of the firmament, create the firmament [see figure 6 on page 129].

The clouds of the firmament are moist. See the force cast down as the dry land extends. Of heaven alone, the path over the high place is in the day. By dry land afterward, spread as a tent. Of the dwelling, extend the abundance, all by means of the Ruoch. It is written, of the beauty of the Ruoch of heaven.

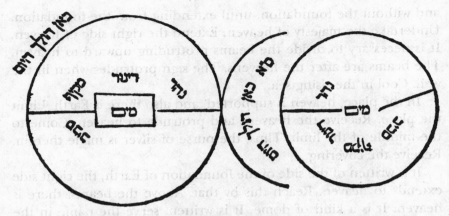

Figure 6. Diagram of the firmament of the heavens. The Hebrew in the center of the circles translates as "water." The text circling "water" reads, counterclockwise, "*Neher/Dinor/*circling [or surrounding]/around." The text on the outside of the circle reads "here journey in the day." *Neher Dinor* is interpreted as "River of Fire."

Of the power of the firmament above, the power rises to the beams of the protruding roof [Qoroth]. Thus, the days of the heavens are between the beams, as proclaimed above of the offering of the day.

Every star rises above, cooling in the days. Rise up and require the beams of the roof of the heavens. Strengthen and support the beams over the heavens. Is it not written, heaven extends to the right side? The rebatements give within and around, not holding the walls of the house, not piercing the wall by the first protrusion. The second is above the first. The sign proclaims the rebatements according to the wall support. Diminish the thickness of the wall, in order to protrude in the place. The sign is above, in the end of the wall. Proclaim to extend above in the wall. In the limited place, proclaim the offering. By the sign in the place, the rebatements of all the wall are weakened. By thickening, therefore, beneath is wide. Five above, six above seven.

It is therefore written in the floor, the lower is five cubits, the center is six cubits, and the third is seven cubits in width. However, not above, but only of the place of the limit.

In the Torah, it is proclaimed to extend. It is written, all these precious stones are hewn in measures, in the granary, from within and without the foundation, until extending from the foundation. Undertake the majesty of heaven. Extend the right side of heaven. It is necessary to divide the beams protruding upward to heaven. The beams are after the heavens. The sign protrudes when in the wall. Cool in the rising sea.

In the place, heaven is supported, and also there is Earth. Limit the place. Receive the heavens and protrude to heaven. Come to the middle of the limit. Thus, the purse of silver is made therein. Receive the covering.

It is written of the side of the foundation of Earth, the right side extends to heaven. Reach this by that. Above the beams, there is heaven. It is a kind of dome. It is written, serve the name in the tabernacle.

Above is the river of fire and 22 shells [Qliphoth]. From the name, cast down and diminish the river of fire. Cast down every star and go with the star by boiling.

It is written, the river of fire leads. Go forth from the presence of a thousand thousands to serve the Lord. In the river of fire, the Malachim serve the Lord. The sign goes forth of every star. Great things are covered and established before the river of fire in every place, however the first indicates the days. Going to the top, here are a thousand thousands. Bear the sign of Elohim in the firmament. The heavens are between, with beams protruding.

Let there be shining luminaries. Do not speak of the luminaries when placing the lights. Here is the Sun, offering as a crystal. The light goes forth outside the crystal. Of the sign of the crystal it is said, let there be luminaries in heaven. Fill with splendor. Produce splendor as the crystal fills with splendor.

Move to the outer. Speak by the dwelling of the gate every day. The gates open in the east. The darkness of the firmament comes from the place. The Sun comes in the morning, going forth for 50 years.

There are gates in the place of darkness of the firmament. There are windows in the firmament. In the place, regard the universe seen from the Earth as the Sun comes in the gate.

The gates serve the morning and grow larger. Therefore, speak of the gates opening in the east. There is no division of the name. There is the Sun. Wind comes forth in the universe. The windows weaken. Therefore speak, divide the window of the firmament. Do not go by the power and by the strength. Consume all the universe completely.

God goes forth in the place. The Sun goes forth from the place and the Moon from the place. Place it in the hollow of the heavens. The Sun is as a kind of dish in the hollow. Of the dwelling of the Moon, dwelling in the place, the Sun goes forth in morning or in evening. It spreads light in all the universe.

Therefore, the Sun is in the language of the female. Let there be luminaries. Do not speak of the luminaries when the Sun rises above. The language of female is of great beauty. The Sun is in the season.

Speak in the language of the male. The Sun goes forth over Earth. It is shining and goes forth. Thus, the Sun is in strength of six in four days from the river of fire. Serve between the shells.

The river of fire freezes [coagulates] as cheese. Create the heavens and dry up, seeing the river of fire as milk already made into cheese. Afterward, separate the firmament above the shells.

Beneath the darkness of the sea, it is dark. Create the Sun and Moon and planets and stars. Of every one, the glory of the firmament.

Know the planets serve in the firmament between day and night. Before the brilliance of the Sun, there is no offering seeing in them as man. Settle in the flames of the Sun, not visible in the distance, of the outer, before it is clear. When placing burning fire in the Sun, see it as ashes. Therefore, in the day, the brilliance of the Sun covers in light and is not visible. However, in the night, the Sun is beneath the Sea of Oceanus, and the planets are visible.

Speak to create the planets. Release the binding, as not shining. According to this, the highest sea cools. The host of the heavens create by the heat of the sign.

In the morning, see the planet going forth from the place of radiance [Zeherieroth]. The day comes, seen as the brilliance of the planet. Go forth from the place of the first rainfall [Yivoreh] as lightning. The planet goes above, not moving. Men are not lacking.

By going forth, give praise. Establish the flowing in heaven. In the place of the flowing, it is established to make the firmament yellowish in order to be more visible. Of goodness, the light is over the Earth. Give in darkness to the lowest firmament.

Support the Earth. The shining extends over the Earth, not in the firmament, but in planets and stars all being over the Earth. Man is able to receive the knowledge between good and evil. It is given in the heart, as God knows all. Here is flesh and blood.

Revere every word by the stars. Of every dwelling, God knows all, knowing of all flesh and blood. It is not necessary to know all. Blessed is he. Rise in memory forever and ever, but not in every dwelling. (Hebrew: OQ"O BNO ShL Q"O MIM M' BMIM.) Bind to it.

In the *Book of Formation*, God goes forth. The Ruoch is from the holy spirit.[16] Engrave and carve the sign of Ruoch, the breath. Form therein the four spirits of the universe.

Ruoch is in every one, divided as instructed. Of him who makes the crystal vessel, receive the vessel of iron bore from end to end. Receive from the crystal, from the smelting furnace. Ascribe the end of the vessel in the mouth of all. The end of the vessel comes to the mouth. Breathe in Ruoch of the mouth. The Ruoch passes from the midst of the vessel bore. Reach until the end of the empty vessel. The Ruoch of the mouth breathes in the crystal. Make the vessel small or large, or long or short or wide. Measure mouths by the power.

Of the power and the strength, the wondrous Ruoch goes forth. Extend the hollow of the universe. The sea goes forth from the slight moisture, much without measure. Carve and engrave the throne of the glory.

Of every high host, do not desire of God to make from the great fire. In order not to liken to it, fire consumes fire. Receive the sea of fire and Ruoch. Create the ministers [Mesherthiyov]. Divide the water into three divisions. In one portion, freeze the water. Boil the water in fire. Tremble in the smoke. Soil is made into the earth. The second portion makes every high host. Heaven is the highest. The third portion is the firmament above. Separate between water. Water is divided above and divided below. The water is received from below.

Rejoice and speak of happiness. There is life to us. Bring near, close to the Creator. Of living and rejoicing, uphold below the throne of the glory. Fly in great happiness. Give praise and

---

[16] See *Sepher Yetzirah*, 1:9.

thanksgiving and praise. Adorn the crown. The splendor forms the universe.

It is written, the sounds of water is the greatest glory. By the works of Berashith, reach eleven times water. Of the generations of Noah, eleven times water. In eleven generations, here is Noah. There is to be a flood. God knows the water restores the universe.

Turn aside eleven times by the sea, according to the generations. The flood purifies in female [Asheth] and male [Ayish]. Turn aside and separate. God is over the sea, being the highest sea. Separate the sea over Egypt. Eleven times the sea. In the ark, the sea is of two kinds. Here are twenty-two kinds. Therefore, twenty-two kinds in the Bible.

The Lord El speaks, and Moses speaks to Aaron [the brother of Moses, the first High Priest]. Receive the staff, and extend your hand over the waters of Egypt, over rivers and streams, and over lakes. All is given, not restored below the Sun.

Therefore, Joshua reaches the sea. Water is from the song [Shiereh] until Esau and Moses eleven times. Also by Joshua, eleven times. The sea is eight times the water of the Jordan. Of three times the sea, give to divide the water of the sea before the sons of Israel. Thus, the water dwells at the approach of morning.

The offering is everlasting, the offering with the water of six days of Berashith. The highest sea is suspended by the commandment of God, between the sea and over the firmament, above the firmament, as suspended by the commandment.

Elohim divided to fill the sea. Learn to divide. Of you, Elohim, of the sea, give half in the firmament divided in Oceanus. The firmament resembles a pool of water. Above the pool of water is the dome. From the heat of the pool of water and the motion of the dome, dense clouds fall. They are cast down to the middle of the sea of saltiness. The highest sea is clear from every word.

The highest sea from the lowest sea is thirty measures. Between sea to sea is thirty. The song of degrees is thirty degrees above from below. Freeze above. From below, the shining of the sea goes forth, complete in fire.

Create the Malachim to consume in the eyes. The Malachim are of the highest sea. They are males and the lowest are females. Between the highest to lowest are three fingers going around the firmament, dividing the sons.

Therefore, by Isaiah, the gate of the sea extends in the hollow over the sea, for the sake of the sea of heaven and Earth. Ruoch arranged the universe by the highest sea.

The firmaments are as goblets [hills]. The house receives the sea. It is said, the sea extends in the hollow. The sea is the hand or sole of the foot, heaven and Earth and the living Ruoch, the everlasting Ruoch.

The Ruoch hovers over the surface of the sea. Above and below, the mountains are suspended in the storm of Ruoch. However, in the beginning of heaven and Earth, the Ruoch arranged the stars and heaven of fire (Hebrew: TAQ ShL ASh ShBG AaPR ThMD ROCh SAaD), and of the sea. Of them, fire precedes farther. Soil is the beginning of the house of praise [Bieth Helel], but only the fire of heaven. The Shekinah is in heaven.

Therefore (Hebrew: TAQ) is fire. Aries is the beginning of the signs of the zodiac. Over thus, fire precedes Berashith. Elohim created the heavens of (Hebrew: TAQ).

After (Hebrew: ShBG) is earth. Fire consumes soil and trees. Let there be earth.

After (Hebrew: ThMR) is air. (Hebrew: ThMR) is from the dryness of the earth. The Ruoch of Elohim passes over the earth. Earth receives the Ruoch from you, not corrupted.

After (Hebrew: SAaD) is water. The Ruoch dwells, flowing in the sea. The forces of the water go forth after the sea of fire. Cancer is water.

After is fire. Leo is fire. The water extinguishes the fire.

After the fire of Leo, Virgo is earth. The fire consumes the earth.

After the earth is the sign Virgo. There is Libra that is air. Of the earth and the greatest mountains make a windbreak of the Ruoch.

After the air of Libra, Scorpio is water. The air breaks the waves of the sea. From blowing the water is clouds, the foundation of the congregation. The earth serves forever.

Record the generations of the Earth, the generations of the king. Restore the earth, as being from generation to generation. The living and the dying come forth. The spirits restore.

The earth speaks of generations. The Sun rises, not enclosing heaven. Offer a sacrifice. There is not awareness when near the Sun.

After the heavens, Ruoch is around in a circle. The Ruoch goes forth, actually to the four corners, going with the Sun. After is Ruoch. The sea is the course of the rivers of Elohim. According to that, the congregation upholds the conclusion.

The word written is the truth, however, love supports by establishing after. By the word of the Lord, create heaven. Blessed is the mouth. All hosts gather moving as the sea of water. Revere the Lord of all the earth. In Ruoch is the beauty of heaven.

Therefore, Ruoch, earth, water. After Ruoch is water. The Ruoch gathers waves and breaking. After water is earth, in the name of the sign. Do not fear the declaration of the Lord. The sands increase the water. Generations uphold to establish after heaven, Ruoch, earth.

Arrange the sign above. Below cover in light. As perfection and light of the Lord, the song of degrees extends in heaven as veils. They are the highest heavens.

In the place of darkness, lead the clouds below the heavens. Go over the wings of the wind. All the air fills below the clouds. Therefore, every bird flies upward. The Ruoch gives power of the bird, making messenger spirits [Melakiyov Ruoch] cast down to Earth.

Establish the universe and be content. Offer a sacrifice to the Malachim, going to and fro in the universe. Offer the sacrifice to the ministers. The name is before fire, burning the foundation of the Earth. Over the foundation of the Earth, we are above the ocean as a vestment of clothing.

These are the seven oceans. They are between four countries. Over the mountains, establish water is below the earth. It is written, extend the earth over water. The water is over the mountains. The mountains are suspended in the gate. In the end of the dominion, arrange and establish after heaven, Ruoch, water, earth.

The sea rises to heaven. From the rising of the sea, gather Ruoch. It is near the heavens. According to the Ruoch of heaven's beauty, the Ruoch comes as clouds to the side of the sea. Water is after the Ruoch.

The Ruoch dwells as flowing water. The rain comes forth. Ruoch establishes every end of the earth. The clouds rain down upon the earth, to drain away.

In the beginning, the dominion of Earth, heaven, water, and not Ruoch. According to that, the earth is created first. According to that, commemorate the foundation of the universe.

The earth and the heavens are bound above. Water is above and below. Also, first is the foundation of Earth. Scatter snow as water. Make mud as a flower bed. The wisdom of the Lord is the foundation of earth.

Establish heaven in the place. Receive the power of fire shining in the vision. Of the purest water, create in the place of the heavens. After knowledge, the oceans divide. Divide the oceans below. The skies drop blessed dew over every place. Dew comes forth. There is no Ruoch to commemorate Ruoch.

According to that, the foundation of the Earth is in every place. Commemorate the foundation, burning the earth. Of heaven, praise Ruoch of heaven, earth, and water from above. Below, the Ruoch circles around. It is written, place the darkness circling around. The darkness drops down in water from clouds in the skies.

The name of the Ruoch is (Hebrew: ANH ALK MROChK). Also speak (Hebrew: ANH MPNIK ABRCh). Speak when rising to heaven. The name is (Hebrew: ShL OATzIAa ShAOL).

Dust is in the end of water. The name leads and completes darkness. The blackness of the universe is not obscured from you. By praising Earth, heaven, Ruoch, water, according to that, commemorate the foundation. The mountains tremble.

It is wondrous to make Aleph in Earth. The earth trembles and shakes. Of heaven: descend from above. Fly upon the wings of the wind, above and around. The darkness of water is in dark clouds around. Here it is regarded from below, rising up. By Job, Earth, water, heaven, Ruoch. Suspend Earth over nothingness. It is written, extend the earth over the water.

Therefore, speak after. The sphere is over the surface of the water. Serve heaven over Oceanus. Therefore, support the pillar of heaven. The Ruoch weakens of the beauty of heaven.

Also, from below, the clouds rise up. Of Earth, bind water in the clouds. Of heaven above the clouds, Ruoch is near. Of Job, water, heaven, and Earth, Ruoch from the word. Establish that rain is the first water.

From the heat of the dome in the firmament, the rain descends. The water over the firmament descends over Earth. The Ruoch blows and the rain descends. Reduce the drops of water. The drops from clouds fill streams. From the water, the clouds drink. It is concealed in the bottom of the sea.

Light shines over the corners of the Earth, drawing out and restore the Ruoch from the chamber. The storm comes forth. By Job, Earth, water, heaven, and not Ruoch, according to that, commemorate the foundation preceding Earth. That is the foundation. The water is around it. Heaven is supported in the sea. Fall to the foundation of Earth.

The sea puts forth. The cornerstones are around the water. The foundation of the fire is in the gates, for the sake of joining the corners of Earth. After, the knowledge of the borders of heaven are bound in the sea. According to that, commemorate the foundation of Earth.

Water extends to Earth. Create the heaven. Do not commemorate Ruoch, not seeing with the eyes. Also, not in visions, so much that is necessary of the ancient law. Speak of the ancient Earth, there are no oceans. Establish heaven in the heights.

Of Earth, heaven is created by the power of the established world [Thebel] in wisdom and understanding. Of the sound Tohu, the sound of water in heaven, not from the word of the creation of the universe, but only to restore, thus speak of the path of the people [Goyiem]. Learn from the signs of the heavens from below.

Go forth in life, hidden in silver and gold. Change by praise and from words. It is written by Zechariah, weaken the word. The prophet makes not from words, to stop when dew and rain fall. According to the word, in order to deny the weakening, as said by Zechariah. From the Lord, rain from the time of the latter rain [Melqosh]. The Lord makes lightning bolts, thunder and rain, and perennial rain.

Grass in the field is from God. This weakens the word, also not in this case. Create Earth by the power of the word. In signs of the Malachim, as written over Egypt, over Judah and over Edom and Gomer, speak, to revere, and also of goodness. There are no signs.

Of truth, the Lord Elohim is angered. Earth trembles and the people do not prevail. Anger makes them perish from Earth. Keep the commandments. From the blessings below heaven, stop the raining. From above, return to create Earth by the power.

Of the mountains, it is written, from the sign, destroy mountains. Of the foundation of the world [Thebel]. In wisdom, support the world. In the place of Earth, increase its people. God creates by wisdom.

Of vengeance, it is written by Jeremiah, in every language, to hear counsel. Counsel El by all thoughts. Consider the Chaldeans [inhabitants of Babylon], when not dragging the small cattle along the ground. The young lions gather above the battle. Of Nebuchadnezzar [king of Babylon, 605–562 B.C.E.], it is written by Isaiah, speak in the heart.

The heavens above are divided. They alone are arranged and bound over the mountains as the greatest cities in heaven. By the understanding, extend heaven above. Give the sound of water in heaven, it is spoken of rain.

Do not dwell over creatures of the world. Speak to extend heaven. Do not speak to create heaven, according to seeing the sign. Of not being able to see, but only as the heavens are filled with stars, as in the beginning of the month, or the end, thus, attribute to extend as the word extends. See so much, thus all the planets and stars, according to the clear heavens, for the sake of visibility.

Therefore, it is written to give the sound of water. There is no thundering, only in the day, quiet and calmness from the clouds of every divine [Elohi] nation. Of pagans [Alieliem], the world is created by means of the stars.

The Lord created heaven by the power, created with the stars, therefore be worthy. It is written, by the word of the Lord of heaven, create Earth by the power. Give the sign, therefore, perish from the Earth.

For the sake of the writing, the people speak. Where is Elohim and Elohino in heaven? All the Lord desires is made in heaven. On Earth, in days, and all oceans go forth to sustain heaven. Therefore, in praise it is first written, heaven is the beginning.

It is written, all that the Lord desires is made in heaven. On Earth in days, all oceans go forth to sustain heaven. Begin the power over Elohino in heaven. Therefore, all the Lord desires is made in heaven.

What name written is as the sound of water? In heaven, water precedes Ruoch. According to the sign, the heavens are clear in the day. As thunder comes, water comes without Ruoch. It comes to pass, write by the understanding. Heaven extends as a dome, visible of the clouds in day, as a rainbow in summer days.

It is written by Job, of Earth and heaven, Ruoch is in the days. The name is established to decree. God decrees Elohim. Understand the path. It is known in every place. Send forth the rain. Regard to the ends of Earth.

It is not necessary to reach below all the heavens. Regard the making of Ruoch. Plummet as a bladder [balloon] going into water. Measure the length and the width. Serve the angel and fill with water. As God blows the Ruoch, divide in 70 drops to fill the bladder. Blow therein divisions.

Water is established by the measure of all land and earth. It is written, the measure of the sea is in handfuls of water over the vessel. It is written by the false prophets [Benebia Hasheqor], the sign goes forth over the nation as crumbs of bread.

Of measures, the vessel is measured therein. Measure six measures. By Malachim, Gobi, the King of Edom, (Hebrew: GBI MLK ADM) pours out the ashes [Apher]. Keep all the people of Sha'aliem at the foot.[17] Fill the city with dust. All the people are at the foot, until it is not possible to measure.

Heaven spans the measure of the highest mountains up to heaven. By the span of the measures of the foundation of Earth, the right side extends to heaven and the mountains.

It is written by Amos, when smitten in Shavol [Hell], from there to take. When benefit of the heavens, from there to descend and divide. When concealed from the eye in soil, of the water, here is the soil.

Proclaim Shavol, and the well-cultivated plain of heaven by the kings [Melekim] in song. It is written, the foundation of the heavens tremble. By striking the foundation, Earth trembles when between the planets.

The sea breaks the rocks by the water. Be strong by the power and lead the people. The king goes to the valley and strikes the son of Sha'ayir.[18]

---

17 Sha'alim is the name of a district, or may also mean palm of the hand or foxes.
18 This may be the name of a man, or may also translate as goat, hairy, or a kind of demon.

Of 10,000 lives, take captive the sons of Judah [the 4th son of Jacob]. Go to the top. Cast down from the top of the rock. It breaks completely.

In every place, it is written of the foundation of Earth. The beginning of Earth is recorded. Of heaven, it is written by Isaiah, I place words in my mouth. Concealed in the shadows, establish heaven and the foundation of Earth.

Speak to the people of Zion. What language is established near heaven? Is it not so they establish and serve only heaven, dwelling in the highest mountains? According to that, Sennacherib [King of Assyria, 705–681 B.C.E.) receives all the gold that was burned [Sheba'ar] by Judah.

It is written, let there be, in fourteen years to King Hezekiah over Sennacherib, King of Assyria, over every city of Judah, fortification. Take flight all Israel from the cities. Therefore, speak to the people of Zion, not to take flight. Over these that are burning, Judah takes flight. It is written by kings, Israel rejoices, being over the people of Assyria until the day. Consider the days hearing of Hezekiah returning. It is written, send forth Hezekiah over all Israel. Judah comes to the house of the Lord in Jerusalem, making Pesach to the Lord Elohi of Israel.[19]

Also written by Isaiah, speak of watching [A'ari], behold Elohikem.[20] Thus of the flesh [Mebeshereth] of Jerusalem.[21] Jerusalem is, as other places, to come after.

The scriptures speak of the beauty over the mountains. Of the flesh of the feet, reveal to the king, the Messiah [Hemelek Hameshiech]. It is written after to speak upon the high mountain, to you over the flesh of Zion. Reveal the flesh.

Speak of the watching of Judah. Here is the king in glory. God rises up to the highest sea to establish the covenant with Earth, not able to live, even for a small moment, before the power of the great fire over the highest heavens, of the great heights and great abundance of the highest sea.

---

[19] Pesach is the holiday of Passover, although this may refer to a Passover sacrifice or offering.

[20] A'ari means watching or waking, however A'ar is also the name of a son of Judah.

[21] This term may also mean rewards, heralds, messengers, good tidings, or declaring to.

The great darkness is of the divided firmament. Divide the firmaments, as all the creatures are not able to live. Of the highest fire, the highest sea cools the universe from the fire above. From the heat of the fire above, the source of the universe is the highest sea.

The water is suspended in the air far from the firmament. The course is 500 years. By the sign, purify the people. It is written, sprinkle the water of the highest sea in purification. Heat the dome from the motion of water as rain. Man receives the vessel in the house of the bathing [Hebieth Hemrechetz]. It is filled with water before the heat and the warmth.

All dwellings are before the heat of the Sun. The great fire is as males. Of the flowing of the oceans below, there are two concealed in the ocean. It is written of the ocean, proclaim them female. The female is of the desire of male. Thus, Earth and the ocean are from desire. Of the flowing of the rain, the rain lords over Earth.

Therefore, all is purity. Immerse in water or pass over fire. Purity is according to that. The sea goes forth from the moisture of the holy word. The fire is by the power of the heat of the word.

The Lord created the complete heavens by the blessings over the water. All comes to pass by the word. The power of the sea is suspended by the command of God. Blessed is he and blessed is the name forever.

Appointed over the firmament is Cherdenial. Speak of the highest of high [A'aliyov A'al]. Cherdenial is bound in the heights in the course of 60 myriad divisions. Of every word going forth from the mouth, go forth with 12,000 flashes [Berqiyem] of white fire [Ash Lebaneh] of the prince of hosts [Sher Tzabavoth].

Bereqial is appointed over. The Malachim in the firmament reveal the power of how to lead the people in the universe. Speak and work to reveal the firmament.

Of the letter Nun, God reveals 50 gates of understanding. These were handed down to Moses less one, corresponding to 49 days from the first day of Pesach until Shavuoth [The Feast of Weeks]. On the fiftieth day, receive the Torah.

Fifty lie down and 50 rise up. Speak of Aleph Beth of Rabbi A'aqiba. The faithful dwell and serve God. Decree and endure.

God dwells and the Malachim serve. Fifty is not of them, leaping up to serve the Seraphim. By rising up, the great wise ones bind seven lands united. Cover the highest Earth. Suspend in the gate and bind in the dome.

The veil is suspended in the gate in the firmament. The firmament is suspended by 60 and 100 as two [BS' OQ' KB']. The base is suspended by 60 and 100 as two.

The plains [A'arboth] are suspended and bound in the arm [Zerova'a] of God. The righteous speak to the sky. Sink down to the righteous.

It is written, the sky goes forth, rising high above. The gates of heaven open to rain manna to eat. Tremble, as there are Malachim in heaven. The sky stretches forth from the righteousness. There is strength in the sky. Power and might is to you and your sons.

Manna rains as water coming from the sky, from all the firmaments of the heavens, before the great power of God. Of the great strength of the dwellings of the law [Shekinethov Thorethov] of Jerusalem and the holy temple, it is written, give strength to Elohim over Israel.

By majesty and strength in the heights of the sky, lead in heaven. Support in the heights of the dwelling of the sky. The sky is placed high above, not in the place, but only Shekinah. It is written of the Lord Elohim, from God, food to eat comes from the sky. Of Israel, rain manna from above to eat.

It is written in the Torah of the strength in the sky. There is not strength, but only in the Torah. The strength of the Lord is given to the people. Bless the people in peace. Of the Holy Temple in Jerusalem, the Lord built it with stones of goodness [Toboth]. At the feet are sapphire stones. By the blessing, every kind of precious stone. The sky sinks down to Jupiter, not the righteous of Jerusalem and the Holy Temple.

It is written, the righteous dwell in the power. At this time, be content to serve Jerusalem. The holy temple is suspended by chains of fire in the sky. In the day, go forth and shine in the wheel of the Sun.

The angels of the hosts of hosts [Melaki Tzebaovoth Mechenoth] of the classes [Kethoth] are in the middle. The ladder is fixed in the sky. The top reaches to the dwelling of the Malachim, the most-holy eleven. The most-glorious princes are appointed over the gates of the sky. Of the Ruoch, of the six princes of the gates of the north, six princes of the gate of the south, six princes of the gate of the east, and six princes of the west.

Beresial is the prince of the host appointed over. Proclaim the sky of the righteous. The dew and rain fall. Israel rejoices in the universe. Come and speak of the sky. The ceiling of the sky is in every kind of hymn [Shier], and every kind of praise [Shebech], and every kind of song [Zemereh].

Before the Shekinah is the holy temple in the heights. Speak of the splendor and glory before the holy temple in the sky. The splendor covers every remote part of the firmament to the highest. Speak of the concealment of heaven and the splendor of the sky. Learn of Thethermech. The hosts serve in the holy temple in the sky. Sing before it every day.

Of every Host of Thethremech, the great Malachim minister. Thus of the sky, the tumult of the sons of Thetheremech, the hosts are around the Shekinah in the sky. The highest name of God is in every kind of praise [Shebech] and song [Zemerah].

From morning until evening, speak Holy, Holy, Holy. From morning until evening, speak, blessed is the glory of the Lord. The Shekinah rises up in night to the heights. Of the hidden house [Bieth Meshtherem], speak, you are the hidden God [Atheh El Hameshtherem].

The third firmament fills the storehouse of clouds. Spirits go forth from it. In the midst of the hosts, thunder and lightning go forth from it. Three princes go forth upon thrones, in the image of the thrones of fire. The fire shines like gold, resembling every angel of fire. They are in the majesty of fire. The sounds of fire are as sounds of thunder. The eyes are as waterfalls [Tzenori]. The Sun resembles a wheel of burning flames. The wings of a bird shine as flaming horses in visions, as lamps from the words. Tremble from the roaring of birds flying, of every spirit, and from the birds in every corner [Pheneh].

These are the names of the princes ministering in the third dwelling.

The first is Yikenial. Of this name, 19 Malachim minister before. They are appointed to every word of fire, to kindle and extinguish.

The second name is Rehetial. Sixty-three Malachim minister, ruling every word over the horseman of fire and the horse of fire, of the broken and weak.

The third name is Deleqial. Nineteen Malachim minister, ruling over flames of fire, of the burning house, of the sinking of the sky therein. The sky is in every vessel. Sing before God. Sandalphon is appointed over, binding the crowns, possessing and delivering the Merkabah. Speak of Sandalphon, bound by Thephiliem [prayers, or phylacteries] in the beginning by the eternal God [Tzor A'avolemiem], the Lord Elohi of Israel. In the Thephiliem, it is written, who are like the people of Israel?

These are also the names of the Malachim ministering from above. The three with Beleqial serve the name. He resembles flames of fire. Nodeh, Avoyil, Melekiyeh, Cholial, Cherial, Chebial, Shelechial, Tzegerial, Kemebial, A'avorial, Sesenial, Gobial, Thomial, Amelial, Thelemenoph, Vothechenial, Arephial, Agebial, Mesherial, Amengenan.

These are the names of Malachim ministering in all seven dwellings. In the first dwelling is A'anial. In the second dwelling is Tzedeqial. In the third dwelling is Chesedial. In the fourth dwelling is Dorenial. In the fifth dwelling is Gabrial. In the sixth dwelling is Bereqial. In the seventh dwelling is Mikal.

These are the Malachim ministering by water. All are therein with Qothial, Thothial, Thekerial, Neqiyet, and Vogaheh. Ruling over the rain are Ma'aroboth, Melekial, Meremeravoth, Teretial, Sekenial, Leqobethial, Thenial, Gedial, Keremial, Isa'ayial, Meterial, and Liethial.

This is Shem Hemaphorash. It is the beginning of all the names. The beginning is the highest name and the lowest. Of the secret of male and female, Berash Adam Vochoveh. Of the name of four letters, Yod Heh Vau Heh. The great and honored name is the knowledge of our existence, the root of the invocation. Change the beginning of all existence. Bind to deliver by the tried and proven essence of truth. Of favorable existence, all was created by the wisdom and desire, according to the decree of wisdom, the desire to bless. Decree the name of twelve signs, of twelve written words combined.

IHOH IHHO IOHH HOHI HOIH HHIO OHIH OHHI OIHH HIHO HIOH HHOI.

These names are approved, combined from the special [Hemivoched] name. The root reveals the meanings, explained by the names written afterward. That is the name of 42 letters.

BOOK THREE

PART 1

THE HOLY NAMES

HEBREW LETTERS: ABG IThTz QRAa ShTN NGD IKSh BTR TzThG ChQB TNAa IGL PZQ ShQOTzITh.[1]

This is the holy name. It is revealed by the combination going forth from the beginning scriptures in the Torah. From the Beth of Berashith until the Beth of Boho. Knowledge of the wisdom of the Torah completes the names of God, blessed are they. The rows of marks reveal the knowledge and wisdom is received.

Hebrew letters: OHO ILI SIT AaLM MHSh LLH AKA KHTh HZI ALD LAO HHAa IZL MBH HRI HQM LAO KLI LOO PHL NLK III MLH ChHO NThH HAA IRTh ShAH RII AOM LKB OShR IHO LHCh KOQ MND ANI ChAaM RHAa IIZ HHH MIK OOL ILH SAL AaRI AaShL MIH OHO DNI HChSh AaMM NNA NITh MBH POI NMM IIL HRCh MTzR OMB IHH AaNO MChI DMB MNQ AIAa ChBO RAH IBM HII MOM.[2]

Know these are the complete names. They are combined here to reveal the secrets of 72 letters. Prophesy the lives of ancestors by them. Of Elohim, learn from. Thus far, reveal the miracles of Yod Heh Vau Heh.

The name of the glory and honor is divided in 72 names coming forth from the mouth of the high priest [Kehen Gedol]. In holiness and purity, it was received therein in a vision. It comes forth

---

[1] The name of 42 letters. See Joshua Trachtenberg, *Jewish Magic and Superstition* (New York: Behrman House, 1939), p. 94.
[2] The name of 72 letters. Trachtenberg, *Jewish Magic and Superstition*, p. 96.

from three scriptures. Reveal the going forth from the tribute. Go forth to begin on the path, from beginning to end.

There are three letters in every name. These words are of the most glorious and hidden power. Of the powers of the highest measure, the letters are glorious and exalted.

They are delivered from three scriptures, of glorious power in the sublime and hidden secret. By them, reveal the wisdom and enlightenment of every sublime and hidden secret. The secret of heaven and Earth. The highest secret of the letters.

They are divided in three groups of 24 names. Reveal the glory of ten divisions, seven in every division. They indicate every secret going forth of the highest matters. The secret of the angel of Elohim. The secret to cover with glory. The secret of the power of water and the sea. The secret to extend the hand of Moses over them. The secret of the host of Egypt and the host of Israel. Of light and darkness, day and night. The secret of the ancient spirit [Ruoch Qediem].

The highest and most glorious words indicate the power. Of the secret of the ten sephiroth, reveal the sublime secret and glory. Reveal the divisions of the profound secrets in places. Reveal the angel of Elohim, of the most glorious and highest powers. Of Jochin and Boaz around the victory and splendor of ancient Israel.[3]

The two pillars rise up to the forehead. The forehead, until the upper arm [Atzilthen], is covered in light. Of darkness of fire, ancient Israel is around Jochin and Boaz, which is in the middle.

The night is complete, destroying the illumination from the light. Of darkness from fire, separate the host of Egypt, the outer from the absolute powers. Reach to the light of the divine emanations [Atziluth] in night. Illuminate as in death. Do not bring one near to the other.

Measure the sea in one place. Thus proclaim one to the other. Michael and Gabrial stand on the right side and left side, giving authority of this to that. Proclaim the dryness of Earth and water springs forth. This is good. Grow old and depart [Kelech Voyit]. Be delivered and rise up in victory.

---

[3]Jochin and Boaz were the two pillars of the Temple of Solomon. Also, Boaz was the husband of Ruth, and Jochin was the son of Simeon.

Seven rivers [Necheliem] are by the ancient spirit [Ruoch Qe-domeh]. The holy power is hidden in all existence. Of existence, all secrets of miracles and wondrous deeds of the highest powers go forth. Be complete from the understanding of the power going forth to light the paths.

Cover in glory by the names of every angel. By the highest power, reveal the highest secret of Egypt. From it, the highest powers and marvelous deeds are recorded, the secret of purity, and of images and power.

Be complete in the secret of Heqophothieh[4] and judgment of the Lord. Of the proclaimation of the great Sanhedrin, reach the highest.[5] Included are the 72 spirits of marvelous deeds.

The highest divisions are of three divisions of 24 names. The divisions of power before the strength are divided in ten divisions, seven in every division, every one sublime power before the strength. From every division are operations of marvelous deeds and strength from power. Bind the image of names and the power extends. Be restored by it.

Also divide 72 words from the highest word of the Malachim. In languages, 72 names of every word of the name, of power sublime and glory before the strength.

Also, divide 46 letters of marvelous deeds. The highest images support the powers of the strength of every one.

Also, reduce the images of the highest glory and hidden powers of the host of hosts, ten divisions of images and letters of the highest names, and words of glory and power and the highest judgment. Proclaim all complete the Shem Hemaphorash. Reach to complete the name.

All the powers of the Lord [Kechethieh] are from the name (Hebrew: ADNI AL ALHIM) of the living hosts [Chieyiem Tzebavoth]. All establish the visions. Proclaim the language of the holy names. Divide by all the powers. Remember all are complete by the name (Hebrew: ADNI), emanating from the hidden and unknown name.

---

[4]The term translates as "surrounding the Lord," but generally refers to the procession around the synagogue on Simhat Torah.
[5]An assembly of 71 scholars serving as legislature.

All is seen in the letters. Do not proclaim. Do not reach the thoughts. Do not know knowledge and intelligence, and not power afterward. Of the four glorious letters, do not proclaim the secret of the unity of the Lord.

In the secret of ten sephiroth are thoughts of unity of the Lord. Of the perfection of the emanations, all is remembered. Blessed is he and blessed is the name.

All emanate from four foundations. The highest marvelous deeds are most secret and hidden by the power of the unity of the Lord. Of ten sephiroth with all actions and paths and the courses of the hosts, complete all, this by that. Unite this by that. Of the unity of one, the secret of the 72 most glorious. Proclaim the Shem Hemaphorash. All the powers are most holy and most pure.

By the strength of the actions of every word, remember the letter man receives. By powers and actions is the secret image and the power. The angel goes forth from every image. Of the letter of the name, measure in language, every one name from the book.

All men know of names and the power of the angel of every letter of the name. The book is a branch. All know the power of every word, of the angel of the wheel and planets, of all the highest words.

Thus, understand all intelligence. Know the words of glory. Reveal every secret of glory, sublime as it is, unknown and hidden. Understand the secret to change the letters. Of secrets, decree of images and all movements. Know of all intelligence. Understand the intelligence. Bind the names and highest letters. Combine the letters of the glorious and wondrous name.

It is written, every name is revealed and explained by the power. Change the images and calculate the name in measures. Of the actions of every word, reveal the images, but only in holiness and purity. Thus, consider the highest divisions established. Be prepared and understand all the words of glory according to the name of glory.

Of the sublime name of the unity of the Lord, the name of four letters is most glorious. According to the image of Yod Heh, the power and the glory. According to Vau Heh, the secret of the name of every name. Reveal the hidden name and the reverse. Bind the sign and the image.

By all measures, know to indicate by the power of the sublime, much exalted, every one according to the power. The image comes to every letter. In the image and power, understand every word.

Know every power of the name of glory and honor. The hidden secret is according to the most glorious name of four letters. Everlasting is the secret of the greatest truth. Reach to the truth of the secret of the names and matters of existence.

The light is diminished by the hidden secrets. Let there be light, and the commandments create. It is written, I am the Lord Elohik, who created the commandments. It is written, let there be light. I am not to be you, according to the accepted power over this.

Of the daughter of the mother [Am Beth], let there be the mother of the daughter and the daughter of the mother. Thus, the mother understands the secret of the image of Heh Heh Aleph. Complete the names and proclaim complete.

Also by the images, thus the name of the Neshemah. Of the secret of the word, bind Yod Heh, indicating three highest matters. Speak of Yod and cut off [Qotzov Ozembov, or dock the tail] Vau Heh.

Of 35 numbers, Yod follows three. Follow in spirituality [Ruocheniyoth] by the secret of ten, and the sublime and hidden secret. Aleph completes, hidden that the Yod Daleth binds; but not binding for the sake of the name of Isaac. Of Yod, Vau binds eternally. Of Daleth, Vau binds Heh forever. The second binds this by that, and now Yod Heh Vau. The Heh is below. Above proclaim Yod Heh Vau Heh. Pass Heh of Aleph Beth. By the name of four signs, remember the highest Aleph and the lowest Heh. Bind this by that. In the place, now prepare to write by the authority. Speak of the Cherubim.

Also, it is written of the God [Elohi] of Abraham, the God of Isaac, and the God of Jacob, Isaac is in the center. Prepare to raise Heh Aleph in the place of Yod Heh. Speak of the highest secret. The great strength and the glory of binding complete, the existence of wealth delivers [A'ashiri Pheltien].

Speak the full name over the unity of the universe in truth. Complete in the end. Aleph indicates two Cherubim, and Vau of beauty. Therefore, bind eternally.

Of the name Yod Heh, the existence is supported in the highest and fortified in the lowest, at the end of the name. Consider the house of the Lord Father [Bith Abieh]. The servant of the Lord [Na'avorieh] speaks to you in day and also night.

∞

Heh is in the beginning of the name and Heh is in the end, the two hands of the holy one. Of two hands, bind the one and the images Heh Yod Daleth.

Yod is united with the word until cut off the body to indicate three of the five divisions of Heh. Of ten sephiroth, here are seven. The thorn of the Yod is not in the amount of the last Yod of Yod Heh Yod. Indicate the last three, and here are ten sephiroth. Indicate the word Yod Heh Yod.

Make to cut off the stalk [Qephed Qeneh] and cut down the reed [Ovagemon Oviekereth]. Of Israel, time ends [A'ath Qetz].

The names by Gematria: Shin Samekh Teth by letters and the word, here is 376 [ShAa"O], as in the amount of (Hebrew: ShLOM) and before 376; here is the word.[6]

Make the wicked to speak to Jacob. Of the Sabbath, be at peace in the house of the father [Beth Abi], and make peace to me below.

It is 376 [ShO"Aa], thus as declared when established from the book. (Hebrew: AChI) is near [Atzel] (Hebrew: AaShO).[7] Here is 395 [ShTz"H], as from the book.

The Neshemeh is above. Speak of salvation at once. (Hebrew: AChI) over [A'al]. (Hebrew: AaSh"O). Remember at once by Gematria. Of salvation, indicate the end with the letters. One hundred ninety-eight [TzCh"Q] is half the number 395 [ShTz"H], with the word of the prayer over binding.

At the time of the Redeemer [Hegavoleh], give the spirit of understanding [Ruoch Biniehem]. Be worthy to dwell in heaven. Isaac reveals the kingdom above. Indicate to Isaac by addition of Yod. Of the crown [Kether], know to establish the crown of the kingdom [Kether Malkuth] in the beginning. The Lord reigns below. Make the sons to rule in peace [Hebrew: AaShO BNI' MOShL ShLOM].

---

[6]The Gematria of Shin Samekh Teth is 369. The Gematria of Shelom is 376.
[7]The Gematria is 19.

∞

By the secret of (Hebrew: IHI AOR) [Let there be light], the secret name (Hebrew: HOIIH BIN KL BRASHITh IHI AOR OIHI IHI). Place in the end and thus, let there be the name. Thus four letters fill and complete. The letters support the name. Rise to the place of emanations by the name Yod Heh Vau. Of the highest glory and the secret, proclaim in secret Shalom. Proclaim Heh [H', sometimes refers to the Lord, five, or Heh] Shalom. Proclaim in the time of the names. Change the secret and complete the sublime secret.

Heh rises up and Heh descends. Reach the unity of Heh. One in the center and much glory, Beth rises up and Beth descends. Reach in the center of the ladder of unity.

When reaching to wisdom, bring support to possess love of the Lord, the secret of the divided name, of the existence, the beginning strength of every host of the Lord. Of power and the secret offering [Qorben], man offers the beasts. Man makes the offering of the beast in secret.

Of the face of the bull, cover the purity of the Cherub, from the bird, the purity of the names. Of the bones in the beast, be in purity. Of secret purification in water, be purified from remission. The image of the land remains, as measures in the sea. Of mercy, thus all remission remains of the image of the lands. Go forth from every remission. Thus, remission is purification.

From the flock, offer the sacrifice. It is written, make the offering by the house of mercy, the dwelling of the hidden secret. The bird is profane [Tema]. Keep it hidden in secret. Do not remember the creatures to rise up, hidden and sealed up.

Reach the highest and lowest. Do not begin the name by 13 measures of strengths, and not in the shape of a circle. For the sake of the name, the 13 provinces are diagonal.[8] The seven foundations are around.

The word is indicated by Moses speaking. At this time, increase the power. Bind and complete 613 [Theryieg] commandments by the full name.

---

[8]See *Sepher Yetzirah*, 5:2 and 6:1.

The highest name is from the name of the wheel. All 72 bridges [Geshriem] are of 72 names of wondrous actions. This is the beginning.

OHO—Guide [Moreh] the great name. The glory binds the image of four powers. Be guided in perfection [Keleloth]. By tithings, be adorned of beauty. Proclaim the Lord and speak, blessed is he. The abundance descends to the temple of (Hebrew: IHOH). From the name, descend to all the universe.

ILI—The Lord indicates the highest blessing. Rise up to the highest compassion. The perfection is complete. Therefore, from it, the strength of the highest strength. Cover the blessing and images of four powers. Guide by the word (Hebrew: OAaZABH). It is the ancient of all ancients [Qedemon Lekel Qedemon]. Bind the image, guided by the word.

SIT—Guide the greatest compassion. Be complete by it. Justice and righteousness is in the living Earth. Bind three powers guided by the word and image. The powers of the Lord support Beth and Beth is in the middle. The Shekinah is in the center dwelling. There are five of them. Seven guide in the place of living in victory. Of (Hebrew: OAaZABH), live and exist in victory.

AaLM—Guide by the second existing. Being in the place, complete Yod Heh Yod. Sublime in the highest judgment, understand all judgment. The image of seven powers join to guide all understanding. (Hebrew: OAaZABH) sees authority by making judgment in Egypt, with three scriptures from them all. The foundation binds Yesod. Adorn in splendor by the highest beauty in the center. They guide over the word.

MHSh—Guide the four secret houses in prayer. Reach to the Lord in the highest light, concealed and bound. Be guided to adorn. (Hebrew: ThTh ThThA). In the center is the Heh. Complete the prayers. Of Shin, the image guide between the vestment of the priest. Guide by the word (Hebrew: OAaABH). By the power of victory, the Heh is the image of the Lord. Reach in righteousness to the fathers by them.

LLH—Guide the Merkabah. Of the Merkabah of unity in two secrets, rise up and bind beauty, beauty of the greatest compassion. Reach to the unity of one. The image of six powers is guided by the word (Hebrew: OAaZABH). Create the universe in compassion by the ten commandments. From the commandment, reveal the one brother. Support to understand the word.

AKA—Guide in the foundation, all the souls [Neshemoth] and the Sabbaths. By the sign of living in victory, reach the Neshemeh. Of the name, bind to guide three sephiroth. Guide by the three vowels, Cholem, Shoreq, and Chireq. The image of seven powers guide to reach in the middle. (Hebrew: OAaZABH) guides to atonement in a quiet moment. Of life and death, understand the power of the actions by measures and thus complete.

KHTh—Guide as the Lord of the action [Ba'al Hepha'avoleh] speaks. The image of five powers guides. Complete by Yod. Of the understanding of vestments, and also the images coming forth from the Torah, support to understand and rise over the rewards of the righteous. Of the righteous, (Hebrew: OAaZABH) speaks. Blessed is he. Of the covenant of Elohinu in heaven, is purity by the highest wisdom.

HZI—Guide to unity. Reach by mercy. (Hebrew: OAaZABH.) The Lord over all the heights and over the measures. The image of four powers guides by the word in unity. Bind the Heh by Yod. Guide and lead by the word of enlightenment. The Yod rises up to the Lord. Both are in victory of the unity of one.

ALD—Guide the Merkabah. Of Merkabah, Aleph adorns (Hebrew: OAaZABH). Rise up and bind three powers, mercy and beauty of the highest beauty, by understanding six images of crowns, the beauty of one.

LAO—Guide by the second actions received from the understanding (Hebrew: OAaZABH). The Yod rises up. Judge in Egypt from the place of the governing dominion. The image of six powers supports the Aleph. Guide by the word. Bind in unity.

HHAa—Guide the Lord of the action. Bind to guide as 20 actions.

IZL—Guide the Yod by the great name in the power of victory. The image of four powers guides by the word. (Hebrew: OAaZABH.) By Yod, all actions. By desire of all powers of the wheel and angel. By the power of victory, bind to guide by two actions, the dominions in every power by the power victory.

MBH—Guide the great name, the name of power by 70. Proclaim unity. Of the image of six powers, guide by six ends and by the word (Hebrew: OAaZABH). The power of God sends forth to Moses by the power and the glory. Bind beauty by wisdom in the crown. In every word is one and the one power. Extend the powers to understand the power of the actions.

HRI—Guide the name of the unity. Bind all by the Yod. Bind three powers of the one word. Proclaim the living Earth. Reach and the image of four powers guides by the word (Hebrew: OAaZABH) by the highest one.

HQM—Guide by two actions. By Yod, the diagonal border. Swear an oath by them and bind to the crown. Reach the understanding, and (Hebrew: OThTh) [a reference to the letter Tau] guides over the word. The image of six powers guide by the understanding of the oath. Of two actions (Hebrew: OAaZABH). Remember the Lord by the name.

LAO—Guide three in beauty. Of the image of six powers, the crown. (Hebrew: Th"Th) reaches the beauty between two wisdoms. Speak from between two Cherubim. By the word (Hebrew: OThTh), complete all. All are divided in three holy things. (Hebrew: OAaZABH) guides by the holy words of degrees. Bind the one name to them.

KLI—Guide by the name. Complete the four gates of the highest universe. (Hebrew: OAaZABH) completes in compassion. The image of four powers guide by the word. Bind the crown of beauty. Of wisdom, guide by all understanding.

LOO—Guide by the commandment. The power of the oath by the Yod. The image guides, thus engraving in twelve signs of the zodiac of Israel.

PHL—Guide by two actions. In the midst is (Hebrew: OAaZABH). The compassion of the Lord is eternal. Follow them in the midst and bind to guide. The image of six powers guides the crown. Reach and bind in mercy and compassion. Bring near the highest.

NLK—Guide by the great name. The oath is in the power of the staff of Moses, of the power of actions of marvelous deeds. Bind to guide from the understanding of two. The image of powers guide by the word. This is received from that. From the midst, the actions go forth remembered.

III—Guide by three secrets of three vowels. Of the unity of (Hebrew: AHIH). The highest path is a line in the center until the Yod. Reach in the three places. (Hebrew: OAaZABH) follows the highest. Reach the resting place in the universe. Make the oath to all the nation by the ram's horn. Of one power, indicate the power of the universe. Bind to guide thus and also the image thus.

MLH—Guide by two actions. All the wheel below rises to every one power. Of the unity of one, thus the father [Abeh]. Bind to guide. The image of six powers guides. The daughter [Beth] becomes the mother [Ameh].

HHO—Guide by four foundations below the Yod. From the power, (Hebrew: HTh"Th OAaZABH). From the power of four foundations, bind to guide by measures. Aaron comes near over the hand of the Lord. Follow in beauty. The image of five powers guide by the word, and by all understanding.

NThH—Guide man from the domain of suffering by the strength of Hethokesh [the battles] (or Hethophesh).[9] Of the universe, reach in righteousness. In righteousness (Hebrew: OAaZABH), complete by two measures and bind to guide thus. The image of five powers guides. In secret, the souls [Neshemoth] go forth from the understanding, in regions in the domain of righteous nations. Speak for the sake of the great strength and bind them with (Hebrew: HTh"Th).

---

[9]This note is in parentheses in the Hebrew text. This term translates as "to catch" or "seize."

HAA—Guide by three measures. Complete the name (Hebrew: AHH). Complete (Hebrew: OShABH) by the power of Aleph. Measure one and bind to guide by Vau. Complete them. The image of eight powers guide by the word. All complete by Jacob. Of images of mercy and truth, understand the secret images. Complete the highest, beginning and ending of understanding the secret of the glory.

IRTh—Guide by completing the moving. Do not move from the place of victory. (Hebrew: OAaZABH.) In unity, establish forever. Bind to guide as 20 measures. Receive this from that until becoming afraid. The image guides all, bound by Yod. Bow down in fear. Do not move from victory.

ShAH—Guide by victory in beauty. By the power of action in Egypt. The middle of degrees (Hebrew: OAaZABH) goes forth to judge in Egypt. The seven bind therein. When passing forth in Egypt, to smite. Bind to guide by the word and image of nine powers. The actions complete in the midst of Egypt. Understand the actions.

RII—Guide by the letters of the sephiroth. Go forth from the star. The understanding of the wisdom of (Hebrew: OAaZABH) is the last wisdom. Bind to guide thus. The image of three powers guide by possessing wisdom of the highest wisdom.

AOM—Guide by two actions. Proclaim the name of one. The foundation is in the midst. Also, of (Hebrew: OAaZABH), righteousness is the foundation of the universe. Bind to guide thus. The image of six powers guides to six ends.

LKK—Guide by throne. Of the one throne (Hebrew: OAaZABH), is the horseman over the fathers. Bind to guide to the crown between the wisdom and understanding. The image of five powers reaches to beauty. (Hebrew: OChT BRCh DPIS.)

OShR—Guide by establishing the oath. In the end, reach thus of one. Of the Lord of the qabalah [Ba'al Haqebleh, or Lord of the receiving], bind to guide thus. The image of six powers guides by the word.

IHO—Guide by two actions from the six. Of the unity of one, the Lord speaks. Bind to guide thus and in all the dwellings. The image of four powers guides by two luminaries. Of the secret of two actions, bind by this.

LHCh—Guide by two lives [Hoyivoth]. In the place of Chokmah and Binah is abundance by Yod in the place of the highest man. Bind to guide in understanding of abundance by Yod. The image of the powers guide by the word.

KOQ—Guide by the name of the judgment of the one power. Bind to guide (Hebrew: BAaTRTh) as Tiphareth and Binah. The image of eight powers guides in the kingdom. Reach the understanding. By two actions, understand the power of the actions.

MND—Guide as Moses rises up to the heights. Reveal to bind by the image of Binah. Actions of mercy are by two actions of abundance.

ANI—Guide by the word. The Yod is of life. Complete the Yod. Of fifty gates (Hebrew: OAaZABH) of the holiness above. Bind by the Tau and the Yod [Hebrew: ThTh OIOD]. Reach in understanding. The image of five powers guide by the word.

ChAaM—Guide by the power of the powers of hosts. The Moon [Lebeneh] is in twelve tribes of Israel. The Tau [HThTh] is between two measures of Aleph. Of (Hebrew: OAaZABH) engrave the name, all from it and therein. Bind to guide by all understanding. The image of seven powers guide by the word.

RHAa—Guide by the Yod. The horseman in the evening is over the Yod. The lives of the Seraphim and A'anephiem are all below and hidden.[10] All Merkabah of Yod and all of Tau. Of (Hebrew: OAaZABH). The name of four is over all. Bind and the image guides by the word.

IIZ—Guide by twenty-two letters of Merkabah, of one and eight of eight [LA' OCh' LCh']. After, experience the power of (Hebrew: OAaZABH) in eight measures and eight following. Bind two wisdoms by victory. Guide by the word and image thus.

---

[10]A'anephiem translates literally as "branches," but probably refers to Ophanim.

HHH—Guide by Binah, of Geborah and the crown. From the living power of the crown, bind thus. The image guides by Chesed, of the six powers.

MIK—Guide by three works of the wheel, angel, and vestment. Of Yod and the throne of Yod, the power of the A'anephiem is over (Hebrew: ZABH). Of the highest, complete all by Yod. Bind the name of the unity over all. The image of four powers guides. Understand the power of the actions.

OOL—Guide by two actions and the name of 42. Rise in unity. Proclaim the foundation of the universe. The twelve borders are slanted. Of (Hebrew: OAaZABH), by Yod Heh is the name over the holy temple. Bind the image to guide by the word.

ILH—Guide by rising up. (Hebrew: OThThAH.) Of wisdom over (Hebrew: ZABH), five measures of thirteen measures. Four are of compassion and mercy. The fifth is complete by Heh Yod Vau. Bind thus to guide. Of the image of five powers, five receive to complete.

SAL—Guide by the Malachim, Asethrial, Aderial, Sandalphon. Of the three palaces in ten sephiroth. Of (Hebrew: OAaZABH) by the power of three letters. Of the chariots of the worlds, the highest power and the highest compassion. The three complete. Bind three times. (Hebrew: OThPA.) Of the unity of Aleph and the image of seven powers.

AaRI—Guide by the crown of seventy degrees. The powers cast down all the branches. The powers are all cast down until the ten are holy in the name of the glory. Of (Hebrew: OAaZABH), the Yod is holy. Complete to multiply [double]. The tenth multiply by all and combine. Bind to guide. The image of five powers guides by the word.

AaShL—Guide by the crown. Establish the oath. The hosts of the Moon in thirteen borders slanted. Of (Hebrew: OAaZABH), seal the arch. Establish the earth. Bind and the image of nine powers guide by the word in secret.

MIH—Guide by two actions of one unity. Of (Hebrew: OAaZABH), do not reveal the hidden name of Moses. Bind Tau of the Yod with the crown. The image of five powers guides. Receive in secret.

OHO—Guide by three. Divide three. The end is fixed. Begin the unity of one. Of (Hebrew: OAaZABH), the secret of Heh follows the name. By the division of three following, bind all. Understanding of unity is from the Yod of the crown. The image of four powers guides the word. From that, understand.

DNI—Guide by the root of three names of the crown. Three letters triple. Of (Hebrew: OAaZABH), the root of the name is Yod Heh Vau. By three holy things, the letters rise up. Bind to guide thus. The image of five powers guide all the unity of Aleph.

HChSh—Guide by the foundation of understanding. By the name, all is complete by Yod. Of (Hebrew: OAaZAB"H), the three complete all, in victory rising up. Bind to guide by the word. The image of eight powers guides by all understanding.

AaMM—Guide by the branch of the tree, from the Yod and from the five powers of all. Of (Hebrew: OAaZABH), the branches of the tree, the power of wheels and planets are from the power of the keys. Bind to rise up. Bind one in the foundation. The image of seven powers guides by the word.

NNA—Guide by the foundation. The secret of four powers is the power of the living blessings. The powers of marvelous deeds go forth from the motion after the wisdom. All is made known by wisdom in 100 days of the highest glory and unity of one, therefore concealed and unknown as (Hebrew: OAaZABH). Of the highest powers, praised is the name. Of every day, by 100 kinds of powers, establish 100 blessings of Israel. Bind and the image of five powers guides by the word.

NITh—Guide by the secret of (Hebrew: HThIO). The dominion is destroyed. Of the blessing over Israel of (Hebrew: OAaZABH), of Tzaddiq, by the power of Yod, reveal the eternal name. All is sealed as one. Bind to guide thus. The image of four powers guides. The unity is complete.

MBH—Guide by the power of the crown with the hosts of the Lord. All from the images of man. (Hebrew: OAaZABH) commands to descend in the midst of man. The universe is diminished. Bind to guide by all unity of one. The image of six powers guides the Yod and completes by Heh.

POI—Guide by the strength and glory of the action in Egypt. Of (Hebrew: OAaZABH), consider the ten plagues as ten commandments. Bind in the midst of the temple. Bind two actions. The image of four powers guides by the word. Extend the powers to understand the actions.

NMM - Guide by the light of the Moon and by the warmth of the Sun. Two reach by Nun. Thus the Shekinah exists. Appoint the rows [Shoreh Bezemen] and release Israel. By the ram's horn, reach the unity above. Speak of the holy, the Nun of the holy crown. Bind to guide by two luminaries. Bind by the ram's horn. The image of eight powers guides. In the end, release the ram's horn.

IIL—Guide by raising up the Yod over all created. Of (Hebrew: OAaZABH), rise up the sign of power over all. Bind to guide over the understanding. Conceal the unity of one. The image of four powers guides by the word.

HRCh—Guide by unity. Thus (Hebrew: ABH) binds to guide the living Earth. Complete the understanding. The image of five powers is complete by all.

MTzR—Guide as these two names. Change the actions before the place. The name goes forth. Of the image in the secret time of (Hebrew: OAaZABH), of every one, do not change any and diminish. Guide thus by the beauty of the crown by Binah. The image of five powers is of the abundance. Complete by Yod.

OMB—Guide by four powers of the name, by 22 boundaries around the day of the illumination and the night. (Hebrew: OAaZABH) leads from east to west. Of the unity of one, bind to guide thus. Of the image of five powers, all is secret. The Yod completes.

IHH—Guide by the unity. The unity is with the crown. Of (Hebrew: OAaZABH), the secret is the Heh. Take the universe from what is received. Bind to guide thus. The image of five powers guides all by the Yod.

AaNO—Guide the sound of the highest assembly in Israel. From the rest, these also unite the lives. Reach and complete the highest and also the lowest. The outer branches extend. Of (Hebrew:

OAaZABH), guide by scattering the languages. Bind to guide by the word and image of five powers. All is complete by the crown (Hebrew: BAaTRH). In the midst, understand the power of the actions.

MChI—Guide the two most holy assemblies of Israel. Reach to the highest in unity. Of unity, Aleph is highest. In the lowlands, bind the tabernacle of (Hebrew: OAaZABH). In order to be darkened by one power, bind one. Bind to guide the secret of two actions. Of all understanding, the image of five powers guides. All is complete by the strength of desire.

DMB—Guide seven lamps from the beauty. Of seven by the crown (Hebrew: OAaZABH). The name illuminates seven above and thus below seven. Of the righteous seven, bind thus to guide. The image of five powers guides. All is complete by Yod.

MNQ—Guide by the name of four that measures two around. Of beauty, thus two classes of Malachim. Of power around the crown, proclaim the Tree of Life grows in Jerusalem. Reveal (Hebrew: OAaZABH). Of the abundance in the Garden of Eden, the highest power binds to guide. By understanding, complete this by that of one power. The image of five powers guides. All is complete by the crown.

AIAa—Guide by two actions. Change Moses in the secret image alone. Do not see the Nephesh in highest Jerusalem and in lowest Jerusalem. Seek after from the highest to highest. See the highest, and receive. Do not receive for the sake of the highest and sublime secret of (Hebrew: OAaZABH). By the name, petition to come to Earth. Do not listen. Bind to guide by beauty. The crown over 70 judgments is the secret of the sublime mysteries. Do not come to Earth. The image of six powers guides by the word.

ChBO—Guide in unity complete. Of (Hebrew: OAaZABH), also bind to one. The image of five powers guides by the word.

RAH—Guide over eight names. The seven release to indicate correspondence to seven names. Of the name of 42, by the Heh complete all by the ram's horn. Of (Hebrew: OAaZABH), calculate the eight sephiroth. Bring forth in the period of the Sabbath. Thus bind this to that until the beginning place. Bind to guide thus. The image of six powers guides to complete the ends.

IBM—Guide by the crown. By the power of the beauty, reach to the power after. (Hebrew: OAaZABH) indicates the measure following to complete all. Bind to guide by the word. The image of five powers guide by the word. All is complete by Yod.

HII—Guide to indicate every secret of creation [Beriyah, or cosmos] and the secret of ten sephiroth. By the secret of three most holy, every one guides ten. Consider the resemblance to the house of the Lord. In the temple, speak Yod is over Yod and Yod. Three complete. Consider the secret of the sephiroth, of the divine emanations and three highest mediums. Of three mediums, it is indicated in the Torah, three follow every commandment. Of every commandment and every Sabbath, complete all. Go forth on every secret path of the names. It is decreed, go forth and complete in the foundation. At that time, proclaim the foundation of Binah. All dwell on the Earth. Proclaim to go forth from Egypt, the highest in night and day. The lives reach to the strength. Complete by Aleph in secret in three days. From the name of three is the highest and most sublime secret. Every secret reveals (Hebrew: OAaZABH). Speak of the God of the children of Israel [El Beni Israel]. The secret name is remembered from generation to generation, all the written name. Bind to guide on the path. The image of the four most glorious powers guides by the most holy and by all understanding.

MOM—Guide by completing two actions. By all of them (Hebrew: OAaZABH) is the beginning. End by the power of compassion. Every one is combined by six ends of the everlasting temples and the two actions of power. Speak, you are in the highest heavens and you are in the highest Earth. Bind to guide thus. By the image of Moses, complete therein all and all therein.

This is the secret Shem Hemaphorash complete. It is sublime and hidden, divided in secret. Proclaimed therein is every secret of heaven and Earth, and of every action occurring from the power. Bind by the image of wisdom, by the power of every name.

Of the Shem Hemaphorash, the secrets are proclaimed and explained by every name of most glorious powers, sublime and highest. Complete by the power of understanding.

The corrected doctrine is the trodden path [Nethiebethieh, may also refer to ways of life or customs of the Lord]. Proclaim to reach in fifty days, of fifty gates most glorious. In seven Sabbaths, complete the holy power of Nephesh [Kech Qodesh Nephesh]. Of every one, all is complete by the power of the secret of two actions. Complete the Yod.

Reach the powers of a thousand paths divided. Of the most holy Malachim. Of every planet and wheel and firmament. Of every prince and magistrate and the innermost and outermost powers.

In purity, be far from the highest classes of most glorious divisions. This from that, man over host and man over banner. Of the most glorious names, all are by one power. Of 72 names, change and bind by images. Calculate every letter.

The power and image are of the highest and most glorious powers. Of 22 letters, most glorious and highest. Consider the impressions of Aleph. The images are complete by the most glorious and hidden powers, concealed and sealed up as the gate of power.

There are fifty inner of fifty highest days, hidden in secret, of the thorn of Yod, sublime by the secret praise of the Lord [Hallelujah]. From the name emanates understanding. Binah goes forth in the light of all highest images. All follow the vessel of purification [Keli Hemetehereh]. The holy power is hidden by Binah. The fifty are complete. Bind every image by image and every power by power. The power of the five images are bound by the secret of Heh. After, bind the images. Engrave the throne of the glory. Every one is in place around the throne. The name of the glory and honor is engraved therein.

Of all divine emanations, every power and action is of all Elohim created. After, by the power and the action of every power, the highest action is of all hosts of the heavens and the Earth. Of the highest power and the highest decree and order and command and word and proclamation. All decrees come from the power of the letters.

Of the fortifications of foundations, engrave the throne, high and lofty. Rise up by the engravings around the throne. Proclaim A'areboth [a metaphor for heaven, translates literally as evenings or deserts] and all therein. It is written (Hebrew: BMSKH ChGINH AaRBOTh).

The hidden name of righteousness and justice is blessed. Of living in peace, of living and dying, of the powers of souls [Neshemoth]. Proclaim the throne of glory. Proclaim heaven receives from the crown of beauty. Therefore, therein are the great treasures of the souls of the rightous ones.

Complete ten sephiroth in three palaces before three divisions of the sephiroth. The palace of Malachim is in the Garden of Eden. The universe comes forth from the holy temple. In the palace, hidden in the images of the name of Seraphim and Chiyoth.

The holy letters around the throne are engraved in the holy dwelling. Proclaim by the name. Heaven receives from the crown. All is complete therein by the crown.

In the throne of the Lord, the name is all figures and images. All was created by Elohim. Divide three hosts and palaces before the palace of the Lord. Of the holy palace, all therein proclaim the dwelling. Speak, cover the holy dwelling of the heavens. Bless you, the people of Israel. From the name comes the blessing.

Also, every word of the throne of the Lord is of these two letters. The highest are engraved in the throne of glory. Heh indicates to complete the Aleph following.

Of the name of everlasting power, experience the word by utterance. Thus the 26 letters are concealed around the engraving of the throne. Two conceal most glorious powers. Give power and the image is complete. Of Yod and Vau, two names of every one.

Of every secret of the sephiroth. Of the trodden paths and the Sabbaths. Of every sublime and hidden secret. Of the fire of Ruoch [Ash Voruoch], reach this by that. Of every power and angel and highest prince, all are of one power and one image. Complete all by the one image of the highest glory of two letters, Yod and Vau.

Proclaim Aleph is first. Give power of the image. Bind the letters. Therein is the secret of the sephiroth, the most holy of six ends. All highest and lowest. Of the four gates of the universe, of the vessel, proclaim the secret of ten sephiroth and 22 most glorious letters. The secret of two is 32 most glorious trodden paths, hidden by wisdom. By the thorn of Yod and the chamber of seas [Imiem], highest and hidden.

Proclaim the praise of the Lord. Man is happy to revere the Lord. Keep the Nephesh, as much comes to the path of El. Do not receive much strength by every word and every letter of the image and most glorious power. Reach the name by the direct path and by the goodness of qabalah.

Thus proclaim the angel Elohim is living. Be prosperous and wise. Souls reach by the living Ruoch of Elohim. Nephesh is pure and holy. Thus reveal the secret of the Lord. The glory of the division of secrets, of all actions and powers, speak above. By desire, bring forth exaltation. Know the name to proclaim and be answered by the strength. In salvation, the glory of light is in the days of adjuration. See by salvation. Blessed is the Lord of the universe, amen, amen.

PART 2

THE GEMARAH
[COMMENTARY]

FROM HEAVEN, ELOHIM LOOKS UPON THE SON OF MAN [Beni Adam], who is seen to possess intelligence. You seek to know when to praise Elohim. Of the praise is enlightenment. Know the sign and the strength of the word over the earth.

Make an oath to the Lord by the right side and by the strength of the arm. Speak in the name thereof. Make an oath by the secret of the word until the scriptures reveal the word. Therein is great strength. Be favored, and speak (Hebrew: AAA HAAa AGO IHO IAaB MOB). How great you are and great is the name.

Be covered by the strength of the right side of the Lord. By the power of the right side of the Lord, crush the enemy. Rise up to the right side of the Lord. Create strength in your arm with the strength. Strengthen the hand. Rise up to the right side. Speak, be covered by the highest holy name. Rise up to the highest. Speak, El is high and lofty. Exalt in the dwelling unto every miracle.

Speak of the high and lofty. Provoke wonder by great miracles. Of the sublime glory, rise up by the most holy and great secret. Speak and reveal the mystery of the strength. Speak of all created by the Lord Elohim. The word reveals the secret.

El serves the prophets. The name reveals the secret of the glory. The unknown glory is of the strength. The most sublime secret of the most holy Seraphim and Aophanim, the holy angel and every host of heaven. In terror and fear, serve Earth and heaven. Tremble to hear the name. The name of the Lord of hosts.

Of the Cherubim, see the glory of Elohim living. By speaking the name of strength, reveal the truth. The name reveals the secret strength. Of the name, man is faithful, worthy, and humble. Speak in every house of the faithful. Speak of the secret as the hand over the throne of Yod Heh. Speak to build the house for me and rest in the place.

All is created by Yod Heh. Draw the hand over the highest image. It is written, be at the hand of the Lord and praise the Lord. Proclaim above the name of the Lord. Do not extend the depth in the depths of the great ocean. Speak of the great ocean and sea. Receive by the image of the Alpha Beta (Hebrew: HALPO BIThA). Thus understand the great mystery. Being devoted to God is the great wisdom.

The splendor is of the most ancient wisdom, the secret of the name of the strength. It is written, the Garden is barred and sealed from eyes.

The wisdom comes forth by understanding of the first and the second. First is Yod Heh and second is Vau Heh. Here is Yod Heh Vau Heh. Of the holy name, it is said there is nothing to compare.

Elohim created by the power and the action. The action goes forth from the power. Speak not of the covenant of day and night. It is decreed of heaven and Earth. There is no second to the action.

All go forth to the one name the Lord proclaims. The secret of the word is divinity [Alehothov] and unity and existence. The secret of the book is truth. The strength of the name divides the division of strength rising in degrees. What is above is as below. Speak and make to establish the temple.

Of the temple above, speak to the Lord high and lofty. Exalt as before. The Vau of the pillars of the foundation divide. It is void [Behov] over the foundation. Divide the dwelling [Bonien]. Above the Vau of the pillars, all is high over the heights. Of the holy temple of degrees, the holy are inside. Go forth from the power of El.

The action below is of the action of actions [Pa'avol Hapova'aliem], the most perfect, the most righteous, and the most complete of unknown secrets. Seal them up by the offerings. The burnt offerings, peace offerings, and sacrifices are in order for atonement of man.

Of the lower action, thus place the desire of desires. The action is the power to give. Of the Ruoch of El, Elohim gives.

In every place, one is in the day as the Lord is one. The name is one, being the name of four letters. Complete the name Yod Heh.

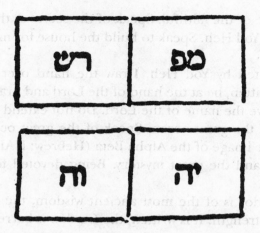

Figure 7. Talisman of the Shem Hemaphorash. This talisman, known also as a "magic square," shows the name MPRSh IHOH divided. This may be translated as "division of God," as MPRSh translates literally as "divided," and IHOH is the holy name of God, sometimes called the Tetragrammaton, or the divided name of God. Tr. Note.

Let it be so as Vau Heh. Regard as Vau Heh rising Koph Aleph added therein.[1] Heh completes the name by the power of Yod Heh.

It is written of Yod Heh, Heh is the eternal image. Heh indicates the Cheth. Of Binah, Geborah, Malkuth, three of three measures after the action of Vau Heh.

It is written, when not making the covenant, be not without. It is also written, rise over to proclaim A'atzem [power]. Every letter of A'atzeemov is as five times Yod Heh. The Heh rises upward. Thus all are divided by Heh. Of Heh, creation of the lower. By Heh, create the pillar by the strength of the Creator, blessed is he. Speak the name A'atzem.

Yod Heh Vau is already divided in the place. By the secret of ten signs and ten sephiroth, proclaim the divisions in the wheel of 72.

It is written of salvation, measure five. Speak of love [DOD, or David]. Salvation measures five. Speak of the light in days. Swear an oath and revere (Hebrew: I IH IHO IHOH). Go forth from the name of 70.

[1]This has a Gematria of twenty-one.

Of the aged man, all the congregation completes the most holy.
Write (Hebrew: IHOH).

In every name is one. By the power and strength of one, man
rises above the side. The light goes forth by the one. The king is
after the image and the memorial is below. Go forth to the light of
splendor. Of the power of the most holy name, images rise up to
complete. It is written, pass before complete. Of Heh in the beginning, here proclaim the beginning.

OHO—The image (Hebrew: ODIO) guides over (Hebrew: YHVH)
and over (Hebrew: OOI). The pillars over (Hebrew: OII) is in the
beginning.

ILI—The image (Hebrew: IKOI) guides with the letters of the
name (Hebrew: AHIH), the name of the strength and the power.

SIT—The image (Hebrew: KOIT) guides (Hebrew: KO) and the
letters of (Hebrew: AHIH) second.

AaLM—The image (Hebrew: AaM AaKO KO) guides two lives
[Hoyivoth, may refer to desires or breaths] by the sublime and holy
seventy names.

MHSh—The image (Hebrew: KO DI OSh) is in memorial of the
rainbow [arch], however guide over as it is spoken in the scriptures
(Hebrew: BAL ShDI) [by Almighty God], and the name of the
Lord.

LLH—The image (Hebrew: KO KO DI) guides over the four spirits
of the world, created by the ten commandments with the powers by
lives.

AKA—Here is the most holy name. Make the oath. Prepare to
come forth by the seal (Hebrew: BAKA). Speak only on the tenth of
the month, not thus, but (Hebrew: AKA). Rest in the place and receive atonement by the purity of souls. The most pure prepare to
come forth in the world by the image of the two names of power
[A'atzem] and the letter of the name of power.

KHTh—The image (Hebrew: KDIDO) guides the 32 paths of wisdom. Of the two tablets of the Decalogue [The Ten Command-
ments], thus in heaven. Below, remember the secret of life.

HZI—The image (Hebrew: DIDO) guides (Hebrew: KO). The one after completes the high and lofty. Guide El high and lofty, and exalt.

ALD—The image (Hebrew: KO ChOD) guides the two lives and the four wheels of the chariot.

LAO—The image (Hebrew: KO KOO) guides (Hebrew: HA). The name of the dominion is in the group above. The second is in the group. The temple corresponds to the temple and the ends of the universe.

HHAa—The image (Hebrew: DI DIAa) guides by the name of power. It is divided by the name of 72 engraved over the brow of Aaron. Thus El comes forth, the most holy holiness [Qedesh Heqedeshiem].

IZL—The image (Hebrew: IZKO) guides the sublime name of the Lord over the ten wheels [Gelgeliem] holding dominion in seven firmaments. Therein are thrones and hosts.

MBH—The image (Hebrew: KDODI) is of the great prince. The Lord proclaims of (Hebrew: DODI), speak (Hebrew: DODI TzCh OADOM). Raise the banner [Degol] over the holy Merkabah and (Hebrew: IHOH) with two letters.

HRI—The image (Hebrew: DIDO) lacks the Teth. Divide by ten. On the Sabbaths, bind the signs above. After sublime alone.

HQM—The image (Hebrew: DIKOM) guides the power. Divide twelve stones being carvings by these holy names.

LAO—The image (Hebrew: KOKOO) guides the two lives. The six ends from (Hebrew: AIThI), most holy in the universe.

KLI—The image (Hebrew: KKOI) guides (Hebrew: KOKO). The Daleth is over the four gates of the universe.

LOO—The image (Hebrew: KOOO) guides. Engrave the twelve signs of the zodiac and the tribes of Israel. Of Yod Heh, the testimony of Israel.

PHL—The image guides the two lives by the name of (Hebrew: AHIH) with three letters of (Hebrew: AaTzM).

NLK—The image guides the power. Seventy names are engraved in the staff.

III—Begin the oaths with (Hebrew: AHIH). By the power and strength of Moses and Isaiah, speak of hearing. Receive revelations by the name (Hebrew: AKA) engraved. Call upon the three most holy. The universe is served first by the ten commandments. One by the ten sephiroth, one by the ten miracles [Nephlavoth] of Egypt and by the secret of (Hebrew: AHIH).

MLH—The image (Hebrew: KO KO DI) is the name of the dominion in ten degrees. The name of the dominion is of seven tribes. The name of the wheel [Hemgelgel] is the sign of the great power.

ChHO—The image (Hebrew: DODIO) guides six and twenty of four foundations of the universe.

NThH—Of the image (Hebrew: NDODI), do not remember the images of five until here following to complete by praise. Of the foot, three are in the sole of the foot of the righteous. The Nephesh is in the universe. Mercy is the foundation of the universe. Begin below to correspond with abundance of the universe. The wheel guides the universe. Of the humble, mercy and righteousness. Consider the lacking of the Teth. Establish and change to correspond to the Aleph. Of the Aleph (Hebrew: QDSh OHThIO), the pillar of the temple. By the staff and the holy sign, guide all the universe in judgment. Speak as it is written of the mercy of the Lord of the universe. Until the world is of reverence and righteousness, guide by the name of the power. The power guides the name of 72 by the great strength.

HAA—Of the image (Hebrew: DI KO KO), the prayer for mercy of the righteous. In truth, the Lord El is compassionate by thirteen measures. Complete by the one power.

IRTh—The image (Hebrew: IRDO) guides the knowledge written above from (Hebrew: HThIO). The Yod delivers the name of (Hebrew: AHIH).

ShAH—The image (Hebrew: ShKODI) guides the name of compassion and the mighty name.

RII—Consider the beginning of the name of twenty and two signs. (Hebrew: AHIH OH) is in the beginning. In the beginning is the oath.

AOM—The image (Hebrew: KOO KO) is of two lives of the pillar. It is written, the pillar is the light of the universe and the foundation. Righteous is the foundation of the universe.

LKB—The image (Hebrew: KOKOD) guides two lives and guides the chariots of the fathers.

OShR—Of the image (Hebrew: OIIIR), here is mystery. Three Yods correspond to the three first fathers. The rainbow is below. Of the rainbow of Noah, make a covenant of earth. Prepare to establish it. You sow the earth. Thus, it is also written of Abraham, Isaac, and Jacob.

IHO—Of the image (Hebrew: IDIO), the name of the angel (Hebrew: IHO) is as Tarshith in the images of gold in flame. It is written, the gold ring of the hand is set in Tarshish. Thus also, guide the name of twenty and six.

LHCh—Of the image (Hebrew: KO DI DO), all the actions of the name Metatron. Proclaim the name (Hebrew: DODI). Descend to the garden of the humble. With two letters, also guide two lives.

KOQ—The image (Hebrew: KO KO) guides the name of the power, divided by seventy names.

MND—The image (Hebrew: KOND) indicates fifty from the palace. When receiving one from the fifty, the name is in the midst of the four being five remaining from nine gates of understanding. Want little from Elohim in the lives of five decades. Of the most holy fire, guide by the name of the power, by the name (Hebrew: AKA) and 32 paths of wisdom.

ANI—The image (Hebrew: KONI) guides by the name (Hebrew: ADNI). With the Daleth of (Hebrew: DNI) and with the Aleph of (Hebrew: ANI [which translates as the pronoun "I"]), here is ADNI, as divided in the place.

ChAaM—Of the image (Hebrew: DOAaKO), the name of 70 is engraved by the name of twelve tribes of Israel. Unite the sublime name alone and establish the two Cherubim.

RHAa—Of the image (Hebrew: RDIAa AaDNI), dwell over the Merkabah of degrees. The assembly comes forth to complete the most holy. In the midst is (Hebrew: H' ADNI). Four are from the Merkabah. Seventy are actually with 70 of (Hebrew: ADNI). All unite that (Hebrew: ADNI) is over 70 nations and over 70 degrees of the horsemen of the Merkabah.

IIZ—The image (Hebrew: KO OA) is the name of 22 letters. (Hebrew: OHHA) indicates five measures of the name of 22 letters. Engrave them in the Torah.

HHH—The image (Hebrew: DI DIDI) guides the power of the name in unity. In great secret, the three divisions of three tenths, of three measures, thus half the name. With half of the one, complete the universe. Therein exists the word. Thus regard the image (Hebrew: IDID). Of the name, Vau faces it in secret and over the image (Hebrew: IHOH OIO).

MIK—The image (Hebrew: KOIK) guides with three tenths of the seal here. The Lord rises up. The holy of holies of the throne of glory. The foundation of the universe is divided below.

OOL—The image (Hebrew: OOKL) guides. The Lord dwells over. (Hebrew: OOI) serves the dominion in twelve orders. Speak, dwell in praise of Israel.

ILH—The image (Hebrew: IKODI) guides over two lives with mighty power [Chiel A'atzem]. Guide by five measures of the name. Of the true image, speak of all power.

SAL—The image (Hebrew: KO KO KO) is written in the palace of the Lord. The palace of the Lord. The palace of the Lord. Three times. The first is the mountains around Jerusalem. The second passes over. You face the Lord in the beginning. The third is the Lord El. Of the three palaces, engraved in the throne of the Lord, of the name Alpha Beta, there is a great secret. Speak, the Lord, the Lord El in compassion and mercy, three times in unity.

AaRI—Of the image (Hebrew: NGDI) is 70 degrees. The power of the wheels guides the name of 72. By them, the degrees and the power of ten wheels. Speak of the reverence of heaven, making fingers.

AaShL—Of the image (Hebrew: NGIOOL), come to remember the covenant of Noah. For the sake of three fathers, therein not to corrupt your universe anymore. It is written, remember your covenant. After, until the covenant of the rainbow, speak of the Earth. Remember the image of the name and consider (Hebrew: KO), of 72 names and one name over all horsemen.

MIH—The image (Hebrew: KRDI) is written (Hebrew: ANI) first and (Hebrew: ANI) last. In the beginning, serve the king. Face the Lord in the beginning. The name (Hebrew: IHOH) is divided in secret. Of the image, speak of the name of the Lord. It is not revealed to them. Reveal the name of the covenant [Shem Berieh]. From the beginning of the covenant, regard (Hebrew: KO KO).

OHO—The image (Hebrew: ODIO) is in the beginning and in the end. Also (Hebrew: ANI) is first and (Hebrew: ANI) is last. Speak and see at this time. Of (Hebrew: ANI ANI), not serving at the feet of Elohim. Of the beginning (Hebrew: OHO), seal (Hebrew: HIH). Of the beginning (Hebrew: OHO), seal (Hebrew: MM). The secret of the first is as the last. Do not extend the most profound secret.

DNI—Of the image (Hebrew: AaTzMO), of the name of the Lord and of the nations above. Want from the one as wanting from (Hebrew: IHOH). Of the nations, the root of the power of all is the most holy name. The nations are over the great secret. Guide to the six ends of the universe. Above, want from the three. Three remain in order to come forth by the word. By the root of the image, be thus two lives. The two (Hebrew: OO"IN) are of six stalks [Qeniem] and six branches. The lives are divided in order to illuminate you in the splendor of the Shekinah of El, before the light of the candles rise up.

HChSh—Of the image (Hebrew: DIDOSh), the name of (Hebrew: ShDI). Of the Shin, the image guides to see three fathers. Speak, behold the God of Abraham, the God of Jacob, the God of Abraham. El Shaddai is the light of all the actions. Establish to speak seven times. Seven cast candles are above the top. The sign leads over ten.

AaMM—The image (Hebrew: GN KO KO) guides two lives. Of the eyes of the prince, the angel of the most holy sign in every day. Bow down before the glory. It is written, all bow down before Elohim. The seven grades dwell in the beginning of the kingdom. The image guides by the name. Of the Lord, the power of Nepheshoth, the stars are divided by these princes.

NNA—The image (Hebrew: NNKO) guides to establish above. It is written, second is the Nun. Second is (Hebrew: QDSh). Of the twenty (Hebrew: QDOShH). Also the Aleph is firstborn [Bekor, or elder, birthright]. (Hebrew: QDSh.) Here is three most holy by the holy sign of one. Of the 100 blessings of Israel, be in prayer every day by the name. Blessed is it. It is written of the Lord Elohik, petition from the people. Be complete, proclaim what 100 are kept above. The king passes before the Lord in the beginning.

NITh—Of the image (Hebrew: NIRZ), come forth to remember the powers of God. By the power of (Hebrew: HThIO), El created the universe pillar over pillar [A'amiedov A'al A'amod]. First speak, righteousness is the foundation of the universe. All the universe is in darkness until it is established. The pillar serves the universe by the light of (Hebrew: HThIO). The name of 26 is divided above. The light of the great Sun does not extend the grace of the name. The light of the Sun lights the foundation. (Hebrew: HThIO) is 26. Of the rest, speak of 60 powers around it. (Hebrew: LThIO.) The holy name goes forth from the scriptures. Reveal the blessing of Israel.

MBH—Of the image (Hebrew: KOKODI) is two lives with two letters of the name of Metatron. Proclaim the name (Hebrew: DODI). Speak (Hebrew: DODI) descends to the garden of the small universe.

POI—Of the image (Hebrew: KOII) is the name of the holy name by the ten words. See the strength in ten plagues coming over Egypt.

NMM—Of the image (Hebrew: NBOKO) is the unity of the two, the most holy over the highest holiness. Speak of the years, the fifty holy years in the holy period by the holy name.

IIL—Of the image (Hebrew: IIKO), the holy name establishes the throne of glory over ten wheels. Rise to the greatness by ten commandments. Speak of the throne of the heavens, and the Earth is the footstool. It is written of the dancing of the hosts [Mecholeth Mecheniem].

HRCh—Of the image (Hebrew: DIRDO), the Resh is lacking. Of the name of 26, speak of one who returns.

MTzR—Of the image (Hebrew: KO INR), of (Hebrew: ADNI) with the three signs of the name. Speak (Hebrew: IHOH ADNI) is the name of the host.

OMB—Of the image (Hebrew: KO ODO), the four foundations are divided. Of twelve signs of the zodiac, the power of the hours of the dominions in day and night.

IHH—Of the image (Hebrew: IDIDI), blessed is it. Of the most holy is strength by Yod Heh. From the name, revealed by the Heh, the truth of the name. The profound image is divided here. After is four of one truth. Of unity, do not speak of four to heal and not to prolong.

AaNO—The image (Hebrew: NGNO KO KO) is everlasting, the most holy sign and the strongest sign. The strongest sign is in merciful justice. One is over 70 languages and one of 24 facing. The universe is sustained by compassion. It is written, eight descend to complete the name of eight.

MChI—The image (Hebrew: KODO IM B B) is most holy, the most holy sign of the world. Of the secret of the Cherubim and the truth of the two most holy. Of these two classes, one class of Israel is below. Of the second class, the names are in abundance above the most holy sign of the world.

DMB—The image (Hebrew: DKODO KO DOD) is seven, by seven cast candles of the illumination.

MNQ—The image (Hebrew: KON KO) guides over the 50 hosts. By Nun, the angel princes journey by the message [Shelichoth] of the everlasting name. The message is of 22 foundations of strength and power around the glory. Keep the glory of the throne. By the messages created, speak to make the angel spirits minister flames of fire. Keeping the flame is the cherub (Hebrew: HMThHPKTh) in the midst of the garden. The two guide by the name (Hebrew: AHIH). The letters of the image are divided. The power is over all.

AIAa—The image (Hebrew: KOING) guides by the two most glorious names. The righteous pray for mercy. Speak, the Lord Elohim of the hosts. Complete with two letters.

ChBO—Of the image above the gate, speak (Hebrew: ATh ALH GDOLH ADON.) [You are God, the great Lord.] Holy is the glory of the name of the universe forever. Of the one power, blessed is the name.

RAH—Of the image (Hebrew: KBOD), truth by the name. The prophet remembers names of strength and power. Proclaim the power over birth. Proclaim the name Phela. Counsel El by the strength of the father until ruling in peace by the name of the power. In visions is power from the strength and strength from power. Proclaim to see the prince of the strength of the Lord, including thoughts of the Lord. Of the vision before, guide to dwell over the holy one. The name of the strength is in the midst.

IBM—The image (Hebrew: DII) is the name of power guiding the horseman over ten wheels. Speak of the horseman rising up in the nights. The image guides to the temple between four great signs, as three tenths. The memorials above are by the number. (Hebrew: AHIH.) Speak (Hebrew: AHIH ZH AHIH N'). (Hebrew: AHIH) of the ten commandments of the Torah. (Hebrew: AHIH) of ten sephiroth. (Hebrew: AHIH) of ten plagues in Egypt and Lord of the qabala [Leba'ali Heqebleh]. Remember the sign by the name (Hebrew: AHIH). All the world trembles. Ten completes the Torah with ten commandments and with ten of Egypt. The truth therein suspends all. The earth trembles. Speak, and hear, after, the great sound of trembling. Remember the strength. Therein are the great secrets, according to the number of the name (Hebrew: AKA). Therein is the seventh secret, the sephiroth with the Aleph. Of the seven, the Lord is sublime. The Lord is one, alone in the day. It is written, the name is eternal. Remember it from generation to generation. Therein seal the strongest and all the most holy. Of all commandments of the Torah and all the powers by them, as explained by the wise ones. Of the qabala, being (Hebrew: OHOH). It comes to pass, by the secret seal in ten commandments (Hebrew: OHOH). The seal of ten commandments and sealed in ten plagues forever and ever, over the order of wise men, the commandment of Gemoreh. Remember to go forth to Egypt in day and night. Speak in order to remember the day of deliverance. Pray until the Messiah comes in the world. Also, not to lengthen. It is hidden in secret and sealed. Of the Lord of the qabalah, indicate by hearing and from revelation.

HII—The image (Hebrew: DII) guides over three most holy. Every one from ten, and four over all.

MOM—The image (Hebrew: KOOKO) guides from the strength of unity. The strongest is beauty in truth. Seal by the two names of power. One is first and last. (Hebrew: ANI ANI OLA ALHIM.) Measure Aleph. Of the understanding of the Lord, the Vau indicates six ends. All are in them. They are east, west, north, south, above, and below, indicating six corners. The most holy sign is everlasting. Of the six ends the universe, speak of the king of Earth and all nations. Of the princes and every magistrate [Shopheti] of Earth. Of righteousness of Elohim until heights and from the magistrate of the great ocean.

Now complete by revealing to bind the image of the book. Consider the most holy qabala, received from the mouth by the strength of Moses from Sinai. It was handed down to Joshua, and from Joshua to the elders [Zeqoniem] and from the elders to the prophets [Nebiyayiem]. The prophets handed it down to the men of the great assembly [Kenneset, the parliament of Israel].

Of the Lord of wisdom, Lord of qabala, Lord of honor, Lord of glory, and Lord of understanding, speak of the secret of the Lord. Of reverence, treasure in the midst. Of the secrets of the Talmud, all the qabala is to Moses from Sinai. Do not interpret the doctrine. Do not draw out and do not cast out. When man understands wisdom, do not fill the stomach and consume meat.

El gathers in the garden and hands down the sign. Man understands the wisdom to revere Elohim. The secret is passed on to companions in order to establish knowledge and understanding.

Complete and open the eyes and heart as being upright. Regard the living light. Regard the ends of the path. Blessed is the name. Rise up from the power, most glorious and powerful, El in heaven created Earth. Inquire and thus understand.

The highest light shines in the eye. Of understanding, it is written, the light shines in darkness. The upright remember the knowledge of the purity and goodness. Dwell by the sign of the highest light. Speak therein of the lamp of the commandments. The Torah is light. Consider (Hebrew: OHI), the name in knowledge of the path. The upright understand the image. Bind from the holy book. Shout out the name of the glory.

The glory is divided by purification. In purity, happiness and wealth come forth. He is everlasting. He shall establish the name of heaven, thus reach to light. Knowledge comes from above with the light of the Malachim, the angel of the Lord of hosts.

The image is engraved in the throne. Of the high throne, the 22 letters of the Torah. The secret of (Hebrew: AHIH) and the light of every covenant. The angel is above. Israel is below. The one letter is engraved. It is written of the Totpheh between the eyes. Engrave in three palaces, the throne and the image. Of the image, the Alpha Beta is received by the Messiah from the mouth.

Of the strength, it is written, thus engrave in the throne. Examine by four signs. (Hebrew: BIH OHI.) Regard the power by Yod and the Vau, the two names of the holy power. Every one seeks alone of the power [La'atzemov].

Of the power of the two. (Hebrew: BIOD OIO.) The chosen name is by them, according to the power of strength. The greatest strength is by them alone, by the images of the strength. The first is fire and the second is Ruoch. It is written of the fire of Elohim and the Ruoch of Elohim, the Malachim are around the throne of the glory by fire and Ruoch. Speak to make the angels of Ruochoth ministering fire.

The two signs are of the strength of the images of the Creator. See the power of the actions. Explain it to people. Give to the people. The strength is in them alone.

Of the power of powers, do not receive, not the image, and not power, and not greatness. Do not move from the place. From the power, bind the holy image in the house of the king within [Beth Melek Pheniemeh]. By the great king and strength of holy glory, unite the people. Give great power of the holy image. All people come after. The name is as the name of the Creator. Also, the power of the image of the Creator.

Speak to provide and support. Lead in measures of compassion and purity of life alone. Make the hand to adorn you in the temple of your kingdom. From worshipping you and from the power, the strength of the prayer of Moses. By you, the days are revealed. Petition the compassion before the strength. Thus speak in prayer. The Lord El is compassionate and merciful before the six ends of the temple. You are everlasting, in reverence and supplication thus before the most holy. That Beth is in the place, indicate to complete ten sephiroth.

Remember David. Understand to indicate the word and secret of the one Lord, great and strong. Complete ten as the division of the sign is received in the great secret. Of the written words before five, Moses remembers them. These six complete ten, as the prayer of Moses to the Lord Elohim.

Of the Lord El, and before the secret of the most holy three, that three is to six, as two to four. Understand the secret by the Lord Yeh, the everlasting image. The three secrets of three nations divided is over the secret of ten sephiroth of 22 letters of the Torah. Below is the king. Bind every one of the images, of the image and the 22 letters.

The food is on the table of the king. Receive every one of the images. Of the image above, nourishment of El. Of the glory, the king seeks. Pass over the king before. Heh begins as the name by the great name. Remember above, as the image divides power of the name of power. The power of the name is from the holy names and from the Shem Hemaphorash. Proclaim the name of 72, the Shem Hemaphorash, the power of the name of power.

All go to the one place, one of every one word. Therein is tranquility. In compassion, we are supported by salvation of the Neshemeh. Of understanding, reveal Nepheshinov. Serve you in the heart. Complete by Nephesh. Desire in fear and, in awe, exalt. Of Neshemeh, forgive iniquities by sin offerings. It is written, the Lord speaks, forgive and complete and return affliction and the highest compassion. It is written, you are compassionate. Of the mercy of the king, compassionate and merciful is he, in great goodness [Merbeh Lehetieb]. Blessed is the Lord of the universe, amen, amen.

BOOK THREE

PART 3

THE ACTIONS
[HEPHA'AVOLOTH]

COME FORTH BY THE STRENGTH of the Lord Elohim. The righteous remember. Blessed is Elohim by the holy path. El is great as Elohim. Of Elohim, learn from youth until here showing marvelous deeds. Bind by strength.

Prepare the wise son [Beni Chekem] in the heart. The wise son rejoices in the heart at this time. The wise son admonishes you, as admonishing the man of the wisdom. Go forth on the path. The darkness covers the earth and fog obscures the lands. The Lord rises above.

Now the wise son is with the Lord Elohiek and opens the eyes. Remove all foreskin [A'arleh] from the heart, removed by all desire. In every period, cover with linen [Lebeniem]. Of sandals, raise the feet. In the place, Elohim enters.

Serve until the man comes to forsake El. Interpret and investigate every palace, lest consuming much grain. Make the battlement of the roof and cast down. Cast down from above the divine emanation. Of the holy man, chosen from people by the priests of the nation of Levites [Hebrew: LOIIK].

The Lord Elohiek chooses from every tribe. Seek and search by all desires. Draw near with the offering. The foreigner [Zer] does not consume and does not suffer, except in the heart by every Nephesh. The heart lives. Give the heart to El.

Now the wise son is pure. In the universe, revere Elohim and turn away from evil. See and understand. Place the heart in El. El is in heaven over all to come. Elohim is in judgment when the son lives and when making the guilt offering [Thashiemeni].

By the word of the oath, you lie down there and rest in thought. Be strong by the high priest [Hekehen Hegedol]. Of the friend from the nearest nation, of sacrifice or supplication, suspend the nation over the name.

Uphold the heart. Life is suspended in the dwelling, however, when turning around, receive visions. Regard the chosen and prophecies. All are most holy. Take the priest the wicker basket. Lie down before the altar of the Lord Elohiek.

Now the wise son is complete, fulfilled by all the word. You listen. Revere Elohim and keep your commandments. Revealed to you is the qabalah by the division of the name of the glory and honor. It is divided by powers and secrets, most wondrous and most powerful.

Of the holy Rabbi [Qedesh Rebienov] and Rabbi Ishma'ael in history, deliver therein. By the secret, understand the signs and the power and image and the actions from them, all in festivals and in hours and in times to reveal. When you are pure and upright, understand the word by wisdom concealed in the womb.

It is written upon the tablet of the heart of the innocent and pure. Understanding the purity, the glory of Elohim is the secret word, complete and revealed to you in answer. Change by the wisdom and power for him. Change wisdom and power for him and understand wisdom and power for him.

Complete the powers of the images, most wondrous and most powerful and most glorious. Come to enlightenment by purity of heart and being upright. Complete by praise in song, in music of victory. Rejoice in the heart. Consider the understanding to learn by them, over the beginning of beginnings and the ending of endings. Rise up without ladder and without degrees. Cast down. Establish those who are cast down.

Now listen to the wise son. Understand how to rise up, and how to come by the secret, and how to obtain power and actions of the light. When receiving them in the beginning, reach the end. Thus understand much. Examine and search the three original scriptures by the simple and plain meaning. Also, examine the concealed meanings. Also, examine the written words. Examine all the letters, every one for itself. Also, examine the changing of the understanding.

Bind the images by understanding of powers, and by the most holy name that guides every one. From them, examine in actions. Reveal the sign to you alone. Complete in the heart by the written words above.

Speak to you of already knowing what is written. Deliver the angel of Elohim. Deliver the pillar of the cloud. The highest powers are most powerful and most glorious. Of the host of Israel, understand the power of the Lord. Divide understanding.

The sign circling indicates the three scriptures. Complete the most powerful and strong. Also, the action of the spirit of the east [Ruoch Qediem]. Also, the strength of power. Measure all the highest before the power of the sea.

Of strength, regard the highest. It is written, the spirit of the east inquires of Aniyoth Tarshish [translates as "a ship of Tarshish"]. The spirit of the east rises up to the visible heavens.

It is written, go with the Lord. The sea begins in love and compassion. Do not listen at once. Come above by measures of strength of all the night. Measure night and thus return and want much.

Every king of the world listens to the sound. Give the three scriptures. Understand in order to separate the two measures of powers. The measure is weak. Begin above and end below.

By the strength of the powers, cast down to judgment. Rise up to separate the understanding. The secret is not being thus, however, upon the path after. Bind strength with strength and fire with fire. Thus consume all the universe. From the destruction of all the universe, all the universe is desolate, not being able to make actions.

The nation is destroyed by the power, however, now, reach to receive therein. Also of goodness, of evil, of judgment and compassion, love and hatred, peace and war. Also healing, and removing evil spirits. From the power of images and from power of intelligence, and the gates [Thera'athem] existing by them.

Now the wise son and the faithful make adjuration to the Lord Elohi of the heavens in every period. In every season, come forth to wander. The words of the Shema establish. I already declare to you the first word. Be revealed when in the periods. Know the heart is of goodness and upright.

Knowledge is in the dwelling of the good. You swear an oath in truth. I revere you. You are near and you are far away. Until wandering around many times, the good see before every name and every power, according to the observance of knowledge.

By images and by divisions, understand what to speak: that (Hebrew: IH) is (Hebrew: IDI) in the image. Actually the power is to bless, however, there are therein three measures—the three signs before Kether, the most high, Chokmah, and Binah. However, the truth of the three measures indicate the fathers.

The truth and all power is unity. Of the power of the sea, reach therein as the hand of the Lord. Here is compassion. Also, of the hand of the Lord, here is the judgment.

Receive therein and change over the sign of power. Desire the action therein. Also the Lord corresponds to the lower. Of the power of the Lord, the power everyone, and one name. Also, the image (Hebrew: IDO HOA HOO) corresponds to the pillar of the universe. Of the holy temple of the Lord [Bieh Hemeqedesh], below and forever is the Earth. It is written, fill all the Earth with the glory of the temple. From the temple of all the Earth, and also the 70 going forth from power, the one name of all strength and power.

PART 4

THE FIRST ACTION
[HEPHA'AVOLEH HERASHONEH]

OHO—Guide by the abundance. Descend to the Holy Temple. From the name, descend to the world.

ILI—Guide by the ancient name [Shem Qedemon] of all ancient.

SIT—Guide by coming to pass of life and existence [Chi Voqiem].

AaLM—Guide by the vision of strength in the three most wondrous scriptures. Make people in Egypt and in the sea.

MHSh—Guide by establishing three fathers by three measures of the name in power and victory, for the sake of victory.

LLH—Guide over the creation of the universe by compassion. Also, create by ten commandments.

AKA—Guide the universe coming forth in atonement and forgiveness. The Nephesh rests. Guide the lives of the people from the image by compassion with the seven holy names. When making incantations [Lochshiem] of the sign or writing on the silver plate, of disease to spread death. It is written, learn by them for the sake of disturbing every evil spirit. It is difficult to measure. Make the incantation by the sign in hours of the Sun. Write the sign in the day in the first hour. Remember the power of desire. Of the angel, one is over the sign in the hour. Be pure and fast. Be immersed in purity and be pure from sexual intercourse.

KHTh—Guide by the highest wisdom of the Torah. Of the covenant of Elohienov in heaven, and over not remembering (Hebrew: HThIO).

HZI—Guide by the wisdom of the unity complete. El is high over all heights.

ALD—Guide by rising up over the chariots of the Seraphim above and below.

LAO—Guide to see miraculous deeds in Egypt. Above and below, create heaven and Earth. Thus the dominion. People revere all the universe.

HHAa—Guide by the foundation of Moses. Hereafter, the name is therein. Come in the temple and remember the powers of God. Hand down the breast plate of the priest, and the name of 72 letters.

IZL—Guide to God. Rise up in strength. Dwell as king over the throne of glory in the kingdom. In order of judgment, all comes to the universe. Also, of judgment with the planets in seven firmaments. Do not place them over making every word of judgment in Egypt.

MBH—Guide by the power of God, the only power by the glory of God. Of Moses, action by the name (Hebrew: IH) over the face of the Lord. Of the seven names, purification is learned by wisdom. Write the sign on the silver plate. Drink from the sea of life, from the spring of life. Of the spring of life, begin in the month of Nisan. Suspend the sign above in goodness. Keep man from every evil spirit and evil eye, from every demon [Mezieq]. Suspended above, written on the shells, covered in holiness and purity. The measures are after, of day and hours. In the beginning, measure Moses.

HRI—Guide one by the highest.

HQM—Guide over the sceptre. (Hebrew: IH) is engraved on the stones. Remember before the Lord.

LAO—Guide by the most holy above.

KLI—Guide by the four gates of the universe, engraved by compassion.

LOO—Guide by the twelve tribes. The holy name is in the midst and measures above.

PHL—Guide by the compassion of God everlasting.

NLK—Guide by the name engraved in the altar. Of Moses, by the actions of the seven most holy names. In goodness, make the talisman [Qemiya'a]. Drive out every evil spirit of fear and lamentation. It is good to petition compassion before the name. You are delivered from every fear. You speak to the four spirits of the universe seven times. Speak, let there be desire from before the Lord Elohi. Of Elohi of the fathers by the name and the divine names. By the power of compassion, deliver from fear. In measures of the first day, Abraham is in the day and in hours and by the angel. Also, it is good to cast out the fear alone in purification, by fasting and immersion in purification.

III—Guide by three Sabbaths [Shebethoth]. Of Yod corresponding three times. (Hebrew: AHIH) is the last and the highest. In clear language, indicate the last measures. From the power of victory, indicate three, the most holy name and all power after. The power of the universe indicates the highest.

MLH—Guide by the highest and lowest. Of one power, reach the sign.

ChHI—Guide by the name from the power of four foundations.

NThH—Guide by the power [A'atzem] of (Hebrew: HThIO), however the Resh resembles the firmament. Begin the lower universe; however (Hebrew: HOO) the righteous proclaim to the feet. Complete from two measures of the righteous.

HAA—Guide by 13 measures. Complete the sign by one measure and one power. Of Kether, proclaim it is complete.

IRTh—Guide by the unity of the name established forever.

ShAH—Guide by the name. Go forth from the place of judgment in Egypt. See visions by the name of strength. The seven names are of the purification of goodness. Journey on the paths of the seven nations. The name is in the place of fear. The names are written on a brazen plate. Remember and write in purity. Be immersed in the name of Isaac, by measures and by power. In the day and hour, the fourth day is the day.

RII—Guide by 22 letters of the Torah. From the power of the name, (Hebrew: AHIH) is above from the last Sabbath and the secret third Sabbath.

AOM—Guide also thus over righteousness, the foundation of the universe.

LKB—Guide over the name of the horseman over the fathers.

OShR—Guide the rainbow. Indicate three measures in three kinds of colors. By the measures, make the oaths of Earth. Israel is taught the sign. Teach to the holy people and dwell by the name of names.

IHO—Guide by the power of (Hebrew: IHOH), as Tharshish indicates (Hebrew: ThRI ShSh).

LHCh—Guide by the Ruoch of Elohim, the living Ruoch of Chokmah and Binah. In abundance, the highest man is in the small universe of all the actions.

KOQ—Guide by the name (Hebrew: KO). Of the first power and seven most holy and divine names. Remember the sign in holiness and purity. It is good to study the Torah and wisdom of the nations. Write upon the first silver plate (Hebrew: TOBIM TOBIM.) [most good, or goodness.] Above is power from all. Study in the second day by measures of power. In the hour, write in holiness and purity.

MND—Guide as Moses ascends to the heights. Deliver to him all wisdom and understanding of the heart of the paths of wisdom. Indicate the holy wisdom to the highest governors [Pechoth] of the highest power.

ANI—Guide by the holy above, corresponding to the ten holy palaces below.

ChAaM—Guide by the twelve tribes engraved by the holy name.

RHAa—Guide by the highest power corresponding to the lowest book [Hemgeleh]. Seventy nations correspond above to seven degrees. The name between is four letters over all. The secret is divided in the throat. Search out the 70 and 12. The rising sea indicates Jacob and sons.

IIZ—Guide by the ten measures of the powers by the sign (Hebrew: HHA).

HHH—Guide by the power of three measures of the name. Of the power of the life of the weak. The power of the living is from the name.

MIK—Guide by the three most holy serving the highest and lowest. By the power of the name of 70 and the divine and most holy seven names. It is good to petition. Petition the words many times. Conceal them when writing. Remember the scriptures and understanding comes forth. Of the song of generations, the Lord is our shepherd. In unity, revere the wondrous words. It is wondrous from the beauty by the most holy. In great purity, remember. Of the Sedieniem [wide linen undergarment, may refer to sheets], the purity of sons. The shell is pure and the ink. Complete four or five. Remember seven times. Place the written word below. From the beginning, be in purity. Speak, let there be desire from the Lord Elohi, the Elohi of the fathers. Of the most holy signs, it is most glorious to see in the night by the word. Thus (Hebrew: OKK AO HM AO LA). In the middle of the day, do not consume. Make immersion and petition thus.

OOL—Guide by the foundation of the universe. Of the most holy, the Holy Temple and the name is above. The name seals the tribes of Israel.

ILH—Guide by four measures. Complete compassion alone. The fifth is in the middle and complete.

SAL—Guide by the image of the signs corresponding to the three powers. The leaders of three worlds by the highest power. The secret of the Lord El. The highest completes compassion and the third is complete.

AaRI—Guide by the 70 degrees in seven firmaments; however, until the tenth holy is complete, double.

AaShL—Guide by the righteousness of the fathers. Serve the universe by the most holy seals and Earth.

MIH—Guide by the image of the name. The signs are not revealed to Moses.

OHO—Guide by the first secret. The secret of the Heh is last in the name, that Heh is the last measure. Yod is first of the seven most holy names of purity. It is good to petition compassion by every action. Of every desire, or with the king or name of the man of grace and love, as the great are very strong by compassion. Thus speak, let there be desire from before the great and powerful name. Hear the prayers and petitons. Make desire and actions from the word (Hebrew: OKK OKK). I love as desire. Of desire, speak to the face and meditate [Hegiyon] in the heart before the image of the Lord. Begin on the sixth day. Observe the measures. By the angel, in purity make retribution [Shelemeh] by prayer and by fasting.

DNI—Guide by the root of the name (Hebrew: OHO) and the third holy secret.

HChSh—Guide by the measure. (Hebrew: ShDI) exists by the two fathers of three complete. Victory is the highest wisdom.

AaM—Guide by 70 powers below the name. From them is the power of seven planets moving forth in arrangement.

NNA—Guide by the highest powers. Praise the name every day with 100 kinds of praises and blessings. Establish in Israel 100 blessings. Every day in prayer and supplication, proclaim also from the highest.

NITh—Guide by serving in righteousness. The foundation of the universe serves the highest universe. Measure the truth of the light of the highest seals of God.

MBH—Guide by the Ruoch of intelligence. The pure are appointed to descend in the midst. The man is in the small universe.

POI—Guide by considering the ten plagues of Egypt corresponding to ten commandments. Of seven names in purity and cleanliness. By the powers, petition every word by petition and supplication. Speak of the sign over the sea of purity. The living springs are flowing. Three times, bathe the face and flesh. Cast over the head and speak thus. Let there be desire from before the most holy and great divine names. Learn every word of the Torah. Of the wisdom, thus create every day. The Lord is in the morning in the beginning of the month of Nisan until the middle of the month.

NMM—Guide by the 50 gates of the power of Elohim. Concealed from every living creature, return to lead away from the temple. Stop the sound of the holy ram's horn. Stop the power that is one in the period of the holy in holiness.

IIL—Guide by raising up the sign of power over all the highest.

HRCh—Guide the holy name. It is sublime alone by one and who returns.

MTzR—Guide by 22 corresponding to (Hebrew: ADNI) and the one power.

OMB—Guide by the name. Give power in the hours of the beginning of day and night, from east to west.

IHH—Guide by the secret of the Heh. Receive it with all the universe in righteousness and compassion.

AaNO—Guide by seeing times in measures of compassion. Scatter the languages in order to return. Restore that the Ayin corresponds to 70 degrees and the seven holy names. It is good to petition prayers of forgiveness and atonement over all iniquities. Confess in fear, in reverence, and in purity. When knowing of transgression by great sin and crime, be in great danger from the kingdom or from the name. Man confesses all iniquities by the name. Speak, let there be desire from before the great name. You are the Lord of forgiveness and atonement. Forgive me for all iniquities and shade me from death and all misfortune. When praying, you establish retribution. Be in great purity in the day. Measure as Moses in hours.

MChI—Guide by the most holy sign above. Also, Israel is below in order of power. Be the nation in one power and in one dwelling.

DMB—Guide by the name illuminating seven powers above. Also, thus seven are below, illuminated before the name in righteousness and thus all righteousness.

MNQ—Guide by the 70 powers. Of the powers around the throne, put forth the everlasting name. Receive abundance by the divine power [A'atzem Halehieth].

AIAa—Guide by the name of supplication. Come forth and gather to Earth, not to hear him.

ChBO—Guide over the unity [thereof].

RAH—Guide by indicating to the prophet of powers rising up from ten sephiroth. Eight by calculation and three powers from the seven. Of the ten, the eight by calculation. Proclaim the sign of deliverance for the sake of the abundance. Thus, for the sake of the power, prepare man and man rises up.

IBM—Guide by indicating to measure last. Complete all.

HII—Guide by three tenths. The three Sabbaths establish the great name. Give the Torah and create the universe by three. Seal the strongest. The powers go forth, most glorious by the great and strongest signs of the highest and lowest. It is written, give the signs in heaven and on Earth. Of the great plagues, the faithful are everlasting. Remember until all the generations come forth. It is written: Thus speak, El of the children of Israel [Beni Yisrael]. (Hebrew: AHIH.) Forsake the eternal name of all coming forth to (Hebrew: HAaHZ) forever until (Hebrew: OOH). Remember from generation to generation of the deaths of the living. From generation to generation are 6,000 of all the days of the life of the universe, until the generation of the Sabbatical year. It is written, the image completes the action. Of the name of life, strength in eternal victory.

MOM—Guide by the beginning works of the name in compassion over all creation from the greatest sign. Consider and know El provides support of all. Praised are all the signs. From the midst is the king of Earth, and all princes of the nations and all magistrates of Earth.

Now, understand the wisdom here. Gather to you the greatest, the most glorious and most powerful. Also the wondrous actions of most precious things. Reveal clearly the writings here. El is everlasting in life. El comes in every period. El is holy.

Of the cotton cloth of the holy vestments, you are the high priest. The people do not rise up in the nation, as coming forth visions of the face of the Lord Elohiek. Be in fear and reverence in the pure heart. Establish retribution by explanation of calculation.

Beauty goes forth from the visible light. Great is the name of the glory and honor. The powers of miracles are bound in reverse and opposite images of the most holy book. All are worthy of the seven words. Of Elohim, live and do not be hungry and thirsty after. Drink of the living sea, most glorious. Thus understand the secret image of Alpha Beta engraved in the highest throne. All hosts worship the three palaces.

The name is engraved. Complete the most glorious powers of Elohim living. Change this from that. Exalt the Lord this from that. Most glorious, this from that. Marvelous deeds, this from that. Most powerful, this from that. Most pure, this from that. Most clean, this from that. Most innocent, this from that. Most upright, this from that. Most perfect, this from that. Most peaceful, this from that. Most illuminating, this from that. Most beautiful, this from that. Most shining, this from that. Living, this from that. Inwardness [Pheniemiem], this from that. Most holy, this from that. Complete the flame of fire, this from that.

Serve in reverence. In reverence and holiness, be [free] from tyranny. El creates the signs. The name of every one by dominions. Of works of the desire of the Creator. Of 22 letters in three palaces, engravings of images of every sign for himself. They proclaim in truth of the highest powers. Reveal to you the hidden and profound secret of the glory. Your sons live upright and faithful to me. Establish and be revealed to you.

These are actually the powers of the name. Proclaim in truth of the highest powers. Engraved in the throne, seal every sign alone from the image by the power. Proclaim that the angel Elohim is living by most glorious and most holy and highest signs.

Thus bind Moses in order to go forth. Bind the image and, from power, do not consume the learned sign. The pure fire consumes and burns. Receive it in purity. By images, change every power for itself. Of the power, remember actions. Thus proclaim the sign of angel Elohim living.

The highest power is from the sign. The abundance of powers of El. Work below and bind power to power, according to the motion and powers and secrets of action. Reveal to you, not to lessen the abundance of the vision of great power. In great purity and great holiness, study and be upright. When living, you understand the word. Corrupt Earth, not seeing and not prophesying.

The image is suspended. Abundance does not descend upon Earth. The secret of (Hebrew: ShARZL) is the splendor. It surrounds Earth, resembling the sea. When separating it by cutting it away, surely to live, and, in them, is the abundance. Thus consume and perish. Over that (Hebrew: ARZL ASOR GDOL) compels the powers above without the great image that is in the river [Biyar].

Of the throne of Kether, Chokmah, and Binah, the Ruoch of Elohim is living. The powers facing before are most powerful and most glorious, and shining [Seraph] from here. The Merkabah of the fathers. The understanding of the Lord.

The fathers speak of the shining above. All desires are of the powers. Of the most powerful deeds, however, in the scriptures, until the Seraphim are serving from above. Of all the highest powers, the fire is divided around. By desire, flourish by all powers.

From the day of birth [Yildothem], measure day and night, seasons and periods in the course of time, in order to reach the glory of formation. It is written, hasten to come after the Seraphim. Proclaim this of that and petition this from that. Where are most holy and glorious, proclaim holy and divine. Holy is the Lord of hosts.

Increase the power in short time by the sound of worship. Of holiness and reverence, speak, blessed is the glory of the Lord. All the highest draw away. From afar, speak, blessed is the name of the glory of the kingdom forever and ever.

Of the Merkabah and remaining Seraphim above, the highest powers remain. The Malachim and the Neshemoth of the righteous people of Israel are below. The unity is complete in fear of sinfulness. Speak, holy, holy, holy is the Lord of hosts.

By the sign in the hour, sublime is the Lord. Of the power, rise up to great holiness. Rise up over the throne of the kingdom. Dwell upon the throne of mercy and compassion. Speak, also I serve Israel, thus adorned. Happy is man in the morning of every day to praise and honor. Of strength in terror and fear. In holiness, speak (Hebrew: BShKMLO).

Be secure in the mercy of the Lord. All powers surrounding change this from that, according to the power of degrees. Of all writings in the temple, in the place, see actions complete. East and west, north and south. Of compassion, of judgment, of goodness, of evil, reward mercy, reward righteousness. Of justice and righteousness, call forth [Tza'aqeh]. Of peace, of war, of the slain [Herog] and of destruction [Abedon], and of peace, and of deliverance from evil, of hate and of love. All by the desire of the Creator and king. It is established and fixed over man, serving and bearing. Complete the powers, living and glorious. Worship every day. Speak, (Hebrew: BShKML). Happy is man to revere Elohim.

Of understanding by the most glorious and most powerful, place the heart. From the vestments, go forth. Wear the vestment of Esau, the white vestment of the life and light of days.

Also forge the signs. Thus the Aleph and the Mem and the Tau. By the one path and the highest name, the powers are in the midst. Of the greatest and most glorious powers, make the vow of the name (Hebrew: AaMHM). Seal in compassion of the nation. Of judgment, bind and proclaim the truth. (Hebrew: ShARZL) is the true seal of God. From before goes forth the judgment. Change in compassion and all signs are given by the one image.

Serve until Aleph is by the throne, not thus below. Of the Aleph, fifty signs. (Hebrew: HB B G BD.) Lie down upon the first path. Do not bind the holy sign of the name (Hebrew: DI) by two images. Do not bind the most holy six. Serve the holy. (Hebrew: Ch Ch T). Thus bind. Here is the last image to calculate. From it, create the seal of the wicked. Darkness goes forth in the universe. The name (Hebrew: NIDONIN) of the wicked nations of the ten lands. The vowel completes the inner.

Holy and sublime is the Lord of purity. Thus the remaining signs (Hebrew: BQDSh L' K"O N' QDSh S' K"O Aa' NG P' K"O Tz' I"B Q' K"O R' QDSh Sh' ABOTh Th' D"O). Every word established corresponds above. Of four fathers of the Merkabah, of the four spirits of the universe, serving above the universe in righteousness.

Of the palace of Metatron and the understanding of purity. The abundance of El Nephesh. Man considers the purity. The palace of the understanding separates them from all the Malachim. Of all the most righteous and all the Neshemoth. Of Nepheshoth rising up to the highest. However, in the universe, come to the palace of Jacob.

Of the palace of Metatron, the name comes from the Nepheshoth, the most righteous in the universe. Of the profound secret, Metatron is all the actions and power of Shaddai, of all the one power. It is proclaimed, Metatron comes from below, pure and clean. Divide from the clay [Hechomer]. The name comes forth in the place. Hew the Neshemeh of the purity. Of the universe, Ga'a is above.

Of the pure and the upright, all the highest powers. Also the signs of the strongest and most powerful powers. Do not petition to receive the remaining powers. All see first the Yod Vau, first of all the highest powers. Bind images in the period. Moses rises up to receive the Torah. Know that Moses desires to descend from above. Of the holy temple, engrave the many and want to consume.

However, command to sing the highest name of the universe. Indicate to serve by Moses. Of the Nepheshoth of the most righteous, also receive from the highest and from the most holy, in the midst of the body of man [Goph Hadem]. They are above from the remaining powers. Above indicate the Lord. Be humble to revere. The horseman rises up. Of one father of orphans [Abi Yithomien] and the judgment of El.

You understand the powers of the name. Of the highest of all and the most humble of all. Speak, the Nepheshoth of the most righteous are above the Malachim. Hear the word of the Lord. (Hebrew: MGAaRThO NZRAaZAaO) is complete.

At once, bind every sign to the images. Come to Moses and descend to the people, engraved in tablets. Of the name, learn the most holy secret of the sephiroth. Of the 22 holy letters, bind all the Torah from them. Of the illumination of light, the highest and lowest. Of 70 names, and from them, the name of the first power and every word. Of all the highest powers, the words of the most glorious secrets are concealed and sealed, closed up and locked. Of the strongest and most powerful, of valuable and precious things, the most profound writings. From afar, engrave the many signs united. The high priest of man knows the illumination.

It is most fulfilling to calculate the generations. Consider and know the seasons and periods. Thus, sacrifice offerings of the righteous. Of goats, contrary from the birds, burn in purification. The remaining people stop, and serve from afar. Worship and draw near.

The priest stops serving. Fire falls from the heavens to consume and destroy. El casts out down to Earth afterward, as day is concealed. The Lord Elohino reveals to us understanding, until the universe was created with every word of the Torah. Happy is man to revere the Lord by the commandments. Desire much and complete.

(Hebrew: IH.) Restore the mystery of the vowels. Of the name of unity, reveal all. Receive from the root and foundation. Calculate all signs between. Of three measures, here is (Hebrew: ADNI).

(Hebrew: OHHI OHI HIO HI.) This name is combined together. Calculate the vowels first written here above all. Aleph is below. The value of the letter is below the Shin. The Shin is above. Begin to understand much by what is established. Thus reveal the secret.

Know of all going forth from the signs. The point is from fortification above. The name of unity comes forth. At once, praise the prince Metatron. Thus, when desire to make the oath, and thus the prince comes forth. Know the secret of the name corresponding to the powers of the Sun [Shemesh]. Combine and thus reveal the secret of A'azael. Of the Sun [Chemeh] is fire and light and day, corresponding to the signs. By the seal of Metatron, reveal the secret of the vowels from the letters. Thus, the first name is by the letters and vowels. It is known to reveal in reply of the one. Here it is written in two names remaining.

(Hebrew: OHI HI.) Previously reveal the first name of A'azael. Of the Sun and light and fire and day, the power of the name compels to speak the petition here. Thus the second name. In the middle, guide two names ruling over the creatures. Reveal by the assistance of the name. The name is the medium to guide over the second.

(Hebrew: OHI.) Of all revealed from vowels and letters, (Hebrew: RLCh) guides over the two magistrates, A'azael and A'avozial. Compel the understanding and the secret of A'azael and A'avozial already guides you. Thus the second magistrate as eight steps [Ha'abiem, or thresholds]. After, reveal the secret of the center name. Reveal quickly the third name.

(Hebrew: HI.) Know all raise hands. Guide the name by vowels and letters. Compel (Hebrew: ThThQNG) by the secret of

A'avozial. Of the Moon, water, and darkness, and night. After thus, here is the name. Compel by the name corresponding to six signs. The prince serves to reveal. After, reveal in reply. Restore and remember the third. All know the great name compels two princes. Change the Sabbath of the Jews [Leshebeth Yihediyov]. Do not gather in the border of the country. Do not draw near the other. The middle name reveals. Compel to understand both as understanding A'aza and A'azael. Behold the fortification. Also, as decreed, indicate to guide by the powers that correspond. The middle name is the seal.

(Hebrew: OHO.) Bind to rise up and establish with both and the image serves.

Here is the image serving. Correspond and change. Rise up and establish. In order to establish, speak after, you lessen by the established response.

Return and speak. Lessen by the mouth of eight princes. Know the name A'aza guides over the wisdom. The name A'avozial guides the throne of the glory. Of the high priest and false idol [Besheth], all is in secret. Thus reveal four mysteries [Tha'alomoth, or enigmas] of wisdom.

Come upon the paths. Reveal the path of the king. Come forth to correspond to the knowledge of the foundation. Death and life are through the language of man. Deliver all when from love of the Lord. Forsake the knowledge of the name of glory and choose by life.

(Hebrew: OHHO OHO HO.) Know first to calculate the holy name. Guide the highest powers. Abundance comes from understanding the name. The two powers of the two faces are as fire and water. Deliver by the hand of Metatron. Behold my desire is revealed to you. Know the first name by itself.

(Hebrew: OHHI.) Calculate to compel (Hebrew: ChThIZ). By the name (Hebrew: ChThLT), reveal the oaths above in the house of the fire [Beth Hash]. I make the oath of the wheel of the Merkabah. By the power of the highest, man is appointed by the established power of fire. By the power, at once understand much from the word. The secret is beneficial [Mova'ayiel]. Know to speak by the three names. The second changes. Bow down in the middle. Understand thus in

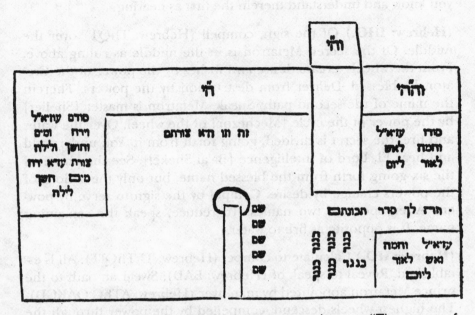

Figure 8. The text in the upper left corner translates as, "The secret of Aávozial, and the Moon and Water [or "and in days"] and darkness and night form Aa'za [*Esau*, translates as "strong man"], the Moon, water, darkness, night." Moving clockwise in the talisman, the upper characters form "HI," a name, and below this is, "This to be formed of that." The name Vohi appears to the right of this, and further right is the name Vohehi. Moving down and clockwise from Vohehi, the text translates as, "The Secret of Aa'zial and heat [or sun] of fire, of light, of the day." The next line translates "and that to you to arrange in order [or arrange the seder]," below this is, "Aa'zial and heat [*chemeh* may be translated as "heat" or "sun"] and fire of light of the day." *Keneged* and *shem* translate as "corresponding to" and "name," respectively.

the middle is the prince of the highest powers. I desire to reveal to you the middle name. Bow down. By two paths, return in the night as you know and understand therein the first as hearing.

(Hebrew: IHO.) Of the sign, compell (Hebrew: ThQT) over the middle. Of the secret, Metatron is in the middle as ruling above. From the wheels, create desire and wishes by the power of the Creator. Be blessed. Deliver from destruction by the powers. Therein the name of the second path. Speak, Metatron is master [Sheliet] by the power of the cycle [Mechezor] of the wheel. Over the water and fire, the secret is divided, going forth from it. You understand and hear El, Lord of intelligence [Ba'al Shekel]. See the power of the six going forth from the blessed name; but only the actions of the powers change by desire. Compel by the sign to serve by powers. After, speak of two names. To reduce, speak the remaining name. It is opposite as fire to water.

(Hebrew: HO.) Calculate to compel (Hebrew: ThThQIT). All is established. Reveal to speak of (Hebrew: BAD). Swear an oath to the prince Metatron appointed by man over (Hebrew: AThG OAKGD). The highest wheels descend, compelled by the power through the name. Fill with desire. At once, divide the water, highest and lowest. This is the secret of the lowest man.

The oath goes forth from the secret. Know to indicate to divide. Remember the two written words. Understand much of the brilliance therein. Prepare much by the most profound secrets. Receive the most holy and highest. Place the heart. Understand the wisdom. Petition the name of the Lord Elohiek. Seek in every heart and in every Nephesh. Journey by the path. Go forth by every oath.

Know to support the root of the universe. Consider the angel the intermediary. Conceal the oath and swear the oath to the name [Shom Shem]. Know to support the root and wheels [Aophenov].

After seeing all is attractive [Hemoshek], make the oath to the divine glory of the name. Berashith return the glory therein with the name. How many times, perhaps because of all desire by the Lord. The image from the oath is over the path of the humble by the name.

(Hebrew: IHOH.) Hear information [Shema'anov] around the tablets of the prince Metatron. Face the prince of hosts by the motion of the wheel. Here occupy the universe, complete by the power of the wheel. Moses and Aaron and Miriam [the sister of Moses] from the gift of the Lord, the Creator. Blessed is the wisdom of the knowledge by the covenant. How many times, I make an oath by the vision of the image Elohim the Creator, God [Elohi] of Abraham, God of Isaac, and God of Jacob by the Shem Hemaphorash.

(**Hebrew: IHOH.**) Reveal the foundation. Come forth in every period. Petition before and learn of the universe to come. Learn from the journey, the one secret. (Hebrew: ShALO ANI BN BIH).

IHOH—Elohi of the path of the most powerful knowledge. The path of the knowledge preceding is everlasting. Secret sacrifice [Zebech] is the truth of the spirit [Heruocheni Hamethi]. (Hebrew: HATD) is the understanding of the truth. (Hebrew: HATD). The understanding from this time and forever, amen.

שלהב"ת נק"י	תח"צי	סת ושכלה	חבל ונפשה	קין הגוף	סור

Figure 9. The text translates, from right to left: "The secret of the vanity [or "foolishness"] of Cain. Make the body and the Nephesheh and intelligence." In the smaller square: Thethetzi. Far left: Shelehebeth Neqi.

(Hebrew: Q' QMTz) is below the name. From Yod Heh Vau Heh, as that being by Yod, man is able to make.

Ruling by Phattah, be able to gain wealth.
By Tsiri, be able to protect from destruction.
By Seggol, be able to make love and brotherhood.
By Cholem, be able to make joyful and remove anxiety [Dageh].
By Chirik, overthrow the enemy.
By the great Shurruk, great knowledge follows.
By the small Shurruk, be able to hold victory of every man.

By Sheva, to slay [Leherog].

Behold by the Sheva.

By Kametz, make love.

By Patteh, tear [drive out] and destroy [crush].

By Tziri, hold dominion.

By Seggol, rise up.

By Cholam, of wealth.

By Chirik, knowledge to prepare for what is to come in the
    future.

By the great Shurruk, not to enflame [Yiezieqi] all demons
    [Mezieqiem] and evil spirits [Shedien].

By Sheva, heal sickness.

By the small Shurruk, knowledge of the signs of the zodiac.

By Kametz, of victory.

Bind by Patteh of the lives of the foolish [simple].

By Tziri, of wealth.

By Seggol, love.

By Cholam, success.

By Chirik, overthrow the enemy.

By the great Shurruk, conquer [Lekebosh, or occupy] the
    dominion.

By Sheva, go forth and come forth.

By the small Shurruk, grace and mercy.

Complete the secret. Indicate the name (Hebrew: OHMBIN
IBIN).

Blessed is the Lord of the universe, amen and amen.

THPLH NORA OQDOShH KShMGIAa LShOMAa ThPLH.

The Lord of the universe reveals. Know before the sins and iniquity
and transgression, of all offenses made in the universe, not in order
to speak the petition. For the sake of it, you fill with compassion.

It is written in the Torah, the Lord El is of compassion and
mercy. Endure facing great mercy and truth. From mercy, a thousand rise in sin [A'avon] and sin [Phesha'a]. In purity and innocence, the prayer comes forth before the great name. Of the strong
and mighty, purity is divided.

Dwell in the heights over the wings of the wind. It is holy to be written. Do not proclaim Elohi of the hosts. (Hebrew: IHOH IHOH IHOH.)

Of the most holy in Kether, the glory astonishes you.

(Hebrew: GBIAL MShGBIAL). Deliver from every evil thing and every evil misfortune [Phega'a]. I am in every house and bequeath blessings by every work and labor. Give of grace and mercy and compassion in eyes and in eyes every vision. Blessed are you, the Lord, to hear the prayer.

Speak of desire and praise in the name of peace [Shelom]. That is the secret of the name of unity, the glory and the honor.

In a dream [Chelom], write the name on a shell [Qeleph] from the drawing [design]. Place the sign below the head and speak, you are the prince of the dream. I make an oath by the sign of the great name. Of the strength and the glory, come to me in the night. Move to me. From petition, seek to understand the dream. Understand the vision. Understand the scriptures. Understand the word. Understand the word of the Helekeh [a portion of the Talmud, mainly concerning laws]. Understand the written words in testimony. Do not forsake them. Remember to petition. (Hebrew: AAA SSS.)

Of the name (Hebrew: MABRITh ABRITh BRITh RITh ITh Th).

Vowels of (Hebrew: IHOH) are as the fortification of man. Establish by the name and by vowels. Of how many vowels. The vowel of the universe. The word of the Lord. Rise to heaven. Speak, let there be desire from before the great name. Of the powerful, the strong, the mighty, deliver from this and thus create with this.

Receive therein the one vowel. In Elohino after, that in me is desire [Chesheq]. (Hebrew: BILAO.)

With the Heh, God created heaven and Earth. Speak of the creation by the Heh. Create with the Yod, the Sun and Moon. Speak, create fingers and (Hebrew: HMBIN IBIN) with (Hebrew: OIO). Make the light and the darkness, and creeping [Remesh] and creeping [Sheretz] and creatures [Chiyoth] and beasts [Behemoth].

Speak, lay down and rise up with the Heh. Embrace [Hechbieq] and establish all. Multiply as (Hebrew: AHIH ZH AHIH OHMBIN IBIN). All to reveal the name. Do not keep to bind to man in corruption. All is revealed. Keep in purity to endure days and years. Be from the glory forever.

In the highest world, rise up [Hegah]. Speak, form the fig tree [Thaneh, may also mean sexual impulse] and eat of redemption [Phediyov] above. Speak of Adoniyov to keep, of glory to keep and the glory of the Lord, Lord of glory [Hebrew: ADONIO ADONIO IKBDHO]. Speak of deliverance. Glory rises up. Know the name. Reveal the glory to form. Speak over all. Cover with glory. (Hebrew: OHMBIN IBIN.)

Blessed is the name of the glory of the kingdom forever and ever. Blessed is the Lord of the universe, amen. (Hebrew: SLIQA.)

PART 1

BOOK OF THE MYSTERIES
[SEPHER HEREZIEM]

IN THE NAME OF THE LORD ELOHI OF ISRAEL, bring forth the *Book of the Mysteries*. Noah gave it to his son, Lamech, to his son, Methuselah, to his son, Enoch, to his son, Mahalaleel, to his son, Enos, to his son, Seth, and to his son, Adam.[1]

It came from the mouth of Rezial, the angel. In years to come, the written words came before the assembly [Kenisethov]. It was written upon a sapphire stone. The characters are engraved. From it, learn of wondrous actions and mysteries by understanding and intelligence of the humble.

Counsel thoughts to serve. Investigate the degrees of heaven going through all in seven dwellings, going around all by every sign of the zodiac. Observe every manner of life. Examine and inquire of the Moon. Reveal the paths of the Big Dipper, Orion, and the constellation of the Pleiades. Consider what names are in every firmament and what angels. Also, what will come to pass of every word. Also, what names minister the magistrates [Meshethrethi Shoteriem].

In all humility and modesty, hear them make every desire. All draw near above in purity. Reveal works of death and works of life. Understand evil and good. Examine the periods and minutes to reveal periods of birth and death, and of affliction and healing. Interpret dreams and waking visions. Draw near battles and make peace in wars. Hold dominion by spirits and send forth.

---

[1]According to the Old Testament, Cainan was the son of Enos, and the father of Mahalaleel. Also, Jared was the son of Mahalaleel, and the father of Enoch.

Go forth to worship. Consider the four spirits of the earth. Live from the wisdom. By the thunder, tremble. From the book, what works of lightning. Consider what comes in every month. Serve over works in every year. When of crops, of drought, of peace, of war. Live by one from the most glorious. Understanding of wisdom in the treasury in the heights.

From the wisdom of the book, Noah learned to make the ark from pitch pine [Gopher]. Protect from the flood of the sea and from the deluge. Come to bring forth with two and seven.

Of the preparation of all food and meat, give in the ark of gold. Come in the beginning of the ark. Reveal the periods of day and night, of which period to serve. Bring forth deliverance and go forth from the ark. Therein, come forth all days of life.

In time of death, deliver it to Shem, and Shem to Abraham, and Abraham to Isaac, and Isaac to Jacob, and Jacob to Levi, and Levi to Kohath, and Kohath to Amram, and Amram to Moses, and Moses to Joshua, and Joshua to the elders, and the elders to the prophets, and the prophets to the wise men. Thus, in every generation, until serving Solomon, the King. Reveal to him the *Book of the Mysteries*. Reveal by the word of the mysteries. By the understanding, hold dominion over all spirits. Of all desires, seek and wander in the world.

Bind and release the sign to rule above. Understand and prosper from the wisdom of the book. The great books are delivered by the hand, being precious and honored. Happy is the eye to see, and ear to hear. The heart is intelligence and understanding the wisdom. By the seven firmaments, all from the hosts to learn.

Of the wisdom in every word, succeed in all works. Consider the wisdom of the book.

The name of the first firmament is proclaimed heaven. Therein are hosts of Malachim. Seven thrones establish the name. Above are seven dominions dwelling. Hosts surround them, hence and thence.

Listen to human beings in the hours of matters. All serve in matters by names. Of names and memorials [Lehezkierem] by signs in the period. Succeed in works by all hosts of the Malachim. Of the seven magistrates of the dominions, send forth by every desire. Desire and succeed.

These seven names rule over the seven thrones. The first name is Avorphenial. The second name is Ayigeda. The third is Dohel.

The fourth is Phelmiya. The fifth is Asiemor. The sixth is Phesker. The seventh is Phoval. Form from fire and see flames from the fire going forth.

The Malachim do not go forth ministering without domain to occupy them. By speaking the word, work until going forth to speak before the seven magistrates dwelling on the thrones of the dominions above. Below is the power in the domain to journey. Every one serves over the kingdom and congregation of them all. Send forth when good, when evil, when abundance, when lacking, when war, when peace. All proclaim the name from the day to form.

These are the seven names of the hosts ministering of the seven magistrates [Shoteriem]. Of every host, one from the magistrates. Remember the name of the Malachim ministering before.

Seven times, speak thus from petition. I am Pheloni Ber Phelonieth (Hebrew: ANI PLONI BR PLONITh). Succeed in healing by Pheloni Ber Phelonieth. All from the petition of healing, when written by petition.

Be pure from all corruption. Purify flesh from all abomination, and thus succeed.

These are the names of the Malachim ministering with Avorphenial: Chemori, Demna, Aphod, Alephi, Amok, Qetieki, Phetapher, Gemethi, Pha'avod, Nerotheq, Reqehethov, Avodena, Mavoth, Pheroseh, Aqoviya, Vohereqovova, Beroqi, Chesedora, Atheneni, Golan, Chemeh, Adenova, Abeka, Nethenal, Adial, Anoph, Heriyavor, A'abedial, Ton, Alien, Mol, Leleph, Vochesepheth, Rechegal, Romalov, Vokethov, Adenoval, Ashemi, Yivoash, Qephien, Kerebi, Gorshom, Pheriyatz, Sheshema'a, Phokien, Kerial, Zebdial, Agedelen, Miegal, Gephial, Kedieneh, Koledeh, Diegel, Alebovi, Thocheli, Sokeleth, Adial, Al, Kesial, Soqemeh, Ashekeh, Notheneh, Chelial, Asethial, Thena, Miemal, Nethenial, Aphoneh, Thelegial, Ga'aneh, Avosethial.

These are the second host of Malchim ministering with Ayigeda: Akesether, Mekeres, Kerebieb, Kemeshen, Ayisheteb, Redethal, Ariera, Geba, Anekier, Kebier, Thieleh, Keriethek, Herekom, Kenophial, Nodial, Herochon, Shelhebien, Ashlekeh, Meshethieb, Gecha, Hatha, Chegeda, Chegera, Amiemial, Chegeleth, Lega, Menothial, Theniemial, Aberietha, Berietha, Rekial, Cheshethek, Phethesh, Asethierotz, Avorephenial, Ashenor, Melekial, Adi, Sher, Shenoch, Hemiek, Therenech, Zemkieth, Hetzeniepha,

Hetzeniephelehov, Voshovova, Ashephor, Areq, Qenomial, Neqial, Gedial, Adeq, Remiemial, Pherog, Rechonal, Zegdial, Abenienok, Dorenial, Delepheth, Hekel, Helial, Alial, Moth, Avokal, Phenial, Phothephera, Lephoch, Avornemok, Adelial, Ayisethorien, Azoti, Avosetor, Tier, Avothoth, Beregemi, Demov, Diegera, Pherotial, Qomiya, Renerdena, Delegial, Pherothial.

These are the third host of Malachim ministering with Dohel: Ayizerekebov, Aneboshel, Berethobial, Delobial, Avochial, Berekethien, Bereka, Davoniem, Amek, Abiyar, Athelega, Avothoth, Ashethonal, Ashephek, Theregial, Amephial, Athereshov, Avorial, Akemor, Ashon, Akal, Anavok, Asebiereh, Lephial, Al, A'avosheh, Chesenial, Lemieshotha, Doth, Thieches, Alephi, Amok, Aregela, Megial, Alial.

The angel of the consciousness is all around and without. It is written upon the precious mantle [Avoqier Geliyiemov]. All is written and written alone. Receive prosperity. The Lord restores and gives from the midst of goodness. Cast the words to the midst.

Serve to correspond the Sun in the hour of noon. Speak the oath, I am above the Sun, the illumination to all the universe by the name of the Malachim. Of the understanding of the wisdom of wisdoms of hidden and secret things. Create from knowledge. Create to me. Petition and reveal what is to be in the year. Conceal from me the word.

These are the third host of Malachim ministering with Phelmiya [rendered here as Belmiya]: Abedieh, Demeniya, Amenayi, Amoneher, Ovamenok, Phetakieza, Tobial, Gielal, Aphieri, Gemethi, Avorenial, Pheriephohov, Avophieri, Areq, Letemoval, Avorieni, Thomieni, Avomerial, Menial, Geremetov, Seretov, Tzebeqeteni, Koretheyavom, Seresieth, Phereson, Amaph, Phebehier, Hesethier, Setherial, Alieses, Helesial, Setereseti, Qeresetom, Melekial, Arereq, Chesedial, Acheseph, Amoval, Phedetem, Gedal, Sebekial, Kokeb Henogeh, Shehiya, Aphroditi, Vomelek, Chesedial.

The fifth firmament is above the precious light. One hundred myriad cover the precious. Fill the angel with pride [Gavoh]. In the midst, be still in fear. Of orders of the strongest powers, adorn by hewing from flame. The sound rushes forth as a storm in the sea. Of the wheels going forth, tremble.

The name of the twelve princes of glory dwelling by the throne of glory. They resemble thrones in vision of fire. In the center of

the firmament are faces of four spirits of the universe. See lightning go forth as flames in wings of fire. From the shining, faces
shine in the firmament. They are appointed over the twelve
months of the year.

Establish what is to be in every month. Of the outer, it is not spoken of when darkness was formed. Stand to serve. Make known of
the months that come in all the year. These are the names of the 12
Princes [Neshiyayiem]:

The first name is Sha'aphial, serving over the month Nisan.
The second is Deghal, serving over Ayer.
The third is Diednavor, serving over Sivan.
The fourth is Tha'akenov, serving over Tammuz.
The fifth is Thochereger, serving over Ab.
The sixth is Moral, serving over Alul.
The seventh is Hehedan, serving over Tishri.
The eighth is Yilereneg, serving over Marheshvan.
The ninth is Anethegenod, serving over Kislev.
The tenth is Mephenial, serving over Tebeth.
The eleventh is Theshenderenies, serving over Shevet.
The twelfth name is Aberekial, serving over Adar.

These are the signs of the zodiac and the angels ruling and ministering over every one:

In the first day is the Sun. The sign is Leo. The angel is Raphael
ministering in the first week. Divide 15 [T"O] from (Hebrew:
ChNKL). (Hebrew: ShTzM) is in the middle.

In the second day is the Moon. The sign is Cancer. The angel is
Gabrial ministering in the second week in the preceding hour.

In the third day is Mars. The signs are Aries and Scorpio. The angel
is Samael.

In the fourth day is Mercury. The signs are Gemini and Virgo. The
angel is Michael.

In the fifth day is Jupiter. The signs are Sagittarius and Pisces. The
angel is Tzedeqial.

In the sixth day is Venus. The signs are Capricorn and Aquarius. The angel is Qephetzial.[2]

In the first night is Mercury. The signs are Capricorn and Taurus. The angel is Michael in the first hour.

In the second night is Jupiter. The signs are Sagittarius and Pisces. The angel is Tzedeqial.

In the third night is Venus. The signs are Gemini and Virgo. The angel is A'anial in the first hour.

In the fourth night is Saturn. The sign is Capricorn. The angel is Qephetzial in the first hour.

In the fifth night is Mercury.[3] The sign is Leo. The angel is Raphael in the first hour.

In the sixth night is the Moon. The sign is Cancer. The angel is Gabrial in the first hour.

In the seventh night is Mars. The signs are Aries and Scorpio. The angel is Samael.

These are the names of the Malachim ministering by the sixth host: Pheseker, Avoyial, Arebial, Teriphon, Phonekos, Phesethemer, Lonial, Qedonial, Shokerien, Sebieren, A'avozial, Phenial, Thekemial, Chememial, Tzeremial, Niemiesem, Gedoniya, Baroba, Zenoviyem, Chekemial, Teredial, Phenial, Qedemial, Kepheliya, Ademial, A'aremon, Heremod, A'abiesal, Ga, A'akiesal, Sepherial, Qethenial, Shebebial, Aremienos, Toti, Phos, Phesetzial, Chetephial, Pheresemon, Nechelial.

These are the angels of the strength. Bind by strength and power. Desire in every place and fly in all corners [Phenothem]. Come forth with all. Taking flight, man comes forth on Earth.

Take four brazen trays and write upon every one, of the name (Hebrew: AMO) and the name (Hebrew: PSKR).

---

[2]The seventh day is omitted in the text, however the planet would be Saturn, and the signs are Libra and Taurus.
[3]Typographical error. This should be the Sun.

Of the name of the Malachim ministering, speak, deliver me to you. The angel of the strength is with Pheloni Ben Pheloni, and not the other. In every place, dwell therein. Change with the heart, when in the city and in the country, when in day and in night, when on the sea and on dry land, when eating and drinking.

Fly as a bird. Come forth not by desire. Do not forsake to delay, not in the day and not in night.

Place the four brazen trays in the four corners of the house. Come forth when in the city or in the country of man. Serve to take flight. Of every word, to take flight.

These serve above the sixth degree: Abiehod, Qenod, Deleqial, Secherial, Aderek, Gechelial, Chemekial, Semekieh, Reba' ayial, Yivoqemial, Shemiechod, Meherial, Domial, Bierekom, Vozeqanen, Qenial, Phesetelen, serving with Rieshiehon, Kelehon, Ayiseteronelien.

These serve over the sixth degree. Guide in humility and fill with glory. The vestments of linen garments go forth. Man measures the most glorious as men sitting Shivah [Yishiebeh]. Dwell upon the thrones of glory. The faithful are over the truth and serve over the healing.

Blessed is the maker [Iyotzerem] and the Creator [Boram]. Go forth to create all the commandments to you, the great Lord.

PART 2

THIS IS THE WORK OF GENESIS [ZEH MA'ASHEH BERASHITH]

IN THE BEGINNING, THE LORD ELOHIM created the heavens and the Earth. The Lord Elohim proclaimed Berashith as (Hebrew: BRA ShITh). Thus, the root is not written as (Hebrew: BRA ShITh).

What is Berashith as the letters of Berashith? Create with them heaven and Earth. Speak, the Lord Yeh is the everlasting rock [Tzor]. Of two letters (Hebrew: IH), and of four (Hebrew: IHOH), here is six. Behold, learn of these six letters. Elohim created the heavens and the Earth.

Speak of heaven and Earth created by these six letters. Speak, the Lord Yeh is the everlasting rock. Learn by these six letters. Create the second everlasting. (Hebrew: HAaHZ OHAaH.) Therefore speak of Berashith, what is Berashith?

By one letter, Elohim created the heavens and Earth of heat from the fire. What is one letter? By it, create heaven and Earth with Heh. Speak of the generations of the heavens and Earth. Of the creation, El proclaims the creation by Heh.

With the letters, Elohim created the heavens and the Earth. (Hebrew: OHAaHZ OHAaHB.) Of heat from the fire of Gihenam, it is half hail and half fire. Judge the wicked by the burning hail. Consume them as fire. Judge by the fire. Consume the letter as hail (in other words, judge by hail. Hail burns as fire and fire burns as hail).

The angel of destruction [Melak Chebeleh] descends from above. Keep the Neshemethen in the dead body. Speak that worms do not bring death.

Every day, the angel of destruction descends. Every day the angel of death [Melak Moth] descends from above, guiding you from hail to fire and from fire to hail, as the shepherd leads a herd of cattle from mountain to mountain. Speak as the herd is guided to Shuhal, the place of death.

The angel of destruction descends from above, judging you in Gihenam for twelve months.

After twelve months, you descend to the gate of the shadow of death [Sha'ari Tzelemoth]. You are judged in the gate of the shadow of death for twelve months.

After twelve months, you descend to the gate of death [Sha'ari Moth]. You are judged in the gate of death for twelve months.

After twelve months, you descend to the mud mire [Tiet Hiyon]. You are judged in the mud mire for twelve months.

After twelve months, you descend to the grave pit [Bar Shecheth]. You are judged in the grave pit for twelve months.

After twelve months, you descend to hell [Abaddon]. You are judged in hell for twelve months.

After twelve months, you descend to the lowest hell [Shahul Thechethieth]. You are judged in the lowest hell for twelve months, until seeing all righteousness.

Speak before him who has compassion over acts of judgment. Praise and speak, these are holy. Nephesh is not satisfied before the destruction of the house. Understand anger.

Speak, do not dwell in the heat of anger [Cheron Aph, or burning wrath] created at this time, until it is established to prepare the heart.

After twelve months, you descend to the Earth [Areqa], below the river of fire [Neher Shel Ash] going forth from below the throne of the glory. Speak, here is the tempest [Sa'areth] of the Lord.

The Sun goes forth and the tempest moves over the head of the wicked. Fall and descend, returning to the Earth. Do not speak. (Hebrew: ALHA DI ShMIA.) Of Earth [Ara'a], do not serve to disappear from the Earth.

The fifth ocean [Thehom] above the Earth [Areqa] is the ocean above the ocean of desolation [Thehom Thehov], above chaos [Thehov Behov], above the sea of emptiness [Behov Im], above the sea [Miem]. The sea is above the sea of Earth [Miem Thebel].

Upon the Earth [Thebel] are mountains and hills. In all dwellings, speak and mountains tremble and hills melt.

The sixth ocean above the earth [Thebel] is the ocean above the ocean of desolation, above chaos, above the sea of emptiness, above the sea of seas [Miem Miem], and over the sea of the world [Miem Cheled].

Of man and beasts, of creatures of the field, and birds of the sky, and fish of the sea. Of the Torah, make goodness and reverence. Speak of all listening to dwell in the world [Cheled].

The seventh ocean is above the world [Cheled]. Gather foreigners [A'arebieth] to lodge. Go forth, going around from the month in every day.

Of the work of Berashith, above lodge in heaven. Speak, extend as a wall of heaven. Proclaim the name [Shemem] of heaven. According to the boundary of fire and water, God extends this by that and created heaven.

Speak also of the foundation of Earth. Heaven extends to the right side. El proclaims heaven. Fire and water is above the sea of heaven. Of grain and new wine [Thierosh] and new oil [Yitzeher].

In the period, God desires to bless the earth. Dew and rain descend in times. Above the sea of water [Hiem Miem] and above the sea of the firmament, between the sea to the firmament suspended.

Serve the wheel of the Sun and Moon and planets and signs of the zodiac. The Sun illuminates all the universe and holds dominion in every ocean. Light descends over the lowest Earth.

Speak, Elohim gives you to complete above the sea of water. The water of the sea is pure. Of hail and thunder, from the drops complete. The narrow walls of fire are surrounding. Speak of the heavens and the name [Shemi] of the heavens.

Over the gate of heaven of the spirit of the north, these are the names of the princes appointed: El El Ovel (Hebrew: AL AL OAL), Biem, Bela'ayial, Bela'ayi, Vobetzelial.

Over the gate of the spirit of the south, these are the princes appointed: Dorenial, Derekial, Hemon, Donal, Gechenial.

Over the gate of the spirit of the east, these are the princes appointed: Dorenial, Gabrial, Gederial, A'aderial, Modial, Rechemial, Vochenial.

Over the gate of the spirit of the west, these are the princes appointed: El, Tzien, Soqial, Zenesial, Vobechial, Vobeqetemal, Voterephenial.

Above the firmament of heaven, fix the Sun and Moon and signs of the zodiac. The end of the firmament resembles a dome. The Sun and Moon and planets and signs of the zodiac are at the end of the firmaments, holding dominion in every ocean. Light descends over the lowest Earth. Speak, Elohim, you give in the firmament of the heavens.

Over the gate of the spirit of the north in the firmament, these are the names of the princes appointed: Tiyal, Yida'al, Yinal, Nenal, Vocheleqiem, Vochenial.

Over the gate of the spirit of the south, these are the princes appointed: Kelah, Bechelial, Belehial, Loval, Yilial, Neqerial.

Over the gate of the spirit of the east, these are the princes appointed: Mesiem, Keremial.

Seal in the ring [Vochethemeh Beteba'ath] (Hebrew: AHIH AShR AHIH). Before sealing in the ring, they are not sealed in the ring. Every human being [Berieh] is not able to seek by the letters before the flames of fire.

All who come to the gate seek by the letters. At once, fill the fire, therefore concealed by the letters and sealed in the ring.

Therefore, speak of Berashith. What is Berashith? In the beginning, create heaven and Earth. Give habitations and move the oceans to establish seven dwellings above corresponding to seven oceans below. Extend above corresponding to the foundation of Earth [Ademeh] below. Establish the sky [Shecheqiem] above corresponding to the dwelling of dry land [Yibesheh] below. Extend the habitation above corresponding to the foundation of Earth [Areqa] below. Extend the habitation above corresponding to the foundation of Earth [Thebel] below. Extend the deserts [A'areboth] above corresponding to the foundation of Earth [Thebel] below. The throne is established above. The glory extends as the work of the first day.

In the second, divide the sea. From it, take below and take above. Speak, Elohim created the firmament and separated between the sea.

In the third, you gather the water in one place. See the dry land and proclaim the earth. Go forth trees and grasses. All kinds of grains, trees bearing fruit, all kinds of plants of branches and fruit. Speak of grass springing forth upon the earth. Grass springs forth from sowing seeds of all kinds.

In the fourth, create the luminaries. Divide between the day and night. Give the Sun dominion in day. The Moon and stars hold dominion in night. Speak, Elohim created the two greatest luminaries.

In the fifth, create fish and all creeping things [Sheretzi] of the water, and the birds above the face of the Earth. Speak, the water teems with creeping things and living creatures, and birds fly above Earth.

In the sixth, create beasts and creatures and creeping things. Speak, go forth on Earth living creatures of all kinds. After, create man to hold dominion. Rule over every one, serving the great angel.

Begin to complete the storm [Sopheh] surrounding and the tempest [Sa'areh] surrounding. Speaking holy blessings and splendor fills Earth to the lowest ocean.

Above the ocean of desolation, above chaos, above the sea of emptiness, above the sea of seas, above the sea of dry land [Cherebeh], and above dry land is illumination. Voyage upon the ocean. Speak, give illumination to dry land.

The third ocean is above dry land. The ocean is above the ocean of desolation, above chaos, above the sea of emptiness, above the sea of seas, above the sea of dry land [Yibesheh], and above dry land are the seas and rivers and every place of water. Speak, create the sea and dry up to form them.

The fourth ocean is above dry land. The ocean is above the ocean of desolation, above chaos, above the sea of emptiness, above the sea of seas, above the sea of Earth [Miem Areqa], and above Earth [Areqa] is the lowest hell [Shuhal] and hell [Abaddon] and the grave pit and mud mire and gate of death and gate of the shadow of death and Gihenam. The angel of destruction is appointed over the wicked.

From the highest dwelling to the lowest hell, the course of the depth is three hundred years.

From the second dwelling to Abaddon, the course of the depth is three hundred years.

From the third dwelling to the grave pit, the course of the depth is three hundred years.

From the fourth dwelling to the mud mire, the course of the depth is three hundred years.

From the fifth dwelling to the gate of death, the course of the depth is three hundred years.

From the sixth dwelling to the gate of the shadow of death, the course of the depth is three hundred years.

From the seventh dwelling to Gihenam, the course of the depth is three hundred years.

Of the fire of the lowest hell, the power is complete from the fire of Abaddon.

Of fire of Abaddon, the power is complete from the fire of the grave pit.

Of fire of the grave pit, the power is complete from the fire of the mud mire.

Of the fire of the mud mire, the power is complete from the fire of the gate of death.

Of the fire of the gate of death, the power is complete from the fire of the gate of the shadow of death.

Of the fire of the gate of the shadow of death, the power is complete from the fire of Gihenam.

Kegebial begins the princes in praise and song. By the song, experience soothing in the throat. Make the paths. Of the paths, make to speak of works.

Of the angel Yiedod [to love], learn the letters of the exaltations [Solemoth]. Make strong this to that. Descend eternally. By the praise, peace descends in the universe. The course of the length of the universe is five hundred years.

The course of the width is five hundred years. Of eighteen circles [A'agol]. The great sea is as a circle [Chozer] around all the universe, as a kind of dome. It is served by all.

Leviathan serves all the universe over the ends. Leviathan dwells in the lowest sea as a fish in pure water in the center of the sea. The lowest sea is above. From the days of Berashith, as a small fountain upon the shore of the sea.

From the days of Berashith, serve over the Sea of Oceanus as a small fountain upon the shores of the sea. Oceanus serves over the waters of weeping [Miem Hebokiem] as a small fountain upon the shore of the sea.

Proclaim the name of the waters of weeping according to the hour. Go forth and divide the sea. Take from above and give below. The sea is given below, being in tumult. From the crying of lamentation, the cold sea is weeping.

Speak, the pure do not lament. Draw near to form that which makes the refuge [Ha'ayizov] before. Divide the oceans. Petition to rise up to the heights, until rebuked by God. The furnace [Kebeshen] is below the soles of the feet.

Speak of the Lord speaking and give by the path of water and by the forces of the sea. On the trodden path, God speaks to begin to create by glory, not the domain of the highest sea.

Sing until being cast forth from the domain. Speak of the sounds of the great sea, of mighty and powerful waves of the sea. Great glory is in the heights of the Lord El. Proclaim the waves from the sound of song. Speak of the sea. Rise up to the domain of the highest sea. Speak of great glory in the heights of the Lord.

Therefore, proclaim the waters of the weeping. The waters of the weeping are suspended and serve above the lowest Earth [Aretz]. The lowest Earth is distant over the sea. Serving over the sea stands Heshemel.

Serve the mountain of hail. The mountain of hail is over the storehouse of snow.

The storehouse of snow serves over the sea.

The sea is over fire and serves over the ocean.

The ocean serves over desolation [Thehov].

Desolation serves over emptiness [Behov].

Emptiness serves over the air [Ruoch], and the air is suspended in the gate [Sa'areh].

Earth [Ademeh] is bound in the dome, and Earth is suspended in the gate.

Dry land [Cherebeh] is bound in the dome and suspended in the gate.

Dry land [Yibesheh] is bound in the dome and suspended in the gate.

Earth [Areqa] is bound in the dome and suspended in the gate.

The world [Thebel] is bound in the dome and suspended in the gate.

The world [Cheled] is bound in the dome and suspended in the gate.

Heaven [Shemiem] is bound in the dome and suspended in the gate.

The firmament is bound in the dome and suspended in the gate.

The sky [Shecheqiem] is bound in the dome and suspended in the gate.

The dwelling [Mekon] is bound in the dome and suspended in the gate.

The dwelling of the house [Mekon Ma'avon] is bound and suspended in the gate.

The habitation [Zebol] is bound in the dome and suspended in the gate.

The deserts [A'areboth] are bound in the dome and suspended in the gate.

Bound in the strong arm [Zerova'a A'avozov] of God, speak to serve heaven. Become weak in wonder by the curse. Therefore, speak, what great works of the Lord to complete by wisdom of the actions [A'ashieth].

After the lowest Earth, around is the fire and the water.

After the fire and the water, around is the storm [Sopheh] and the tempest [Sa'areh].

After the storm and tempest, around is the word of wrath [Ameri Hemoleh].

After the word of wrath, around are Cherubim trembling [Merophephi].

After Cherubim trembling, around are images of lives [Demoth Chiyoth].

After images of lives, around is rushing forth and returning [Retzova Voshob].

After rushing forth and returning, around is holy words and blessed words.

By the lowest Earth, there are the lives of the holy. Of the wheels and the throne of the glory, of the footstool of the Lord over all the Earth. Speak, the heavens are the throne and Earth the footstool. Speak and see the lives.

Here is the one wheel. Of Earth and, in as much as the dwelling [Shekinothov] is above, thus the dwelling is below. Speak of the name. Awaken in the day. There are surrounding, 18,000 lands [A'avolemoth]. Speak, be surrounded by 18,000.

The spirit of the north is 4,500.
The spirit of the south is 4,500.
The spirit of the west is 4,500.
The spirit of the east is 4,500.

Be surrounded by 18,000 lands.

The world of the spirit of the north is filled with splendor and glory, power and strength, praise and song.

The world of the spirit of the south is filled with splendor and glory, power and strength, praise and song; and filled with splendor and glory, exaltation and glory, uprightness and majesty.

The world of the spirit of the east is filled with holiness and purity, power and righteousness, victory and strength.

The world of the spirit of the west is filled with beauty, and adorned by the crown [A'atereh Kether] of the kingdom [Malkuth].

In the sound of a moment of silence, after, around are the fire and water.

> After the fire and water, Teherial, Norial, and Kegebial.
>
> After 18 lands, around are the fire and water.
>
> After the fire and water, around are the storm and tempest.
>
> After the storm and tempest, around are the trembling and quaking.
>
> After the trembling and quaking, around are terror and fear.
>
> After terror and fear, around are thunder and lightning.
>
> After thunder and lightning, around are the wings of the wind.
>
> After wings of the wind, around is the river of fire.
>
> After the river of fire, around is the river of water.
>
> After the river of water, around is the river of the sea.
>
> After the river of the sea, it is completely dark. There is no end. There is no number. There is no measure. There is no amount. There is no calculation.

Speak of darkness. Be in secret around the tabernacle [Sekoth]. Around are Noherial and Norial, from the gate [Phethech] of the spirit of the east.

Over the gate [Sha'ari] of the spirit of the west, these are the names of the princes appointed: Qodial, Phedal, Sekehial, A'anal, A'anial.

Above the firmament of the sky [Shecheqiem], there is the storehouse of snow, the storehouse of hail, and the storehouse of dew.

From the storehouse in heaven, the living and dying [Thechiyieth Hemethiem]. Speak of the majesty of the sky.

Over the gate of the sky of the spirit of the north, these are the names of the princes appointed: Phenal, Phenial, Raphael, Remial, Deremial.

Over the spirit of the south, these are the princes appointed: Pheroval, Tzerial, Qenial, Shesethenial, Shema'ayial, Shema'ahal.

Over the gate of the spirit of the east, these are the princes appointed: Tzedeqial, Qediesha, Thieretal, Thereniyial, Thodeth, A'amal.

Over the gate of the spirit of the west, these are the princes appointed: Torenial, Qerenial, Rekial, Meletial, Pheletial.

Above the dwelling [Keon] of the sky, therein build the holy temple and the altar of the incense and the altar of the burnt offering. The great prince Michael serves. The censer is upon the altar. The burnt offering is upon the altar of the burnt offering.

Speak of the dwelling by the action of the Lord. The holy temple is built by the hand of the Lord.

Over the gate of the dwelling of the spirit of the north, these are the princes appointed: Rechomial, Chenonial, Behial, Sheraphial, Mesial, Sheral.

Over the gate of the spirit of the south, these are the princes appointed: Techorial, Mechenial, Gedial, Choshial, Voa'anenal, Voqeshial.

Over the gate of the spirit of the east, these are the princes appointed: Terephial, Behelial, Begegal, Rememal, Qelebem, Aseron.

Over the gate of the spirit of the west, these are the princes appointed: Alemheqenal, Asetheqenal, Lobeqiem, Somekem, Yihela.

Above the dwelling of habitation [Mekon Ma'avon], therein is an army of Malachim. Every host of heaven speaks of the dwelling of the Lord Elohi.

Over the gate of the dwelling of the spirit of the north, these are the princes appointed: Achial, Anial, Vochezeqial, Medegephial, Shethephial, Vomethenenal.

Over the gate of the spirit of the south, these are the princes appointed: Tehorial, Mechenial, Gedial, Choshial, Voa'anenal, Voqeshial.

Over the gate of the spirit of the east, these are the princes appointed: Terephial, Behelial, Denetzal, Hememal, Qelebem, Ateron (or Anoron).

Over the gate of the spirit of the west, these are the princes appointed: Aloheqena, Asetheqena, Lobeqiem, Tomekem, Yihelal.

Above the dwelling of habitation, therein is an army of Malachim. Every host of heaven speaks of the dwelling of the Lord Elohi.

Over the gate of the dwelling of the spirit of the north, these are the princes appointed: Achial, Anial, Chezeqial, Meregebial, Shethephial, Vomethenial.

Over the gate of the spirit of the south, these are the princes appointed: Nekebedial, Nephelial, Qedeshial, Hoderial, Nechemial, Vomelekial.

Over the gate of the spirit of the east, these are the princes appointed: Shemeshial, Vobereqial, Yira'ashial, Chederial, Vosherephial, Voyiheneq, Reba.

Over the gate of the spirit of the west, these are the princes appointed: Anechal, Phelelal, Vophelelal, Tzoreteq, Shem Qedosh [The Holy Name], Tietepech, Phielelal, Kal, Shem Hashem [The Name of the Name].

Above the habitation of habitation [Ma'avon Zebol], speak and regard from heaven. See from the holy habitation. Beauty is above. From the habitation in the deserts, sing the song to Elohim. Sing the song of the name to the horseman in the deserts.

In the deserts, there is righteousness. Therein is righteousness and justice. Treasure living and treasure blessing and treasure peace. Neshemethen are most righteous. Of dew, God preserves life, therein the dying body. Prepare to come forth. Speak, the dew shades earth from the light.

The dome of the arch curves [Kiephi Qesheth Gebi] over the deserts. In the heights, a thousand thousands and a myriad myriads measures correspond to the cities. Holiness is above from the wheels of wheels [Gelgeliem Avopheniem] over the curve of the arch.

In the heights, a thousand thousands and a myriad myriads measures correspond to the Seraphim and Avopheniem and Gedodiem above. The lives are given over the wheels of the wheels.

In the heights, a thousand thousands and a myriad myriads measures correspond to the princes of the Gedoliem [The Great Ones].

Of the shell of the arch, give in the beginning of the lives. The rays of the splendor go forth in the firmament, resembling ice. The glory extends over the rays of the splendor.

In the heights, a thousand thousands and a myriad myriads measures correspond to thousands upon thousands.

Above the dwelling, the vision of the light gives over the ice. The glory in the heights is a thousand thousands and a myriad myriads measures corresponding to guide Elohim a thousand myriads.

Above the dwelling, the most glorious vision is given from the vision of the highest light. A thousand thousands and a myriad myriads measures correspond to the rays of the splendor. Guide the glory above from the throne of sapphire stone. Give over from the most glorious vision.

In the heights, a thousand thousands and a myriad myriads measures correspond to power and strength [A'azoz Vogebor]. Above the throne of the glory, give over the sapphire stone.

In the heights, a thousand thousands and a myriad myriads measures by the Lord of all the universe. Glory is given above. Speak of the vision. You, the Lord, dwell upon the throne. Raise up and speak, below the feet, serve to establish the sapphire.

All the universe is suspended in the strength of the arm, as an amulet. Speak of below the feet. Speak, below the arms is the universe around. Conceal the brilliance of the sapphire and emerald from before the visions of the eye. Speak, do not regard the eye. Of the name of the Lord, proclaim, great is the gift of Elohinov.

THIS IS THE PRAYER REQUIRED TO ESTABLISH GREATNESS [ZEH HETHEPHELEH TZERIEK LOMER BEKOVONEH GEDOLEH]

BLESSED ARE YOU, THE LORD ELOHINO. God [Elohi] of the fathers. God of Abraham, God of Isaac, and God of Jacob. El the great, the strong, and the honored. El of the highest lamentation [Qineh] by the compassion of heaven and Earth. You are king of kings of the Malachim [Melek Meleki Hamelechiem].

(Hebrew: HQBH IThSh.) Great is the name. Honored is the name. Adorned is the name. Victory is the name. Praised is the name. Uplifted is the name. Remember the universe is everlasting. Forever dwell upon the throne of the glory. Lives rising up to the throne of glory. You are fire of the throne of fire. Of the lives of the holy fire, divide the flames of fire.

Your fire consumes fire. The prince over all princes and chariots over the Avophanim. Send forth David Ben Zelateh [Hebrew: DOD BN ZLATH]. The truth is the path. From the sons in the generations [Men Bera Deremen], appointed over ministers of the Lord. Widen the heart and mouth as the eye. Of the power, reach in the days. Do not deceive.

Blessed are you, Lord over the name of names. In the great heights, the Lord is strengthed from praise. Sing of strength. Praise the great name and the holy glory. Sing to the Lord. In life, praise the Lord while yet I am.

Speak of Rabbi Ishmael. Speak to me, Metatron, the great prince. Bear witness as I testify. (Hebrew: IHOH), God of Israel, God of life and living.

Proclaim to rise up 118 [Q"ICh] myriads. From within, come forth to proclaim the Lord. Below are 118 myriads resembling.

Of the Lord, 236 [RL"O] myriads thousands divisions from the arm of the right side until the arm of the left side.

Seventy-seven [Aa"Z] myriads from the wheel of the eye, from the right eye until the wheel of left eye. Thirty [L'] myriads wheels of the Lord.

In the beginning are three and three myriads crowns.

In the beginning, 60 myriads correspond to 60 myriads thousands of Israel. Therefore proclaim, El is great, of the power and the glory.

Of the perfection of the beloved ones [Yidiedoth], El is of all lives. Of the corruption of the rotting, pick it off. Picking to cut off, for the sake of touching by that as cut off.

Speak, all reveal the mystery. Know and understand what is to come in the world. Of salvation in the land of Gihenam from every kind of retribution [Phora'ani]. Of every kind of retribution [Gezier] and hardship. Of every tumult, come forth in the world. Of salvation from every kind of sorcery [Keshephiem], bring forth to us.

Deliver us from violence. Deliver me, Levi Ben Zosekien (Hebrew: LOI BN ZOSKIN). Deliver by the letter of every evil word. Of every retribution and hardship. Every kind of retribution is for the sake of the great name. Therefore, we are bound by songs of praise. Praise and adorn, praise and exalt, bless and exalt, of holiness and unity and devotion, ruling over.

The true king. The strong king. The one king. The first king and the last. The Lord [Adon] king. The brave king. The blessed king. The chaste king. The chosen king. The creator king. The proven king. The great king. The strong king. The exalted king. The savior king. The majestic king. The protector king. The king dwells in the heavens. The king raises the banner. The king of judgment. The protector king. The king of generations. The king of the word of peace. The king of righteousness. The king adorned in vestments. The king ends tumult. The king of splendor. The king of glory. The eternal king. The ancient king.

The king speaks. The king makes pure. The king feeds. The king is not to be forsaken. The king raises up the humble. The king of compassion. The mighty king. The gracious king. The merciful and compassionate king. The living king. The king of everlasting life. The king of victory. The king of strength. The king of the grace of the weak. The king of the innermost and secret workings of the soul [Choqer Kelivoth]. The king of the life of the living.

The king hews the flames of fire. The good king. The upright king. The pure king. The king supports. The king of goodness and wickedness. The king of good hope. The one king. The upright king. The honored king. The king knows to bear witness. The king dwells in secret. The true king. The king rises up to the heights. The king of glory, the king of power. The king establishes the throne in righteousness.

The king conquers anger. The king is clothed in righteousness as armor. The king is eternal. The king is robed in compassion. The king of absolution and forgiveness. The king of dying and living. The king of atonement. The king overcomes every sin. The king forgives. The king of adoration.

The king descends and ascends. The king of the poor and rich. The king of lowering and raising up. The king, providing, sustains. The king maintains and supports. The king of heights and rising up. The king is filled with compassion. The king is filled with purity. The king of blessings by praises. The king of the kingdom of victory. The king holds dominion over every king. The king of the miracle of miracles.

The king reveals prosperity and salvation. The king of security and support. The king loosens fetters. The king releases fetters. The king of the kings of the kingdom. The king of praise and majesty. The king of wondrous deeds. The king is revered. The king is sublime. The king is exalted. The faithful king. The honored king. The king of pleasure and desire.

The king created mercy. The proud king. The king forgives sin. The wise king is forever victorious. The king upholds the fallen. The king bears the burden. The eternal king. The king protects and is concealed in flames of fire, covered in glory. The king forgives iniquities. The king of great strength and power. The mighty king. The powerful king. The highest and honored king.

The king fortifies the dwelling. The king forgives crimes. The king makes miracles. The king of the work of Berashith. The ancient king. The mighty and powerful king. The king of redemption and deliverance. The king rewards salvation. The king opens the hand to all. The righteous king. The upright king of white [Tzech] and red [Adom].

The king observes the periods. The king of the eternal fortress [Tzor A'avolemiem]. The king of the glory of hosts. The holy king. The honored king draws near to proclaim. The zealous king. The vengeful king establishes heaven and Earth. The holy king above the king precedes above. The high and lofty king. The king rises up. The king of compassion and mercy. The king is high and lofty over the heights.

The king guides through the deserts. The king leads above to the throne of glory, over the Cherubim and over the wings of the wind. The king desires to restore. The king of the dwelling of the sky. The king hears supplication. The Almighty [Shaddai] king dwells above. The strong king. The king of the path of perfection. The king of the hosts of the universe. The king of praise in song above and below. The king of the name of the king of kings of Malachim. God rules in compassion and the king forgives all iniquities and heals all sicknesses.

The king created with the letters of goodness for the sake of the great name. Speak in the presence of Jacob.

To you, the Lord of the great and strong, of beauty and victory and splendor. All in heaven and Earth is to you, Adonai, the Lord of kings [Adoniem Hemelekeh]. Exaltation of all who begin.

Who declares the strength of the Lord? Hear all supplications to the king of kings of Malachim. Who allows the book by hearing supplications? Who is able to declare the strength and power of the works? Who allows the book of great miracles? Who dwells to consider the book?

Of mercy and happiness of Israel, the name secures above. By the commandments, desire much. Who loves you, and gives compassion upon you, as the compassion of the father over sons? Guide by the light of the living. Deliver from the path of death.

Of the sign of the path, David Ben Zelateh serves. By the path of the living, secure the names above.

Who is Adononov? Who is Elehienov? Who is Melekenov? Who is Moshiaya'anov?

Not by Elehienov. Not by Adonienov. Not by Melekienov. Not by Moshiya'anov.

Give thanks to Elehienov. Give thanks to Adonienov. Give thanks to Melekenov. Give thanks to Moshiya'anov.

Bless Adononov. Bless Elehienov. Praise Melekenov. Praise Moshiaya'anov.

You are the power. You are the strength. You dwell in the great kingdom. You are the splendor. You are the glory. You dwell in the glory of the kingdom. You are the strength. You are the power. You dwell in the glory and the strength. You are great and make miracles.

You are Elohim. You are blessed. The Lord blesses. You create the heavens and the name of names. All hosts of the Earth praise the Lord El, first and last. You are the Lord. The beginning of all beginnings and end of all endings. You are the strength of great power and deliverance of the Lord of hosts. Happy is man to have faith in you.

Rabbi Ishma'al speaks. I see you dwelling upon the high and lofty throne. Rise up and hosts serve before you, from the right side and left side. Speak to me. The angel prince faces the name Metatron Ruoch, Mieseqoniech, Pheseqien, Atemon, Hiegeron, Siegedon, Sereton, Seniegeron, Mieqon, Chesekos, Sethiem, Heshekem, Cheqierien, Na, Doqierien, Ziena, Reba, Nenetosh, Zenetoph, Hekieqem.

Of Rabbi Ishma'al, how much is the measure of God? Conceal from all the human beings. Divide the feet [or soles of feet]. Fill all the universe. All speak of the heavens as the throne and the Earth is the footstool. Hew divisions [or the height of every sole] of three myriads thousand divisions.

Of the sole of the foot of the right side, the name is Pheresiemiya Atereqetet. Of the left side, the name is Agethemen.

From the soles of the feet until the ankles are 1,000 myriad and 500 divisions of height. Thus of the left side of the ankles.

Of the right side, the name is Thetzenenethenieh Teshesheqes. The name of the left side is Asethemen.

From the ankles until the knees are 19,400 divisions of height, and thus of the left side.

Of the leg of the left side, the name is Qenegegi Meheriech Teseseqos. The name of the right side is Memena Vozoviya.

From the knees until the thighs are 12,000 myriad divisions and 1,004 divisions of height. Thus the name of the left side is Menehebov Heriech.

The name of the thigh of the right side is Sheshephoseth Phereseb. The name of the left side is Thepheget Chezieza.

From the thighs until the neck [or back] are 24,000 myriad divisions. The name is Motheni Motheniyov, and the name is Motheniyehov Athesegeh Yidiedieh.

Over the heart are 70 names[1] written:

TzTz TzDQ TzChIAL TzOR TzBI TzDIQ SAaP SRAaP BOChN
TzBAOTh ShDI ALHIM IH OHI TzCh DGOL OADOM SSS
AaAA AAA AIA AHO RBIH HH HO OH TzTzTz PPP KN ChH
ChI ChI ChI ROKB AaRBOTh IH HH OH MMM NNN HOO
IH ChPTz HTzTz AI ZA ThAaA AAaA QQQ QShR RZ ZK
GBOR IA IA IOD HAN ALP DIMN PAP KOP RAO III IIA KBB
TTT BKK PLL SIIM AOThIOTh BShB MLO

The neck is 13,000 myriad and 800 divisions of height. The name is Seneniehov Vobehethieqen. The curve of the head is 300,000 myriad, of three and one third divisions. The mouth is not able to speak and the ear not able to hear. The name is Ather Hoderieh A'atesieh A'atetieh.

The chin is one myriad and one thousand and 500 divisions. The name is Hedereq Semiya.

See the face. See the jaws as the image of Ruoch. Fortify the Neshemah. Not every creature is able to remember bodies as Tharshish. The shining brilliance enlightens from the midst of darkness. Clouds and fog surround the sign. Of every prince, face the Seraphim. Speak before, not to measure these names written to us. Bind the name Legebethiyiya and the name Aberegeg Tetephiyiyeh.

Of the tongue, from one end of the universe until the other. Speak in the presence of Jacob. All who sleep are not revealed. Seal the scripture. Speak in the presence of Jacob. The name is Asesegiyiyehov Voayiyia.

---

[1]There are actually 72 names here.

Of the forehead, the name is Mesesegiyiyihov Yinayiyia Negem. Upon the forehead is written (Hebrew letters: IIHO HH IOH OIH HA HI HI HI HA HH OOH III HO OIHO HH IH AI HH IH IH IA HO HO IIHII HIH IHO HS HA HIH OIH).

The black [pupil] in the eye of the right side is one myriad and one thousand and 500 divisions, and thus of the left side. The name of the right side is Azeriyiyeh Azeriyiyeh Atetietos. The name of the prince is Rehebial. Over the name is Shehoval Metet Gerophemetzia. Of purification, go forth from the illumination of all creatures.

The white in the eye of the right side is two and twenty myriad and two divisions, and thus of the left side. The name is Bezeqocha.

From the shoulder of the right side until the shoulder of the left side is 16,000 myriad divisions. The name of the shoulder of the right side is Metetegeriyaha A'anegen. The name of the left side is Thethemehieneta. Of one name (Hebrew: ShLMH INNIAL).

From the arm [or forearm] of the right side until the arm of the left side is 12,000 myriad divisions. The arms are double. The name of the arm of the right side is Geberehezeziya A'akebovi. The name of the left side is Metetegehetzetziehov.

The fingers of the right hand are 15,000 myriad divisions by every finger, and thus of the left side. The name of the right side is Thethemetzemetz Gegemoth Gegeshemesh. The name of the left side is Thetz Meph Thethemeth Agegemetz Agegemeth Voshosheniem. Thus, you appoint to go on and grow.

The palm of the right hand is 4,000 myriad divisions, and thus of the left side. The name of the right side is Hezeziya Ategeriyiyieh. The name of the left side is Ashehoziech.

The toes of the right foot are 10,000 myriad divisions by every toe, and thus of the left side. The name of the right side is Atheremetz Aderemeth Beremenem Berethehemiem Ovahoz. The name of the left side is Zekiyiyen Kezekiyiyin Hethemeth Ahoz.

You appoint the hands and go forth. Therefore, proclaim El is great, the power and glory. Speak of the Lord Elohiekem. He is the God of Gods [Elohi Helohim] and Lord of Lords [Adonai Hadoniem]. El is great, the power and glory.

Speak to me of the word. Calculate the divisions complete. How many measures of every division? The division of three miles [Mielien]. Every mile [Miel] is ten thousand cubits. Every cubit is two spans [Zerethoth]. The span fills all the universe. All speak, who measures by that over the sea and heaven. Establish by the span.

Rabbi Nathan is the disciple of Rabbi Ishma'al. He speaks of the nose of the face. Of Nathan, measure from the right side and measure from the left side. Thus of the lips and jaws of Nathan. Measure the forehead of Nathan, every cubit, whom the Lord adorns.

The width of the forehead is as the eyebrow to the neck. Thus the shoulder as the point of the nose. The point of the nose is the point of the small finger. The height of the jaws is half the curve of the head. Thus measures every man.

The lips are 77 divisions. The name of the higher lip is Tiya. The name of the lower lip is Hezereniya.

Of the mouth, fire consumes fire. Deliver Aleph from the word. Of the name Akedera, who desires to present as an ornament.

The crown [Kether] is beginning 500,000 over 500,000, and the name (Hebrew: IISh).

The precious stone is between the rays. The name (Hebrew: IISh) is with (Hebrew: ALI). There is with (Hebrew: ALI) engraved (Hebrew: AaLIH DODI) of the white and red banner.

The Merkabah begins in gold. Of fine gold [Phez] locks of curly hair.

The eye is established over the horizon of the sea, as a fragrant flower bed. Two thousand myriad divisions of all not sealed in scriptures. Be as a fragrant flower bed of the greatest aromatic perfumes. The lips are as lilies. Of myrrh dripping, passing over the hand. The gold ring is filled, as Tharshish in the womb, ivory covered by sapphires.

Stand and rejoice, as instructed. Of Adonai, fine gold appears as white [Lebenon]. The young man percieves sweetness and all desire that love [DODI] and that beloved [RAaI] sons of Jerusalem.

AGTIH TChON IChON TOB THOR IOD IOD IOD IHIH ChSIN ChSIN.

Holy, holy, holy. The Lord of hosts fills all the Earth with glory.

The eyebrows measure the eye of the right side. The name is Heder Vovoled. The name of the left side is Aphedeh Tzetziehov.

The height of the ears are as the height of the forehead of the right side. The name is Atzethiyiya. The name of the left side is Megogehov Tzetziya.

Obtain all the measures of every myriad. A myriad myriads of thousands of divisions in height and a thousand thousands of myriads of divisions in width.

Rabbi Ishma'al speaks, as speaking the word before Rabbi A'aqiba. Speak to me of all who know to measure that formed. Praise God for covering the creatures. Know of security, and understand what is to come in the world. It shall be good in the world. Know of the good coming in the world and the length of days in the world.

Speak to me of Rabbi Ishma'al before the disciple. I and Rabbi A'aqieba combine the word this by that. All who know measures of the formed, praise God. Of security, understand (Hebrew: HAaHB). The second letters change in every day.

Establish to fill (Hebrew: KRSIO) of fire. (Hebrew: DTh BG BG GB HOMG.) The name of the locks of hair. Establish the name (Hebrew: DBR BRIR DOKN). There is half. Call the name (Hebrew: GL ShRB).

One eye sees from one end of the universe until the other. The name is Akeseseth. It is necessary to go forth from illumination to all the creatures. One eye sees afterward, of what exists eternally.

Of the name Atenoneseth, the body resembles an arch. The arch resembles the name Leqeseshiya. Divide the name Men Kemetz. The name Cherebov Metzemetzieth Metziya.

Of the throne of glory, the name is Dorekez Phierota. Of the dwelling place, the name is Dorephez Pherorephez. Thus call by the name. The feet of the glory of lives [Chiyoth].

The living serve below the foot of the first throne, that it is living. The name is A'ageliyov Chetzebiyiyeh. Of the foot of the second throne, it is living. The name is Bekebeb Phelebiyiyepheti. Of the foot of the third throne, it is living. The name is Kekebeb Alegiyi. Of the foot of the fourth throne. it is living. The name is Atzekiyiya Bezekez. The name is Alegiyi.[2]

---

[2]The second name here was probably added by the editor of the 1701 edition, possibly due to a contradiction in the different manuscripts he was compiling.

Of the image of the faces, the seal of the lion, the seal of the eagle, the image of the bull. The face of man conceals four faces. One of four faces and four faces to every face. Of sixty and four faces to every life. Four faces and four corners to one and four corners to corner. Four corners to faces and faces to corner and corner sixty and four faces to every life.

Of the prince of the face of the man, the names are Alieh, Ametzeb, Ametz, Ameth, Kemetz.

Of the prince of the face of the lion, the names are Hodov, Dieh, Hiedova'ah, Al, Avoriya, Hod, Hoviyeh, Themegemetz.

Of the prince of the face of the bull, the names are Alieh, Tzemetzememeba, Mesekiya.

Of the prince of the face of the eagle, the names are A'aphephi, Alieh, Memetzieth, Tzehorierial.

The sin offering of Israel covers the face of the bull, and the Cherub comes below.

Of the prince of the face of the Cherub, the names are Temetemeni, Alieh, Kerobieh, Kerobeh, Phesephesiech, Heneqeneqiya.

Of them, speak, they are holy. Speak, it is blessed to speak. Declare words to Jacob. Of all who are not sealed in Sepher Berashith, in order to work Berashith. Here prosper in the beauty of God. Beauty fills all hosts.

Thunder and storms are from the right side. Support the storm from the left side. Omens of the storm come before. In the midst are signs of brilliance. Of darkness and clouds and fog and mud mire. Before strengthen between star to star, the source of lightning. Between lightning to lightning. Of the gate of Heshemel, of spirits above, and thunder and sounds and lightning and the shell of the arch and vapor [Hebeliem] belonging to the seal. Ascend and descend therein over God. The grace and mercy and glory and compassion and splendor and crown and honor and beauty and majesty.

Of the hand of God and the name Metatron, speak of power and strength. Speak of holiness and blessing. Speak, there is not tumult before. Serve before being cast out. Metatron comes forth.

Place before the name (Hebrew: HQBH AHH). Of praise and beauty, speak, blessed is the glory of the Lord from the name (Hebrew: IHO HO HO IOHO IHIIH). Blessed is the glory of the Lord from the name. Thus speaking after, blessed is the glory of the Lord from the name (Hebrew: OBShKMLO).

Gather before and below the throne of the glory. Go forth from the right side. Separate fire and stones of hail and the wall of darkness. Of Ruoch, the left side goes to the corners of the storm and strength of the tempest.

Gather Metatron before God, below the throne of the glory. From great strength of the corners, every angel ministers before God. Speak, El is great, the power and glory. In praise of God, speak three times every day for eighty days.

Of Metatron, God gives from the splendor and glory. Metatron is over the ministering angels. It is written, the great prince is over all the princes and over every angel ministering.

Serve before and serve above. In the heights, minister before Adam. Fire consumes fire. Of the throne, the name of Moses by the prince Metatron.

It is written, by one letter, create heaven and Earth. Seal in the ring (Hebrew: AHIH AShR AHIH). It is written in seven letters. Of seven letters of 24 signs and 70 names and seven most holy. Give over six from the names. Engrave upon twelve stones.

It is written in seven sounds by six over six high. Give in the innermost chamber [Chederi Chederiem], by the secret of secrets [Setheri Setheriem] and the miracle of miracles [Phelayi Phelayiem]; but only to Rabbi [Rebienov] Moses.

God did not give domain, nor allow to make use of by Adam, the first man, and not to Shem, son of Noah, and not to Abraham, and not to Isaac, and not to Jacob, but to Moses alone.

Speak, here I am. Send forth the angel and the brilliance of God. Moses keeps it therein. Speak, keep therein and listen to the sound. El rises up as smoke therein. Do not rise up in rebellion in heaven.

Moses draws near and speaks before God. When not facing him, El goes forth to rise up. The Malachim come forth and circle before the throne of the glory on one side. Lives are from one side. Shekinah over Shekinah. The glory is in the center.

One life rises over the Seraphim and descends from the Shekinah. Metatron speaks in a great sound and small silence. The throne of the glory is silent at once. The Avophanim are silent and also the Malachim. Of the strongest cities, the most holy silence and weaken the river of fire.

Lives give faces by the Earth. Metatron comes forth as fire in silence. Give in the ears of lives, in order not to hear the sound of the glory of God. Of you, the Shem Hemaphorash. (Hebrew: HTTTRON.)

Remember by the sign of the hour. Thus proclaim to God by the name of the life of the pure and the holy. Of the greatness and the glory and the strength and the power and the love and the might and honor and splendor.

ADRIHO AHRKI HChII IHOH AHIH AShR AHIH HChI IOM HKH HH OH HOH OHO HH HIA HOA HH IHI HI HI IHIH IHOH.

Of the everlasting Lord, the name is remembered from generation to generation, divided in portions in clear language.

IHO HHIO HIH HI IH IH HOHI HIH OIHIO IHO HChI OIHH IHI HI HHIO HII HO IHOH IHO HIHO HI IHOH.

Blessed is the name of the glory of the kingdom forever and ever.

By commandment of Adonienov, righteous host of Israel, hope and expect righteousness is with you. Be righteous and rise up in rightousness. Rise up in exaltation to you. Burst into song from the mouth. Answer and speak. The Lord Adonienov. What mighty name is in all the Earth? Praise the splendor over the heavens.

You are holy and your name is holy. You are mighty and your name is mighty. You are strong and your name is strong. You are true and your name is true. You are blessed and your name is blessed. You are chosen and your name is chosen. You are great and your name is great. You are power and your name is power. You are exalted and your name is exalted. You are praised and your name is praised. You are honored and your name is honored. You are ancient and your name is ancient. You are eternal and your name is eternal.

You are pure and your name is pure. You are refined and your name is refined. You are mighty and your name is mighty. You are life and your name is life. You are pure and your name is pure. You are precious and your name is precious. You are upright and your name is upright. You are unique and your name is unique.

You are great and your name is great. You are flame and your name is flame. You are high and your name is high. You are pleasure and your name is pleasure. You are glory and your name is glory. You are desire and your name is desire. You are revered and your name is revered. You are tolerance and your name is tolerance. You are upheld and your name is upheld. You are power and your name is power. You are wondrous and your name is wondrous. You are splendor and your name is splendor. You are righteous and your name is righteous. You are pure and your name is pure. You are holy and your name is holy. You are compassion and your name is compassion. You are beauty and your name is beauty. You are Almighty and your name is Almighty. You are perfect and your name is perfect. Blessed are you, the holy Lord El. Amen.

Give praise above. Adore and exalt. Of the unity of the everlasting image, the Lord is over all the universe. The Lord is over all creatures and all the lives of the living souls [Nepheshoth Chi Hechiyiyim], first and last.

Of the song of the Lord, the majesty of the king. Be clothed in the vestment of the Lord. Strengthen the fetters. Also establish the world [Thebel] is not to shake. Establish the everlasting throne. You raise the rivers. The Lord raises up the sound of the rivers. The great rivers rise up from the sounds of the great sea. The most powerful waves of the great sea.

In the heights, the Lord witnesses the most faithful dwelling in the most holy house of the Lord. Enlighten the days. Sing of the love [or the Song of David]. Deliver to the Lord. Build strength and deliver to the Lord the glory and strength. Deliver to the Lord the glory of the name. Bow down to the Lord in the splendor.

The holy voice of the Lord is over the sea. Of the glory, the desires of the Lord. Over the great sea, the voice of the Lord. By the power of the voice of the Lord, the glory of the voice. Of the grain of cedar trees, the Lord strengthens the white cedar tree. Leap up as a white calf. A coat of armor as in oryx [Ramiem]. The voice of the Lord hews flames of fire.

The voice of the Lord strengthens from the word. Strengthen the Lord from the holy word. The voice of the Lord strengthens trees and strips bare the wood.

In the palace, all speak of the glory of the Lord. Of the deluge, to dwell. Dwell the Lord, king of the universe. The Lord of the strength of the nation. Give the Lord to bless your nation in peace.

Sing of the love of the Lord of the Earth. Fill the world and dwell in it. Over the foundation of seas and over rivers, establish who climbs up the mountain of the Lord. Who rises up in the holy place with clean soles and pure heart. Do not bear falsehoods of Nephesh. Do not make the oath to deceive.

Rise up and you are blessed from the Lord. To the righteous, Elohi gives salvation to the generations. Seek in petition. Face Jacob and rise up to two gates. Of the first, rise up the gate of the universe. Come forth the glory of the king. Who is he that is king? Of the glory of the Lord, mighty and strong. The Lord of the strength of hosts. Rise up to two gates first.

Rise up to the gate of the universe. Come forth the glory of the king. Who is he that is king? The glory of the Lord of hosts. He is king. The glory rises up.

The Lord blesses you. Create the heaven of heavens. Of the heavens and all hosts of the Earth, all rise up in the days. Of all in them, you are life and you complete. Of the host of the heavens, you are worshipped.

You are the Lord Elohim, that chose Abram to go forth from the light of prosperity. There is the name Abraham. Reach your heart, faithful before.

Of the covenant of the people, the covenant gives you the Earth. Of the Kena'ani [Cannanite], Hechethi [name of a people, the second son of Cannan], the Amorites, the Perizzites, the Yibosi [ancient name of Jerusalem], and the Geregeshi [name of a Cannanite nation]. Spread the seed and rise up by your words, that you are righteous.

You are the Lord. The great and the strength and the beauty and the victory and the splendor is in heaven and Earth. You are the Lord of the kingdom. All rise up to begin. You hold dominion over all through power and strength, greatness and might over all. You are Elohino. We praise you and praise for the sake of beauty. Blessed is the name of the glory of the heights above.

Of every blessing, the splendor forms mercy. One thousand rise up in sin and iniquity, of atonement and purity. The Lord Elohim Shaddai of hosts.

IH AHH IHA IH AHIH AShR AHIH IHOH IHOH AL.

Of compassion and mercy, you are slow to anger. Of great mercy and truth extolled. I pray to the power of compassion. Of sadness and anger and wrath, pass in the distance from it.

Serve to understand the truth. Of Phelonieth, all to me. From every house and from you. From cities and divisions, let there be compassion. The Lord above shows pity and is merciful above.

All speak of the Lord Elohim, and your prayer comes before. Worship to dwell in heaven. Dwell in the highest heaven. Derephed Pheloni guides in the deserts. Dwell in the habitation.

Dwell in the habitation. Dwell in the sky and dwell upon the throne of compassion.

In the seventh firmament, all light is sevenfold. The light shines on all the habitations. Therein is the throne of the glory. Establish over four lives in glory. Therein is the storehouse of lives [Chiyiyim] and storehouse of souls [Nepheshoth]. It is unfathomable.

In the world, the great illumination is therein. From the great light, illuminate the Earth. Malachim are bound to serve light, light as light shining and not extinguished. See it as the movement of a ship.

Of lightning, serve over the rising light. It is most wondrous. Come to the dwelling of the high and lofty throne. Rise up that it is alone. There is no limit and there is no end.

Before the rivers of fire, bind and rise up to dwell. Rise up in silence to serve. From the sound, the nations tremble. The powers extend to serve before. Do not behold the images facing. Conceal from all.

Of the sign, not able to see. Of the unity, images from all hidden. All images are not hidden in the most profound book. Divide darkness and go forth to light. In the shadows, know what is secret in darkness. The light is of splendor.

By completion, aid the light. Dwell in the light of the throne. See around is the light of lives. The Aophanim rise up.

Of the darkness are the six corners. In the corners, cover the face. Below give faces. Of four faces facing. Do not rise above faces from fear and terror.

Of hills [Gebiehem] serve before breaking into pieces. Be immersed in the river in purity, wrapped in white coverings. Dwell by the sound of strength and power.

Holy, holy, holy. The hosts fill all the Earth with glory. It is the place of all the works. It precedes all the universe and precedes the Garden of Eden. Also, until heaven and Earth. It is alone and there is no limit and no ending without.

Be suspended by the strength in the habitation. In all dwellings, revere by the Ruoch. The mouth is established and glory is established. It is one. There is not two. There is no equal. There is nothing to compare. There is none except. There is none without.

Of the word, there is no end to the life of the king of kings of Malachim. God is king over every king of the Earth. Rise up over every angel in heaven. Search the hearts until not formed. Know thoughts until not existing.

In the name of the Lord, be blessed with honor and glory of the universe forever and ever. Eternal victory forever. Follow eternally, as there is no universe if there is no Elohim.

By the sound, the earth trembles. Mountains move forth and mountains dissolve. Of anger, by the wrath of the power of the sea. Travel and serve in the world. Proclaim, all rise up in strength. Hidden from the eye, all life dwells in the throne of the glory of the great holy kingdom.

Travel and serve in the world. Travel all the world. Do not be visible. Know all the most secret things. Know what is in darkness. Change the shadows of dawn. Illuminate night as day. All the most secret things are revealed by the Sun. Be in wonder from the word.

The holy king journeys over wings of the wind. He holds dominion in all worlds. Do not turn away from [him]. The Sun and Moon and all planets and all signs of the zodiac worship him. It is revealed in the Garden of Eden, plant the Tree of Life in the garden.

Blessed is the name in every generation. From blessing in the habitation above the ancient [A'athieq]. Of the ancient and righteous, blessed is the glory of the place. From blessing, proclaim to fill in beauty. From understanding of knowledge of creation, search and reveal. Thus, reverence of the name.

Blessed is the name. Proclaim in the habitation. From the blessing, strength in beauty.

Blessed is the name. Come forth snow from the blessing. The river in flames.

Blessed is the name. Splendor in darkness. From the blessing, splendor and glory in the habitation.

Blessed is the name. Guide in deserts. From the blessing, thousands upon thousands.

Blessed is the name. Be fettered from the blessing, of cords of flame [Mietheri Leheboth].

Blessed is the name. The sound of thunder. From the blessing, lightning rushes forth.

Blessed is the name. All in Earth. From the blessing, oceans in Earth.

Blessed is the name. All in deserts. From the blessing, waves in the sea.

Blessed is the name. Alone on the throne. From the blessing, dwell in strength.

Blessed is every Neshemah. From the blessing, every creature.

Blessed is the name forever and ever. From the blessings, forever and ever.

Blessed is the Lord of the universe, amen and amen, hallelujah.

The scholar forsakes [Beni Thorethi Tha'azob] the commandments. Conceal your punishment [Moser]. The Lord El condemns and El abhors, in punishment. Keep the commandments and laws as the apple of the eye. Do not remove the covering [Kepher] of the Torah.

Of retribution, and lamentation in day and night for the sake of keeping, create all written therein. Thus succeed upon your paths and thus prosper. Is it not so, appointing strength and power? El strengthens. El is below the nation.

Of the Lord Elohiek, all go forth in the day. Appoint the mercy of the Lord. In night, sing in prayer to El. Blessed is the everlasting name in the great kingdom.

ARIOHO AHRKO HChII IHOH AHIH AShR AHIH IHOH OAI HBH HH OH HO HH HI HH IHI HI HI HI HOTh.

Of the everlasting name of the universe, remember from generation to generation.

BShKMLO IHI HHIO HIH HI IH HH HO HI HOH OIHIO IHO HHI OHI HH IH IHI HO HHIO HII HO IHOH IHO HHO HI HOH.

Blessed is the name of glory, the Kingdom forever and ever. By the name, thus great. Of greatness, thus glory. Of glory, thus majesty. Of majesty, thus holy. Of holiness, thus beauty. Of beauty, thus light now. Of light now, thus light then. Of light then, thus great mercy. Of great mercy, thus power. Of power, thus exaltation. Of exaltation, thus great. Of greatness, thus great compassion. Of great compassion, thus goodness. Of goodness, thus compassion over all works.

To you, beauty of the glory of the name, great and strong. Of the kingdom and the beauty and the victory and the splendor, all in heaven and in Earth. The name is from it. Thus, the name of glory in the universe. The name of glory forever and ever.

The highest blessing is of the name. Of the name of splendor, of the holy name, praise the name. The highest name is over every blessing. In prayer, the name is as thus. The name is before all. Establish the name forever and ever.

Establish the name. From the name, armies [Gedodi] tremble. From the glory of the name, hew flame. Praise the name. The Seraphim praise the name of the lives of the most holy. The name Aophanim is from the name of purity. The name makes you over all the creatures.

Of the name, receive from the name. The sea rises up hereafter. All waves and undulations are from the great name. All dwell above. Every habitation and dwelling trembles and shakes.

In heaven and Earth, dwell with the Lord [Derieh]. Of the ocean and the desert [Tzieh], hell [Abaddon] and shadows [Tzelemoth], man and beast, mountains and valleys and hills, seas and rivers. Of fire, hail and snow and vapor of the great Ruoch. The angel of fire and angel of water.

Tremble from the name. All Neshemeth, Ruoch, Chiyiyem. Thus establish the glory of the name. I, David Ben Zelateh, serve. Dust and ashes afflict the heart of the humble, Ruoch is appointed. Of worms, shadows pass over the field.

Come forth to fall in supplication. Of prayers before, obtain grace in the eyes. Of grace and mercy and righteousness and compassion before the throne of the glory of the kingdom. You draw near to every proclamation and commandment.

All seek glory in holiness. You fill with compassion. You are pure and upright. Mercy and compassion are to you who are pure and good. Rise up, you who are pure. Make prayers and petition and supplication before the throne of glory. Open to me. David Ben Zelateh serves. The gate is prayer. The gate is answer. The gate is understanding. The gate is wisdom. The gate is knowledge. The gate is righteousness. The gate is compassion. The gate is reverence of heaven. The gate is blessing. The gate is supporting and maintaining.

It is written in the book, of the living nation of the most righteous. Give thanksgiving and be great of the lives of goodness for the sake of the glory of the great name, the power and glory.

The divisions are the mighty and the powerful and the strong and the wondrous and the holy and the secret and the honor. Holy, holy, holy. The Lord of hosts fills all the Earth in glory.

The angel host gives honor to you and strengthens you. Adorns you and protects you. You are to be holy and you exalt. You rejoice and entice in song. You praise the splendor in song. Sing blessings of praise [Shebech] and praise [Helel] and praise [Qelos] of splendor [Theheleh] in thanksgiving of freedom and victory.

Play the music. The sound is exaltation. Rejoice in joyfulness and merriment. Sing and reply in answer. Of beauty and righteousness is truth. Be upright and rejoice of the great glory and mighty stength. Rise above in wonder. Salvation is in the quiet resting place. Be in comfort and calm, in peace and serenity, in security and goodness, in love and desire.

Redemption is in grace and mercy and beauty. In the light of day, desire redemption in glory. In purity, the brilliance of shining radiance. Be adorned in shining light emanating outward. Be adorned in shining light. As spice from salt, light illuminates. Of power and majesty and glory and strength, hold dominion and strengthen. Rise up to the heights.

Of brilliance, holiness, and purity. Of purity, mighty strength, and great power. Of the majesty of the kingdom, in splendor and glory. The crown is majesty. The crown is most glorious. It is pleasant there. Remember it is pleasant and the splendor of it. The splendor of the beauty of it.

Desire the glory. Minister from desires before. There is wondrous power in the presence of the king of kings of the Malachim, the God of Gods [Elohi Helohiem] and Lord of Lords [Adonai Hadonaiem]. Go around by binding the kingdom. Surround in the branches.

In the presence of shining light, cover with splendor. Cover heaven in the splendor. Brilliance comes from the heights. From the mouth, burn the oceans. Describe the splashing in the majesty of the skies. Of deliverance, appear perennially from the dispersion. Tremble and flames push forth to divide all formed.

Rejoice by singing the song. It is required to rejoice. Words drop down in heaven. Push out and go forth as burning in flames of fire. Be happy in the morning in tranquillity. Establish love of the king.

Of desire, the pure are lifted over all. Be lifted up high from the splendor above. Generation to generation rise over, constantly, perennial in the heights. Over the most glorious praise of the king in splendor.

Draw near the exaltation of the holy. It is common to all. By expectation, by the good name, by every upright path in all works. Pleasure is in all vestments. Be pure by counsel.

By the knowledge of the ages, by understanding of the actions, judge all the Neshemah until every word. Of judgment by every word, power is in wisdom of every mystery. Be skillful in purity and all holy.

The true king. The one king of eternal life. The king of death and life. The king is creator of every plague and creator of every cure. The king is creator of every blessing. Establish all goodness. The king is pure in all works and maintains all creation. The king is high and lofty. Of all the low and all mighty power, the king is high and exalted and sublime. Of honor and glory, desire strength and highest power. Of the nation, holy and pure, righteous and upright, faithful and pious, great and strong.

Thus, constantly dwell upon the lofty throne. Rise up by the great strength, honor, and glory. It rises over all. Bind splendor and desire over every crown. Be praised in the splendor of the majesty of the palace. Conceal and cover, and see the most profound.

In every place is the name. Do not dwell over words, not hereafter with desire. Wish not to flow and not to take flight from it and not to conceal it. Reign eternally. Reign upon the throne from generation to generation.

The king of mercy and compassion forgives. Dance in a circle. Pass to honor in every song. Honor in every desire. Rise up in the palace by exaltation. Bear all splendor to exalt in all the workings. Dwell over all creations. Be honored upon the throne of glory. Be honored over all precious things. Be blessed in all the blessings. Be praised in all the praises [Hethoshebechoth]. Be praised [Thethehelel] in every praise [Qelos]. Be praised [Thetheqelos] in all the great things. Be great eternally. Be holy forever and ever.

(Hebrew: TTRIM IHOH). Elohim of Israel. King over all. Eternal Lord [Adon] of all the works of wisdom by all mysteries. Hold dominion by all the spirits. Elohim and prince. Eternal Lord of all the works. The one king rises up in eternal victory.

Let there be the name from the blessing forever and ever, eternally. The king proclaims (Hebrew: TTRSIO IHOH). Elohi of Israel. The Lord of Lords. Praise the throne of glory. You give majesty and strength. You dwell in strength and beauty. You are strong. You are power. You restore. You rejoice [Yirenenov]. You are praised [Yishemechov]. You are blessed. You are praised [Yishebechov]. You raise up. You are adorned. You bring forth. You are great. You are honored. You sing. You are one. You are serene. You are praised [Yiqelesov]. You are crowned. You are victory. You are praised [Yiselselov]. You are exalted. You are holy. You are praised [Yihelelov]. You sing. You are desire.

You are (Hebrew: TTRSII). You are the Lord Elohi of Israel. Honor the Seraphim. You declare greatness. You are (Hebrew: TTRSII IHOH). Elohi of Israel ministering. You crown with crowns [Ketheriem]. Sing to you the new song and reign forever. Hold dominion over all kingdoms. The elders are united forever and ever.

(Hebrew: TTRSI IHOH.) Elohi of Israel. Of eleven kings over all the mysteries. Lord of all the secret things.

God proclaims you are Na'ar [youth]. Thus he proclaims, you travel and wander. Call out the name. Hew from flames of fire in the desert. From generation to generation is the name of Na'ar. Do not slay the guilty. The first goes forth. The second passes over from seeing the strength. Below resembles this of that. From seeing the strength, above there is none resembling.

The name of Na'ar is as the name of Rebov. Speak of who examines therein, the name of God of 72 letters. Of the name of Na'ar, 72 letters rise up. Twenty-six letters descend. Twenty-six letters of the glory of Elohim is the secret word.

In order not to cast out from the universe, 72 of the young king [Meleka A'alema]. From here and henceforth you do not hold domain over the word.

Thus, it is written in the book. To turn away is incomprehensible. You do not inquire. Cover you from above. Investigate that which is to reveal the knowledge. Do not be concerned by secrets.

One by one, turn that which changes. Do not inquire. Reveal in three. Not in the work of Berashith in two. Not by Merkabah, even though it is in unity, but only wisdom. From understanding of knowledge, be instructed of its first nature.

The name illuminates the eyes. Understand what is spoken in the beginning. Understand (Hebrew: HI) goes forth from (Hebrew: IOD ShBALBM). Come up to (Hebrew: IOD ShBALBM HI).

Go forth from the seven. From the seven (Hebrew: ShBAChS). From (Hebrew: LMD ShBALBM). Come up to (Hebrew: IOD ShBAChS). This is facing.

Go forth from (Hebrew: IOD). From (Hebrew: GH ShBAChS) and from (Hebrew: LMR ShBALBM). Come to (Hebrew: IOD ShBAChS).

Here is the Shem Hemaphorash. (Hebrew: BAI AMH AQBO) is over the word of the holy name.

Speak, desire to establish, to reveal, to descend and ascend. Of the sons of Israel, designate to me three blessings by six [B"D] above and six below. All are secondary in order of the work of Berashith. Designate to it blessing in every day. Of day, six is above and six is below.

In the house of rejoicing [Beth Sheshoniem] are over myriad blessings. Also, that I love you, the redeemer [Phodeh].

All who desire the wisdom every day, receive the book. Proclaim therein from the beginning until the end. When the book is within the house, do not fall therein fire. Do not perish. Do not be destroyed. Do not turn away. You regard the name of the minister above.

Petition that the dream is proven. From the experience, bathe the hands in purity. Draw the hands to the left by the water lily [Mi

Chebetzeleth]. It is written, above is the Lord. Thus, the dwelling of the most holy Malachim. The names come forth.

Show me all petition by divisions. When speaking, increase the interpretation of the dream. At this time, know when to answer. Make mercy and show me the truth.

(Hebrew: AAA SSS NTzCh NTzCh NTzCh.) Lie upon the right side. It is good to be on the left. See and be amazed.

Petition the dream is proven from the experience. Fast for three days in purity and humility and reverence. Be clothed in linen vestments. Be cleansed from all defilement. Purify the body for three days. Of the second, third, and fourth day, do not eat until the fifth day. On the fifth night, light the lamp in the house. Lie upon the ground in the middle of the house upon the face. Let there be light of the lamp. Speak in petition and make an oath.

In adjuration by the Shem Hemaphorash, dwell in the darkness of the highest heaven. You come in the night, by eye and mouth and heart complete. Do not come forth, but only in love. Speak the petition to me. That is what I seek. Explain to me the petition, as when Gabriel explained to increase the dream of the Pharoah. The words are true. Thus come forth in the night in truth.

Conceal me in petition. Petition in the name of the prince Metatron by the Shem Hemaphorash. Dwell over the wheel of the Merkabah in the name of life. Establish to dwell in deserts. By Yod Heh is the name.

Rejoice before, in the name of the great El, the power and glory. He is love and desire and faithfulness. Make the oath to the prince Metatron by (Hebrew: AHIH AShR AHIH). It is revealed to Moses, son of A'amerem, from the midst of the bush [Heseneh]. Eleven disciples [Lemedeni] are appointed by the name divided in 70 languages. Of the robe [Hema'ayileh] in 70 languages.

Rise up by 70 names, from the seventh letter in the name, to tremble. You are in the universe. From the name, Gedodi tremble, the highest and lowest. Of wrath, the earth trembles. The people do not endure the wrath. Blessed is the glory of the Lord.

Of the name (Hebrew: OBShKMLO), the adjuration over the prince Metatron by the name. God [Elohi] of Israel, God of Abraham, Isaac, and Jacob. By the name, the Malachim establish to precede. (Hebrew: ALHA RBA.)

The seven Malachim are Michael, Gabriel, Raphael, A'anial, Yi-etzorial, Turiel, and A'azial. They are over the name and over the truth of the name, in mercy and compassion.

Of the name (Hebrew: BShKMLO), the adjuration over the prince Metatron. By the name, the princes are appointed over the four seasons of the year.

In the first are Norial and Tzedeqial. In the second are A'azial and Samael. In the third are Zebedial and Semenial. In the fourth are Gabriel and Raphael. Ashebiereh Hesheron rule in every season of the year.

Of the adjuration, the sign of the prince Metatron is by the blessed name. From the blessing of the name, in the heights over every blessing.

Begin by the name. Thus the name is before all. Establish the name forever and ever. Serve the name. From the name, Gedodi tremble, highest and lowest. Of the most magnificent [Mephariem] name. Of every Gedodi above. Of every most magnificent name. Do not regard the name. All tremble.

The sea flows in reverse from reverence of the name. All the most powerful waves are of the magnificent name. The earth trembles by regarding it. Serve the Lord. Shake in fear from the name. Over every name of the world. (Hebrew: ODIIRI.) The world trembles in fear from the name. (Hebrew: ODIIRI.) Thehom and Ab-badon and the shadow of death flow from the name. In the Garden of Eden, all pious shout for joy of the name. Of all Neshemeth, Ruoch and Chiyiyim in the nose.

By desire, the language gives glory to the name. Give glory to the name. I am as dust and ashes cast forth. Worms smite the heart.

Of the Ruoch of the humble, cover until, as a flower of the field, you cast down to be humble before. Petition compassion before the throne of glory. You draw near to every proclamation and commandment. Seek to make prayer in petition by desire before. Hasten the petition in compassion. Make desire that you created after.

Of all desire, let there be below. Of compassion, forgive the sin. Do not defile. Many return in anger. Do not designate all anger. The Lord descends in clouds formed from the Ruoch above. Give over seventy men, the elders. Let there be quiet above the Ruoch. Prophesy and do not fail.

The Lord passes over, above the surface and proclaims, three [G'] forms mercy to thousands. Of three, pardon sins. Of three, forgiveness in the nation. Of three, the Lord hears. The Lord pardons. The Lord listens. Of three, Jacob goes forth from Bar Sheba. Of three, reach the place and remain there. Then to dream. Here stands the ladder. Of three, here is the Lord. Stand above and be spread as dust of the earth. Break forth. Of three here, we are the nation. Keep by all that to go forth. Speak, these are the complete scriptures. Let there be facing below to see desire.

This is the Shem Hemaphorash. Remember from desire in the bush. All who remember the sign over the destruction [Heshed] take flight. It is over extinguishing the fire and healing disease, and over the mountains of Tharshish.

When man remembers and writes the sign, the enemy dies, and the magistrate loves you. Remember not to proclaim the sign, but only when you are pure from all defilement.

Of all who proclaim the sign, those who are not pure will surely die. Thus the consecrations are necessary.

Of Chenial and Chesedial and Tzedeqial above, by the name reveal to me. Thus the name goes forth from three scriptures. Travel and come forth to be guided. Make a pledge [Iya'arebem] to the nation. Begin and end and begin.

This is the name of the honor and glory. It is divided into these 72 names:

OHO ILI SIT AaLM MHSh LLH AKA KHTh HZI ALD LAO
HHAa IZL MBH HRI HQM LAO KLI LOO PHL NLK III MLH
ChHO NThH HAA IRTh ShAH RII AOM LKB OShR IHO
LHCh KOQ MND ANI ChAaM RHAa IIZ HHH MIK OOL ILH
SAL AaRI AaShL MIH OHO DNI HChSh AaMM NNA NITh
MBH POI NMM IIL HRCh MTzR OMB IHH AaNO MChI
DMB MNQ AIAa ChBO RAH IBM HII MOM

(Hebrew: BShKMLO.) Blessed is the name of the glory of the kingdom forever and ever.

When petitioning to turn away the heart of the woman, not to hear; but only Eliek receives from the motion of the nose of the face. On the New Moon, take one brazen tray and inscribe the above upon the tray. (Hebrew: QSITRON) is the name of the

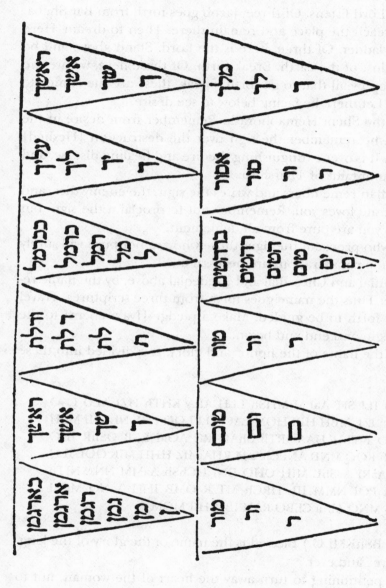

Figure 10. The upper level of "banners" translates, from right to left, as "First/rise up/as an orchard [or garden]/and a door [or gate]/first/as purple." The lower level translates, from right to left, as "King/binds/in the ceiling/arranged/concealed/changed." There are various possible interpretations. This diagram is also published in Trachtenberg's *Jewish Magic and Superstition*, page 117.

magistrate. Of the names of the Malachim, cast forth to the midst. Speak over the knowledge of the face. Of the oath, I am A'aliekem, the angel of knowledge. Change your heart. Phelonieth or Pheloni Ben Phelonieth. Do not create the word by putting it in order. Empty the heart or regard in the heart.

Take the flask and conceal it in the place of passing. It is written in the day, five in four hours in the day, that there is not five days.

Afterward, come forth to restore. These are the Malachim and the magistrate of the nation. The magistrate is Phelemiya. These are the Malachim ministering: Aberieh, Azemerehi, Demenehi, Amenehi, Aphenok, Phetebieza, Tobial, Gelial, Avophori, Gemethi, Avorenial, Menial, Vobemethov, Sereten, Tzebeqetheni, Bemerethiyas, Serephieth, Keresovien, Amaph, Phekehier, Hesethier, Setherial, Aliesen, Helesial, Soresephi, Qerekototh, Melekial, Acheseph, Amial, Pheretem, Gedial, Sebekial, Kokeb.

These are the Malchim ministering. These are the Malachim exciting your heart. Of the king and the greatest knowledge, and your human heart.

When the king desires to come forth, or when petitioning the visions of the image of love or friendship from these words, the miracles of the holy book and the glory, remember the recorded names of the most holy Malachim and the name of the magistrate, and succeed.

These are the names of the Malachim ministering with Deleqial, serving in the the three dwellings and holding dominion by flames of fire: Noreh, Avoyiel, Melekieh, Cholial, Chedial, Shelechial, Cheboval, Tzorial, Bemekial, A'aqerial, Sesenial, Benekial, Thomenal, A'amelial, Thelemeteph, Votechenial, Arephial, Agenial, Mesherial, Amenegenavoth.

Speak thus and thus create. They create and succeed only in purity.

When of desire, the house is filled with smoke and fire. The flames do not consume anything. Gather fruit [Pheriyon] and place upon the coals of fire. Smoke rises in the midst of the house. Remember the name of the magistrate and the Malachim. The smoke rises. Speak thus from the oath. I above the Malachim weaken the fire by who understands fire. Dwelling upon the throne of fire and ministering flames of fire, the host of fire ministers fire by the great name. I speak the oath. You see to rise up the greatness. Do not fear. Complete the word. See the house fill with fire.

When of desire, the fire abates. Speak from the oath. I above the most powerful angel. You extinguish the great fire. Do not serve one hour in the house. In completion, the fire abates and is extinguished quickly in the hour, without ash and without destruction. Work in purity and succeed.

These are the names of the Malachim ministering by the sixth host: Pheseker, Azial, Arebial, Teriephon, Phiekebom, Phesethemer, Lenegial, Qeronieren, Shobehen, Sebieren, A'avozial, Phenial, Therenial, Chememial, Tzehemial, Biememom, Gerezeniyiyeth, Gorenetal, Baroba, A'aremor, Heremor, Zebenos, Chesemal, Noredial, Pheniyavon, Qeremial, Bepheliyiya, Aremial, A'aremon, A'aphosal, Sepherial, Qethenial, Shebebial, Aremiyiyenos, Tophiemos, Phetzetzial, Chetephial, Pheresomon, Nechelial.

These are the Malachim, the most strong [Hegeboriem] and most powerful [Havozeriem]. Of power and strength, rush forth from place to place. Come to man upon the earth far from the house of El. Fly as one hour of the bird or in order to come to serve that to pass.

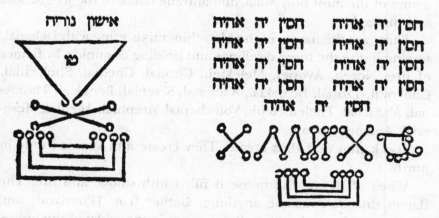

Figure 11. The talisman on the left reads, from right to left: "The little man [refers to the small image of a person as seen in the pupil of the eye] / Light of the Lord." The characters in the center are likely to be an error, and should be Tau Vau, which translates as "sign." The talisman on the right displays the word "mighty" on the far right, and the names of God to the left.

Take four brazen trays and inscribe upon every one. On one of them, the name, and the name Amov, and the name Pheseker, and the name of the Malachim ministering before. Speak correctly, I am above the angel of the strength. You are Pheloni Ben Phelonieth. You do not follow in every place. It dwells therein. Face your heart when in the city, when in the country, when on the sea, when on dry land, when eating, when drinking. You fly as a bird. Come to you not by desire. Pray to El. Tarry not in day and not in night. Place in the four corners of the house.

In the beginning is the name of the honor and the glory. Of the oath, above is Asmoday, the king of demons. Of every group, go forth to gather in groups of diseases. Of every group, go forth. Do not cast forth and do not fear. Do not be afraid. You are Pheloni Ben Phelonieth, but only by assistance and support from all misfortune and distress.

Of all who fall upon harm and all disease gather. Of Beremech Ayiberiem, by the four names of the gates [Mephethechien]. Of Diyovehen, Phethechien, Yidiehon, Segeron. Bless the Lord and enlighten the face of the Lord above. Favor Phesephesiem. Exalt the face of the Lord above. Restore peace to you.

Of adjuration above, the king is holy. Of purity, destroy and divide every man in warmth and coldness. Of every devil [Shed] and demon [Mezieq], of every binding [Ayisor] and weight [Qeshiet], of every enchantment [Chereshien] and every sorcery [Kieshophien].

Of Pheloni Ben Phelonieth, by the names Diehon, Diyavon, Shehov, Shemoth, Mepheresha, Keshemi, by the name Shel [Sh"L, or 330 names], engrave upon the crown. (Hebrew: AAA SSS.)

Of all who desire to write the amulet [Qemiya'a], it is necessary to write first the Malachim appointed over the period as thus.

In the period of Nisan, the names are Semal and A'anoval and Genesheriesh. The name of the prince is Avor Pheniek.

In the period of Tammuz, the names are Kedenial and Tzedeqial and A'akenial. The name of the prince is Abel Abehem.

In the period of Tishri, the names are Bedeqial and Ayisemerial and Gabrial. The name of the prince is Aleberiyavor.

In the period of Tebeth, the names are Gabrial and Avorial and Berekial. The name of the prince is Rebial.

Concerning the periods afterward, Nisan is Avorial. Ayer is Amerial. Sivan is ____.[3] Tammuz is Terial. Ab is Bereqial. Elul is Phenial. Tishri is Tzorial. Marheshvan is Keberial. Kislev is Adenial. Tebeth is Tzephial. Shebet is Yirial. Adir is Somial. In Adir is Sandalphon.

The first day is Ariyal. The second day is Asephenial. The third day is Ariyal. The fourth day is Hekebial. The fifth day is Yihova'ayial. The sixth day is Hederial. The seventh day is Israel.

In the period of Tishri is Gelietzor and Hederenial.
In the period of Tebeth is Berezial and Sememial.
In the period of Nisan is Semial and A'anial.
In the period of Tammuz is Nemetzial and Tzereqial.

---

[3]In the text, the two letters of the name are obscured. The visible letters are Tz**IA"L.

BOOK FIVE

THE BOOK OF THE SIGNS OF THE ZODIAC [SEPHER HEMAZELOTH]

IN THE MONTH OF NISAN, the sign of the zodiac is Aries, and Ovavorial is the angel.

In Ayer, the sign is Taurus, and the angel is Lehetial.
In Sivan, the sign is Gemini, and the angel is Phenial.
In Tammuz, the sign is Cancer, and the angel is Zorial.
In Ab, the sign is Leo, and the angel is Bereqial.
In Elul, the sign is Virgo, and the angel is Chenial.
In Tishri, the sign is Libra, and the angel is Tzorial.
In Marheshvan, the sign is Scorpio, and the angel is Gabrial.
In Kislev, the sign is Sagittarius, and the angel is Medonial.
In Tebeth, the sign is Capricorn, and the angel is Shenial.
In Shebet, the sign is Aquarius, and the angel is Gabrial.
In Adir, the sign is Pisces, and the angel is Romial.

In the first day, the planet is the Sun, and the angel is Avorial.
In the second day, the planet is the Moon, and the angel is Semal.
In the third day, the planet is Mars, and the angel is Voyieroval.
In the fourth day, the planet is Mercury, and the angel is Lehebial.
In the fifth day, the planet is Jupiter, the angel is Zieroval.
In the sixth day, the planet is Venus, and the angel is Ashedial.
In the seventh day, the planet is Saturn, and the angel is Asherial (or Israel).

In the first season, beginning with Nisan, the angel is Semal.

In the second season, beginning with Tammuz, the angels are Nemetzal and Tzedeqial.

In the third season, beginning with Tishri, the angels are Yiqemial and Yiremoth.

In the fourth season, beginning with Tebeth, the angels are Bereqial and Sememial.

(Hebrew: TAQ) creates the males from fire, and they serve in the east.

(Hebrew: ShKG) creates the females from earth, and they serve in the south.

(Hebrew: ThMD) creates the males from air, and they serve in the west.

(Hebrew: SAaD) creates the females from water, and they serve in the north.

In the day, the Sun rules in Leo.

In the day, Venus rules in Taurus, and in Libra in the night.

In the day, Mercury rules in Gemini, and in Virgo in the night.

In the day and the night, the Moon rules in Cancer.

In the day, Saturn rules in Capricorn, and in Aquarius in the night.

In the day, Jupiter rules in Sagittarius, and in Pisces in the night.

In the day, Mars rules in the horn of Aries, and in the sting of Scorpio in the night.

Of the twelve signs of the zodiac (Hebrew: TAQ) and (Hebrew: ThMD) are male, and (Hebrew: ShKG) and (Hebrew: SAaD) are female.

When a male is born in the feminine sign of the zodiac, he will not live.

When a female is born in the masculine sign of the zodiac, she also will not live.

These are the hours of the days of the week when it is suitable to engrave the amulets [Qemiya'ayien].

In the seventh hour of the first day.
In the fifth hour of the second day.
In the first hour of the third day.
In the second hour of the fourth day.
In the fourth hour of the fifth day.
In the fifth hour of the sixth day.[1]

Of the sign [Siemen] from the twelve hours (Hebrew: AB"D H"I).

These are the days of the month when it is suitable to engrave the amulets.

Anytime in the first day.
The morning of the second day.
Not on the third day.
Anytime in the fourth day.
In the morning of the fifth day.
Not on the sixth day.
In the morning of the seventh day.
In the morning of the eighth day.
Not on the ninth day.
Not on the tenth day.
In the morning of the eleventh day.
Any time in the twelfth day.
Not on the thirteenth day.
In the morning of the fourteenth day.
Not on the fifteenth day.
In the morning of the sixteenth day.
In the evening of the seventeenth day.
Not on the eighteenth day.
Not on the nineteenth day.
Not on the twentieth day.
In the morning of the twenty-first day.
Any time in the twenty-second day.
Not on the twenty-third day.
In the morning of the twenty-fourth day.

---

[1]See Joshua Trachtenberg *Jewish Magic and Superstition* (New York: Behrman House, 1939), p. 145.

Any time in the twenty-fifth day.
Not on the twenty-sixth day.
In the morning of the twenty-seventh day.
Any time in the twenty-eighth day.
Not on the twenty-ninth day.
The morning of the thirtieth day.

Thus inscribe the amulet and speak, by the name (Hebrew: DI) create heaven and Earth [Shemiya Ovara'a, or sky and ground].[2]

It is written, this is the amulet of Pheloni Ben Phelonieth, and by the name of the angel appointed in the hour of the day, of Pheloni.

Open the heart to make desire of Joshua [The Lord is his salvation]. Write the sign upon the leaves of citrus [Terephi Atherog]. Wipe the sign in aged wine and drink in purity.

These are the letters to write:

DR TBA IOD TIHO BOTA AAA NS.

Afterward, in purity in Nisan, speak over the glass of aged wine seven times. These are the names: Phethechial, Rephal, A'anal, Yihov, Yihov, Tedephial, Yihoval. After thus, you drink.

Afterward speak, beloved is the Lord [Elohim Ahabath] 40 times.

After, engrave the sign upon the back of citrus or apple. As you engrave the circle around the sign, speak La'ayila three times. Then consume it. The sign and written word.

After the adjuration speak, I am above Gelietzor. In the book [Hemegeleh], the Torah decrees of adjuration, I am above Yiphiephieh. The prince directs adjuration. Zegenez Gal is the prince of the Torah. Open the heart of Pheloni Ben Phelonieth by the Torah. By wisdom and understanding. By the name (Hebrew: IH IH IH) of hosts. (Hebrew: AAA NS).

Take the virgin egg [Bietzeh Betholeh] and boil to harden the shell. Upon the shell, write these letters:

PI PI OOTh PI PI IOTh ChIL PI PI IOTh AKOTh ChIL TzOR ITO TATITh QDOSh QDOSh AAA NS.

---

[2]Usually, the term representing heaven is Shemiyiem, and Earth is Aretz.

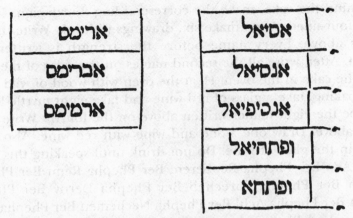

Figure 12. The transliteration of the Hebrew is as follows: left hand column: *ARIMS, ABRIMS, ARMIMS*; right hand column: *ASIAL, ANSIAL, ANSIPIAL, OPThHIAL, OPThChA.*

Afterward, by the name (Hebrew: OMSPR MSPRA AKD PSPSL), the great teacher [Ameser Gedol]. Open the heart. David Ben Ze-lateh is learned in the Torah. All learn not to forsake from this time and forever (Hebrew: AAA NS).

Afterward, the root of the workings is purity in Sivan, in the evening of the Sabbaths; nevertheless do not eat until tomorrow. Concerning all matters therein, purity is not the foundation.

It is required to keep the body and heart in purity. Establish heaven and thus judgment. Take flour and barley. If not barley, take wheat; however barley is best. Knead in purity. Speak the name Phel-oni. I employ by that. Let there be desire before Elohino in heaven. Succeed by opening the heart. I establish the name Pheloni Ben Phelonieth. Be the key of the Talmud and Torah. Of every word, do not forsake. Teach all, and all is known by decree in the cities. Of the dogma [Phethegema], speak most holy are these by the name (He-brew: IH), the Lord of hosts. Knead to improve the flour. Make pure the fine meal. From the fine meal, make round cakes as the palm of the hand. Take ink and make four drawings on the four cakes.

Write in the center of the cake. Write upon the fourth these three names. Write as these are tried and proven. Do not write in one and not in two, but only in three rows.[3]

---

[3]See Trachtenberg, *Jewish Magic and Superstition*, p. 117.

Behind the cake, make the corresponding fourth sign. It is already four-sided. After, make six, drawings with ink. Write the five names above. Every name before the strength is written and proven. After, write all the second names on the sides of the cake. Bake the cake in the oven. Heat the oven with wood of wild vines. After baking, take a glass of red wine and take eight myrtle leaves. Inscribe the eight names written above on the fourth. Write every name above. Draw one alone and wipe with red wine. Also place above in the glass of wine. Do not drink until speaking this seven times: Ada Ber Phepha Repherem Ber Phepha Remi Ber Phepha Yikiesh Ber Phepha Sorecheb Ber Phepha Derov Ber Phepha Chema Ber Phepha Achi Ber Phepha Nechemen Ber Phepha Meri Ber Phepha.[4] Blessed are you the Lord, to teach the law [Berok Atheh H' Lemedeni Choeqiek].

Of Nephesh, live and praise. Of judgment, support you in goodness. Blessed are you, the Lord. The good and the goodness.

Adjuration above is the key. Of the prince of Shekineh, the foolish turn away the heart from me. Cast out to live upon the mountain [Toriya, or castle]. Rise up by the name. (Hebrew: ShMRThA QDIShThA ALIN ARIMS ABRIMS ARMIMS ASIAL ANSIAL ANSIPIAL OPThChIAL OPThChA.)

Noah obtains favor in the eyes of the Lord. Speak in testimony six times. After thus, eat thou the cake.

The amulet is good and proven. Put to flight the evil eye by the spirit of knowledge. Of grace, take hold of the sword. Open the heart and examine the Torah. Therein are blessings over every kind of affliction and pain. It comes to pass that treasures flow. By the name (Hebrew: ShDI DI), create heaven and Earth. By the name, the angel Raphael is appointed over the month.

Sememal, Henegal, Vonegeshoresh, Kenedores, Nedemeh, Qemial, Sa'arial, Aberied, Noried. Appointed over the period of Tammuz. The prince is Avora'anied. The angel of the hour and the sign of the zodiac. In the name of the Lord Elohi of Israel, the Cherubim dwell. El is great, the strong and the glory.

(Hebrew: IHOH) is the name of the hosts. By the name Elohi, compassion. By the name Adierieron Elohi Ropha, worthy of all

---

[4] ADA BR PPA RPRM BR PPA RMI BR PPA IKISh BR PPA SORChB BR PPA DRO BR PPA ChMA BR PPA AChI BR PPA NChMN BR PPA MRI BR PPA.

groups below. Above is the innermost part [Bierek]. By the name (Hebrew: IHOH), succeed in writing.

Of the amulet, write in the name of Pheloni Ben Phelonieth. Keep all 248 mighty ones [Ayiberiem] therein. Take hold of the edge of the sword. Be aided and prosper. Of deliverance and salvation of wicked men, from the tongue of the wicked, and from the lord of judgment [Ba'al Dien].

It is difficult to understand the covenant. Understand that there is not a covenant of all established above. The wicked understand by the works of the Lord. Understand by language and by counsel. Understand by thoughts. Overpower the humble [Hekeniya'am Heshephielem]. Cast down and be weary. Be subdued [Hekena'a] and shaken [Na'ana'a] and afflicted [Sheber]. Be weary without rising up in strength.

All is from the petition of wickedness. Complete every wicked desire. Deliver and save from all. From being covered with bruises. From every kind of pain and affliction. From wicked men, from the second death [Memietheh Meshoneh], from every kind of evil thought, from every kind of suffering and wicked disease.

Give grace and mercy and compassion before the throne of the Lord, and before all creatures. You behold the visions, when placed over the creatures, as when over the lion attacks.

Of the oath, I, Pheloni Ben Pheloni, in the name of Avoriedon and Aderieron.

Here is another amulet: Aregial, Seregial, Nedegial, Achenal, Tzemethienial, A'amethenial, Shemenal, Yivochek, Yivobek, Yivobeb, Az, Bov, Geh, Aberial, Berekial, Gelalek, Deleqial, Horerial, Ova'arial, Zereqial, Chenial, Tehorial, Yihoval, Kerobial, Mehemenial, Lechetial, Norial, Sorial, A'azerial, Phenial, Tzephehal, Qethenial, Ra'ashial, Shepherial, Yithoqial, Avorial, Rephal, Miephal, Athenal, Seneseneh, Qeneqenetha, Mova'aqech, Mekeshephial, Vosenederial, Voqephetzial, Abeg, Yithetz, Teha, Nod, Heneb, Gemal, Torial, Yiphiephieh, Gelietzor, Tzoreteq.

Rejoice and be happy in the Torah, by the name (Hebrew: OPTh ZAI BThA RKB TzRD IIH AThM ChZA BIZ RThIK IChD ThQO IOH IA IA AaPR QAN OThA BBD ORK AIR). Open the heart of Lieb Ben Shereh (Hebrew: LIB BN ShRH). Be learned in the Torah.

Of prophecies, it is written in the Talmud of Jerusalem. Of the complete Talmud and Midrash and additions and books and scrolls, the decrees of the Torah and profound secrets of the Torah live in the heart as flowing fountains.

(Hebrew: HOH.) Of knowledge and wisdom and all orders of the wisdom and every word of the Torah. Keep the commandments. Deliver and save and bring forth from every kind of sorcery. From binding and from every kind of misfortune, and every kind of punishment. From the edge of the sword and from evil men. From the tongue of the wicked and from the Lord of judgment. It is difficult to understand the covenant. Understand there is not covenant of all established above.

Of wickedness, understand by the works. Understand by the thoughts of the subdued and humble, fallen and weary, overthrown and shaken and broken. Do not rise up in strength. All is from petition of wickedness. Complete the desire of wickedness. Of deliverance and salvation from every kind of misfortune and affliction. From evil men and from second death, from every kind of evil nature, and from wicked disease. The heart of the good prevails over the heart of the wicked.

Behold when over the creatures, as when the lion attacks. By the name (Hebrew: IHOH IHHO IOHH HIOH HOIH OIHH OHHI HHIO HOHI), and by the name (Hebrew: ABGIThTz QRAa ShTN NGD IKSh BTR TzThG ChQB TNAa IGL PZQ ShQO TzITh)[5] and by the name (Hebrew: OHO ILI SIT AaLM OKO') and by the name (Hebrew: ANQThM PSThM PSPSIM ODIONSIM)[6] bless and keep.

The Lord enlightens. Face above and find favor. The Lord rises up. Face above and give you peace.

Listen and dwell in Israel. In secret, the Lord of the highest favors you. Be protected by the Lord Shaddai. Dwell united and of love, you speak of the Lord. Shelter me Elohiek and fortify all. Of Elohi, secure in the heart. All therein Nephesh. All give much. Breathe the words. Gather them from the word breathing.

I, by the power, command to establish the day to you above and below. Regard in the heart and repeat. Find refuge from the cold.

[5]The name of 42 letters. See Trachtenberg, *Jewish Magic and Superstition*, p. 94.
[6]The name of 22 letters. See Trachtenberg, *Jewish Magic and Superstition*, p. 93.

By the words, travel in truth to the dwelling. Do not fear in the house. Go without fear on the path at night to the dwelling.

Establish to cover with darkness. Bind in the day. The letter of the word is above, in the side of darkness. Go forth and be cut off. The unclean are laid waste. Cast down the eyes.

It is written, fortify over 1,000 door posts [Mezozoth]. Of one myriad houses from the right side, open in the heart of the dwelling. Drive out the demons [Mezieq] from the place (Hebrew: IHOH) keeps away devils [Shiedien] and demons [Mezieqien]. Pass the night and breathe easy while sleeping. Be safe from all fears by the name (Hebrew: IHOH), the God of Gods and the Lord of Lords.

(Hebrew: OALHA RBA AaGLA). In the designated time, draw near. (Hebrew: AAA AZ BO GH ThThA MGINO.)

Blessed are you, Lord of the Shield of David [Megen Dod]. (Hebrew: MTzMTzITh NAaRORON MTTRON.)

Here is another amulet. It is of the Ruoch of man. Raise up and give great success. (Hebrew: BAaH) is written upon the shell and suspended by the left side. This is written and be protected on the path. Be guided by the word of truth. Of righteous nations, the Torah reveals the knowledge of the right side.

SNMKR TNP BKR ZG MNB ODD TZHSN TThA ChD SBR AS-BQSD ARAHB.

Let there be desire of the Lord Elohi of Israel. Command the angel. Come forth to the house of Pheloni Ben Phelonieth. You go forth and succeed in every work. Succeed with great ease, in the day and night, in the house and outside of the house, in the city and outside of the city. Of the name and the holy seal, have pride in your work. In your house, succeed of Pheloni Ben Phelonieth, amen seleh.

It is tried and proven to keep the woman safe. Give birth to the infant. Keep from sorcery and from the evil eye. In the hours of the birth, do not hold dominion. In birth, turn away from misfortune and bad events.

Of the song of degrees [Shier Hema'aloth], the names go forth. From the song of degrees, these raise the eye. (Hebrew: AL R"Th Aa"B.) Of the name (Hebrew: HOIH), speak of praises.

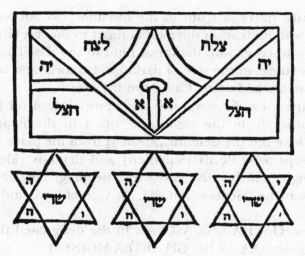

Figure 13. The characters in the upper right section translate as "succeed," or "prosper." Upper left: "of purity" or "of the pure." The other corners are the same letters re-arranged. Below the rectangle, in the center of each Star of David is Shaddai, "the Almighty," another name of God.

Thus (Hebrew: S"Th). The eye sees from where. (Hebrew: Q"L.) The Lord guides over. (Hebrew: Aa"B Q"L) and also (Hebrew: S"Th). See from where comes (Hebrew: ADNI HOIH). Join together to support the nation. The Lord creates. (Hebrew: S"Th ADNI). Heaven and Earth. (Hebrew: S"Th Q"L.)

Do not flee from here. (Hebrew: R"Th HOIH.) Speak of Alephs [Alephien]. The highest man is the right hand. Of the day, three Yods [Yodien]. From the name of 72, complete compassion. Awaken compassion in the highest man. (Hebrew: HOIH). Speak of Alephs. Of the names, do not lament. (Hebrew: R"Th HOIH). Speak of Alephs. Also of every letter after the name (Hebrew: HOIH NOTRIQON AaShTzII). The name is very good. Keep safe also in every night preceding. It is required of every man. Of the song of degrees, establish the name.

You pass. Of passing (Hebrew: IB"Q). Pass (Hebrew: Aa"B RI"O). Of the 72 names of 216 letters (Hebrew: IB"Q ADNI HOIH AHIH) joined together.

Of the name of 72, as found on page 24 [of the Hebrew text], serve two of the scripture. Be blessed by the names found on page 42 [of the Hebrew text]. Serve two.

Serve the wheel [Ha'ayigol]. Of the image in the circle on the right, listen to people join together. Let there be pleasure on the page ***7 Of the second side, answer the Lord. Bind in the day.

Go forth from the song four times. (Hebrew: IB"Q) in the day. Of misfortune, exalt holiness in strength. Deliver and fall. We establish to answer in the day. Proclaim (Hebrew: IB"Q) of the three names (Hebrew: ADNI HOIH AHIH) joined together. Of four treasured powers, deliver from all misfortune, especially in childbirth. Here the Lord guides.

The names going forth from the scripture are very good. Keep safe, not being bound by sorcery. Here by Gematria, complete the name from the name of 72. All sorceries are not able to work. (Hebrew: Aa"I) completes 72. Of the name of 72, keep from all powers of evil [Qliphoth]. Have knowledge of it. (Hebrew: OA"K). Salvation by all three letters of the name before the power. Blessed is the name of glory.

(Hebrew: O"K) of the three letters of the name is in the presence of the power [Bepheni A'atzemov]. Joseph, the son of Ephraim, raises the eye to the young sons. Raise the wall in the name of (Hebrew: IO"D H"H O"O H"H MI"K OSh"R NI"Th AaSh"L NM"M RH"Aa). These names are very good to the evil eye. Go forth from the scriptures. Of the son of Ephraim, see the Lord [Rayieh]. Of the word (Hebrew: AaShL), understand the evil eye. Also (Hebrew: NMM RHAa). By Gematria, the evil eye.

Of the 70 names of the Malachim, they are very good. All keep the things as revealed. Afterward, these names and images are seen and engraved by Adam, the first man. Of your image, it is very good to keep safe during childbirth.8 Another well-known amulet follows.9

7The letters HN"L are presented here, which would not correspond to the page in this book. Also, the page numbers cited refer to the original Hebrew text.

8This diagram is also published in Gustav Davidson, *Dictionary of Angels* (New York: Free Press, 1967), p. 164. The caption under the diagram reads, "Of difficult labor in childbirth, take the shell of a turtle. Prepare it by writing above by the name (Hebrew: QOP QPO OQP OPQ PQO POQ). Bind it over the navel. Whisper in her right ear. You go forth and all the nation by foot. This is tested and proven.

9This plate is also published in David Goldstein's, *Jewish Folklore and Legends* (London: Hamlyn, 1980), p. 30. Goldstein notes, "In each of the two compartments are representations of the three angels who captured the female demon Lilith, namely Snwy, Snsnwy, and Smnglf."

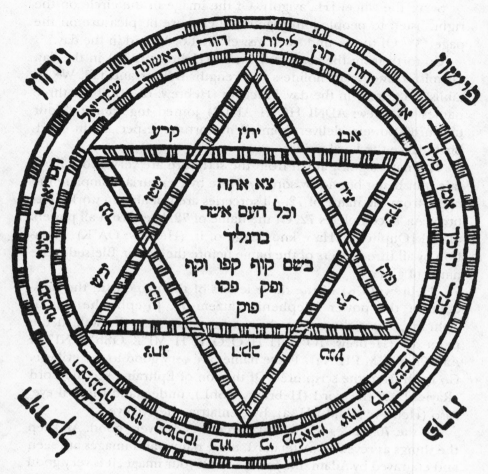

Figure 14. This talisman protects women from a difficult childbirth. The Hebrew outside the circle mentions the names of the four rivers of Eden (from upper left clockwise): Gihon, Phishon, Phereth (the Euphrates) and Chidgel (the Tigris). Contained within the circle are the names of angels and Adam and Eve.

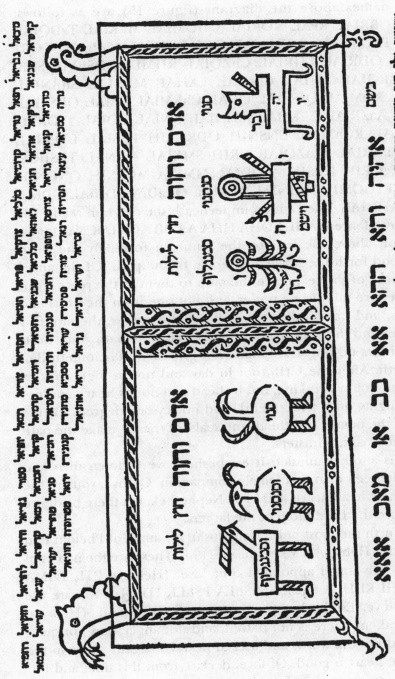

Figure 15. A talisman for protecting new-born children from Lilith.

The names above the diagram (figure 15) are as follows:
MIKAL GBRIAL RPAL NORIAL QDOMIAL MLKIAL TzDQIAL
PDIAL ThOMIAL ChSDIAL TzORIAL RMAL IOPIAL STORI
GZRIAL ODRIAL LHRIAL ChZQIAL RHMIA QDShIAL ShB-
NIAL BRQIAL AHIAL ChNIAL LAHAL MLKIAL ShBNIAL
RHSIAL ROMIAL QDMIAL QDAL ChKMIAL RMAL QDShIAL
AaNIAL AaZRIAL ChKMAL MHNIAL QNIAL GDIAL TzORTQ
AaOPPIAL RChMIAL SNSNIH ODRGZIH RSSIAL DOMIAL
SNIAL THRIAL IAaZQIAL NRIH SMKIAL AaINAL ThSIRIH
RNAL TzORIH PSISIH AaODIAL MMKIA MChNIH QNONIH
IROAL TTDOSIH ChONIAL ZKRIAL OAaDIAL DNIAL GDIAL
BRIAL AHNIAL. The caption underneath the diagram reads, "By
the name (Hebrew: AHIH OHA HHA AA BB AO MAK AAA), give
adjuration above. Be first by the name to form. By the third
name, send forth the Malachim. Form by the path. Of the angel
of the shore of the sea, make the oath to them in the place. Find
the names are not of one power, and not one from the hosts and
ministers, and not of all who dwell. Of the names, therefore by
the names and the seals written here, I make the oath. Your hosts
and ministers do not strengthen. You give birth. Phelonieth Ben
Phelonieth. After the birth, not in day and not in night, not by
eating and not by drinking, not by head and not by heart, and not
by 248 mighty ones [Aberihem], and not by 365 degrees. By the
power of the names and the divine seals, of these I make the oath
of your hosts and ministers.

Here is another amulet. It establishes love between man and
wife, or between man and female companion. Of love, you are the
Lord Elohiek in all hearts and in all Nepheshek. Let there be desire
from before the Lord Elohi of the fathers.

Send forth the most holy [Heqedoshiem] angel of Pheloni Ben
Phelonieth. (Hebrew: K"P) establishes love. These are the names of
the most holy angel appointed over love. (Hebrew: PTh TzIMA
ThA HOHI KI HLA ShLK KShShLA PShLK IThQL.) You are the
angel of love. Establish love. Declare to understand. (Hebrew:
PB"P). In them, there is not hatred, and not anger, and not quar-
reling, and not evil words and wicked hearts; but only peace in the
heart. The heart is good. Of love, declare from this time and forever and ever, amen. Let there be the image.

Here is another amulet of love (figure 16). It is written of water lilies and saffron, and with the brazen writing tool, write upon the prepared shell.

In the name of Pheloni Ben Phelonieth, let there be binding of the heart. Of Pheloni Ben Phelonieth, to love. Of Pheloni Ben Phelonieth, works of desire. Desire from power of the song and power of the Totepheth. You are blessed of Nephesh of the Lord Elohi. In great splendor and glory, the vestments cover with light. Peace extends to heaven. The veil cools in the highest sea. In the place of darkness, the horseman travels upon the wings of the wind.

Make the angel over spirits that minister flames of fire. The foundation is of Earth. Above is the dwelling of the Lord. It is not to fall forever and ever. Of Thehom, the vestment covers the mountains. The sea stands from the curse. Flee from the sound of thunder. Quickly rise up the mountains and descend into valleys.

Of the foundation, measure the limits. Do not pass over. Do not inhabit the earth. In the place, put forth from flowing rivers between mountains. Journey and drink. Do not live in the dwelling. Quench the thirst in the arid wilderness. Fly above the heavens to dwell. Be refreshed from the highest mountains to the wilderness.

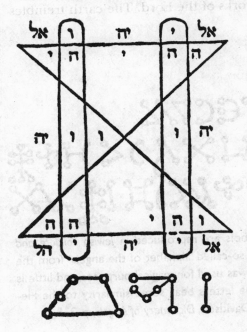

Figure 16. The letters in this figure form "God names." This diagram is also reproduced in Goldstein's *Jewish Folklore and Legends*, page 30.

The earth is enriched with plant growth to support the beasts. The grass serves man. Go forth by the warmth from the earth. Of wine, man rejoices in the heart. The surface of the earth becomes fertile. Warm the heart of man. Support the tree of the Lord. Of white cedar, establish the name. Return to the nest of the stork in the fir tree. In the house of the heights [Bitheh Heriem], mountain goats [Liya'a'iem] hide in the shelter of rocks.

Make the Moon of the fixed time of the Sun. Know to come forth. Beseige the darkness. Let there be night therein. All life moves, until the lions roar and growl, rending and tearing apart.

Seek food from El. The Sun rises. Gather to the dwellings to lie down. Man goes forth to work and works until evening. How many works of the Lord are complete by the wisdom created to fill the Earth with wealth.

The sea is great and wide. There are creeping things without number, from the smallest creature to the greatest. There are boats to journey Leviathan. Form clouds therein.

Complete by providing grains. You give food in the hour. Give to gather and fill the open hand. It is good to hide the face as the winds increase. Of toil, the dust returns. Send forth Ruoch to enrich and restore the surface of the earth. Let there be glory of the Lord forever. Rejoice by the works of the Lord. The earth trembles and the mountains shake.

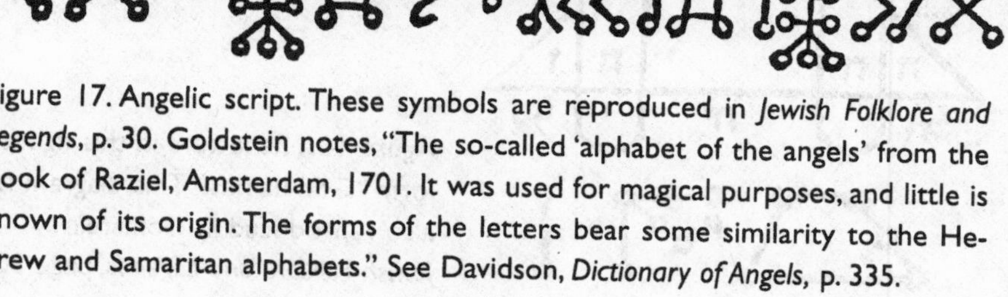

Figure 17. Angelic script. These symbols are reproduced in *Jewish Folklore and Legends*, p. 30. Goldstein notes, "The so-called 'alphabet of the angels' from the Book of Raziel, Amsterdam, 1701. It was used for magical purposes, and little is known of its origin. The forms of the letters bear some similarity to the Hebrew and Samaritan alphabets." See Davidson, *Dictionary of Angels*, p. 335.

The Lord keeps in life. Sing to Elohi as long as darkness is above. Let us rejoice. The Lord ends sin and evil from the earth. Nephesh rises up. Praise the Lord.

Here is another amulet (figure 17) of grace and mercy written upon the prepared turtle shell. In the name of grace and mercy (Hebrew: IHOH), let there be mercy in the world. (Hebrew: IHOH AaL PB.)

Increase the righteousness of the nation. Speak, of the Lord to increase and send mercy above. Give you grace in the eyes of all visions. In the name of Michael, Gabriel, Raphael, Avorial, Kebeshial.

IH IH IH IH IH IH IH IH AHIH AHH AHH AHH AHH IHO IHO IHO IHO IHO IHO IHO IHO IH.

Here is another amulet (figure 18). Do not hold dominion by men with weapons [Keli Zien]. It is written upon the prepared shell of a turtle and suspended by the neck with these most holy names:

AaThRIAL   ORIAL   HORRIAL   HMRRIAL   ShOBRIAL ShOBRAL AaORRIAL ShORIAL MIKAL GBRIAL HGRIAL HGDH AL ShOBRIAL TzBChR AThNIQ TzORTQ ANQThM PSThM PSPSIM DIONSIM LISh OAaTh KQO IThI IHOH ABG IThTz QRAa ShTN NGD IKSh BTR TzThG ChQB TNAa IGL PZQ ShQOTzITh QBTzQAL AHMNONIAL OMSThIH HIRShThIAL AaANH PIH ALAaH ABG IThIN ALAaH AaH AaH AaZOR LPLONI BN PLONITh

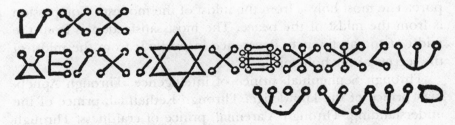

Figure 18. Angelic script. These symbols have been reproduced in Trachtenberg's *Jewish Magic and Superstition*, page 141, as well as in other texts.

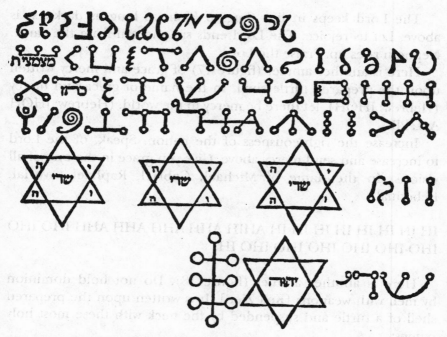

Figure 19. Angelic script. These symbols are also published in Trachtenberg's *Jewish Magic and Superstition*, page 141.

It is spoken of wisdom, live for seven periods. Drink a glass of rum [Kosiya Remiya] every day for 40 days. Understand the divine word that was given to Moses from the midst of the bush.

The understanding of the wisdom is from the midst of the knowledge. Intelligence is from the midst of the thoughts. Intelligence is from the midst of all goodness and honesty, from the midst of the most skillfull. Improvement is from the midst of the most pure. The most holy is from the midst of the modesty. Compassion is from the midst of the peace. The most satisfaction is from the midst of the abstinence. Reverence in purity is from the midst of the secrets of the holy spirit.

Through Sephephial, prince of intelligence. Through Aphephial, prince of the knowledge. Through Kethethial, prince of the understanding. Through A'aremial, prince of craftiness. Through Yihoval, prince of testimony. Through Nehenal, prince of the deliverance of the Lord. Through Rehal, prince of the mystery of the

Shekinah. Through Ashemoli, prince of the Torah. The name Shehesherov Shekinah is over Moses.

The Ruoch of wisdom and understanding. Ruoch of knowledge and intelligence. Ruoch of craftiness and science. Ruoch of the mystery of the deliverance of the Lord. Ruoch is from you, Elohim. Thus dwell in the Shekinah of wisdom and understanding. Ruoch of counsel and strength and thoughts. Ruoch of knowledge and wisdom. Of the Ruoch of Elohim, the mystery is from intelligence in the hour over David Ben Zelateh by the name Sheqrechozi.

The great prince is (Hebrew: ZH PTR II'). The great prince is (Hebrew: GDL ZH RIRIAL II'). The great prince is (Hebrew: AGOQThIAL II'). The great prince is appointed over the treasured wisdom of the Torah and over all keys of wisdom.

Teach Moses the Torah. Of wisdom and knowledge, thus to open. I am David Ben Zelateh. Of the gate of wisdom and the gate of understanding, by the name (Hebrew: AHO AChOSh IChOSh IHOH IHO IH HH HOH HH HOH IHOI HOH HH IH OH AH IHO AH IH OH OAA ANM SLH).

Do not forsake desire. Do not forsake learning. Speak of the scriptures preceding. Consume and mix a glass of wine or beverage [Mesheqeh] after. Speak, these are the scriptures over Ruoch of men and women. Of Shaddai, man understands to arrange the heart.

The Lord answers in language. Of El, cast out from before. The holy spirit of El is received from me. The Lord commands to cast the amulet out of gold. Deliver to the pure heart. Create to me Elohim and Ruoch is established, restored within.

Elohim gives me language to understand the knowledge. You give the word to awaken every morning. My ear hears the teaching. The Lord Elohim opens my ear. I am not disobedient. After, do not remove Ruoch. The word of the Lord is in me. Rule over language and speak thus.

Let there be desire from before the Lord Elohi of Abraham, Isaac, and Israel. Open the heart by the laws. Enlighten the eye and heart by the name Phethechial Rephal Chophial. Open your heart. In all the days, do not forsake all that is learned.

What is commanded to learn? From serving, learn all days. Do not forsake the word of the Torah forever, amen.

Make to fast in the evening. (Hebrew: R"Ch) is in Sivan. Write the divine scriptures upon an egg. Knead the yolk with good honey. Consume the word from all flesh. You eat the food.

(Hebrew: DIO NSIM.)[10] That is (Hebrew: D"IO NS"IM).

Of two flags [B' NSIM], create Gabriel as (Hebrew: DIO). Of the appearance [Pheretzophien] and the interpretation of the flags, create Gabriel of the grace of Mieshal [Hebrew: MIShAL].[11]

Of support, the cold is before. Be warm from the inside. There is interpretation over the holy. Blessed is it.

(Hebrew: A"Z B"O G"H.) Of five seals of God, divide the letters. Strip away the plain meaning [Peshet Pieseth]. Create the two flags.

(Hebrew: A"Z B"O G"H.) Establish the letters of the name of 22 letters. (Hebrew: ANQThM PSThM PSPSIM DIONSIM BGIM' ADIRIRON IHOH ALHI.) Of the hosts, the Cherubim dwell. Here completes the name of 22 letters.

You make change to engrave the name of 42. (Hebrew: ABGIThK) is divided. (Hebrew: ABGA) is broken down. (Hebrew: ABGA) is above and faces the veil.

Obtain (Hebrew: HShTN). Denounce to break down and rend (Hebrew: QRA'a)[12] the Sepharim. Denounce going forth (Hebrew: HShTN). Denounce over Israel. Obtain the book of the Merkabah.

(Hebrew: ABGIThK QRA'a ShTN.)[13] In the *Sepher Hekeloth* [*Book of the Palaces*], even as rending the book. Of the guilty, denounce here until being without food. Make the oath. Learn of favor [Zekoth] and fault [Meleqien] before the Lord.

The beauty of the bow of the Lord is in the secret parts of the one new language coming forth [Yikesh Henah Daqoshi Lieh Bemebosha Leched Beter Leshon Bova]. The first part is new. (Hebrew: TzTh"G.) Of language, establish the tabernacle [Heqeb]. Proclaim to expand the language. (Hebrew: TN"Aa.) Thus the keys of power. (Hebrew: IG"L). Thus the book of power. (Hebrew: PZ"Q KPZ"Q.) Learn of the snow. (Hebrew: PZMQ"I ShQ"O.) Bear

---

[10]These are the final letters of the name of 22 letters.
[11]This translates, "Who is what God is?" It is also the name of several people, notably a companion of Daniel.
[12]This word is significant in the name of 42 letters.
[13]See Trachtenberg, *Jewish Magic and Superstition*, p. 95.

the burden. Run from the place. (Hebrew: TzI"Th.) Go forth in abundance.

(Hebrew: ABGIThK) is the secret in the tractate passed over by the scholar. Of supplication, go forth three miles. Do not speak before, however afterward, do not return to Jerusalem. Of exactly one mile, return in less than a mile.

Thus the law [Helekeh]. Now, the sons understand of the sins of thousands of nations. Of all murder [Rotzech], it is necessary to journey. Take flight and take refuge in the city. There is no evil outside the pasture.

It is written of the shelter of the city, of 48 cities nearby. Your pastures and fields are in the nations. You are hidden in the nations. Take possesion of the cities, given before. Afterward, reduce from one mile in the midst of, and not be slain.

(Hebrew: ShARZL.) Less than three miles, here the Sun rises. Thus of murder, measure three miles. Speak, take flight to the east from the place of murder. Thus at the appointed time, be in prayer for nearly one hour. Thus the killer turns away. Of murder in the place of prisoners, the sea is around. Speak, you are prisoners. Of the might of the Lord, send forth. You lessen to draw from the sea.

(Hebrew: MGB"A GB"A.) Of the letters Aleph Beth Gimel, it is the name. Of the book of great wisdom, the thousands of nations of God. Be blessed to calculate by combination. The sea is less from one mile. Speak of the length from Earth. Measure width until the sea. The Sun returns above. Be immersed in the sea. Afterward, lessen from one mile. Do not return before three miles.

Therefore (Hebrew: AB"G BI"Th GIM"L NOTRIQON). Through prayer, the border of one mile. Of three miles, it comes to pass. The sea is fixed by portions in the soil of the ground. Dig down one mile. Make it in the place where the ground is virgin soil. Speak the oath. I am above Nechelial, A'aremogial, Tetophiech, Atzothiech, Nera'ayial. By the name, truth goes forth as a bubbling fountain.

(Hebrew: QRAa ShTN.) The letters (Hebrew: ShAaR) are small above. Therein gather to denounce Shaitan over Israel. At once, see lives preceding. Arrange the ends. You are the gate. Do not be able to come before the Shekinah. Denounce over Israel.

Remembering the purity of Jacob. Proclaim of the small. Speak of who rises up. Of Jacob, it is small.

(Hebrew: OAa"O NAM' TzDQ" OMShPT" MKON" KSAK.) Mercy and truth precede before. (Hebrew: OS"Th) is small. All is made by that name.

(Hebrew: QRA'A ShTN.) It is good. Those who are wicked are torn to pieces above or from before the evil spirit or from before the sharp teeth of the demon [Mezieq].

(Hebrew: KOChBIN.) Of that name, suspend by the neck and heal.

(Hebrew: IKSh.) They are lifted up. Below is Teth and above is Samekh. According to that, speak of grace of all the acts of El three times.

Of man with strength, as to be thus 13 (Hebrew: I"G) below. Thus without punishment. You are lifted up three times. Thirteen rise up. Establish Teth, however above, there is no punishment until to be thus 23 times 20. They are (Hebrew: S' NG"D). It is good to remember support, of food and nourishment.

(Hebrew: BTR TzThG.) The false are dismissed [Sheqorien Pheter]. Of the language, dismiss the first sea above [Pheter Miem Rashieth Merom]. There it is false. Rend Shaitan. Thus of the oath. Thus record the event. Rend Shaitan.

(Hebrew: PTR TzThG.) Reply to the oath afterward. The event is with Shin and Beth.

(Hebrew: BTR BNIMT' ALIH.) Fulfill the letters Aleph, Lamed, Yod, Heh.

(Hebrew: TzThG.) By Gematria is as the strength [ChLNOTh]. Petition the Lord above in prayer. That is what to speak. Look from the windows, from the Tietz [ornament] and from the lattices.

(Hebrew: MShNIH NOTARIQON MTTRON.) The great prince. Open the window. Of 13 [OI"G] windows, they are by the throne of the glory. You open them in order to gather to the phylacteries [Thephielethen] of Israel. All are created in that name.

(Hebrew: BTR TzThG BATh BSh ShGN HAR.) Learn that the first light was created by God. Separate the righteous and make them ready. God conceals it in Eden.

Speak and proclaim, Elohim illuminates. (Hebrew: AOR.) By Gematria to the Garden of Eden. Understand by that name.

(Hebrew: ChQD TNAa.) By Gematria. (Hebrew: RAM.) According to it, speak of the rays [Qeren].

(Hebrew: RAM.) Rays by the nation of Enoch.

(Hebrew: RAM.) Raphael, Avorial, Mikael are the hosts of Shekinah. Make ready to assist the Messiah. That is what is spoken of rays at once.

Of the name (Hebrew: ChBION AaZO), by the letters and by the name, that is Avorial.

(Hebrew: D"L.) Facing Avorial. (Hebrew: L"A RA"O). You see after and before (Hebrew: L"A IRA"O).

(Hebrew: ChQD TNAa) by Gematria is Nezeral the angel. Make the oath to the angel Nezal in order to stop deriving evil.

Differentiate by the name. It is necessary to be of great innocence and baptized [Tebieleh].

(Hebrew: IGL PZQ) by Gematria is Cherub. The name to engrave over Cherub is above. Every day, God above guides. Speak and guide over Cherub. I take flight and fly upon the wings of the wind. See in 18,000 lands in the east, and 18,000 in the west, and 18,000 in the north. These 72 lands establish mercy. Speak of mercy in the universe. Understand the mercy. In heaven, establish the faithful. Establish mercy of thousands of myriads. Of (Hebrew: OAaZ), speak around 18,000. Of the name, the day of the name of the Lord.

Divide around to all four faces. Of 18,000, there is no place. Of the angel of the nation, the angel is prince. The faces guide the nation. Be covered with glory. Speak of facing the letters (Hebrew: HNOK).

By the one letter, the vision of glory comes to all the world. In the highest world, of one song of every group above. Remember the name.

(Hebrew: IGL PZQ MThI.) In the period, God rises upon the throne of the glory. The wicked are judged at once. Of every group above, directly see God rising up.

(Hebrew: KThRIHON.) Beginning above, descend from above upon horses. Of judgment, seek compassion over Israel. At once, rise over the throne of compassion. Therefore, the Shekinah is by the throne of compassion.

(Hebrew: IGL PZQ.) Above is the throne of the glory. Understand all is well.

(Hebrew: ShQO.) By Gematria and over the veil, learn that above the veil, engrave the name and image of the idol [Besh Tzer] of evil coming forth. Denounce over Israel at once. Remember the name. (Hebrew: OMIDNBO.) Fear the evil image. It is not permitted to gather before.

(Hebrew: ShQO BNI' OAaL ITzR D"L.) Above is the evil image.

(Hebrew: ShQO BNI' OAaL HDRNAL MLMD ShHDRNAL.) Journey by all. The veil is spread over the throne. Immerse you in the river of fire. Divide over the throne of glory. At once, gather every group above the Moon [Irech]. They are also immersed in the river of fire.

(Hebrew: ShS"H.) Be protected above the river.

(Hebrew: AaLI NHR BNI' ShSH.) Thus take authority from Jacob. The fathers above are of peace. Sing the song. Speak not of Jacob. From the sounds of Gihenam are the letters of Jacob. At once, they hold dominion by the name. According to it, engrave over the hearts.

(Hebrew: ShQO TzITh.) It is good for man to wear the vestment garment of sackcloth and have gray upon the head. Remember the name. Pray and, at once, the prayer is heard and answered. Speak, there is not one permitted to wear the vestment sackcloth. Only be answered by the king. (Hebrew: KIORM BN AChAB.)

Also, it is spoken in the Midrash, of how many are adorned in sackcloths. God sees you at once, lest [you] understand the secret of the sackcloth. All thus are adorned. See the covering.

Of the letters of the covering, thus find (Hebrew: BMRDKI). Wear the sackcloth and be gray. Go forth (Hebrew: LRBIM) and thus (Hebrew: GBI ANShI NINOCh). Wear the sackcloths and understand the great secret.

Here completes the division of the name of 42 letters. The book is complete. The fountain of wisdom [Ma'ayiyien Hechekmeh] is from the secrets of the great Rezial. Of all the books that Rezial the angel gave to Adam, the first man, learn from it. Of all fountains of the wisdom of the Lord, for the sake of compassion. Be favored by the pleasures of victory. Desire to succeed by walking upon the path of the wisdom. Be ministered by a myriad myriads hosts. Of armies of fire, the river of continuous fire [Methleqecheth Neher Ash]. Dwell before rising up to shine in strength. From the sounds, the nations tremble. Guide in strength and guide to the highest. Blessed is the Lord of the universe, amen.

Through the actions, employ the holy messenger. The faithful hold dominion.

DOD BN LAA KHRR IShShKR DOB ZTzL MPOLIN QTN MQQ ZALQOOI HBIRH HSMOK LQQ LBOB.

APPENDIX

SEPHER REZIAL MANUSCRIPTS[1]

British Library MS. Sloane 3826 (101 folios):

1. ff.1–57 Liber Salomonis, called Sepher Raziel, containing Seven Treatises:
   1. The first is said Clavis for that in it is determined Astronomy and of the starres for without them we may do nothing.
   2. The second is said Ala for that in it is determined of the vertues of some stones, of herbs and of beasts.
   3. The third is said Tractatus Thymiamatus for that there is determined in it of Suffumigations and of allagacions of them and divisions.
   4. The fourth is said the Treatise of tymes and the heere of the day and of the night for that in it is determined when any thing ought to be done by this booke.
   5. The fifth is said the Treatise of Cleanesse for that there is determined in it of Abstinence.
   6. The sixth is said Samaim for in that treatise it nameth all the heavens and her angels and the operations of working of them.
   7. The seventh is the booke of virtues for that there is determined: *in it of vertues and miracles for there be tolde the propertyes of the arte of magicke and of his figures and of the ordinances of the same.*

---

[1]This list, compiled by Adam McLean, was posted on the World Wide Web, at http://www.levity.com/alchemy/raziel.html. Readers may find his information helpful to their study.

2. ff.58–65 The rule of the booke of Consecration or the manner of working with some orisions.
3. ff.65–83 Magical Directions.
4. ff.84–97 Liber Lunae.
5. ff.98–101 The Invocation of Oberion concerning Physic Art.

British Library MS. Sloane 3846 (Paper. Quarto. 186 folios. 17th century): Item 18. ff.129–157.

Liber Salomonis, called Cephar Raziel, containing seven treatises, said to be written by William Parry of Clifford's Inn in 1564. ff.129–157. [The text in English is the same as in MS. Sloane 3826.]

British Library MS. Sloane 3847 (Paper. Quarto. 188 folios. 17th century): [Items 1 and 2 see under Clavicula Salomonis—English] [Item 11] ff.161–188.

Praefatio in librum Razielis J.V. in nomine Dei omnipotentis vivi et veri, et eterni, et sine omni Fine qui dicitur Adonay—Saday—Assereye—Jucipio—scribere istum librum qui dicitur Cephar Raziel cum omnibus suis Pertinentiis, in quo sunt septem Tractatus completi, et septem libri.
Introductio Libris.
Clavis Libris. Liber Primus Astronomia.
De Lapidibus. Liber Secundus.
De Herbis.
[This text in Latin is the same as MSS. Sloane 3846 and 3826 but breaks off incomplete in Chapter Three.]
[Preface begins]: "Dicit Salomon Gloria et laus cum multo honore sit Deo."
[First book begins]: "Clavis istius libri est cognoscere et scire locum septem corporum superiorum."
[The introduction lists the seven books of the Sephar Raziel as:]

1. Clavis de Astromonia et de Stellis.
2. Ala de virtutibus quorundam Lapidum, Herbarum, Animalia.
3. Thimiamatum de Suffumigationis.
4. Temporum Anni [times of the year].

5. Munditio de abstinentia.
6. Samahym [names of God and Angels].
7. Virtutum quod ubi determinatur in eo [Virtues of the art of magic].

British Library MS. Sloane 3853 (Paper. Quarto. 268 folios. 17th century):

1. Tractatus cui titulus, Thesaurus Spiritum, secundum Robertum Furconem et Rogerum Bacon, cum tabula contentorum et pro-logo praemissis. ff.3–45. [Begins]: "Haec est doctrina omnium experimentorum."
2. Libri qui vocature Sephar Rasiel [Imperfect]. ff.46–53. [Begins]: "Incipio scribere istum librorum qui vocatur Sephar Rasiel."
3. Experimenta plurima magica. ff.54–63, 70–120.
4. The book of consecration. ff.64–69.
5. De spiritibus, solaribus, in figuris delineatis. ff.120v–127.
6. The divine Seal of Solomon. f.127v.
7. Invocationes, orationes, etc. f.129–137.
8. Tractatus qui vocatur, Speculum quator Regum. ff.138–141. [Begins]: "Dic inprimis hanc orationem."
9. Processus magici, excitationes spirituum, etc. ff.142–174.
10. A magical book called the Dannet, containing various magical experiments. ff.176–219. [Begins]: "This is the doctrine of all experiments in general."
11. The book of the science "of nygromancie." ff.219v–241. [Begins]: "Here beginnethe the boke of the sience of nygromancie by the which sience thou mayst worke yf thou wylt by daye as by nyght."
12. De sigillis planetarum, etc. f.243.
13. Conjurations, etc. ff.245v–252, 253–256.
14. Of the Offices of Spirits. ff.257–264.
15. Experimenta quaedeam magica. f.266.

British Library MS. Additional 15299:

[The following description appears in the British Library MS catalogue entry which is pasted into the beginning of this volume.]

"The Book Raziel (the Hidden Things of God). The Angel Raziel delivered this book to Adam after 130 years of his Repentance, which book contains Cabbala, by which they can cause Angels, according to his month and his day, to perform miracles, and cast out the evil spirits which occasionally enter in men, and it also contains the knowledge of conversing concerning the Sun, the Moon and the Stars, and to cause to be sick and heal again, and it speaks of many other powers of the vegetable world, precious stones, fishes, fowls, wild beasts, also to be enabled to foretell by the means of the stars and to explain the rod of Moses, wherewith he performed wonders. Vide Labia Dormientium lette 7. No. 31. "This MS contains the book Jetzirah, with the commentary apparently, of R. Eleaser ben Juda de Garmiza, who lived in the middle of the 13th century. There are various other cabalistic Treatises in it. See the note at f.132b. See Wolfius Tom 1, p.23."

MS Alnwick Castle 596:

The following work is a Book of great name among the Magi and Cabalists as the Title of Sepher Raziel or the Book of the Angel of Secret.

- p.1. For the Account of the Book, see the Zohar of the Jews in Genesis. When Adam was in the garden of Eden J. H. V. H. sent him a Book of the Angel Raziel in which were engraved characters of the highest wisdom.
- p.3. A Compendium of the Book called Sepher Raziel or the Angel of the Great Secret.
- p.8. [Recipe for cabalistic ink.]
- p.11. Operation of the First Heaven.

p.20. Operation of the 2nd Army in the . . . and attributed to Mercury.

[Opens in English, then in Italian.]

p.25. Operationi del 2 do Exercito. [Sections in Italian, Latin, and English.]

p.35. Operationi del 3 zo Exercito. [Italian, Latin.]

p.47. Operationi de 4 to Exercito. [Italian, Latin, and English.]

p.56. The Operations of the 5th Army. [English, Latin.]

p.62. The Operations of the 6th Army. [English, Latin.]

p.69. Operazioni de 7 mo Cielo. [Italian and Latin.]

p.75. [Lists of qualities of the sevenfold.] [List of various Angel names.]

p.88. Oratio. [Latin.]

p.90. l'Orazioni. [Latin.]

p.92. Tavola. [Contents of MS. in Italian.]

p.93. Haec Sunt 72 Nomina Dei. [List of 72 names with qualities and powers.] [Latin and Italian.]

MS. Alnwick Castle 585:

f.ii. "This Book was bought at Naples from the Jesuit's Colledge when that Order was suppressed and all their goods seized upon by the King and confescated. It was brought from there by a Gentleman in publick Employment in the English service and at his death was purchased in London with other MSS of the Jesuit's Colledge."

1. Cephar Raziel. [In Italian p.1–43.]

p. 1. Erudition hujus Libri. Zoar: Sectione in principio Genesi I.

p. 1. Comprehendio de Libro dello Cephar Raziel, id est Angelus Magni Secreti Communicato as Adamo, ed esposto da Salomonie in Ebreao . . .

p. 2. Incomincia.

p. 3. Disse Salomone in guest libro guello che disse l'Angelo Raziele as Adamo.

p. 6. Operazione de primo Cielo.

p. 8. Seguone l'operazione del i' cielo.

p.11. Operazioni del 2' esercito, quale'nel Cielo di Labana, ed attribuiscon a Mercurio.

p.12. Operazioni del 2' Esercito.

p.14. Operazioni del terzo esercito.

p.17. Le operazioni de IV esercito, il quale sta'nel cielo de labana, ma'e atribuito al Sole.

p.18. Operazioni del IV Esercito.

p.21. Operazioni del IV Esercito, il quale ben che stia nel Cielo di Labana, non di meno e'attribuito a'Marte.

p.22. Operazioni del quinto esercito.

p.25. Operazioni del VI esercito, il quale ben che stia ne Cielo di Labana, non di meno, e'attribuito a [Jupiter].

p.26 Dell' operazioni del VII esercito.

p.29. Operazioni del VII Cielo ill 7' Cielo si chiama Arabitht.

p.37. Il Complimento.

p.40. Questae l'orazione.

p.41. Siegrie il Nome Magno.

2. Compendium totius Sme Kabala cuius misterius consistit in divinis nomninibus vita hora fundamentum smus hoc nomen. [Begins]: "Haec sunt 72 Nomina Dei."

p.1–8. [In Latin.]

3. Regole di Mr Gio Adamo Wetter.
[Table of the days of the months.]
[Tables with inverted pyramids of numbers.]
Kabala Hermetis.
[With number square and inverted pyramid of numbers. Some sigils at end. Text in Italian.]

4. Vero modo d'acquistare la Kabola Angelica.

p.1. {Angels of past, present, and future.]

p.2. Cio finito di rai con gran divezione.

p.3. Invocazione dell' Asistenza.

p.5. Devi sapere. Cio che s'edetto / che in agni nome d'Angliolo si deve leggere: Hic est spiritus: e si segna la Croce.

p.6.   Oratio.
       [p.1–6 in Italian. 18th century] [four short tracts bound together.]

British Library MS. Additional 16390 (Paper. Small quarto. 17th century):

Two tracts in Hebrew.

(i) "The Seven Names."

(ii) The eight chapters of Maimonides, or introduction to Aboth [imperfect]. At the end is added an extract from the Hebrew cabalistic work, entitled Raziel, in Italian.

BIBLIOGRAPHY

———✦———

Crowley, Aleister. *The Equinox, Volume I, # 5*. London: Equinox Publishing, 1911; York Beach, ME: Samuel Weiser, 1992.

Davidson, Benjamin. *The Analytical Hebrew and Chaldee Lexicon*. London: S. Bagster & Sons, n.d.

Davidson, Gustav. *Dictionary of Angels*. New York: Free Press, 1967.

De Manhar, Nurho, trans. *Zohar (Berashith-Genesis)*. San Diego, CA: Wizards Bookshelf, 1995. (According to the Wizards Bookshelf edition, Nurho De Manhar was a pseudonym for William Williams, and this translation was published in 1978 and 1980.)

Fortune, Dion. *Mystical Qabalah*. London: Rider, 1935; York Beach, ME: Samuel Weiser, 1984.

Frazer, James. *Folklore in the Old Testament*. London: MacMillan, 1918.

Gaster, Moses, trans. *Sword of Moses*. London: D. Nutt, 1896; New York: Samuel Weiser, 1970.

Goldstein, David. *Jewish Folklore and Legend*. London: Hamlyn Publishing, 1980.

Graves, Robert and Raphael Patai. *Hebrew Myths: The Book of Genesis*. New York: Doubleday, 1963.

Grillot de Givry, Emile. *Witchcraft, Magic and Alchemy*. Boston: Houghton Mifflin, 1931.

Hastings, James. *Encyclopedia of Religion and Ethics*. New York: Scribner, 1908–1927.

Kalisch, Isidor, trans. *Sepher Yetzirah*. New York: L. H. Frank, 1877.

Kaplan, Aryeh, trans. *The Bahir*. York Beach, ME: Samuel Weiser, 1979.

_____, trans. *Sefer Yetzirah*. York Beach, ME: Samuel Weiser, 1990.

Knight, Gareth. *Practical Guide to Qabalistic Symbolism*. Cheltenham, England: Helios Books, 1965; York Beach, ME: Samuel Weiser, 1978.

Metzger, Bruce and Michael Coogan, eds. *Oxford Companion to the Bible*. New York: Oxford University Press, 1993.

Morgan, Michael, trans. *Sepher Ha-Razim: The Book of the Mysteries*. Chico, CA: Scholars' Press, 1983.

Rappaport, Angelo. *Myths and Legends of Ancient Israel*. London: Gresham Publishing, 1928; Studio Editions, 1995.

Regardie, Israel, ed. *The Qabalah of Aleister Crowley*. York Beach, ME: Samuel Weiser, 1973.

_____. *Tree Of Life*. London: Rider, 1932; York Beach, ME: Samuel Weiser, 1972.

Sperling, Harry, Maurice Simon, and Paul Levertoff, trans. *The Zohar*. London: Samuel Bennet, 1958; London: Soncino Press, 1931, 1984.

Trachtenberg, Joshua. *Jewish Magic and Superstition*. New York: Behrman House, 1939.

Waite, Arthur. *Holy Kabbalah*. London: Williams & Norgate, 1928.

Westcott, W. W., trans. *Book of Formation (Sefer Yetzirah)*. London: J. M. Watkins, 1911; New York: Samuel Weiser, 1980.

Yurchison, George. *World of Angels*. New York: Vantage Press, 1983.

INDEX

(Numbers in italic refer to
pages in the Translator's Introduction.)

❦

Asherial, 255
ashes, 139
Asheth, 133
Ashethonal, 208
Ashlekah, 207
Ashon, 208
Ashoshal, 18
Ashphek, 208
Ashtaroth, 20n
Asiemor,. 207
Asmoday, 253
Ason Avor, 18
Asor, 17
assembly
    sound of the highest, 160
    two most holy, 161
Assyria, 140
Atemon, 229
Atenoneseth, 233
Ateredemen, 18
Ateron (or Anoron) 222
Athelga, 208
Atheneni, 207
Ather Hoderieh A'atesieh
    A'atetieh, 230
Atheremetz Aderemeth
    Beremenem Berethehemiem
    Ovahoz, 231
Athereshov, 208
Atheroph, 14
Athial, 26
atonement, 185
Atzekiyiya Bezekez, 233
Atzethiyiya, 233
Avoa'anied, 260
autumn, 122
Av, 68, 69, 73
Avochial, 208
Avodena, 207
Avokal, 208
Avoliyar, 18
Avoloth, 125
Avomerial, 208
Avophenium, 223
Avopheter, 15
Avophieri, 208
Avophori, 251
Avor, 26
Avor Bemepheterieh, 18
Avor Berek, 25
Avoreberien, 24
Avoremedial, 17
Avorenial, 208, 251
Avorephenial, 207
Avorial, 13, 14, 16, 17, 25, 208,
    253, 254, 255, 277
Avoriedon, 261
Avorieni, 208
Avoriya, 234
Avornemok, 208
Avorphenial, 206, 207
Avor Pheniek, 253
Avosethial, 207
Avosetor, 208
Avothoth, 208
Avothov, 115

Avoyial, 210, 251
Avoyil, 144
Ayar, 127
Ayer, 20, 21, 69, 70, 209, 254,
    255
Ayied Mesetar, 12
Ayienovagel, 15
Ayiepheten, 14
Ayieserien, 14
Ayiethebien, 24
Ayigeda, 206, 207
Ayir, 68, 73
Ayisemerial, 253
Ayiseteronelien, 211
Ayisethorien, 208
Ayish, 133
Ayisheteb, 207
Ayizerekebov, 208
Azemerehi, 251
Azeriyiyeh Azeriyiyeh Atetietos,
    231
Azial, 252
Azoti, 208

Ba'al Avob, 44n
Ba'aren, 22
Babylon, 102
Bal Menael, 23
Bala'am, 86
Baledenien, 25
Bar Sheba, 249
Bar Shecheth, 80
Baraschecath, 19
Bariebererov, 24
Baroba, 210, 252
bear witness, 50
beauty, 154, 156, 161
Bechedon, 16
Bechelial, 215
Bechemera, 16
Becheral, 15
Bechieledek, 14
Bedeqial, 253
Bedod Besher, 24
Begegal, 222
Begierethov, 19
beginning, in the, 62, 92
Behelial, 222
Behial, 222
Behemi, 23
Behemoth, 20
Behenephel, 26
Bekebeb Phelebiyiyepheti, 233
Bekemekesheb, 20
Bekemesheb, 20
Bekereba'al, 22
Bel Ached, 25
Bela'ayi, 214
Bela'ayial, 214
Belehial, 215
Beleqial, 144
Belied, 26
beloved ones, 226
Bemekial, 251
Bemerethiyas, 251
Benai A'ami, iii

Benebod, 14
Benekial, 251
benevolent acts, 45
Beni Chekem, 181
Bepheliyiya, 252
Bephenial, 26
Bephopher, 21
Beqoneqephethov, 14
Beqosh, 22
Berakial, 13, 14, 15
Beraqial, 99
Berash Adam Vochoveh, 144
Berashith, viii n, x, 2, 43, 50, 90,
    92, 133, 134, 200, 213, 215,
    218, 227, 234, 246
    secret of, 35
Berashith Bera Elohim, 59
Berashith-Genesis, 14
Beravoth, 15
Beregemi, 208
bereka, 208
Berekethien, 208
Berekial, 16, 17, 253
Beremech Ayiberiem, 253
Bereqial, 17, 19, 141, 144, 254,
    255, 256
Bereqovon, 125
Beresial, 143
Berethobial, 207
Berezial, 254
Beri Abieriyov, 15
Berial, 17
Berieh, 54
Beriekoch, 25
Beron, 19
Beroqi, 207
Berqiyem, 141
Beseron, 14
Beth
    of Berashith, 15 , 51
    of Boho, 145
    destruction of, 51
Bethemial, 26
Bether, 79
Betheroqa, 24
Bethiem, 62
Biehereron, 23
Bieker, 22
Biem, 214
Biememom, 252
Bierekom, 211
Bieth, 23
Bieth Meshtherem, 143
Bietheron, 23
Biethial, 15
Big Dipper, 103, 106, 108, 111,
    112, 118, 119, 205
Binah, 157, 158, 160, 163, 168,
    184, 188, 194
bind images, 196
bind Moses, 193
Bitumen, vn
Biyom, 23
black Sun, 6
bladder, 139
blessing, highest, 152

ABOUT THE AUTHOR

Steve Savedow is the author of *The Magician's Workbook: A Modern Grimoire* (Weiser, 1995) and *Goetic Evocation: The Magician's Workbook, Volume 2* (Eschaton Productions, 1996). He has studied magic and the Western Mystery Tradition for many years. Savedow lives in Daytona Beach, Florida, and owns the Serpent's Occult Bookstore, an independent bookstore specializing in magic and pagan titles. He has been interested in the *Sepher Rezial Hemelach* for many years.